JOHN MARSHALL 1860
MATTEAWAN 1901
PACIFIC 1875
KEWEENAH 1894
IVANHOE 1894
JAPANESE JUNK 1833
SOUTHERNER 1854
CONDOR 1901
FLORENCIA 1860
MONTSERRAT 1894
UMATILLA 1884
AUSTRIA 1887
FREE TRADE 1878
ST.NICHOLAS 1808
RYO YEI MARU 1927
TEMPLE BAR 1939
LAMUT 1943
WIDE WEST 1889
SIR JAMSETJEE FAMILY 1886
FERNDALE 1892
ABERCORN 1888
JANET CARRUTHERS 1919
YORKMAR 1952
TORRISDALE 1912
RYBA 1925
LAMMERLAW 1881
G. BROUGHTON 1881
ALICE 1909
NICHOLS I 1954
INTREPID 1954
ROSECRANS 1913
WELSH PRINCE 1922
JAPANESE JUNK 1820
SILVIE DE GRACE 1849
PROTECTION 1900
TACOMA 1887
CITY OF DUBLIN 1878
PETER IREDALE 1906
SPANISH SHIP 1925
SHARK 1846
BEESWAX SHIP 1679
SAN JOSE 1769
GLENESSLIN 1913
LIFELINE 1923
MIMI 1913
ARCO 1909
FRANCIS H. LEGGETT 1914
PIONEER 1900
CARMARTHAN CASTLE 1886
BLANCO 1864
J. MARHOFFER 1910
UNCLE SAM 1876
MINNIE E. KELTON 1908
SEA OTTER 1808
TACOMA 1883
FEARLESS 1889
CAPT. LINCOLN 1852
C.W. WETMORE 1892
CZARINA 1910
SANTA CLARA 1915
CONGRESS 1916
OLIVER OLSON 1953
J.A. CHANSLOR 1919
SINALOA 1917
T.W. LUCAS 1894
ALASKAN 1889
WILLAPA 1941

VICTORIA
HENRY SCOTT 1922
ANDALUSIA 1947
CLALLAM 1904
DIAMOND KNOT 1947
R.K.HAM 1894
PORT ANGELES
WAR HAWK 1883
WINDWARD 1875
A.J. FULLER 1918
MISSISSIPPI 1883
IDAHO 1908
SEATTLE
ANDELANA 1899
TACOMA
HOQUIAM
ROBERT BRUCE 1851
SOUTH BEND
ASTORIA
FELTRE 1937
SENATOR 1875
TILLAMOOK
PORTLAND
ELK 1857
GAZELLE 1854
NEWPORT
COOS BAY
QUADRATUS 1856

WASHINGTON

OREGON

CALIFORNIA

Shipwrecks of the Pacific Coast

By
James A. Gibbs

BINFORDS & MORT, *Publishers*

Portland   •   Oregon   •   97242

ISBN: 0-8323-0013-6

Library of Congress Catalog Card Number: 57-13208

First Edition, 1957

Second Edition, 1962

Second Printing, 1971

Shipwrecks of the Pacific Coast

DEDICATION

To Dad, who but for the will of God
would have sailed on a ship that
foundered with the loss of
all hands

Books by James A. Gibbs

Pacific Graveyard
Sentinels of the North Pacific
Shipwrecks of the Pacific Coast
Shipwrecks off Juan de Fuca

ACKNOWLEDGMENTS

In offering this volume to the reader I wish to make special reference to the kindness of certain individuals who aided in its preparation: Andrew Genzoli, one of the foremost editors of the *Humboldt Times* in Eureka, California, and Carl Christensen, also of Eureka—two individuals who have done much to keep the maritime chapters of history alive in the Humboldt Country.

Keepers of the light with whom I served while at Tillamook Rock Light Station—Oswald Allik, who put in 20 years on "the Rock," and Ed Stith, who recently retired from the Coast Guard.

H. W. McCurdy, president and general manager of the Puget Sound Bridge and Dredging Co., and president of the Seattle Historical Society; the late Wedell Foss of the Foss Launch & Tug Company, of Seattle and Tacoma, and Captain Daniel Hutchings, retired.

I also wish to thank certain members of the Puget Sound Maritime Historical Society—its president, Ralph Hitchcock; J. W. "Bill" Todd, whose Shorey's Book Store is a Seattle institution; Joe Williamson, proprietor of the Marine Photo Shop; the late Capt. N. A. McDougall, whose memory will long remain alive; Gordon Newell, author of *SOS North Pacific* and *Ships of the Inland Sea;* Capt. L. H. Bayers of Juneau, Alaska; Dan Noonan, the Bard of Alaska; Bill Somers, marine historian of Grapeview, Washington, and Lucile Mc Donald, author of many historical books.

I should also like to thank Karl Kortum, who has done such a splendid job at the helm of the San Francisco Maritime Museum, and his cohort, Harold Huycke.

John Haydon, editor and publisher of Seattle's *Marine Digest*, and his entire staff were most helpful.

Allen Knight, former mayor of Carmel, California, and a collector of maritime relics gave a wealth of information as did Mrs. Fred Niendorff of Seattle.

And, as always, the United States Coast Guard Districts 11, 12, 13 and 14, have been of considerable assistance.

The Author

CONTENTS

Death on the rocks. Russian freighter *Lamut* imperiled off Teahwhit Head near La Push, Washington in 1943. One died—54 men and women were pulled to safety. (Coast Guard photo)

Irretrievably lost—Panamanian freighter *Andalusia*, laden with lumber, breaks in two near Clallam Bay, Washington, in 1949.

The Japanese SS *Tenpaisan Maru*, a victim of the sands of Copalis Beach, Washington, December 1, 1927.

SS *Cadaretta* stranded off James Island, Washington, May 28, 1945, was remarkably refloated and beached near Neah Bay, where salvagers could work. (courtesy Capt. Loring Hyde)

PART ONE

SHIPWRECKS OF THE
WASHINGTON COAST

Chapter One

CAPE FLATTERY TO DESTRUCTION ISLAND

CAPE Flattery is an inappropriate title for the most northwesterly point of mainland U.S.A. Perhaps Tombstone Cape would have been more suitable, for below and and around its bold head lie billions of dollars in lost ships and precious cargo. Scores of hardy seafarers have made it their last port of call. In spite of the many navigational aids at the entrance to Juan de Fuca Strait, the staggering toll continued until recent decades. From the erection of the lighthouse on Tatoosh Island, just off the cape, in 1857, man has continued down through the years his battle to safeguard these grim waterways. The entrance to the strait is deep and navigable the year round but the wrath of God dwells at this calamity corner when storms roll in, and turn the so-called peaceful Pacific into a seething, churning, ocean hell.

Fog, rain, sleet, snow, wind, and ocean currents have all played their destructive role here, and woe unto the navigator who finds his ship off course where abound the devilish rocks and inundated reefs. By such hazards has the hair of the most experienced navigator turned gray.

Over 150 deep-sea ships are known to have come to grief near Cape Flattery. No telling how many others went to the bottom unrecorded in the pages of history.

Many Oriental junks have been wrecked along the

1

Northwest Coast, some in recent times, some in ancient times—perhaps two to three centuries before the arrival of the white man.

JAPANESE JUNK OF 1833

The first case of a wrecked junk on Cape Flattery's shores was recorded in the *Journal of Occurrences,* kept at Fort Nisqually. According to this old document, on June 9, 1834, the ship *Llama,* in command of Captain McNeil, arrived on Puget Sound from the Columbia River, having aboard two Orientals picked up from the Indians near Cape Flattery. Several months earlier they had been shipwrecked near the cape, and taken as slaves by the natives. A third survivor was moved inland but the Indians promised to free him on the *Llama's* return trip.

Ultimately all three were taken to Fort Vancouver, where it was learned that they were of Japanese and not Chinese origin as had first been supposed. They were frightened and terrified individuals, for in those years Japan was yet a closed country set apart from the rest of the world. The three survivors were unable to speak or understand new-world language or customs.

It was surmised that their junk had been blown far from its course off the Japanese Coast by a typhoon and carried across the Pacific by the Japanese Current. Most of the crew had perished during the long drift, probably from the scourge of beriberi, scurvy, starvation, or exposure.

The three castaways were ultimately sent back to China and from there to their sacred Japan, where foreign vessels were forbidden.

So fascinated was Mrs. Eva Emery Dye by the tale of these three Japanese survivors that several years later she made excellent use of the episode in the penning of her novel, *McDonald of Oregon.*

Up until 1875, sixty Oriental junks were known to have been wrecked at various locations in the Pacific.

2

They were found derelict or cast ashore as far south as Mexico and the southern Pacific Islands and as far north as Alaska and the Aleutian Chain. Japan is known to have had nearly 22,000 registered junks in 1874.

RYO YEI MARU

In the mid-19th century Japan became on open country with a new lease on life. But the natural wonder known as the Japanese Current has never altered its course. This great river within an ocean still carries floating objects thousands of miles across the Pacific to the shores of western America.

On the gray fall day of October 31, 1927, the freighter *Margaret Dollar* was steaming south of Cape Flattery when a derelict fishing vessel loomed on the horizon. The freighter changed its course until it came abeam of the stranger. The shipmaster, Captain H. T. Payne, scanned her deck with his glasses and on seeing no sign of life ordered a boat lowered, and dispatched a boarding party.

As they approached the mysterious craft they found her hull encrusted with four inches of barnacles. Her rigging hung limp and the masts were badly strained, with but one shred of sail remaining. A cold chill came over the intruders as they clambered over the gunwales. The smell of death was about. Their lips became silent as about them they saw decomposed bodies. Inside the cabin were the remains of the captain. Near him was a thin cedar board upon which was scrolled a list of the crew, the vessel's owner, and the name, *Ryo Yei Maru*.

A small wicker trunk housed two small books—the log of the ship and a diary of the slow, tormenting death of its twelve-man crew.

In substance the translated log read thus:

While being lashed by a sixty-mile gale, the *Ryo Yei Maru* refused assistance from the freighter *West Isom* on December 23, 1926. Our engine was out of commission and the freighter came alongside in an-

3

swer to our distress flags, 700 miles off the coast of Japan.

Captain Richard Healy, master of the *West Isom,* warned us of the seriousness of our situation, but we refused to abandon in favor either of repairing the engine or of getting a tow. Finally the freighter sailed on, leaving us to our fate.

We drifted on, pounded unmercifully by the storms that beset us. Soon the hope of repairing our engine was abandoned. Sails were set but were soon blown to ribbons. The winds and current carried us farther and farther away from our homeland. Six weeks passed and another vessel was sighted but failed to recognize our frantic signals of distress.

On February 5, the first member of the crew became seriously ill. The engineer died on March 9, and two others were confined to their bunks, too weak to move. Food was nearly gone. Between March 12 and April 1, five fishermen and the first mate perished. On April 5, Captain Tokizo Miki caught a large sea bird, which was immediately devoured. The following day, however, another member of the crew passed away. On April 14, a shark was gaffed and hauled aboard after an exhaustive struggle, but by this date those of us remaining were weak from malnutrition and afflicted with beriberi.

On April 19, the tenth member of the crew succumbed and on May 6 the captain became seriously ill. Four days later only Captain Miki and I remain alive. Both of us are too weak to tend the helm.

Finally, on May 11, the last words appeared in the log. "Wind is Northwest. Weather cloudy. Wind fresh. Sea rough. Drifting with remaining sails hoisted."

The *Ryo Yei Maru* drifted on and on, manned by a crew of dead. The vessel had departed Misaki, Japan, on December 5, 1926, and was not picked up by the SS *Margaret Dollar* until October 31, 1927. After drifting well over 5000 miles with the Japanese Current in 11 harrowing months, the derelict was towed into Puget Sound—but much too late. Its crew had all perished. Reminders of their desperate struggle in repairing the faulty crankshaft lay in the sight of tools strewn about the deck. A goodly quantity of fuel oil was still in the tanks. When the derelict reached Seattle it caused great excitement. Thousands thronged to the waterfront to see a real ghost ship. Fabulous offers were made to purchase the vessel as a sightseeing and sideshow attraction. But to the Japanese owners it was no joking matter. The remains of the dead were removed and cremated at a Buddhist service after clippings of their hair were sent to relatives in Japan. Then at the request of the ship's owners the vessel was saturated with oil and burned, much to the dismay of the publicity minded. Well into the night, weird flames crackled, consuming her weathered timbers. After many hours the fire died, and scattered upon the dark waters were the ashes of a ship of death, cremated like the dead that had once manned her helm.

ST. NICHOLAS

The first recorded shipwreck on the coast of Washington was that of the Russian ship *St. Nicholas*, in command of Captain Nikolai Bulagin. The account of this tragedy as recorded by the ship's supercargo, Timothy Tarakanof, has been preserved at the Territorial Library at Juneau, Alaska.

The *St. Nicholas* departed New Archangel (Sitka), Alaska, on September 8, 1808, on a trading and charting voyage down the coast of Northwest America. Under the flag of the powerful Russian America Company, the vessel made frequent anchorages along the coast of Vancouver Island to barter for sea otter skins.

Later, in Latitude 47 degrees 56 minutes North, charting near Destruction Island, a dead calm left the canvas hanging limp. The currents carried the ship toward the rock-ribbed coast, much to the concern of the shipmaster. To further complicate matters a southwest gale was in the making. Before the wind had gained enough impetus to bring the unwieldy vessel about, she was in the throes of a dilemma. Carried by the currents amid ledges of sharp rocks, she was soon hung up near the mouth of the Quillayute River (near Lapush of today). Hopelessly trapped, the ship pounded relentlessly on the reef and all hands struggled ashore with the ebbing tide. In this hour of turmoil Bulagin's first consideration was his beautiful wife Anna Petrovna, who had sailed with him.

Arms, ammunition, tents, sails, provisions, and other usable materials were salvaged between tides and the shipwrecked party settled down for a long, hard stay on little-known, inhospitable shores. Anna, being the only woman, was given special consideration.

Prior to his departure from Sitka, Bulagin had made plans to rendezvous with the ship *Kodiak* at Grays Harbor and he was now hopeful of reaching that place overland.

No sooner had the Russians constructed their shelters, however, than savages came swarming down the hillside, armed with stones and spears, yelling wildly. Bulagin ordered his men to fire their muskets. The shots rang out and two half-naked Indians were dropped in their tracks. The roar of the guns sent the others in disorganized retreat. For the time, the Russians were in command but the savages were playing for keeps, and grave trouble lay ahead.

The days dragged on until the last vestige of the wreck was pulverized by the breakers. It was then decided to make the rugged overland hike to Grays Harbor. Only the necessities could be taken. Accordingly, much of the heavy equipment, including one of the ship's cannon, was thrown back into the sea. A long and arduous journey lay ahead.

With the aid of some friendly Quileutes, the Russians were shown a path through the forests and along the beach, but within a few miles they were harassed by

6

hostile savages and placed on their guard. Bulagin restrained his men from firing except as a last means. To the Russians, muskets and ammunition were all that stood between them and annihilation.

When they reached the swollen Hoh River, natives had to be hired from a nearby bark-hut camp to ferry them across in canoes. Most of the party, including Bulagin, were crammed into one large canoe. In a smaller boat, Anna was placed under the protection of a young Russian officer, a Kodiak, and an Aleut. Midway across, the savages pulled the plug from the bottom of the larger canoe, leaped overboard and swam ashore, leaving the Russians to fend for themselves without the aid of paddles. Scores of natives then assembled on the river banks and began showering spears down on them. The big canoe filled rapidly as the razor-sharp weapons found their mark in the side of the boat.

Half-submerged, the craft drifted to the opposite bank. While the savages took Anna and her escorts as prisoners, Bulagin and his men had recovered enough from the bloody attack to prepare for battle. The muskets that had not been soaked by water were trained on the spear-wielding natives, and fired. Two fell to the ground. Retaliation brought a spear down on one of the Russians. It caught him in the groin and, with a terrible scream, he rolled over and died.

The survivors retreated to a small hill and put in a sleepless night guarding against more attacks. Bulagin was half crazy over the capture of his wife and well aware of the overwhelming odds against his men. The situation worsened as heavy rains began to fall. Food was running low and it was virtually impossible to keep the ammunition dry. While some of the Russians stood guard, others searched for food — mushrooms, berries, roots, leaves—anything eatable.

Confined to their small shelter they became weary, discouraged and famished. Some were gnawing on their shoe leather and sea-lion skin shirts. Despondent and heartsick, Bulagin relinquished his leadership to Timothy Tarakanof. Then, on November 14, the new leader led the others in a daring raid on the nearby Indian village. To their amazement it was empty, the natives having gone hunting. The Russians returned with a supply of dried salmon and ate until their stomachs were filled.

Now fortified with a sort of false security, Tarakanof scouted the nearby hills in search of an escape route. This time, however, his small party was ambushed and two of their number wounded. The savages were finally driven off and the Russians hastily returned to their encampment. Following this frustrating experience, it was decided to give up the plan of reaching Grays Harbor in favor of building a winter fortress at a mountain lake near the headwaters of the river.

Abandoning their crude shelter, they commenced their trek upriver. En route they encountered some friendly natives who traded salmon for beads and trinkets, but still later they were approached by an emissary of the Quileutes who sought ransom for the return of Anna Petrovna.

Bulagin, having lost all sense of reason, conducted the bargaining, and against the wishes of the others, offered everything they had except the muskets, in trade for his wife. But the savages demanded the muskets as well. Bulagin pleaded with his shipmates to give up the guns but they flatly refused to render themselves so completely helpless. Then he pleaded desperately with the red men that he might be permitted an audience with his Anna. The savages agreed and several hours later brought forth the girl.

It was a pitiful reuniting as the two embraced amid bitter tears. Both bore the evidences of their tribulations. Anna's beautiful face was pale and drawn. Her clothes were ragged and her hair hung unevenly over her shoulders. The handsome Russian captain was gaunt and thin and all but broken in spirit. Their rendezvous was brief, for the Indians insisted that Anna would be surrendered only in trade for the muskets.

Despite the pleadings of Bulagin, the natives dragged the girl back into the forest. The outnumbered Russians had no alternative but to continue their trek. When they at last reached their desired haven they set about immediately building a breastwork and later a loghouse with corner sentry boxes for protection against attackers. This had to suffice for their winter quarters. The long, wet months lagged on until at last the first signs of spring appeared. They had managed to construct a boat of sorts during the interim and it was with this that they planned their escape. Only the hope of freedom for his wife had kept Bulagin from going insane.

At last the boat was supplied and the voyage down river began. That they would be like flies in a spider's web there was little doubt, but they had a plan. After the arduous river run they approached the Indian village and immediately seized two Indian maidens and held them as hostages until the tribesmen produced Anna.

Bulagin, greatly heartened, could scarcely await the return of his wife. Then at last she was brought forth but he was shocked beyond words by her refusal to go with him. Anna saw nothing but mass annihilation for all should they attempt an escape. Bulagin was so stunned that in desperation he threatened to shoot her. Still she refused and, stricken with remorse, he threw himself into the bottom of the boat.

Having seen that the other Russian captives had not been ill-treated by the savages, Tarakanof proposed surrender, trusting that a trading ship would eventually come to their rescue. He and four others accordingly gave themselves up, but Bulagin and the others frantically launched their boat and paddled over the river bar toward Destruction Island. A strong wind was blowing and the sea was rough. En route to the island the boat was carried on the rocks. It capsized and all of their provisions were lost. The pursuing Indian canoes were soon upon them and plucked them one by one from the water, taking them as prisoners.

This time there was no escape. All of the Russians

were now in the hands of the savages. Tarakanof was taken by a chief named Utramaka and ushered off to a village called Koonistchat near Cape Flattery. Bulagin was the prize of another chief near Ozette.

In August of 1809, Anna Petrovna died and the chief who owned her, had her body dragged into the forest and left to decay without burial. This saddened the other prisoners and when the news reached Bulagin he no longer had the will to live. In February of the following year he died.

Tarakanof, on the other hand, kept his hopes alive and cunningly kept in good standing with his master. He made tools and flew kites into the sky, boasting to the Indians that he possessed hidden powers. They flocked to watch his Ben Franklin performances. He informed them that he was sending messages to the great white father. The savages were fascinated and awed by this strange man. Thus he ultimately gained their respect, was permitted to build his own hut, and was granted certain freedoms.

In September, 1810, the remaining Russian prisoners were ferried up the Strait of Juan de Fuca by the natives where they endured a hard winter and long periods of hunger.

The following year the American brig *Lydia* arrived on the Strait and, while engaged in trading, the news of her arrival spread among the native tribes. Tarakanof learned of this and managed to escape his master. He made his way to the ship and related his tale of hardship and shipwreck to Captain Brown, master of the vessel. He begged that he and the other Russians be ransomed. Brown readily agreed and immediate negotiations were arranged with the Indian chiefs. The conferences were held aboard the vessel and after long debate the natives agreed to accept in exchange for each prisoner a large quantity of cloth, a locksmith's saw, two steel knives, a mirror, five packages of gunpowder, and five bags of shot. But before final agreement was reached the savages demanded more for two of the Russians. This greatly angered the *Lydia's* commander. He sternly protested. Even more enraged by the surly conduct of the natives, he ordered his men to lay siege to one of their chiefs and hold him as a hostage. The scuffle was short and the chief subdued. Now all they had to do was wait for the savages to produce the remaining Russians. Three were known to be in the area in addition to Tarakanof. Another was believed captive on distant Destruction Island. The *Lydia's* crew succeeded in freeing all the prisoners in the immediate area but freedom for the other survivors was slow in coming. One was later ransomed as far away as the Columbia River, by the crew of the ship *Mercury*. Some had been traded from tribe to tribe and one of them was never found. Of the original complement of the *St. Nicholas*, 13 were eventually ransomed and returned to New Archangel in the summer of 1811. Seven perished in captivity.

So ended one of the many tragic tales that occurred on the early Northwest Coast.

SOUTHERNER

As white settlers drifted into the Pacific Northwest, the hostile acts of the natives were somewhat curtailed, but the danger from the elements never ceased.

The first passenger steamer lost on the shores of Washington was the *Southerner*, a venerable 339-ton side-wheeler of the vintage of 1847. After three owners and three changes of name within slightly over two years she became a ship of little distinction. Her checkered career continued, and five years later after a complete rebuilding she was placed in Pacific coastwise service under the name *Southerner*.

After but two brief voyages she cleared San Francisco on December 20, 1854, in command of Captain F. A. Sampson, making calls at Eureka and Crescent City. She continued northward with but 25 paying passengers and a crew of 19. The ship's itinerary called for stops at Port Orford and Umpqua but at both places rough bar

11

conditions prevented an entrance. The *Southerner* continued northward in a zigzag course like an inebriate after a night of celebration.

The winds continued kicking up from the southwest and the ocean became cantankerous. At 10 a.m. on Christmas Day, Oregon's Tillamook Head was reached but most of the passengers were confined to their cabins with bad cases of *mal de mer*. The Yuletide spirit was forgotten. Three hours later the vessel gained the Columbia River entrance but the winds had made the bar a mass of white fury. While the steamer wallowed about off the mouth of the river the chief engineer summoned the bridge with the news that the vessel had developed a serious leak below the waterline. The passengers were immediately alerted to the impending danger, but most were too sick to care.

Captain Sampson stood off the bar until 6 p. m. Then, conditions failing to improve, he set his course for Puget Sound. All the time water was gaining in the hold in spite of the full output of the pumps. When the situation reached alarming proportions the captain ordered every male passenger to join a bucket brigade. Even those who were green from seasickness were pressed into the task, gagging and moaning as they passed each container. The combined efforts of crew and passengers managed to keep the inrush of water at a level with the engine room floor.

At daybreak on December 26, the engines were barely turning over—the vessel laboring heavily. Fearing the worst, the shipmaster ordered the quartermaster to bring the steamer nearer the shore. Close-hauled to the wind, movement was at a snail's pace until late afternoon. In spite of the efforts to prevent it, water had now reached alarming heights and the stern had begun to drop. The passengers pleaded with the captain to beach the ship. Some even threatened him. But he didn't have to be threatened, for none knew better than he the danger and responsibility resting on him. He shouldered aside the tormenting words of the passengers and ordered his mate to keep a gun handy in case of necessity. When the steamer's. forward progress was all but halted she came to anchor in seven fathoms southeast of Cape Flattery. Her position offered little protection and the seas pounded so relentlessly that she creaked in every joint. Mild panic broke out among the passengers and the mate's hand slipped into his pocket for his gun. But the officer's harsh words were sufficient to keep them under control. Such a severe punishment did the steamer take that at last it slipped its anchor chains and was carried broadside onto an inundated shoal amid screams of terrified souls.

The captain sprang into instant action. He ordered the masts cut and jettisoned. Then her stack was pried from its fittings and dropped overboard. The vessel, thus lightened of some of its burden, was carried over the reef and swept into the breakers. Her decks dipped into the sloshing surf and breaker after breaker swept her higher and higher. The wind was strong, the tide full, and the dying steamer—nearly on her beam ends—thumped over the reef, coming to rest among the driftwood. Frozen with fear, the men and women on the *Southerner* remained almost motionless until the tide ebbed and left the battered wreck in temporary repose. By morning, amazed at their survival, all hands evacuated their wooden prison. There was not one casualty. The *Southerner* had delivered its cargo of humans but the next rising sea, fortified by powerful breakers, pounded the old sidewheeler into submission and she caved in like a straw hut in a windstorm.

The survivors traveled on foot to Neah Bay, many weary miles without complaint. They had been resurrected from the cradle of the deep, and when men are saved from almost certain death they can smile where others would gnash their teeth. The *Southerner* reached the port of no return but her human cargo went free.

FLORENCIA AND JOHN MARSHALL

By 1860, a thriving lumber trade between Puget Sound and San Francisco flourished. From a virgin wilderness, sawmill towns had mushroomed virtually over night. California's gold rush had brought heavy demands for Pacific Northwest timber and San Francisco had opened wide her Golden Gate. The superiority of the lumber soon became known the world over. The entire Spanish Navy was soon equipped with fir spars from Puget Sound.

With the birth of the lumber industry, scores of foreign and domestic ships arrived on the waters of Puget Sound. Many met with ill-fortune in these hitherto little-known Pacific Northwest waterways. Among them was the Peruvian brig *Florencia*. In the winter of 1860 she was loading lumber at the thriving sawmill port of Utsaladdy on Camano Island. Many days later, deeply-laden, she cleared for Callao. Out through the Strait of Juan de Fuca she passed into a howling gale with powerful headwinds. On December 8, after waging a fruitless week-long battle against a powerful gale, the great seas off Cape Flattery caught her broadside and flipped her on her beam ends. She floundered like a dead whale, all hands clinging desperately to keep from being thrown into the surging tempest. The captain ordered the deck load cut loose and the masts chopped away, but so terrified were his men that they would not obey his orders. There was nothing for the shipmaster to do but find an axe and do the job himself. His bravery stirred the crew to the reality that their only hope of survival lay in assisting their captain. To a man, including a passenger doctor, they abandoned their strongholds and joined the effort to lighten the vessel.

Suddenly a sea far greater than the others made a clean sweep of the brig—a driving, twisting avalanche of water. When its course had been run, the gasping crew came up for air, but the captain, supercargo, and the doctor had been swept to a watery grave.

Suddenly the vessel sprang back on an even keel and

14

began drifting northward away from the sinister shadow of Cape Flattery. Near Nootka on Vancouver Island she draped her remains on deadly rocks; and those still walking her sodden deck, staggered ashore seemingly more dead than alive. No sooner had the news of the *Florencia* tragedy reached Puget Sound than another ship arrived at Port Townsend and reported sighting pieces of wreckage from the American ship *John Marshall,* off Cape Flattery. She was long overdue at Port Discovery where she was to have loaded lumber for San Francisco. Her last reported position was off Cape Flattery on November 10, 1860, where she was sighted battling a severe gale. She had not been heard of since.

December passed, then January and February of 1861 with still no sign of the *John Marshall.* Every deep-sea shipmaster leaving Puget Sound was asked to be on the lookout for her but nothing more than a few pieces of wreckage was ever found. Then came the terse announcement from her owners that she must be presumed lost with all hands. And that's the way it stood—another unit of the early lumber fleet had vanished into the graveyard of ships.

PACIFIC

Death clad in all its hideousness rode the decks of the steamer *Pacific* on its tragic voyage in the fall of 1875. Unlike so many ship losses, the circumstances surrounding her sinking were somewhat baffling—no deadly gales, raging fires, or treacherous reefs. Following a collision seemingly of little consequence, scores of passengers perished only hours from their port of debarkation. A total of 277 souls was aboard the *Pacific*—only two survived the sinking—the worst maritime disaster ever recorded on the Pacific Coast of the United States.

The *Pacific,* a big sidewheeler, steamed out of Victoria Harbor, B. C., at mid-morning on November 4, 1875, in command of Captain J. D. Howell, brother-in-law of the

15

South's immortal Jefferson Davis. The vessel's decks were lined with passengers from Puget Sound and Canadian cities.

Steaming out through the Strait of Juan de Fuca, the *Pacific* rounded Cape Flattery Light at four in the afternoon. The wind was blowing fresh from the southwest and there was a heavy swell. The cresting seas slowed her forward progress to a minimum and—while yet in the vicinity of Cape Flattery—night came on cold and black. After an evening of entertainment in the ship's lounge most of the passengers had retired to their cabins. About 10 p. m. they had a rude awakening by a sudden shock that sent them sprawling from their bunks. All were filled with dreadful apprehension. The steamer had collided with an unknown assailant.

All within a few terrible minutes, the *Pacific* with its precious cargo of human souls sank like a rock into the hidden depths. But that fate intervened, there might not have been a single survivor. Though a handful escaped on pieces of wreckage, only two survived the ordeal in those icy, storm-swept waters. One was named Henry Jelley, who some time after his rescue died from the results of his exposure. The other was quartermaster Neil Henley. He was adrift for 80 ghastly hours on a piece of wreckage before he was finally rescued by the revenue cutter *Oliver Wolcott*.

Later his experiences were told under oath at the Court of Inquiry:

> I was off watch and about 10 p. m. was awakened by a crash and getting out of my bunk found the water rushing into the hold at a furious rate. On reaching the deck all was confusion. I looked on the starboard beam and saw a large vessel under sail, which they said had struck the steamer. When I first distinguished her she was showing a green light. The captain and officers of the steamer were trying to lower the boats but the passengers crowded in against their commands, making their efforts useless.

None of the lifeboats had plugs in them. There were fifteen women and six men in the boat with me, but she struck the ship and filled instantly, and when I came up I caught hold of the skylight which soon capsized.

I then swam to a part of the hurricane deck, which had eight persons clinging to it. When I looked around, the steamer had disappeared leaving a floating mass of human beings, whose cries and screams were awful to hear and the sight of which can never be effaced from my memory.

In a little while it was all over: the cries had ceased, and we were alone on the raft, the part of the deck on which was the wheelhouse. Besides myself, the raft supported the captain, second mate, cook, and four passengers, one of them a young lady. At 1 a. m. the sea was making a clean breach over the raft. At 4 a. m. a heavy sea washed over us, carrying away the captain, second mate, the lady, and another passenger, leaving four of us on the raft. At 9 a. m. the cook died and rolled off into the sea. At 4 p. m. the mist cleared away, and we saw land about 15 miles off. We also saw a piece of wreckage with two men on it.

At 5 p. m. another man expired and early the next morning the other one died, leaving me alone. Soon after the death of the last man I caught a floating box and dragged it on the raft. It kept the wind off, and during the day I slept considerable. Early on the morning of the eighth I was rescued by the revenue cutter *Wolcott.*

Such were the plain facts as related by Henley, but one can easily read between the lines and imagine the indescribable suffering endured by those pitiful few who rode that raft of death.

The other survivor, the passenger Henry Jelley, along with four others, seized hold of an overturned lifeboat after the *Pacific* went down. One after another they were

17

swept off until only Jelley remained. For 48 hours he clung until the blood froze in his veins. At last the ship *Messenger* discovered him and took him aboard, but his days thereafter were numbered.

Seventeen persons in all were known to have managed places on life rafts after the ship went down, but all except Henley and Jelley either perished from exposure, were drowned, or took their own lives.

The bodies of many of the dead were later found in Juan de Fuca Strait, having been carried there by the strong inward currents. Some drifted as far as San Juan Island, over 80 miles from the scene of the disaster. The body of a beautiful young girl came up on the beach near Victoria, within blocks of the happy home she had left before sailing on the *Pacific*.

None can ever know all of the dramatic and heart-rending scenes enacted as the ship plunged to her doom. A baby was crushed to death in its mother's arms as they attempted to enter a lifeboat. Spine-chilling death cries, repentant prayers, were heard from every corner of the ship. Many never knew what struck them. Several life spans were relived in a few brief moments. Then all was silent.

When the news of the disaster reached Victoria it was like a mass hypnosis had come over the city. Nearly every family had at least one member who had gone down with the *Pacific*. In the aftermath of the tragedy the following editorial appeared in the *Victoria Colonist*:

> We have no heart to dwell today on the disaster that has hurried into eternity so many of our fellow citizens with whom only a few brief hours ago we mingled on the streets or met in the social circle, as full of life, hope and energy as any who may read the *Colonist* today. The catastrophe is so far-reaching that scarcely a household in Victoria has not lost one or more of its members, or must strike from its list of living friends a face and form that found ever a warm greeting within their circle. A bolt out of

18

the blue could not have caused more widespread consternation than the awful tidings spread far and near yesterday. In some cases entire families have been swept away, in others fond wives returning from a visit to their childhood's homes to meet husbands and younger children in San Francisco have gone down to an early grave. In others the joyous, happy maiden, the sweet, innocent, prattling babe, the banker, the merchant, the miner, the public officer—all, all have found a common grave in a dreadful and tumultuous home, wide opening and loud roaring still for more.

Whether the catastrophe was one that human skill could have averted we cannot now say. All we do know is that a steamship carrying a cargo of precious lives has gone down and that so far as is known only one man, out of 275 persons on board, has been saved. We can only express the hope that the vessels now flying like ministering angels to the scene will return with glad tidings of great joy for some of the hearts that are now bowed down with grief.

An agitated public is a dangerous weapon. Up went the cry loud and clear—"Why?" When it was learned that the *Pacific* had gone down after a collision with the ship *Orpheus* and that this vessel had not picked up a single survivor, the people cried for the scalp of Captain Charles A. Sawyer, master of the ship in question. There are, however, two sides to every situation. Following was Captain Sawyer's testimony on the appended verdict of the coroner's jury:

The *Orpheus* was steering about north, keeping close into the land, with the wind from the southward, and blowing fresh with fine rain, the ship going about 12 knots. Her head yards were braced sharp up but the starboard braces, her main and after yards square, thus leaving the ship in such a position that she could be hauled offshore on a moment's notice, if anything came in view.

At 9:30 p. m. I left the deck in charge of the second mate, Allen, with orders if he saw anything, to starboard the wheel and keep her head to the northwest, offshore. I went below to consult the chart and had just seated myself at the table in my cabin with my oil clothes on, looking at the chart, when I heard the second mate tell the man at the wheel to starboard his helm. I looked up at the compass over my head and saw that the ship's head was rapidly coming up toward the northwest. I immediately went on deck and asked the officer what was the matter, and he said there was a light on the starboard bow.

I let the ship come up in the wind until she headed to the southward of west, and the after sails aback. My ship now was comparatively at a standstill, in just such a position as I would be if I were going to take a pilot aboard. This brought the steamer's light a little forward the starboard beam. I stood looking at her with my glasses. I did not then think there was going to be a collision, but I said to the second mate, "She will be into us," though I did not think she would, for I thought she would see us and keep off. I made up my mind that she would hit us, and shortly afterward she blew her whistle, and immediately struck us on the starboard side in the wake of the main hatch. The blow was a light one. She had evidently stopped her engines and was backing and gave us a glancing blow, for she bounded off and again struck us at the main topmast back stays, breaking the chain plates. She then bounded off and struck us at the mizzen topmast chain plates, carrying away the back stays and bumpkin, main and main topsail braces, leaving me comparatively a wreck on the starboard side.

Before she blew her whistle my wife came on deck and stood by my side. We could plainly see her deck

20

from the pilot house to her bows and not a soul was to be seen there as she passed the stern. I hailed her and asked her to stand by me, but she made no reply. My wife attempted to jump on board of her, and would, had I not grabbed her. We drifted apart and I gave my attention to my ship and gave orders to the mate to cut the lashings on the boats and to the carpenter to sound the pumps. My rail was broken from the fore rigging to the main rigging. The first report the carpenter made was that the ship was half full of water. I told him to take a light and go down the fore hatch and see.

In the meantime I found there was no water in the hold. I then gave orders to the mate to never mind the boats, but to take all hands and secure the back stays and repair damages. All my starboard braces had been carried away with the blocks, etc. Now, while I was attending to the condition of the ship, it certainly took from ten to fifteen minutes, and during that time I never looked after the steamer, neither did anyone else that I know of. We were all busy attending to our own necessities. When, after I found I was not seriously damaged, I looked for the steamer, I just saw a light on our starboard quarters, and when I looked again it was gone. There has been a great deal said about the crying and screaming of the women and children on the steamer. Not one sound was heard from her by anyone of my ship, neither was anyone seen on board of her. Neither did any one on my ship think for a moment that any injury of any kind had happened to the steamer, for at 1:30 a. m. as the sailors were furling the spanker, they commenced to growl, as sailors will, about the steamer, after running us down, to go off and leave us in that shape, without stopping to inquire whether we were injured or not.

At the time of the collision, the *Orpheus* was bound for Nanaimo, B.C. in ballast, where she was to have loaded coal for San Francisco. An 1100-ton ship, built in 1856, she had made ten voyages around Cape Horn but was only on her second in the coastwise coal trade when the catastrophe occurred. The damage inflicted on the *Orpheus* following the crash was temporarily repaired but a few hours later she piled up on the rocks off Cape Beale on the west coast of Vancouver Island, becoming a total loss.

Owing to the fact that Captain Sawyer had a reputation as a hard master, many seized the opportunity to brand him before the facts were heard. Some of his commands had been known as "hell ships," for he always ruled over his crew with an iron hand. Thus rumors were freely circulated that he purposely put his ship aground following the collision so that he would be absolved of blame.

Regardless of adverse comment Captain Sawyer was considered a worthy shipmaster, though in truth a strict disciplinarian. Nevertheless in the intense excitement following the tragedy he was accused of casting his ship away and was arrested on that charge on his return to San Francisco. Deeply sorrowed by the loss of life on the *Pacific*, he brooded for many days. Like a caged lion he paced the confining walls of his conscience, living and reliving the tragic events of that horrible night. His brain was tortured beyond description, for neither he nor anyone else could bring back the scores of dead. Nights were sleepless and days dragged. Over and over he prayed that he would awaken from this nightmare—but, alas, the hands of time never turn back and he realized that he must face reality and with it the awful consequences of being a condemned man. When examined for the loss of his own ship, his testimony acquitted him of the charge. Captain Sawyer's explanation was fully corroborated:

> Cape Beale Light had only been lighted for four or five months then, and I had no record of it. My sailing directions gave Cape Flattery as the most northern light, and the negligence of the second mate in not calling me when he found he could not

steer the course given him caused the loss to the *Orpheus*. I have a letter from Captain Gilkey of the ship *Messenger,* which picked up the man Jelley, saying he mistook Cape Beale Light for Cape Flattery, and had he made the light earlier he would have been in the same fix that I was in, but he fortunately did not get up to it until daylight, and then he saw by the land that it could not be the entrance to Fuca Strait.

Not so easy on Sawyer was the coroners' jury which was convened at Victoria, at the inquest on the body of Thomas Ferrill, one of the victims. Their findings follow:

That the said steamer *Pacific* sank after a collision with the American ship *Orpheus,* off Cape Flattery, on the night of November 4, 1875; that the *Pacific* struck the *Orpheus* on the starboard side with her stem a very light blow, the shock of which should not have damaged the *Pacific* if she had been a sound and substantial vessel; that the collision between them was caused by the *Orpheus* not keeping the approaching *Pacific's* light on her port bow as when first seen, but putting the helm hard to starboard and unjustifiably crossing the *Pacific's* bow; that the watch on the deck of the *Pacific* at the time of the collision was not sufficient in number to keep a proper lookout, the watch consisting only of three men, namely one at the wheel, one supposed to be on the lookout, and the third mate, a young man of doubtful experience; that the *Pacific* had about 238 passengers on board at the time of the collision; that she had five boats, the utmost carrying capacity of which did not exceed 160 persons; that the boats were not and could not be lowered by the undisciplined and inexperienced crew; that the captain of the *Orpheus* sailed away after the collision and did not remain by the *Pacific* to ascertain the damage she had sustained.

Wild tales about negligence on the part of the officers and men of both ships ran their usual course. In spite of it all, Captain Sawyer was later given another command and sailed for many years thereafter. Finally he quit the sea and settled down in Port Townsend where he died in 1894. Though disliked by many who believed him guilty, his faithful friends always maintained that he had done nothing that any other shipmaster would not have done under similar circumstances on that black day in maritime history.

So overcome were all by the great loss of life on the *Pacific* that little was said about her precious cargo. Aside from the regular general freight, including 2000 sacks of oats, ten tons of sundries, 261 hides, ten cords of bolts, 280 tons of coal, 11 casks of furs, 31 barrels of cranberries, two cases of opium, 18 tons of merchandise, six horses and two buggies, she carried a strongbox containing $79,220. None of this was ever recovered. The waters are deep and treacherous where the *Pacific* went down but doubtless the reading of this account may someday stir divers to search for her hidden grave.

It is doubtful that the *Pacific* is more than a small pile of teredo-eaten planks and rusted iron fittings after three quarters of a century at the bottom of the sea. The 875-ton steamer constructed at New York in 1851, had a walking beam engine and two large sidewheels. She also carried sail on her three masts which gave her a fair speed under the right conditions.

There is a sequel to the story of the *Pacific*. In July of 1861, fourteen years before her final destruction, she was on her way down the Columbia River from Portland when she rammed into Coffin Rock in a heavy fog, immediately sinking. At first it was decided to abandon her and if only this decision had been abided by, one of the coast's worst marine disasters would have been averted several years later. But fate intervened. The steamer *Express* came down from Portland with the town's new fire engine and pumper on deck to empty the water out of the *Pacific*. Shortly afterward she was refloated, patched and sent to San Francisco for badly needed repairs. Fate is a strange, intangible thing and frequently leads to the paths of death and destruction.

After yet another decade of service the *Pacific,* tired and worn, was relegated to the mudflats. Then came the gold excitement in the Cassiar district of British Columbia and she returned to the coastwise run in 1874. Supposedly reconditioned and overhauled, she was advertised as equal to a brand new ship. Actually the principal extent of her face lifting was a good paint job and a company publicity director handy with adjectives. That she was unseaworthy goes without saying. The real guilty went untried and unpunished.

As a conclusion, it may be said that many lives might have been spared when the *Pacific* went down had Captain Sawyer's wife succeeded in jumping to her deck following the collision. For a certainty, the master of the *Orpheus* would have then at all cost brought his vessel about and plucked many from the black waters of a demanding ocean.

In December of 1935, Neil Henley, then a master mariner, the only survivor of the *Pacific* disaster, celebrated his fiftieth wedding anniversary at his Steilacoom, Washington, home. Eighty years of age, physically frail but still mentally alert, he told again of the terrible tragedy that chilled the blood of the most casual listener.

UMATILLA

A lightship now guards the dreaded reef where on the ninth day of February, 1884, the splendid new steamer *Umatilla* was nearly lost. And surely she would have been except for the courage and daring of her first officer, Johnny "Dynamite" O'Brien, who was to become an almost legendary figure in maritime annals.

The *Umatilla,* a collier, was in command of Captain Frank Worth on that stormy winter evening. Snow drove with fiendish force. The sea snarled and frothed as the wind whipped it into jagged peaks. Visibility was at a minimum and the ship groped blindly through the murk. With a sudden jolt that threw her crew to the decks she rammed an uncharted obstruction. The ship shuddered from stem to stern. Through the gaping hole, water began to pour. All hands were ordered to the boats. The first lifeboat got away in charge of the second officer. The next boat carried the captain and the remaining crew members with the exception of first officer O'Brien and two seamen. They drew a light raft.

According to the accepted version, O'Brien's raft lost sight of the two lifeboats in the midst of the storm and was forced to return to the *Umatilla*. Those who knew O'Brien personally, figured differently. Though he spoke nary a word when Captain Worth ordered abandonment of the stricken steamer, wheels were turning about in his head. To defy the master's orders would have been insubordination. Call it the luck of the Irish, but O'Brien talked his two companions into returning to the abandoned ship. They scrambled up her iron sides as the raft was raised by the pulsating sea.

By this time the steamer had worked free of the reef and was adrift. Not a moment was lost by O'Brien. In an effort to keep the ship from being dashed back on the reef, the men succeeded in hoisting head sails on the foremast and moving slowly away from the reef. Three men sailing a 3000-ton steamer was unusual, to say the least, but those who knew O'Brien claimed him the equal of ten men.

The *Umatilla* rode low in the water, having shipped a generous portion of the Pacific. The situation worsened but the Irishman gave no indication of defeat. His luck continued, for at 7 p.m. the San Francisco-bound steamer *Wellington* sighted his distress signals and immediately came to his aid. A light line was fired across the ship's bows and by putting the steam winch to work the three men managed to make a heavier hawser fast. The tow commenced. The *Wellington* altered her course, came about, and headed for Juan de Fuca Strait—her goal Esquimalt, B. C. Her work was cut out for her. The

Umatilla was down by the head and sinking lower by the hour. Men on the *Wellington* kept a weather eye on the hawser to cut it instantly should their charge sink. Bucking wind and tide, the towing steamer battled on. Only after many anxious, hectic hours did it gain its desired refuge. Within the protective walls of the harbor the towline was at last dropped. Lower and lower settled the steamer and, then defying all efforts to keep her afloat, plunged to the bottom, 200 feet down. It appeared that O'Brien's folly had failed.

To the casual viewer the whole operation might have seemed a total waste of energy—O'Brien's gallant stand; the tenacious tow by the *Wellington*. But no. Where salvage would have been impossible near Umatilla Reef, the steamship, though on the bottom, was in protected waters where salvagers could work.

The famous Whitelaw Salvage Company of San Francisco was awarded the bid and performed a marvelous salvage feat in raising the ship from the harbor floor. Several months were required and a large crew of men, but by utilizing the tide, slings and cradles, the *Umatilla* was raised. It was well over a year before she was refitted and returned to her run. In the meanwhile there was the intervening hassle in getting the insurance adjusted.

An investigation was held at Seattle and Captain Worth was exonerated from all blame, testimony showing that a very strong northerly current prevailed during the snowstorm, setting the vessel on the rocks in spite of any precaution that could have been taken. Though free of all charges, Worth had a feeling of apprehension about his first officer bringing his command into port. The inspectors commended O'Brien for his act of bravery, which did little to quell the frustrations of Captain Worth. Sizable hunks of salvage money were paid all involved in the saving of the *Umatilla* and the Whitelaw people took home a generous sum of greenbacks. The *Umatilla* was heavily insured, having been built to the highest specifications. Her owners were willing to go all the way to restore her to service.

O'Brien and the *Umatilla* went on to enjoy long and colorful careers, both carving niches for themselves in the maritime hall of fame. The ship bequeathed its name to the reef that almost spelled its doom.

AUSTRIA

Since 1887, a pitted three-ton anchor has rested amid the rocks at Cape Alava, Washington, most westerly point of the United States mainland. As the tide ebbs and flows around it, it seems to whisper its story. This ancient anchor and a few bits of wreckage mark the grave of the *Austria.* Should you be the kind that likes to dig for relics under the sea sands, chances are you can unearth a dead-eye or a rusted spike from the old wreck but the rest you'll have to visualize from the facts that were left behind.

The *Austria* departed from San Francisco in ballast for Tacoma on January 21, 1887. She was wrecked on Flattery Rocks less than a quarter-mile off Cape Alava, nine days later. Following is the account of the shipmaster, George E. Delano:

> We had a fine run of 8½ days to the vicinity of Cape Flattery. The wind had been from the south and east when it hauled to the westward and blew a heavy gale.
>
> We did not calculate ourselves so near the coast until we made Cape Flattery Light when we knew that the current had taken us inshore, the light bearing west by north. Immediately we made all possible sail and headed N. W. by N. The vessel making leeway wore around heading S.S.W. Lost foresail, fore-top-sail and mizzen staysail all new canvas blown out of the bolt ropes. The vessel still was making leeway and drawing nearer the shore.
>
> The sea was a mass of living breakers to leeward

28

and as daylight dawned we realized our dangerous position and did not know how soon the vessel would dash itself to pieces on some hidden rock. Our principal sails blown away, there was nothing left for us to do but steer through the network of rocks to the smoothest place visible and about 7:30 a. m. she struck a hidden rock, part of which must have gone through her bottom, as the tide ebbs and flows through her as she lies upright and apparently uninjured. During the day the wind hauled to the northward and the sea went down sufficiently to allow us to make a landing in the boats. As we approached land the Indians came out in their canoes and assisted us in getting safely ashore. We suffered very much with the cold until the next day when the sea had sufficiently moderated to allow us to return on board and get bedding, clothes, and some provisions.

Later sighted steamer *Mexico* bound northward and hoisted signal flags. She came in close but did not send a boat ashore. We presumed she would send for help. The following day we landed sails, rigging, stores and all movable materials. When everything was removed but the anchors and chains, I walked 30 miles to Neah Bay suffering much from the cold. I left the crew to protect the stores.

On arriving at Neah Bay, Captain Delano learned why help had been delayed. The revenue cutter *Oliver Wolcott* lay at her moorings awaiting a supply of fuel. Her boilers were cold. Eventually the coal arrived, they steamed her up, and hastened to the scene of the wreck. The cutter anchored offshore and sent in her boats for the survivors and Captain Delano did not rest until his entire crew were safe aboard. Then the master of the wreck bowed his head as if saying a prayer for his ship.

With this solemn moment past, he turned his attentions to what might be salvaged, for it was said that he owned an interest in his ship. With the help of the revenue cutter crew, all available salvaged materials were rounded up and later sold for $3000. The wreck was insured for a mere $7900 but was valued at $20,000. So Captain Delano and all parties involved in the ownership of the *Austria* took a financial beating. The 18-year-old, 1300-ton vessel had made some very creditable passages in her time but like so many proud old sailing vessels of yesteryear, the *Austria* was doled out an unkind fate.

Her timbers, anchor and chains still languish in the sands. Romanticists have spun fantastic tales of pirates, bloodshed and cannibalism after viewing the scant remains of the *Austria*. Little did they know that she was but a common carrier of the sea, wrecked without fanfare or loss of life and little noticed in the maritime obituaries of a bygone era.

WIDE WEST

The vicissitudes of the steamer *Wide West* can best be summed up by the simple phrase—from riches to rags. Let us start with the riches. Imagine, if you can, the warm summer day of August 15, 1887, on the Portland, Oregon, waterfront. Thousands had gathered to witness the launching of the mammoth sternwheeler.

It represented the greatest forward step in river steamboating in two decades, The vessel was the largest paddler on the river and the envy of every person who had a yen for steamboating. The name *Wide West* was on the lips of every Portlander.

At the time of her launching, the inland empire was experiencing boom times and every available steamer, regardless of size, shape or condition, was taxed to capacity in carrying wheat downstream, and building materials and farm machinery upstream. So much in demand were steamboats that the *Wide West* was pressed into service before her lavish fittings were completed. Rushed into the Portland-Cascades run, she was loaded to the guards on every trip. Not until the following spring did she get her finishing decorative touches and the installation of the first hydraulic steering gear on the river.

The vessel remained on the Cascades route, becoming the most popular boat on the inland rivers. She was both handsome and fast. While alternating on the Portland-Astoria run she established a record of five hours which stood unchallenged for many years.

Captain John Wolf, her long-time master, always chuckled over the fact that he had once towed the steamer *Oneonta* at a faster pace than it had ever been able to go under its own power.

In 1883 the *Wide West* was making a round trip each day between Portland and Astoria, but she had been worked so hard that age and lack of repairs were fast catching up with her. Her final voyage on the river was to the Cascades in 1887, after which she was relegated to the boneyard. No steamer on the Columbia or Willamette rivers had been worked harder during a single decade.

Then the riches turned to rags. Her house and most of her elaborate fittings were stripped off and placed on the elegant new river queen, the steamer *T. J. Potter.*

In the background of ignominy, the *Wide West* rotted away for nearly two years. She might have remained thus till the bitter end had not the hastily formed Puget Sound Steam Lighter and Transportation Company come into existence. They purchased the engineless hull, and dreamed dreams that were not to be. The new firm headed by a young Seattleite, Captain Frederick Sparling, fitted its purchase out with a small inferior engine and replaced her giant sternwheel with a propeller. This was the beginning of the end of Sparling's steamboat ambitions. Now it may be said he was the kind who had to do things on the spur of the moment. Detail, research and speculation were unknown to him. It was all or nothing, win or lose.

Without the knowledge of the local steamboat inspectors who certainly would have adjudged the vessel unseaworthy, Sparling slipped out of Portland under the veil of night and went downriver to Astoria. After but a brief stop for additional fuel the steamer moved out into the stream and headed for the bar.

No government officials stopped her, for it was a holiday—Christmas Day 1889. Amid the festivities nobody was much concerned about the departure of an aging steamer resurrected from the boneyard.

Sparling's knowledge of steam navigation was somewhat limited. He had mastered the fundamentals but had left the rest to chance. Somehow he was able to get the steamer over the bar but shortly afterwards, when a gale confronted him, his usual luck suddenly departed. The vessel became unmanageable. Then, just to put the sealer on an impossible situation, the engine conked out.

Some weather-beaten sails were run up a makeshift mast but the spanker and boom were carried away. At 2:30 the following morning, while frantic crew members were trying to repair the engine, the propeller fell off. The chief engineer threw up his hands in despair.

The *Wide West* drifted, helpless. Two hours later, driven by powerful winds, she piled up on the bleak shores of Destruction Island, off Washington's lonely northwest coast. The seas lifted her high on the rocks until her entire hull rattled and creaked like a skeleton in a closet. Sparling felt his ship breaking up beneath his feet and cursed the day he had traded cold cash for a floating coffin. He and his men hastily surrendered their "white elephant" to the overpowering forces of nature.

They managed to save a lifeboat and with it rowed to the mainland and then traveled overland on foot, mile after mile, until they reached the Indian village at Neah Bay.

Sparling stood on the beach, disheartened and disgusted. He removed his captain's cap and threw it into the surf, ending once and for all his short-lived role as president and captain of a steamship company.

On September 6, 1956, the Liberian freighter *Seagate* ran aground on Sonora Reef, Washington. Salvage tugs relaxed their vigil; ship drifted free; grounded near Taholah where it broke in two. Fred Rossi and William Waara, with helicopter, purchased wreck for salvage.

Wreck of the cargo vessel *Lake Gebhart* off Toleak Point on the Washington Coast, May 9, 1923. Vessel later foundered, after cargo of salt was removed.

The 3600 horsepower tug *Salvage Chief* pulling the SS *Yorkmar* off the beach north of Grays Harbor. It was thought that the vessel would be a total loss until man's skill and ingenuity intervened. (Ackroyd Photo)

Before salvage, the *Yorkmar* rested uneasily high and dry on the beach. She went aground December 8, 1952. (W. B. "Doc" Heil Photo)

HMS *Condor*, a British naval vessel which was lost with all hands numbering 140, somewhere off Cape Flattery, Washington, in December 1901.

British SS *Temple Bar* wrecked off Quillayute Reef near La Push, Washington April 8, 1939. She was bound for Japan with scrap iron. Ocean currents and negligence of captain were blamed.
(Joe Williamson Photo)

Surrounded by acres of sand at low tide is the passenger liner *Admiral Benson* which grounded on Peacock Spit, at the Columbia River entrance February 15, 1930.

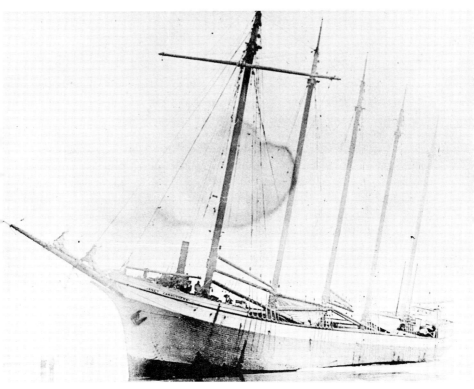

Six lives were lost in this shipwreck. The Canadian schooner *Janet Carruthers* wrecked north of Grays Harbor January 22, 1919. Salvage efforts failed.

IVANHOE, KEWEENAH, AND MONTSERRAT

In late 1894, a weird sequence of events was enacted on the high seas. Three reportedly sound vessels vanished, the only clue being an occasional piece of wreckage cast up on the beaches from California to Alaska. Here was indeed mystery to stir the most skeptical soul —intense drama without logical explanation.

The first victim was the coal-laden ship *Ivanhoe*, Captain Edward Griffin, which sailed from Seattle for San Francisco on September 27, 1894. Twenty-three persons, including two men and two women passengers, were aboard. The 30-year old vessel was towed down Juan de Fuca Strait by the tug *Tyee* and cast off. Later she fell in with the barkentine *Robert Sudden* and was in her company until the following day. Then from the southeast sprang a gale blowing up hurricane-force winds of rain and hail. So thick became the weather that the two vessels lost track of each other. When the atmosphere cleared, the *Ivanhoe* had vanished.

Despite a lengthy search by the revenue cutter *Grant* and several commercial craft, nothing could be found. It was as if an unknown force had devoured the ship and its crew. Then after many days a life ring marked *Ivanhoe* was picked up on the shores of Christie Island in Barclay Sound, B. C. This led to the supposition that the ship had foundered off Cape Flattery as the prevailing northerly currents would have carried the life ring there. Then the ship's name board was picked up by the lighthouse keeper's wife on the north spit of Willapa Bay, over 100 miles south of where the life ring was found. The board was standing upright in the sand, and the gold leaf in the name was not marred, suggesting that it had not drifted far. This caused widespread speculation as to the locale of the sinking.

Commander Farenholt of the 13th Lighthouse District secured the name board and sent it to factors of the Black Diamond Coal Company, owners of the *Ivanhoe*. With it was a letter advancing his theory that it would have been almost an impossibility for a ship to be lost off Cape Flattery and have pieces of its wreckage drift as far south as did the *Ivanhoe's* name board in the light of the prevailing northerly current.

Receipt of this theory started a concentrated study of the situation. Some advanced the suggestion that the vessel was still afloat but the majority were satisfied that she had gone down off Cape Flattery, victim of a sudden gale. None was ever to know. While the experts were seeking an answer an even greater mystery was in the making—a mystery with a plot too deep for the super sleuth.

Two sizable colliers, the steamships *Montserrat* and *Keweenah,* in late 1894, put out to sea within a few hours of each other, coal laden for San Francisco. The former departed from Nanaimo, B. C., the latter from Comox. The *Montserrat,* a well-constructed vessel, was in command of Captain David "Lucky" Blackburn. In all, 26 crew members, plus two or three passengers, were aboard.

Blackburn, a native Nova Scotian, was probably the best-known skipper on the coast, a man of questionable pursuits but one who shared fear with nobody. He made his money however or wherever he pleased. To gain ownership of his vessel he had done everything from blackbirding to salvage.

On the afternoon of December 7, the *Montserrat* and the *Keweenah* came within hailing distance off Tatoosh Island. The *Keweenah,* the older and less staunch of the two vessels, was in command of Captain W. H. Jenkins, and carried a crew of 31. The two steamers were last sighted by the lookout at Cape Flattery Light Station toward evening. They were about ten miles offshore, plunging head on into a southwest gale. The *Montserrat* was in the lead and both were taking heavy seas over their bows. The gale mounted in fury and darkness came on. Then the plot thickened.

The hurricane did not abate its fury for eight days, one of the most severe storms of that decade. Shoreside facilities were damaged from Alaska to San Diego which in itself prevented a search of any magnitude for the missing ships. Several weeks later, on February 28, 1895, a medicine chest stamped *Montserrat* was discovered on the beach at the south end of Etalin Island, B. C. The months slipped by. Then one day a schooner ran into Rose Harbor, in Canada's Queen Charlotte Islands, and her officers found in an Indian village several pieces of finished hardwood. The names *Montserrat* or *Keweenah* were imprinted on them. This lent credence to the theory that the ships had turned before the gale and foundered in an attempt to seek out shelter. Dead men tell no tales—but in this mysterious case not even a body was found.

Two other theories were advanced. One was that the *Keweenah*, the less seaworthy of the two steamers, was in danger of foundering. While the *Montserrat* was trying to get a line on her, an old skill of Captain Blackburn, a collision occurred and both went down. The other theory was that the respective vessels were grossly overloaded and, in the heavy seas with a minimum of freeboard, sank like rocks.

Because of Blackburn's reputation as a nerveless skipper—one who had taken chances that no sane mariner would attempt—and because of his eye for salvage, he was generally thought to have been a definite factor in the disappearance of the ships. But if a thousand theories are advanced none will ever reveal the truth. It must forever remain sealed on the lips of those unfortunate souls who went down with their ships. Until the sea shall give up its dead the truth must repose in its depths.

CONDOR AND MATTEAWAN

Occasionally a fragile clue will turn up after many years to shed some light on a ship posted missing with all hands. The author played a small role in the identity of a teredo-eaten binnacle trawled up from the ocean

35

depths—the probable key to one of the most baffling marine disasters on the Pacific Coast.

The trawler *Blanco,* skippered by Ole Stokke, was fishing for petralie sole approximately 40 miles northwest of Cape Flattery in May of 1949. Suddenly her nets fouled in about 42 fathoms of water. They were immediately raised. The fishermen were astonished to find there entwined an ancient ship's binnacle, the remains of a battered lifeboat, and some other bits of wreckage. The binnacle was hoisted on deck, but the lifeboat, punctured by teredo holes, was too heavy to handle and sank again.

When the binnacle was unloaded on the dock at the San Juan Fish & Packing Company in Seattle, its story made front page news. Letters began pouring in, offering clues as to what ship the instrument was from. Being somewhat of a beachcombing romanticist, I took my turn and ended up hauling the binnacle home, all 200 pounds of it.

The odor of the attached sea life was extremely offensive and the curious remained at a safe distance. My best friends would have no part of me. The teredos had grown fat over the years, feasting on the delicious morsels of mahogany. Countless small holes honey-combed the stand of the instrument. The iron deviator balls and the horizontal sphere, though badly rusted, were still intact. The brass hood was battered and the compass missing. The maker's name plate, however, was still legible and this offered the principal clue to the instrument's identity. It read:

Lord Kelvin's Patents
(Sir William Thomson)
sole makers
No. 9011
Kelvin and James White Ltd.
16 Cambridge St. Glasgow

With old wreck records and charts at hand I located

the vessels reputedly lost off Cape Flattery. Many were eliminated because of the type of binnacle involved and the fact that it was wired for electricity. The first ship in the world to be lighted by electricity was the SS *Columbia* in 1880. This automatically omitted all wrecks prior to that date.

Old chandlery catalogues listed the instrument as the type manufactured between 1885 and 1900, and the wiring placed it in the 1890-1900 classification.

It was the opinion of most that the binnacle was from a steel or iron-hulled steamer, as it was not only wired but also carried the maximum in deviation correctors. Many binnacles were not successfully wired until after the turn of the century, as direct current had a definite effect on a ship's compass needle. Later this was remedied by using alternating current.

Process of elimination narrowed it down to two vessels, one the H. M. S. *Condor,* a British sloop-of-war lost off Cape Flattery in December 1901 with a reputed 140 souls; and the American collier *Matteawan* which vanished off Cape Flattery with 33 souls, also in December of the same year. The two vessels sailed within 48 hours of each other.

Inasmuch as the *Matteawan* was San Francisco bound and the *Condor* en route to Honolulu, the location where the binnacle was recovered would favor the latter. The British Admiralty was then contacted as well as the makers of the binnacle in an effort to establish definite identity. Wrote the Admiralty:

> With reference to your letter of the 25th of August, 1949, requesting information concerning the binnacle carried by the H.M.S. *Condor,* I am commanded by My Lords Commissioners of the Admiralty to inform you that while it has not been found possible to identify the binnacle recently trawled up off Cape Flattery with that on board H. M. S. *Condor* when that ship was lost in that area in 1901, it has been established that the binnacle on

said vessel was manufactured by Messrs. Kelvin, White and James and was of the type you have described. It is regretted that no further information is available from the Admiralty records.

The answer from the makers of the binnacle, whose company name in the interim had been changed to Kelvin & Hughes Ltd., follows:

> We have read with great interest your letter of 27th of May, directed to our old address at Cambridge Street regarding the Kelvin binnacle brought up off Tatoosh Island by the fishing vessel *Blanco.* We have been investigating this matter in the interval but are sorry we are unable to furnish any further information, except to confirm the correctness of your guess that the binnacle was manufactured the decade prior to the turn of the century and was of the exact type sold to the Admiralty.

What happened to the *Condor?* All of the known facts are here presented.

The *Condor,* classed as a screw sloop-of-war, departed from Esquimalt, B. C., December 2, 1901. She was en route to Honolulu where she was to have arrived 11 days later. The H. M. S. *Warspite,* also Honolulu-bound, was scheduled to leave in company with the *Condor* but remained behind for gunnery practice. Toward evening, the *Condor* put out to sea and was last reported off Tatoosh Island. Captained by Commander Clinton Sclater she carried a complement, according to the British Admiralty, of 130, but Victoria, B. C., sources claimed she had taken on an additional ten men before sailing. She was a 980-ton steam-propelled vessel built of iron at Sheerness, England, in 1898. Her dimensions were length, 180 feet; beam, 32 feet, and depth, 11 feet, six inches.

The *Condor's* armament consisted of ten four-inch quick-fire guns and four three-pounders, plus smaller auxiliary fire power. The full output of her steam propulsion gave her a speed of 13 knots and she could carry sail in an emergency. The vessel was commissioned at Chatham on November 1, 1900, and was not the same *Condor* that gained fame when Lord Charles Beresford steamed in under the guns at Alexandria, with the historic signal flown, "Well done, *Condor.*" Rather the *Condor* in question was named for its historic predecessor.

After the *Condor* passed Cape Flattery she ran head on into a southeast gale. She was unreported for several days when a small work boat, similar to those she carried, was found abandoned on the beach at Ahousett, B. C. Other unidentified wreckage was found at Clayoquot on the west coast of Vancouver Island. Several months later at Wreck Bay, B. C., a sailor's cap and a broom were picked up, supposedly from the *Condor.*

The HMS *Warspite,* which was to have accompanied the *Condor* to Hawaii, encountered the same savage gale believed to have claimed the *Condor.* On reaching Honolulu, the *Warspite's* commander reported such terrible seas off Cape Flattery as to tear out one of his deck cannons.

If the binnacle trawled up from the bottom of the sea in 1949 is actually from the *Condor,* it is the first clue to the locale of the iron coffin that holds 140 souls of the Royal Navy. It has been generally theorized that the vessel turned turtle in the throes of the mighty gale and sank in minutes, trapping every Jack Tar where he stood.

The disappearance of the SS *Matteawan* was basically the same as that of the *Condor.* She left Nanaimo, B. C., on December 1, 1901, and sailed out through the Strait of Juan de Fuca in command of Captain H. B. Crosscup. Like the other mystery ships, she signalled the lightkeepers on Tatoosh Island and was never again reported. What strange fate intervened to snatch these ships and their human cargoes from the face of the sea may never be known.

The 3300-ton *Matteawan* was a collier with a length of 324 feet, one of the largest coal carriers on the Pacific

Coast. When she cleared Nanaimo, her holds were filled with 4890 tons of coal. Encountering the same vicious gale off the Washington Coast that reputedly claimed the *Condor*, the *Matteawan* was last seen on December 3, taking a terrific buffeting. Then the curtain closed down on her and never reopened. A staunch vessel, but underpowered for her size, the British-built *Matteawan* was launched in 1893 as the *Asturian Prince*. Later she was accepted under United States registry and was last operated under the banner of J. Jerome and Company.

Within a few minutes of the departure of the *Matteawan* on her voyage of doom, another steamer also sailed from Nanaimo—the SS *Wellington*, under Captain Collin Salmon. She followed in the *Matteawan's* wake out through the Strait but on reaching the open Pacific her master elected to come about and take up anchorage at Neah Bay where she might ride out the impending gale. Had the *Matteawan* followed suit a terrible tragedy might have been averted.

The replacement value of the *Matteawan's* hull and cargo was set at $250,000 but she was insured for only $175,000 and her cargo for $15,000. After being officially declared missing with all hands, the insurance costs were paid in full by the underwriters.

There are several who believed that the binnacle trawled up off Cape Flattery was from the *Matteawan* and not from the *Condor*. The late marine surveyor and salvage master, Captain W. J. Moloney, once served aboard the *Matteawan* as second mate and had recollections of her carrying a similar binnacle to the one in question. Both ships, having been built in British yards, were fitted out with the same make of binnacle, the Kelvin patent being standard equipment on most British ships of the period. Also both ships were electrically wired.

The former Seattle marine surveyor, Captain Daniel Hutchings, has weird memories of the *Matteawan*. As a lad he boarded the vessel at Nanaimo while the ship was loading coal. He asked permission of Captain Crosscup to work his way to San Francisco. When his request was refused he stowed away but was discovered by the mate before sailing time and promptly put ashore.

Shortly after the *Condor* and *Matteawan* vanished, a theory that gained considerable impetus was advanced—that the respective ships collided and immediately foundered. Existing evidence, however, would make such a theory questionable, as wreckage thought to be from the *Condor* was found scattered up the west coast of Vancouver Island, while pieces of flotsam believed from the *Matteawan* were discovered south of Cape Flattery.

Another factor that may have figured in the loss of either vessel was that the Umatilla Reef Lightship was not in position, having been blown off station by the hurricane.

There was an old saying in the days of the coal ships that they stuck their noses under after rounding Cape Flattery and never came up until reaching the Golden Gate. At the turn of the century a large fleet of steamers and sailing vessels was engaged in the trade. Many of them foundered because their reserve buoyancy was so little, due to overloading. The *Matteawan* may well have been such a victim.

So ends this sinister tale of vanishing ships, but there were more that followed and others that preceded. Cape Flattery has a flattering and erroneous title for its role as tombstone over a massive graveyard of ships.

LAMUT

Shrouded under war-time restrictions of World War II was the news of the loss of the Russian freighter *Lamut*. She crashed near Teahwhit Head in the severe gale of March 31, 1943. The usual newspaper headlines that scream a ship's loss were missing. Only those who had a part in the actual rescue or those concerned with the movement of the vessel were notified of its loss.

The *Lamut*, a grubby, gray freighter flying the flag of the U. S. S. R., had an alias. She was built at Ashtabula,

41

Ohio, in 1919, as the *Lake Elpueblo*. Never a headliner, she was just a homely old breadwinner kicking from pillar to post. Like so many aging American ships that had long been forgotten, she ended up in the Russian merchant marine, long the most antiquated in the world.

Thus we find *Lamut* Vladivostok-bound, out of Puget Sound and in the throes of tumultuous gale-whipped seas off Washington's coast. Driving winds and sheets of rain obscured all visibility and fear was outlined on the faces of the Russian crew. The captain was no longer certain of his position, and fear turned to near panic when the ship drove up against the towering Quillayute Needles—the jaws of death. Hopelessly cradled below cliffs that rose plumb from the ocean, the ship sounded its death knell. The grinding and tearing of her steel hull shattered the eardrums as breakers forced her on her beam ends. Aboard, 44 men and eight women scrambled like sheep, violently frightened and not knowing which way to run.

The Coast Guard, alerted by a desperate call for help, failed in getting small boats anywhere near the boiling maelstrom where lay the wreck. Larger craft were even more useless. Rescue must come from the shore. Blazing their way through two miles of thickly-wooded virgin country, Coastguardmen on foot reached the sharp precipice above the wounded freighter. They realized that unless they acted immediately the Russians would all perish. Without suitable gear at their command, the would-be rescuers removed the laces from their shoes and tied them together. These they dropped down the sheer cliffs to the frantic hands on the wreck. A heavier line was attached, pulled up, and made fast. The skeptical Russians meanwhile had attempted to launch a lifeboat but one woman was killed and another injured when a cable snapped dropping the bow of the craft into the sea. This having failed, they turned their hopes to the handful of men above them.

With a heavy line at fast secured between the wreck and the rocks, the Russians, women as well as the men, clung desperately for survival. They worked their way up the rope hand over hand, their bodies dangling over an indescribable chasm. Across the churning hell below, arm and back muscles straining to the breaking point, the weird procession began. Hanging between the black clouds above and the snarling, crashing breakers below, they went. One slip would have meant instant death.

The Coastguardmen encouraged the survivors not to give up. Miraculously, but not without incident, all made it. Some admitted that fear alone impelled them onward. They had cheated death but only by the narrowest of margins.

Russian sea captains who lost their ships often faced the death penalty on reaching their homeland. When the master of the *Lamut* was found not liable, many Americans associated with the case wrote personal letters to the Soviet premier, Joseph Stalin, asking that he not punish the captain for the loss of his ship. The timeliness of those letters is believed to have spared the captain's life after his return to Russia.

From Cape Flattery to Destruction Island the bottom of the sea is filled with the remains of ships which have carried hundreds of souls to watery graves. Authorities say the North Pacific is not as rough as the North Atlantic, but it goes without saying that countless ships have mysteriously disappeared without trace in North Pacific waters. Even in recent years two well-known ships with every modern means of communication have vanished after rounding Cape Flattery Light. One was the Chinese-owned, British-registered freighter *Hai Da* lost with 27 souls in 1937, and the other the States Steamship Company's freighter *Pennsylvania* with 46 crewmen, in the winter of 1952. What ship will be next only the storm gods know.

Chapter Two

CENTRAL WASHINGTON COAST

SOUTH of Destruction Island for many miles, deep-sea vessels give the Washington Coast a wide berth, due to the geographic indentation of the coastline and the many hazards that lurk there. In the absence of suitable bar entrances south of Cape Flattery until reaching Grays Harbor, there have been fewer shipwrecks in this area than on other coast stretches of Washington.

At Grays Harbor the entrance is narrow and very dangerous if the pilot book is not followed explicitly. Several ships have left their gnarled bones to rest on these treacherous bar sands. The shoreline just north-ward from Grays Harbor is marked by long sandy beaches. Farther north, the sand subsides in favor of rugged boulders and terminates in precipitous cliffs that rise sheer from the ocean.

SIR JAMSETJEE FAMILY

The British bark *Sir Jamsetjee Family,* Captain John Thompson, was wrecked near the mouth of the Quinault River, below Point Grenville, on December 1, 1887. Much of this area was then virgin country and the only white people within many miles were the Indian agent and his family.

En route to Port Townsend from Melbourne, Australia, in ballast, the cumbersome ship approached the north Pacific Coast in thick weather, so persistent as to prevent her captain from taking a bearing or an observation for over a week. The vessel was running under shortened sail. Night came on dark and forbidding and Captain Thompson paced the poop nervously. "If only I could see a light," he said over and over to himself. It was as though the ocean was boundless. Then with

44

shocking suddenness the ship heaved and groaned and the fearful roar of breakers beat upon the captain's ears. The impenetrable curtain closed down and the ship's forward motion ceased. It ground upon the shoals amid mighty breakers.

"Where are we?" groaned the captain in despair. "Stand by, all hands, to lower away!"

On the nearby shore, Indians had sighted the ship's side lights and knew that she was in dire trouble. A runner carried word to the Indian agent miles from the spot where the ship perilously lay. Charles Willoughby, the genial agent, lost not a moment, for he knew the terrific odds against sailors unfortunate enough to be wrecked along those hostile shores. With him went several natives, guided by a crude oil lantern.

Gusty rain-filled winds slowed the rescuers as they climbed over slippery boulders and brush-covered cliffs, mile after mile. At last they reached their destination and immediately built a large beach fire to cheer the despairing souls aboard the wreck.

The shipwrecked mariners had become panicky under the apprehension that their ship was about to break up. All awaited the captain's command to abandon. Finally it came. Their futile efforts, however, were short-lived as every boat with the exception of one was either crushed or capsized before it could be manned.

By now the battered wreck was in its death agonies, seas tearing down rigging and masts and breaching the decks. It would not last through the night. The last boat must be lowered. The fire on the shore afforded the only ray of hope. The captain was now fearful of another danger. He had heard and read of ships being plundered and crews murdered by savages along this little-known coast. He had two choices, either to remain with his ship or risk his chances with the natives. He had no way of knowing that an agent had been assigned to the area and that these once-fierce natives had come to offer their services.

The captain made his choice. The remaining boat was

lowered, and by taking every possible precaution, it got safely away from the wreck. As it came in through the high breakers, the Indians waded out to their hips in the frigid water to guide the boat to shore. On seeing them come alongside, the Englishmen beat them off with their oars, fearing their savagery. When agent Willoughby saw what was happening he shouted over the roaring tempest, and the astounded castaways ceased their actions. The Indians guided them to shore and cared for their needs as though they were members of their tribe. They were taken to the home of the agent. Eventually all recovered from their frightful experience and were guided on foot to Grays Harbor. There they found passage home.

The ill-fated *Sir Jamsetjee Family* became a total loss within 48 hours after its stranding. Built in 1864, the ship was named for a Parsee nobleman (a Parsee is a member of a sun-worshipping sect of India descended from the Persians who first settled there in the eighth century A.D.). For a figurehead she carried the bust of a Parsee, head of the Sir Jamsetjee family, but this sun worshipping emblem must have been an evil omen, as the ship was wrecked in one of the rainiest spots in America.

ABERCORN

The tragic wreck of the British bark *Abercorn*, which claimed 21 lives, ironically left a cargo that contributed greatly to the progress of a city.

It began when the *Abercorn* was en route to Portland, Oregon, from Maryport, England, with a full cargo of railroad iron (rails). Commanded by Captain William Irvine, this vessel of some 1262 tons was fashioned throughout of iron and was considered one of the finest ships in the trade. She arrived off the mouth of the Columbia River on January 10, 1888, and took aboard bar pilot Charles Johnson. Before sail could be made, unusually foggy weather closed in on the vessel and bar tugs were unable to locate her. In spite of the splendid reputation of the bar pilot, he lost his bearings and the ship was carried northward by the wind and currents.

Nothing more was heard of the *Abercorn* until three bruised seamen, sole survivors of the wreck, were found struggling along the shore ten miles north of Grays Harbor. Taken in by local beach dwellers, they told how their ship had struck bottom at 6 a.m. on the morning of January 12. The tremendous weight of the cargo held her fast off the beach while the savage breakers uprooted her masts and swept the decks clean. It became an impossibility to lower the boats. One by one the men succumbed to the avalanches of seawater slashing through the terrible tangle of rigging.

Among those who perished were Captain Irvine and pilot Johnson. The sea gave up the corpses of 14 others, strewing them at intervals along the beaches—a tragic display to sadden the hearts of the local inhabitants.

There was, however, another side to this regrettable wreck. At that time there was competition on Grays Harbor. Its little sawmill towns were each endeavoring to gain prominence. Ocosta on the south side of the bay had gained the initiative by winning a railroad connection to give it a link with the so-called "outside." It was the railroad that spelled the difference, and while Ocosta was booming, Aberdeen and Hoquiam were struggling for an existence.

The showdown battle was staged in 1894, six years after the *Abercorn* was wrecked. That was the year that public-spirited Aberdeen citizens banded together to bring the railroad to their city. Every able-bodied man saw to it that he donated ten days of work or the equivalent in cash at the rate of $2 a day to build their own link of the railroad to connect with the main line farther inland. They laid the road bed and cut the ties. Then came the expensive problem of securing the rails. This might have been a pitfall except for the fact that Captain George Pease, taking a much larger view of the situation, had already built a long trestle opposite Oyehut, extending between the beach and the submerged wreck of the *Abercorn*. In a novel salvage operation he managed to remove 2000 tons of rails. His entire take was purchased by two of Aberdeen's leading citizens, J. M. Weatherwax and Charles Wilson, who donated them to the railroad project. This heartened the townspeople, stirring them to new heights. Shortly afterward they celebrated the historic railroad link that was to put them on the map. It proved the beginning of a new era for Aberdeen and Hoquiam and the finale for Ocosta.

There was one drawback, however. The salvaged rails had been submerged in salt water for six years and had become badly pitted. Early-day travelers always knew when they reached the Aberdeen branch of the railroad by the rattle of the train as it wheeled over the pitted rails. But then who were they to complain? After all, weren't the rails donated?

FERNDALE

Not very often does a woman figure as the heroine in a shipwreck. In that of the British bark *Ferndale*, however, one gained international fame. Her name was Mrs. Edward White. On the morning of January 29, 1892, she and her husband came down to the beach from their farm about 15 miles north of Grays Harbor. As they walked along, hand in hand, suddenly amid the parting strands of fog they came to a complete halt. Before them was the dim outline of a great ship mortally wounded and nearly submerged in the outer breakers. Immediately Edward White left his wife and ran over the dunes in search of help. As Mrs. White gazed seaward she saw the form of a man being jostled about in the breakers, too weak to gain the shore. Imperiling her own life, she ran into the surf and pulled him to safety. No sooner had she made him as comfortable as she could than she saw another survivor staggering about in the breakers. Again she braved the towering surf, struggling desperately. Clutching the man, she exerted her full strength, somehow managing to pull him away from the boiling maelstrom.

48

Still no sign of her husband or the lifesaving crew. Then for the third time, still shaking from the cold, she found herself out in the combers in a desperate struggle to save another man. He was by far the largest of the three, a Russian, now in a state of delirium. She battled with him frantically and began making some progress in getting him toward shore when a wave knocked her feet out from under her and sucked her down. Around and around, over the sandy bottom, she was carried until her breath was nearly spent. With sand in her ears and eyes, her body aching from the terrible pummeling, she kept a vise-like grip on the oversized Russian. Twice more before she could get him to the beach she lost her footing but tenaciously pursued her task. It was as if she were possessed of a hidden power. Then, when success seemed assured, the half-crazed man turned on her and began beating her severely. A bitter struggle ensued. She was able to defend herself only because the seaman was nearly exhausted. In a wild disarray he finally sank to his knees, clawing and scratching at the sand.

When at last help arrived, this heroine had the three survivors lying side by side above the reaches of the tide, administering to their needs like an angel of mercy.

These were the sole survivors. Eighteen perished trying to escape from the ship. It was a mournful tale, for but a few hours before disaster struck, the *Ferndale* was 50 miles off the mouth of the Columbia River inbound with coal from Newcastle. On approaching the river entrance she was enveloped in fog and was obliged to stand offshore. It was the oft repeated story. Northerly currents and driving winds took command. At 3:30 a.m. on January 29, 1892, she struck hard on the beach. The rest has already been told.

The trio of survivors owed their lives to the courage of a gallant woman. Nor did the world let her deed pass unnoticed. For her act of bravery she was awarded an elaborate gold lifesaving medal from the Royal Family of England. A gift of money came from the people of the Grays Harbor area. Mrs. White was modest and over-

49

whelmed by the tribute paid her. "I'd gladly do the whole thing over," she said, "if I thought I could save a life."

TORRISDALE

Heavy loss of life was prevented by an almost suicidal series of trips by the lifesaving crew at Grays Harbor on the early morning of December 28, 1912.

The British square-rigger *Torrisdale*, inbound to Astoria from Antofagasta, had fallen victim to one of the severest southwesterly gales in many years. Far off course, she was much nearer shore than her master, Captain G. Collins, had dared dream. With both anchors out, she dragged over the Grays Harbor bar and was buffeted by such terrible seas that she went over on her beam ends and drifted to the south jetty, her crew fighting frantically to keep from being carried overboard into the watery turmoil. It was pitch black and the wind drove mercilessly.

At precisely 2:30 a.m. the watch at the lifesaving station sighted eerie rockets soaring through the night air. This terse message alerted the lifesaving crew and in a matter of minutes all were at their places in the surfboat ready to launch out. Through turbulent seas they pulled out near the jetty but so black was the night that the wreck could not be located. No more flares were sighted, and they rode out the mountainous breakers until the first rays of dawn. Then in the murky veil they made out the half-submerged ship over on its side. The survivors were astride it calling frantically to be saved.

With the ebbing tide, the seas eased off slightly. Risking all, the surfboat crew pulled on their oars, making a daring run around the fringe of entangled wreckage. Dodging about, they worked their way between two fallen masts and thumped up against the ship's hull. One by one the frantic survivors jumped into the boat until it had lost much of its buoyancy. Those remaining were warned not to jump, for they would capsize the boat and all be drowned. Frantic with fear, they held to their perches after the boat crew promised to return. The promise was kept and the boat did return, not once, but twice until all 31 members of the crew were rescued. Repeatedly the driving surf seemed to swallow up the surfboat but it would always emerge like a charging bull. After the last man was rescued, the changing tide brought vehement seas that swept the wreck with such destructive force that no living thing could have survived. That there were no casualties under such extreme circumstances is to be considered nothing short of miraculous—a remarkable feat of seamanship by a courageous lifesaving crew.

One of the largest steel barks operating to the Pacific Coast, the 2316-ton *Torrisdale,* hailing from Glasgow, was 290 feet long.

In the Scotch city where she was built, were many sad hearts when the Board of Surveyors and Underwriters decided that the wreck should be disposed of to the highest bidder. It had settled deep in the sand and was so full of water that nobody could get aboard. The high bidder paid a mere $250, his principal reason being to recover about $2000 in English money left in the captain's cabin.

Within a few weeks the elements had torn the wreck apart and, needless to say, the salvagers did not find the money nor much of anything else but grief. Probably the last memento of the *Torrisdale* is one of her ring buoys which for years hung on the walls of the old Grays Harbor Lifesaving Station.

JANET CARRUTHERS

If ever there was a jinx ship, it was the Canadian five-masted schooner *Janet Carruthers.* She was in trouble of one kind or another from the day of her launching till the end of her career less than two years later. She slid down the ways at the Wallace Shipyards in Vancouver, B.C., on June 28, 1917, during the booming years of World War I. Under the ownership of the Canadian West Coast Navigation Company her maiden voyage was from Vancouver to Adelaide, Australia, with a cargo of lumber. Though rigged as a schooner, the 240-foot *Carruthers* was fitted with a Bolinder oil engine, driving twin-screws and—she cost an exorbitant $150,000.

Two weeks after departing from British Columbia, the vessel was forced into Honolulu with several cracked cylinders and a broken shaft. Here her propellers were disconnected and the cumbersome schooner relied on her sails alone. Next she turned up at Apia, Samoa, disabled and damaged by severe weather. After temporary repairs she put out to sea again. Arriving off Adelaide, she was in such deplorable condition that the vessel towing her into port not only demanded but was awarded $10,000 salvage money.

Limping back to the Pacific Coast, she took on cargo at Tacoma and then departed for Astoria to load lumber for Shanghai. Two days later, on the night of January 22, 1919, Captain Cairny, master of the schooner, mistook Grays Harbor Light for the beacon on North Head. In the fury of a gale of driving rain, his command crashed ashore four miles north of the entrance to Grays Harbor. The fearful crew were too hasty in their evacuation. The first boat to leave the schooner was overturned and six were drowned amid the breakers. The sight of this kept the others aboard. And wise they were, for on the ebb tide the schooner rested in shallow water, allowing them to reach shore with a minimum of effort.

The wreck, very much intact, was not considered beyond the realm of salvage. Her value prior to stranding was set at $200,000. It was purchased at auction by J. H. Price for a mere $11,000. Price was, incidentally, the same man who had designed her faulty engine. He made an attempt to float her by dumping the oil from her tanks and might have succeeded had not the Washington Fisheries Commission stopped him on the grounds that it would seriously damage the clam beds. The claim was upheld, the operation cancelled, and the schooner became a total loss.

RYBA

What started out to be a routine towing job was suddenly and unexpectedly turned into a calamity. The tug *Ryba* of the Allman-Hubble Tugboat Company departed Hoquiam on the morning of April 30, 1925, to take pilot Charles Hanson out to the Japanese freighter *Etna Maru*, lying in wait outside the bar entrance.

With a seasoned towboater in command, Captain Sam Anderson, the tug moved out through the bay and across the bar as she had done hundreds of times in the past. She came alongside the freighter, performing her duties like clockwork. The pilot climbed aboard and the tug tooted her whistle and moved away, heading back to the harbor for her next assignment.

Suddenly and seemingly from nowhere a mammoth swell caught her under the counter and swung her broadside into the full onslaught of the breakers on the bar. Over she went before the stunned eyes of those aboard the freighter. Nor was her capsizing hidden from the eyes of others. The crews of the government dredge *Culebra*, the freighter *Lake Francis*, and the tug *John Cudahy* were all witnesses to the freak accident. Even the lookout at the Coast Guard tower watched the tragic episode. So quickly had it all happened that none could believe what they had seen. On numerous occasions this same tug had battled the vagaries of the fickle Grays Harbor bar under far worse conditions. Now for some unexplained reason, tragedy struck.

All hands were thrown rudely into the vortex. Three were never seen again. The fourth and only survivor, Captain Anderson, was pulled unconscious from the water by the crew of the *Lake Francis*. Taken into port for hospitalization, he ultimately recovered. Two of those who perished were members of the family which owned the tug and, with the sunrise of the next day, the flag over the company headquarters flew at half mast.

All because of one peculiar sea on the Grays Harbor bar, three men died, and a stalwart tug was destroyed.

YORKMAR

The floors of the lanes of maritime trade, wending their way over seven-tenths of the earth's surface, are marked with the decaying hulls of wrecked ships with the most treasured possessions of man. For as long as man has ventured upon the sea, he has paid for his accomplishment by giving to its waters a handsome share of the materials he has put in transit. Disaster, the creator of the salvor's work, has without invitation boarded ships without respect to flag to take an exacting toll. In the wake of each incident, the marine salvor has pitted his skill and cunning against the elements of nature to nullify the deplorable waste that follows. For the most part the ocean comes out the winner, but the law of averages, plus human ingenuity and energy, can sometimes save a ship from destruction in the face of heavy odds. Such was the case of the salvagers who freed the freighter *Yorkmar* from the treacherous sands just north of the Grays Harbor bar in the winter of 1952.

The SS *Yorkmar,* a 7200-ton Liberty-type freighter owned by the Calmar Steamship Corporation, had gone aground in attempting to cross over the Grays Harbor bar, on December 8, 1952. In ballast, she was driven high on the beach on a flood tide. At low water, the vessel rested high and half dry. She lay on a stretch of beach from which only once in history a stranded ship ever gained its freedom.

Immediately alerted was the Astoria-based tug *Salvage Chief.* This mighty craft and her valiant crew had already distinguished themselves on difficult salvage missions all along the Pacific Coast. Ahead of them now lay their biggest challenge.

Because of rough seas the *Salvage Chief* was unable to get near enough to the wreck to be effective, for three days. On December 11 two anchors were dropped about 2000 feet to seaward from the freighter, and about 400 feet apart. The salvage tug then came astern on the steel anchor cables for 800 feet, halting 1200 feet from the wreck. The tug's stern was toward the shore. Savage breakers curled all about, lifting her up on great crests and then dropping her into pitiless troughs. With amazing agility she rode them out. All that kept them from ripping out her bottom was her shallow draft. At slack tide there was less than ten feet of water beneath her keel.

The salvagers doggedly attempted to get lines to the *Yorkmar* but all either got fouled or parted under the strain. Finally a messenger line was floated ashore on an oil drum, retrieved by the Coast Guard, and taken to the stranded ship. A three-inch hawser was then taken back to the *Salvage Chief* from the *Yorkmar,* and the entire operation repeated with steel cables.

The breakers continued their onslaught, causing the starboard anchor cable to snap so that the salvage tug had to cut her towline to keep from joining the *Yorkmar* on the beach. The scores of shoreside spectators shook their heads and went home. The tug proceeded across the bar to Aberdeen to make repairs and procure new salvage equipment for another attempt.

Fred Devine, owner of the *Salvage Chief,* consulted with Walter Martignoni, San Francisco salvage master, for the next three days as to the best way to tackle the problem. The Calmar Steamship Corporation, owners of the stranded ship, felt that the situation was in the hands of the finest salvage men available. Said a company spokesman, "If Devine and Martignoni can't get the ship off the beach, then nobody can."

Meanwhile, back at the wreck the Coast Guard was keeping a constant vigil, ready at a moment's notice to remove the 37-man crew should the ship give indication of breaking up. A heavy surf had threatened the freighter since the departure of the salvage ship and there was much concern for both the ship and her crew.

On December 16 the surf calmed somewhat and excitement gained new impetus when it was learned that the *Salvage Chief* was returning for another try.

She hove in sight and took up her perilous position. Towlines were placed aboard the *Yorkmar* with every bit as much difficulty as before. Night came on and passed. On the following day as the tug kept a strain on the towlines, the *Yorkmar,* with the aid of the tide, moved 200 feet. The thrill, however, was short lived, for on the ebb the freighter once more settled in the sands.

Still the salvage ship kept a steady pull on the hawsers; throughout another night the lines remained taut.

It was now a race to get the *Yorkmar* free, as new winds were beginning to pick up and the weather bureau was predicting a storm.

In Aberdeen and Hoquiam, wagers were being placed as to the fate of the ship. The odds were heavily against success.

On December 18 the *Salvage Chief* still had the pressure on, but was being severely buffeted in the surf. While straining on three towlines she braced herself with three kedge anchors.

The weather worsened. Would time run out? At last the awaited 12-foot tide flooded the beach and afforded the break the salvage crew had been waiting for. Another powerful tug, the *Sea Lion,* was dispatched to the operation. Owing to her deeper draft she was unable to get close like the *Salvage Chief* but took a line to brace the straining salvage vessel. Two Coast Guard cutters also arrived on the scene.

In spite of the cold, the beach was lined with spectators. The tide was well in now and the two tugs were sent the signal to give it their all in a do-or-die effort. The roar of diesels was heard, the combined output of both vessels equal to that of 5400 horses.

It was like the ninth inning of a baseball game, with the bases loaded and two strikes and three balls on the batter.

Then the *Yorkmar* began inching over the bottom toward deeper water. There was anxiety ashore and afloat. Everybody seemed to be grunting with the tugboats. Foot by foot, yard by yard, the freighter scraped over the sands, stern first. Suddenly she was afloat.

As if the tugs were afraid of losing their prize they

refused to relinquish the full output of their engines until the *Yorkmar* was four miles offshore with her own steam up. She was virtually undamaged except for a bent propeller.

It was like a grand parade of victory as the cargo ship and her escort moved along in procession. The elements had been robbed of their victim in a marvelous piece of salvage work.

Still remaining was the investigation into the stranding, and charges against Captain Oscar Kullbom, master of the *Yorkmar*. He was charged with attempting to enter Grays Harbor without a pilot's license.

At the hearing he testified that he endeavored to cross Grays Harbor bar after bar-bound pilots wirelessed him that they thought he could make the crossing on his own. Fearing that his ship could not stand the punishment from the rough seas at the bar entrance, he elected to make the crossing. The empty ship was riding high and difficult to handle. She got out of the ship channel and drove up on the beach north of the bar entrance. She was inbound from San Francisco to load lumber when the accident occurred.

Captain Kullbom was exonerated of the charges. The civil trial examiner for the Coast Guard, James M. Donahue, contended that a "realistic approach is meant in enforcing the navigation laws and the captain acted in a way which his best judgment told him was proper."

After the *Yorkmar* received a complete survey at a Portland drydock she was rejoined by her master. It was back to the intercoastal run for both.

The refloating of the *Yorkmar* went down in the books as the most remarkable salvage feat of the decade.

Chapter Three

SOUTH OF GRAYS HARBOR TO THE
COLUMBIA RIVER BAR

B ETWEEN Grays Harbor and the Columbia River perhaps more strandings have occurred than on any other sector of the Washington Coast. The entire beach area is composed of long sandy stretches piled up by the deposits from the Columbia River and carried northward by the prevailing currents. Lesser rivers and streams also carry their share of sand, which constantly forms dangerous shoals. Because of these build-ups of sand and silt, government dredges must be constantly employed on Grays and Willapa Harbors and at the mouth of the Columbia.

Willapa Harbor was once known as Shoalwater Bay, because of the shoals that abound there. With no jetties to control its bar entrance, channels are constantly changing. Erosion has been nothing short of alarming along its north portal. Hundreds of acres of land have been washed away through the years, destroying summer homes, undermining the Coast Guard Station, and toppling the old Willapa Lighthouse.

The narrow finger-shaped North Beach Peninsula, south of Willapa Bar, has one of the longest unbroken stretches of beach in North America, 28 miles long. With the Pacific Ocean to the west, Willapa Bay to the north and east, the peninsula is but a mile and a half wide. Ancient Indian legend claims that it was once cut in half by the rampaging ocean. Nor is this beyond imagination, as its elevation is no higher than the most elevated sand dunes anywhere along the peninsula. A few years ago, an erroneous report that a tidal wave was headed toward the area started a mass evacuation.

The Columbia River has attracted a heavy volume of maritime traffic for decades and in the days when the sailing ship was still queen of the seas there were many obstacles on the approach to the bar. Conditions had to be right for crossing, for when a sailing vessel was in trouble it had no auxiliary power to keep it off the shoals. The Columbia River south jetty was not completed until 1885, and the north jetty not until 1916. Prior to that time the channel changes were more frequent than those of Willapa Bar. Some sailing vessels were recorded to have waited as long as four weeks to get safe passage when the Columbia Bar was riled by southwesterly winds.

Conditions have greatly improved since the turn of the century and every modern innovation in navigation aids has been employed, cutting shipwreck to a minimum. Bar pilots, however, still stress the dangers of that famous entrance, requesting continually that it be dredged to greater depths. Meanwhile larger and larger ships are being constructed for world commerce. Many deep draft vessels have sustained damage in transit when heavy swells prevailed on the bar. It has been a long, determined battle to secure sufficient funds for the project, but congress is becoming more generous in its appropriations for the vital waterway.

In modern times all ships that negotiate the Columbia and Willapa bars know weather, tide and bar conditions beforehand. It is no longer a case of incorrect charts and thumb-and-nail navigation as it was in the hectic days of yesteryear when the lifesaving crews ran themselves ragged saving lives.

POINT LOMA

A wind-swept beach, driving rain, and white-lipped breakers set the scene as the cry, "Shipwreck!" echoed across North Beach Peninsula. The populace dropped everything and came running. The *Point Loma*, a coastwise steam schooner had washed ashore near Seaview on that stormy 28th of February, 1896.

Some hours earlier, the luckless vessel had become entangled in the most severe gale of the season. She rode out titanic seas, groaning under her heavy load of lumber.

Her destination was San Francisco, but since departing Grays Harbor, Captain Conway, the shipmaster, had encountered nothing but adverse weather. At midnight, the overtaxed engine broke down and the tireless seas opened the ship's seams. The pumps became clogged. Water poured through at an alarming rate, filling the bilge and climbing to the level of the boilers. The black gang was driven topside by scalding steam.

In the terrible blackness the *Point Loma* was completely at the mercy of the wind and sea. The faint beam of Cape Disappointment Light broke through the murk denoting that the dreaded shore was not far off. Flares went soaring into the sky.

The lifesaving crew at Fort Canby hitched up the horses to the beach cart, and with their lifesaving apparatus moved into action. When they arrived on the scene, the steamer was already aground. There were men to be saved and not an instant was lost. The surfboat was removed from the cart and shoved out into the surf. The breakers proved overpowering and the tenacious crew were hurled back again and again. They refused to quit until their boat was up-ended, throwing them into the swirling vortex.

Next they turned to the line-throwing gun. Twice the ball fell short of its target but on the third try it hit the mark. Those on the wreck immediately made the line fast and prepared for evacuation.

Already one of the ship's masts had been knocked from its fittings and the stack bent at right angles. The decks were a mass of wreckage and the cabin, what was left of it, flooded.

The low elevation of the beach and that ever precious factor, time, ruled out the use of a breeches buoy, so a crude raft was hastily contrived and made fast to the lifeline. As the angry seas nipped at their heels, the survivors boarded it, a few at a time. Back and forth across the crashing surf traveled the raft. It took a terrible pounding but held together until all seventeen crew members gained the shore.

It was daylight now, and time for the peninsula folk to begin beachcombing, to see what the wreck had brought them. The steamer's yield was kind, strewing its lumber cargo at intervals along the beach. Everything from scrub brushes to dishpans found anxious hands.

The Grays Harbor Commercial Company, owners of the *Point Loma,* wrote her off their books as a total loss and let the beachcombers take what they would. The remains of the wreck were a tourist attraction for many years thereafter.

PROTECTION

The wooden steam schooners of old, ran an obstacle course along the Pacific Coast. Underpowered and usually laden with such stacks of lumber as to liken them unto a submarine, their mission was a difficult one at best. The mortality rate among this fleet of carriers was perhaps greater than for any other type of coaster ever devised. Developed entirely on the West Coast, the steam schooner played a great part in the upbuilding of the Pacific states. Today they have virtually disappeared from the face of the sea, pushed out by faster modes of land transportation.

The *Protection* was one of the original steam schooners, built at San Francisco in 1888. She was relatively small, only 281 tons, but for a decade she packed enough lumber to build many cities.

On December 29, 1899, she moved away from her Seattle dock, loaded with lumber for San Francisco. Flying the flag of her owner, John S. Kimball, she moved down the coast and headed into a New Year's Eve storm. There was no celebration, as all eyes were peering out at the mountainous waves contorted and twisted by the howling winds, somewhere off the mouth of the Columbia. Came New Year's Day and the *Protection* was taking it green over her bow, constantly losing headway.

That was her situation when last reported. Nothing more was heard. She failed to turn up at San Francisco or any other port. The *Protection* went missing with her entire crew, a mysterious victim of the ravages of the deep. Not so much as a scrap of wreckage was ever found.

ROSECRANS

At the mention of Peacock Spit, shivers ran up the spines of the ancient mariners. On this shoal, which spreads like a malignant growth at the north portal of the Columbia Bar, countless ships have left their bones. Today the north jetty at the river entrance crosses over the spot where the spit formerly..existed. Though a share of the spit remains, its treachery has somewhat subsided.

On the morning of January 7, 1913, the Associated Oil Company tanker *Rosecrans* was battling her way over the turbulent bar, inbound from San Francisco. The wind was blowing a steady 60 miles, driving with determined fury. The tanker labored under the weight of 20,000 barrels of crude oil. Captain L. F. Johnson stood bleary-eyed on the bridge from his endless hours on watch. He was noticeably worried, now that his ship was solid on the breaking bar. As thick weather closed down he lost his bearings and the quartermaster stood at the wheel nervously awaiting orders. The big vessel overran the channel and drifted nearer and nearer to the dread sands of Peacock Spit. Pitching and rolling at unprecedented angles she parted great walls of disturbed water. The wind whistled through her rigging in weird crescendos like a haunted organ in a graveyard. Then came that dreaded moment. She plowed head on against the spit, heaving crazily. The seas swept over her. A distress message crackled from her wireless. The lifesaving station on Cape Disappointment picked it up at 5:15 a.m.—

Steamer *Rosecrans* on bar, send assistance. Ship breaking up fast; can stay at my station no longer.

There was no further contact with the ship. The lifesaving crew prepared for an immediate run to the wreck. Tension ran high. The river entrance was a solid mass of crashing breakers from north to south.

At 8 a.m. the *Rosecrans* broke in two, the sections literally ripped apart, rivets and all. The crew was forced to the rigging. But even in their high perch they were swept off one after another by the rising avalanches of water. Finally, only four remained. Blue from the cold, and half mad, they stared blindly, hoping and praying that rescue would come.

Then the lifeboat hove into sight, but almost too late. As it approached, only a mast rose from the turbulence. One of the four men clinging to it could not stand the suspense and hurled himself into the sea, swimming frantically. The strain was too much. The rescue crew pulled him aboard dead. The others waited impatiently until the boat got under the mast, and saved them. The bar had become so rough that refuge had to be sought at the nearby Columbia River Lightship. The boat in the interim was brought alongside with much difficulty and the men taken aboard. Suddenly a heavy swell struck and the craft broke away, bearing the corpse of the man who had leaped from the mast. It was never seen again.

Several days passed before the survivors could be picked up, from the lightship. High seas persisted even after the storm had run its course. When the rescue boat reached shore, reporters were on hand to get a first-hand account of the disaster, and what caused it. The survivors were each of the opinion that the master of the *Rosecrans* had mistaken North Head Light for that on the lightship and had temporarily lost his bearings. So tragic was the wreck that none of the survivors had a desire to discuss it at length.

In the tanks of the wreck was a cargo of crude oil valued at $200,000. As the sea broke up the ship, much of the petroleum escaped. There was no salvage. From her launching at Glasgow, Scotland, in 1884, the *Rosecrans* was plagued by mishaps—breakdowns, strandings and fires, some resulting in loss of life and abandonment. Each time she was resurrected from her grave. But her fate was sealed when she tangled with the elements at the entrance to the Columbia.

ALICE

A ship buried in a coffin of cement may repose indefinitely in a watery grave. And that in short is the tale of woe of the French bark *Alice.*

On January 15, 1909, the big sailing vessel was bound for Portland from London and Tasmania, with her holds full of 3000 tons of cement. On approaching the Columbia River she got ashore a mile north of Ocean Park, Washington. A boy and his dog discovered the wreck at 7:45 a.m. Strangely enough it was the dog's barking that alerted the lad to the presence of the ship. And more amazing was the fact that this same dog was a survivor of a shipwreck two years earlier, along the same beach.

The boy excitedly ran to the nearest settlement for help. His news brought the Klipsan lifesaving crew hurrying to the scene. But there was mutiny in the ranks. The white horses which usually pulled the surfboat down the beach, balked in the soft sand and refused to go farther. Captain Conick, keeper of the station crew, tried every conceivable means to get his steeds to pull the remaining four miles. But they were more determined than he was. The horses won out, and Conick and his men had to launch the surfboat into the crashing surf and row the remaining distance. They arrived at the wreck dog-tired, only to find that the survivors had already made their escape in the ship's boat.

Conick was unable to get aboard the wreck. It was lying about 300 yards offshore, listing heavily to starboard. The seas swirled madly about the hull causing it to settle deeper in the sands.

Three days later the surf was still running so high that only Captain Aubert, master of the *Alice,* and nine of his 24 hands were willing to join the lifesaving crew in returning to the wreck for their personal belongings.

The Bordeaux-built bark of 2500 tons, was scratched from the register as a total loss. Her cargo of cement, inundated by salt water, hardened within her hull, creating an unbreakable crypt. A single mast remained above the

Ancient photo of the remains of the bark *Austria* wrecked January 30, 1887 on Flattery Rocks off Cape Alava, Washington. In background, Ozette Indian village, now nonexistent.
(courtesy University of Washington Library)

French bark *Alice* stranded near Ocean Park, Washington, January 15, 1909 with 3000 tons of cement as cargo. Total loss.

Burning furiously off the Washington Coast is the Panamanian steam schooner *Salina Cruz*. Fire broke out October 18, 1949. The vessel and her cargo of lumber were a total loss.

(U. S. Coast Guard photo)

A mysterious explosion ripped open the Greek SS *Hellenic Skipper* off Grays Harbor July 10, 1940. She went down in deep water after the crew miraculously escaped.

President Madison, 14,000 ton liner of the American Mail Line, rolled over on her beam ends at the Todd Shipyard in Seattle, March 25, 1933, taking the life of one man. Reason: carelessness.

HMS *Nabob*, Canadian aircraft carrier, ran aground doing 18 knots at Point Roberts, Washington. Damage was heavy but vessel was towed off, under direction of Capt. Loring Hyde, salvage master, and repaired.

Ill-fated *Diamond Knot* a few minutes before going to the bottom near Port Angeles, Washington with a $3.5 million cargo of salmon. Sunk by the *SS Fenn Victory*, August 13, 1947.

It cost $210,000 to repair the luxury coastal liner *H. F. Alexander* after it crashed into Cake Rock off the Washington Coast, August 6, 1922.

constant pounding of the surf for more than 20 years before it finally toppled. It served as a headstone over the wreck. Today all that remains to be viewed, and then only at extreme low tide, is a section of her hull. But if one should be of a mind to dive beneath the surf and sluice out the sands, he would find the cargo of cement still encased within her steel hull.

LAMMERLAW AND G. BROUGHTON

A very unusual tale of a double shipwreck was enacted at Cape Leadbetter near the south entrance of Willapa Bay on October 31 and November 1, 1881. Two barks, the *Lammerlaw* and the *G. Broughton,* both British, and both destined for Portland from Australia, came to grief within a few feet of one another, one day apart.

The *Lammerlaw* stranded after her master, Captain Pringle, mistook Willapa Bar for that of the Columbia. Heavily laden with coal from Newcastle, the vessel was held tight on the sands.

The North Cove lifesaving crew rushed to the scene of the mishap and succeeded in removing all hands safely.

Immediately plans were formulated for refloating the wreck but when the dawn of a new day broke the lifesaving crew were astounded to find a second ship aground but a few hundred feet from the *Lammerlaw*. It was the bark *G. Broughton*. Her master, Captain Payne, had sighted the tall masts of the *Lammerlaw* looming above the sea mist and supposed that it was crossing the Columbia Bar. Accordingly, he followed in its wake.

The lifesaving crew wearily went to work again and assisted in rescuing the 16 crew members of the second wreck.

Immediately after the *Broughton* had grounded, Captain Payne ordered the masts cut and sent overboard in an effort to lighten the ship. But it was to little avail, as she was in ballast, and stranded high on the sands.

The *Broughton* remained on an even keel for three days, then careened over and began digging her grave in

65

the sands. Her value was placed at $40,000. The *Lammer-law* likewise refused to be budged and became a total loss. Her value, $70,000.

When the Board of Inquiry convened, the *Lammer-law's* Captain Pringle was severely criticized for allowing his ship to go aground. They were easier on Captain Payne, since he thought the *Lammerlaw* was crossing the Columbia Bar. In spite of the reprimands, both skippers were eventually reinstated and placed in charge of other ships. Needless to say, both were wiser in the ways of the sea.

ROBERT BRUCE

In December of 1851, the schooner *Robert Bruce* entered Shoalwater (Willapa) Bay, in quest of oysters. Already two vessels had preceded her to take bivalves to San Francisco. The first of these had arrived with the cargo in spoiled condition. The second, the *Sea Serpent*, had delivered them in proper condition. The taste buds of Bay City restaurateurs had been aroused. Thus was the *Robert Bruce* dispatched to the almost virgin land of Shoalwater Bay where existed in the southern arm, vast oyster beds. It was heavily forested about the bay, with much wildlife and an occasional Indian village. A handful of white settlers had come and gone, but for the most part it was too remote and lonely to attract them.

The business of exporting oysters was the brainstorm of Captain Charles Russell, a pioneer from the East who had been taken in on a land swindle. To retrieve some of his hard-earned cash, he collected several of the bivalves and shipped them south for approval by San Francisco chefs. They met with overwhelming approval. There was a definite market for the oysters.

So it was that the *Robert Bruce* lay at anchor in Shoalwater Bay taking on oysters. While the operation was underway, trouble broke out among the crew. It revolved around the ship's cook, a man known only as Jefferson. When the schooner came into the bay he was overheard saying that "she'd never get back out again if I had anything to do with it." He was brooding over reprimands by the captain and crew over his unpalatable meals. His irascible temper had caused him to threaten every man aboard.

The situation reached a climax when the captain informed Jefferson that he would have to turn out food fit for consumption. He mulled over the warning. Then inflamed with revenge, he set out to poison every man in the crew and set the ship afire. The more he brooded, the more determined he became.

One night after all hands had turned in, he rifled the captain's medicine chest and extracted a generous quantity of laudanum, a solution of opium and alcohol, used on early-day ships to lessen pain. He mixed it with the food and coffee and served it to the crew. Suspecting nothing, they all ate of it.

The cook then waited until most of them had lapsed into unconsciousness and proceeded to jettison all the buckets and cooking pans—everything that could hold water. Then he touched a torch to the vessel and escaped in the only boat.

The date was December 16, 1851, a day long remembered.

As the flames gained in fury, the cook looked back at the burning schooner, a sinister smile masking his face. He reasoned that his nefarious scheme was the perfect crime. And to all intents and purposes it could have been had the ship and all hands been consumed in flames. The cook, however, had overlooked a white settler named William "Brandywine" McCarthy. "Brandywine" had married an Indian chief's daughter and lived on the shores of Shoalwater Bay. He spotted the fire, rounded up the tribe, and made haste to the burning schooner, via canoe.

The tide was on the ebb and many of the canoes had to be discarded in favor of wading or swimming to the flaming ship. The Indians braved the smoke and fire and with considerable effort pulled the drugged seamen to safety. At first McCarthy thought they were all inebriated, perhaps celebrating the prospects of a profitable trade. When the survivors came out of their comas however, they blasphemed the name of the cook and his dastardly scheme of revenge.

The schooner burned furiously right down to the water's edge and then settled in the tidewaters of the bay. The crew saved nothing but the clothing on their backs.

Aside from Captain Alexander Hanson, the shipmaster, the crew included Mark and Sam Winant, John Morgan, Dick Milward, Captain J. K. Terry, Frank Garretson, and a seaman known only as Tyson.

The missing cook Jefferson, after his escape, was never seen or heard of again.

Far from discouraged, the castaways, some of whom were partners in the oyster venture, made themselves shelters with the help of the Indians. They proceeded to gather oysters which they ultimately sold to other ships arriving on the bay. Business flourished to such a degree that they eventually were able to purchase the schooner *Mary Taylor,* and accordingly placed Captain Hanson, master of the ill-fated *Robert Bruce,* in command.

Center of the oyster enterprise was at Bruceport, on the east side of the Bay. The village was named for the burned schooner. The Bruceport company became an important oyster-producing firm and its success prompted Captain Charles Russell to quit the trade despite the fact that he had discovered the area as an oyster center.

The Bruceport enterprise eventually allied with similar interests at Oysterville, on the opposite shores. The margin of profit in those early years is worthy of mention. In 1853, bivalves from Bruceport were sold to merchants for $1.50 per bushel and brought $7 in San Francisco.

The oyster business today is still flourishing on the bay, but Bruceport is no more. The last vestige of the burned schooner has also disappeared.

Recently it was contemplated searching for her century-old remains with the purpose of securing a part of her hull for the museum at Fort Columbia. This was prompted by recollections of descendants of pioneer settlers. They recalled hearing of the ship being seen protruding from the bay at extreme low tide. Doubtless her sunken hatches have collected a cargo of oysters but for a certainty they will never get to San Francisco aboard her.

INTREPID AND NICHOLS I

On January 21, 1954, the ocean tug *Tidewater Shaver* departed Honolulu towing the barges *Intrepid* and *Nichols I*. There was nothing outstanding about the voyage. The barges were merely to be delivered to the Columbia River for the purpose of dismantling.

The Pacific crossing, for the main part, was routine until the tug approached the Columbia River. There a severe gale was encountered on February 23, and the barges became unmanageable. The tug's crew were forced to cut the tow lines off Buoy No. 5 to keep from being dragged on dreaded Peacock Spit. Lightened of its burden, the tug fought its way back into the channel and safety.

The unmanned derelict barges drifted northward, unwatched. Above Long Beach they were engulfed in the breakers and swept ashore within a mile of each other.

The larger of the two barges, the 185-foot *Intrepid*, immediately took a starboard list and began to settle aft. Down by the stern, the inrushing tides washed over her quarter deck and the old oaken door to the master's cabin would swing back and forth issuing eerie intonations. This immediately prompted over-zealous news reporters to visualize an invisible sea dog pacing mysteriously about.

In spite of the fact that the *Intrepid* was only a barge, she attracted tourists to the beach in droves. Her hull had an undeniable grace that suggested service far more glamorous than her final lowly role. And rightfully so, for the old ship began life as a trim naval training ship,

69

square rigged and one of Uncle Sam's finest. She was completed at the Mare Island Naval Yard in 1907 and carried 16 officers and 120 enlisted personnel. On her initial voyage she ran into heavy seas and almost capsized, but after alterations and ballast shifting served a long and useful career.

In 1921, the *Intrepid's* navy days were over. At ceremonies her pennant was lowered. Masts and yards were later removed, and her boiler, part of an auxiliary steam plant, was installed in the basement of the Matson Building in San Francisco. And what of the rest? The bare hull went to Honolulu to serve as a sludge barge. Battered and bruised, she pursued her task at the end of a tow rope. Despite the punishment, her hull of Swedish iron remained intact.

In 1949, the *Intrepid* was sold by the Hawaiian Dredging Company, and was kicked about until it fell into the hands of the Independent Iron Works. Several months later they decided that the barge would bring a better price on the scrap market and decided to bring her back to the coast.

They engaged the Foss Launch & Tug Company to make the tow, along with two other discarded craft. Strung out behind the tug were the *Intrepid,* the old steamer *Columbia,* and the lighthouse tender *Kukui.*

The voyage was doomed from the start. The Coast Guard delayed the towing craft, *Martha Foss,* questioning her master over his license. This straightened out, the tug put out to sea with the strange armada trailing astern. Four days out, the *Columbia* broke in two and sank. The towlines to the other vessels parted and the tug was able to retrieve but one, the *Kukui.* She continued on toward the Pacific Coast and radioed for another towing company in the islands to search out the *Intrepid* and return her to Honolulu.

Immediately the Independent Iron Works brought suit against the Foss Company. The case was in the legal courts for many months. Three years later, the federal judge ruled in favor of Foss, defendant, in the suit. They were not responsible for the sinking of the *Columbia*, ruled the judge, inasmuch as it was unseaworthy. The judge also ruled that Foss was entitled to collect expenses incurred in hiring Young Brothers of Honolulu to find the *Intrepid* and tow her back to port.

The barge remained in the islands till late in 1953 when her owners engaged the tug *Tidewater Shaver* of Portland to tow her back to the coast along with the petroleum barge *Nichols I*. As has already been told, the two barges came to grief toward the end of the voyage.

As they languished on the sands of North Beach Peninsula, the local folk hoped that the *Intrepid* could remain as a summer attraction. But, alas, a crafty junk dealer with a brain for business made a fast deal with the owners. He purchased her for a mere $100. The citizenry protested, but the deal was all legal. The owners wanted to be rid of their jinx ship once and for all.

The "junky" took his own sweet time with his cutting torch. He first removed the elaborate scrollwork gracing the ship's bows, at the billet head. Though covered with paint it turned out to be solid copper, pounds of it. Rumor had it that he found a buyer who paid $1000 cash—a nice return on a small investment.

If nothing has been said about the other barge, there's a reason. There's not much to say about it. No glamor, just an ugly, flat-bottomed tank barge built for the Army in World War II. Purchased later and renamed *Nichols I*, it was consigned to Babbidge and Holt of Portland.

When she came ashore the local sheriff posted large signs on her steel sides warning trespassers to keep off. But beachcombers will be beachcombers. The barge's anchor and chain disappeared right under his nose the very first night.

Chapter Four

JUAN DE FUCA STRAIT AND PUGET SOUND

ONE OF the greatest inland arms of the Pacific is the Strait of Juan de Fuca, a deep body of water separating Canada and the United States. Through its portals passes the commerce of the world. It is one of the most frequented waterways in the northern hemisphere. Nearly all ocean traffic coming and going from Puget Sound and British Columbia ports passes through the Strait of Juan de Fuca.

It was named by the English explorer James Cook in honor of Juan de Fuca (Apostolos Valerianus) who allegedly discovered the strait in 1592.

At its entrance and for 50 miles eastward to Race Rocks, the strait has a width of about 12 miles, then a width of about 18 miles for 30 miles eastward to Whidbey Island.

The shores on both sides are heavily wooded, rising abruptly to elevations of considerable height. At their eastern extremity, the waters of Puget Sound have their entrance and run in a general north-and-south direction, amid numerous islands and islets, for nearly 80 miles.

Today these waterways are well marked by aids to navigation. In the past they were the bane of many mariners. Within the last century, over 600 major and minor shipwrecks occurred on Puget Sound and in Fuca Strait. Many of the shipwrecks in the Strait of Juan de Fuca went unrecorded prior to the turn of the century. Today the Coast Guard keeps a constant vigil over the waterways from ashore and afloat.

HENRY T. SCOTT

The Strait was shrouded by fog. The coastwise steamer *Henry T. Scott,* Captain C. Thorsell in command, was

Seattle-bound from San Francisco. As she entered from the ocean, her whistle sounded its warnings at regular intervals. Not only was the fog thick, but a ravaging forest fire along the shore was wafting a choking, yellow smoke over the water.

The freighter was off Neah Bay when it happened. The 12,000 ton cargo vessel *Harry Luckenbach* was feeling her way along at about seven knots. At approximately 6:04 a.m. there was a frantic exchange of whistle signals. At 6:05 the bow of the *Harry Luckenbach* loomed up at the side of the *Henry T. Scott*, ramming her with the impact of a meat cleaver. The blow gashed a gaping tunnel in her port side. Water poured in with the rush of a dynamo and in a scant 45 seconds it was all over. The *Scott* dropped by the head, her stern rose in the air, the propeller spinning like an egg beater. Then, in the flash of an eye, the vessel completely vanished beneath the surface, entombing four members of her crew.

The other 21, including a woman passenger, were ruthlessly thrown into the maelstrom, struggling for their very existence. They bobbed up in three inches of thick oil, clutching blindly at an overturned lifeboat. Captain Thorsell was among them.

Boats from the *Harry Luckenbach*, groped about in the fog guided by their frantic calls. All 21 were rescued, some badly hurt, but all glad to be alive.

ANDALUSIA

Being the captain of a ship frequently calls for hasty decisions. He has complete authority and upon his shoulders rests the entire responsibility, whether it be right or wrong.

At 4:25 a.m. on the morning of November 4, 1949, fire of undetermined origin broke out in the engine room of the 7700-ton Panamanian steamship *Andalusia*. With five million feet of lumber in her holds it was Captain George Lemos' decision to purposely run his ship aground, four miles east of Neah Bay. It took but 90 minutes to extinguish the fire, but the freighter was lodged on a jagged reef of rock, irretrievably doomed. There was imminent danger of her slipping off into deep water.

Captain Lemos had made his decision and it was to cost him his ship.

The Coast Guard motor lifeboat and the tender *Fir* answered the *Andalusia's* distress calls. Immediately 17 crewmen were removed, including a 26-year old woman stewardess.

The vessel took a severe list, but Captain Lemos and nine crewmen remained aboard. Three Canadian tugs were making full speed toward the wreck to attempt salvage.

In a strange sequence of events the *Andalusia* was the third Panamanian-registered vessel to catch fire off the Washington coast within a six-months' period.

As big salvage tugs arrived on the scene from both Canadian and United States ports, efforts immediately were focused on pulling the ship free. There was danger of the ship going down if she was pulled free, but salvage men were banking on the hope that the deck load of lumber would keep her buoyant long enough to get her up on a sandy beach. In one concerted effort seven powerful tugs combined their horsepower to refloat the ship. Still it would not budge.

Four days after the stranding, angry seas prompted Captain Lemos and the remainder of his crew to signal the Coast Guard to take them ashore. A Lloyd's insurance underwriter had already been aboard and announced that the plates in the boiler and engine rooms were badly cracked. He gave salvagers less than a 50-50 chance to save the ship.

Grim red-and-black flags whipped in the breeze at the shore station. A gale was scudding up the coast with 50-knot winds. The situation favored the negative view.

While all waited the outcome of the storm, gossip was freely distributed about Captain Lemos having needlessly run his ship aground. Perhaps his decision had been too hasty. But who was to judge? Had the flames assumed great proportions and claimed lives, he would have been seriously criticized for not having run his ship aground.

Then, too, the crew of the *Andalusia* was of polyglot assemblage. There were Uruguayans, Greeks, Italians, Spaniards, Puerto Ricans, Dutch, and Americans. With but few exceptions all spoke only in their own native tongues. Thus when fire broke out there was a hodgepodge of language which led to utter confusion.

Twice before, in isolated sectors of the world, fire had been reported on the tramp steamer, but each time it was extinguished.

Even as the vessel was abandoned by her crew, huge auxiliary pumps were aboard, working to capacity to rid her of the water being shipped. Then the gale struck and worked the ship on the reef as if it were a teeter-totter. On November 9, it gave a mighty groan and cracked amidships. The following dispatch was sent from the scene of the wreck:

ALL SALVAGE OPERATIONS UNSUCCESSFUL. VESSEL HAS BROKEN IN TWO. AFTER SECTION SANK. DURING HEAVY WEATHER NOVEMBER 9, BROKE ABAFT FUNNEL IN TWO PIECES. AFTER PART NOW SUNK IN 50 FEET OF WATER; FORWARD PART FAST ON REEF. TUGS ENDEAVORING TO FREE FORWARD PART AND SALVE ON "NO CURE, NO PAY" BASIS, BUT DOUBTFUL WHETHER THEY WILL FLOAT IT FREE.

To put it briefly, the entire salvage operation failed. The only benefactors were the local commercial fishermen who realized a bountiful take from the sea after the deck load of lumber drifted free of the wreck. Many of them did a little too much bragging over their good fortune, for the customs' agents were on their trails like bloodhounds. A heavy duty was placed on their take, since the cargo had been loaded in a foreign port.

The *Andalusia* was a pathetic sight, broken, battered,

its grave a quarter mile from shore. Built for the U.S. Shipping Board at Alameda, California, in 1918, her owner at the time of her loss was the Triton Shipping Company, large trampship operators.

DIAMOND KNOT

With the sinking of the MS *Diamond Knot* on August 13, 1947, in Juan de Fuca Strait, a cargo of choice Alaska salmon, valued at $3,500,000, went to the bottom of the sea. Faced with the largest collision cargo loss ever to occur on the waters of the Pacific Coast, Fireman's Fund Insurance Company, with the co-operation of the reinsuring underwriters, supported the proposal to conduct a hazardous attempt to salvage and return the lost cargo to the world's depleted food markets.

On August 13, 1947, the *Diamond Knot,* property of the U.S. Maritime Commission, under bareboat charter to the Alaska Steamship Company, was proceeding toward Seattle from Bristol Bay ports. In her holds, neatly stowed, were 154,316 cases, or 7,407,168 cans of choice Red, Chum, King and Cohoe salmon, enough for a can for every man, woman and child in New York City. The 5525-ton freighter, down to her marks, moved cautiously through the choppy waters amid a heavy fog. Her cargo of fish was the property of three of the world's largest food processors and packers. In addition, she carried cannery equipment, labels, herring oil, salted fish, an automobile, and a small cannery tender.

From another direction, outbound from Seattle, came the 10,681-ton freighter *Fenn Victory*. She carried but 200 tons of miscellaneous cargo and rode high as she rounded Point Wilson and headed down the strait.

The thick shroud of fog that had accumulated during the early hours obscured all lights both at sea and ashore. Six miles north of Port Angeles at 1:15 a.m. the two ships collided, the *Fenn Victory* pushing her stem a full fourteen feet into the side of the *Diamond Knot*. It was the kind of shock that stirs man to the depths of his soul. The

76

sudden stillness of the fog had been broken by a rending crash that bore an undeniable finality. The Coast Guard picked up terse distress messages, and salvage tugs rushed out from Victoria and Port Angeles. First to arrive on the scene were the tugs *Matilda Foss* and *Foss No. 21*. They scurried about like bees around a honeycomb, endeavoring to find the solution for saving the interlocked ships. The *Fenn Victory's* bow had cut so deeply into the smaller freighter's starboard side that her main deck was awash. The big ship's forecastle was entangled with the crosstrees on the mainmast of the *Diamond Knot*. The vessels were locked together at right angles refusing to release their death grip. It was like a fight to the finish between two mighty beasts. Meanwhile the fast ebbing tidal currents carried them steadily westward.

Salvage crews brought burning equipment aboard the *Diamond Knot* to release the steel jaws. After several anxious hours the vessels were at last separated. The *Fenn Victory* started for port under her own power, but for the *Diamond Knot* it was the beginning of the end. Tugs took her in tow, stern first, moving toward the protected waters off Crescent Bay. Here it was hoped she could be beached and her precious cargo saved. It was a race against time, the ministering little giants struggling valiantly with their dying ward. Water was pouring into the gap in the freighter's side, filling holds number two and three. Captain C. N. Goodwin and his nervous crew were finally evacuated from the freighter. It was now completely out of their hands.

Then came more trouble with a capital T, for at the entrance to Crescent Bay abound the strongest currents in the Strait. Flowing off Tongue Point Reef they sweep like a raging river. This seriously hampered the progress of the tugs which were now being strained to the breaking point. At 8:45 a.m. there was a noticeable jerk on the towline. The freighter settled deeper. At 8:55 the towboatmen were forced aft to chop the towing hawsers. The *Diamond Knot* was going down, so near and yet so far from the beach. Mortally wounded, she rolled

77

over on her side. The inrush of water hissed and snarled as it crowded out the remaining air from her interior. Giant whirlpools formed at the outset and the ship slipped quickly beneath the surface. Tired tugboatmen stood on the fantails of their respective tugs, watching, wide eyed. A great cavity opened in the sea and then filled. A strange hush fell over the place. The *Diamond Knot* went to her final resting place in 135 feet of water at 8:57 a.m.

The sinking brought about one of the largest cargo collision losses on the west coast. Insurance companies set in motion machinery to indemnify those assureds who had sustained such staggering losses. The Fireman's Fund Insurance Company and the Sea Insurance Company made prompt payment of claim to one cargo owner amounting to $982,258.55. In quick succession another check was issued for $2,053,366 and a third for $359,767. Then $16,000 was paid for the cannery tender strapped to the *Diamond Knot's* deck and $12,000 awarded the crew for loss of personal effects.

With the task of providing indemnity to its assureds, the insurance companies considered cargo salvage.

Walter Martignoni, San Francisco salvage master, was immediately contacted. He agreed to tackle the job with certain misgivings. Foss Launch & Tug Company was to supply the equipment, and James Gow was appointed as chief cargo surveyor for the underwriters. Diver Walter McCray was in charge of undersea work, assisted by Fred Devine.

On these captains of maritime salvage hinged the outcome. It was a battle of endurance, skill, and ingenuity against the ravages of the sea.

Action was immediate. Delay would have meant the complete destruction of the canned fish. McCray's equipment barge *Diver III* hastened to the scene and anchored over the wreck. A diver was sent down into the frigid depths to chart the wreck's position. He groped around on the dark ocean floor as strange denisons of the deep swam about him. Then he saw the ship, like a ghostly castle of the deep. It was lying on its starboard side. The cannery tender and the automobile lashed to the deck were missing, probably crushed under tons of steel. Then the diver was brought up to reveal his findings.

On Sunday, August 17, a special meeting on the salvage proposal was held at Seattle. Martignoni reported the unfeasibility of raising the wreck, because of the enormous costs involved. Only the cargo could be saved.

A plan to recover the cans of salmon with an electric magnet was abandoned, due to depth and limited magnetism in the cans. Stevedoring methods were ruled out because of extreme tidal conditions. After careful consideration Martignoni suggested usage of two twelve-inch siphon pipe lines which would suck the cans from the sunken ship. Similar devices had been experimented with on a small scale, but this would be the first of such magnitude. Nor could anyone be sure of its success at raising one pound cans from such depths. A decision had to be made immediately. Martignoni smiled and those attending the hearing knew that he was optimistic.

Martignoni then went into consultation with Captain Loring Hyde, renowned salvage expert and pilot. The two initiated plans to recover fish oil in the deep tanks before going after the salmon.

Back at the scene of the wreck, divers with special instructions were sent down to plug sounding and vent pipes to make the ship tight. Attachments were then made on the lower side of the hull at the deepest part of the tanks, to which were secured suction hoses. Above the level of the fish oil, additional openings were made through which air at great pressure was to be introduced. This produced an air pressure over the fish oil forcing the oil downward into the attached hose which reached to the surface. The pressure caused the oil to shoot upward to the receiving barge. This plan was successful and $22,000 worth of oil was recovered.

Now came the time to attempt recovery of the salmon. A mother barge was securely anchored over the wreck and all other floating equipment lashed to it. The siphon plan demanded tremendous volumes of air to be forced through the pipes—a veritable deep sea vacuum cleaner. Large air compressors had to be utilized with powerful fire fighting jet pumps to get high enough water pressure to pull the cans from their cartons. Crane hoists were secured on the barge to control the siphon lines underwater.

The race against time continued. Priority demands rushed to the scene welding equipment, and flexible discharge hose for the top of the siphon lines.

Twelve anchors were set to hold the salvage barge in position. Urgent appeals for more divers were issued in an endeavor to keep the underwater men working around the clock.

Under Martignoni's direction, divers went to work with cutting torches. Burning through the plates leading to number two hold, they found 2,000,000 cans of salmon. The suction hoses were now intact. The underwater vacuum cleaners were ready for work. Air at 90 pounds pressure was forced through the manifold.

Then came the zero hour. The receiving barge became a beehive of activity. Over the noise of the compressors, orders were given to lower the siphon pipeline to the hold of the sunken freighter. With communication phones pressed hard to the diver tenders' ears, instructions were relayed between the divers and crane operators.

The salvage master ordered water released into the manifold with its four jet openings. Water jetted out at 300 pounds to rip cartons and free canned salmon. The pipe convulsed under the strain. Then a sudden charge of water exploded, followed by belches of foam. A raging torrent poured into the barge above. The operation was working! Divers guided the lines on the ocean floor and soon cans were being spewed into the barge. More divers went to work as the siphons spouted the cans. Next they cut holes into the number three hold. Work continued around the clock, day and night.

Wind and rain slanted down, but still the work went on. Sometimes the lines would part or siphons would bend or buckle under the force of heavy seas. Divers were frequently forced to the surface when currents grabbed at their lifelines or tore their suits as they clung to the skin of the sunken ship. Decompression chambers were taxed to the limit.

It was an exciting business. When conditions were at their best, each siphon sucked up an estimated 1000 gallons of water per minute, at the same time depositing nearly 800 cans of salmon on the barge. Before the operation ended, divers working in shifts cut away about 90 percent of the port side of the *Diamond Knot*, plate by plate, hour after hour. Barges when filled were towed out and empties brought in. Each full barge carried about 300,000 cans.

On October 29, the last can was recovered—the air and water leading into the siphon pipeline manifolds shut off and operations discontinued. It was a long job; 77 days had elapsed since the *Diamond Knot* went to the bottom. Out of 7,407,168 cans of salmon aboard the ill-fated ship, 5,744,496 were recovered; 10,000 cases remained in inaccessible sections of the ship. Several thousand cans were scattered over the ocean floor at the time of the collision.

One of the greatest cargo recovery salvage jobs in history had been completed. The cans were barged to canneries around Puget Sound, assorted, tested, inspected, and repacked. Of 5,744,496 cans sucked up from the bottom, 4,179,360 were restored to sound commodity. About 27 per cent were found in spoiled condition.

Man had won a hard earned victory over the sea and its magnitude was destined to remain as one of the highlights of marine salvage. The total gross salvage recovery was $2,100,100.

With an agreement of mutual fault the hearing over the collision was recessed. But there was a final tragic note. Captain Joseph Gaidsick, master of the freighter that sank the *Diamond Knot,* hanged himself in the cabin of his ship after mourning over the blemish against his record.

WARHAWK

A night fire which lighted up Discovery Bay and brought every living soul within a radius of ten miles to its shores, occurred at 1 a.m. on April 12, 1883. The victim was the proud old clipper ship *Warhawk,* which after a brilliant career, was consumed by flames.

The *Warhawk* had arrived at Discovery Bay from San Francisco and was in the process of loading lumber for the return voyage when fire of undetermined origin broke out. Scarcely a soul was aboard, the crew for the most part being at the saloon in the little mill town. When flames fanned her aging timbers, all hands were rousted out of the "gin mill," along with everybody else in town. All were needed to form a bucket brigade, should the fire spread to the lumber mill. Dark forms danced about before the orange flames, trying in vain to put out the fire.

The ship's mooring lines were cut and she drifted away like a flaming torch. Captain Connor, master of the *Warhawk,* and some of his crew had managed to board her but found the decks unbearably hot. The soles of their shoes were smoking. The seacocks were opened in a last-ditch effort to save the ship. But the stay of the boarding party was brief, as they ran the risk of being encompassed themselves by the inferno.

The burning ship slowly settled as the water poured into her, causing a gyration of steam. As her main deck began to flood she slipped over on her beam ends and then went to the bottom, with only the stubs of her charred masts breaking the surface. The fire had blackened her almost beyond recognition before she sank and there was only $9000 insurance to cover the loss of the 1067-ton vessel.

The *Warhawk* was adjudged a total loss. Her obituary

was short. In her last role as a coastal lumber carrier, many had forgotten her brighter years. Built in 1855 at Newburyport, Massachusetts, she took part in the great clipper ship era when America ruled the seas. She made many splendid passages in both the Cape Horn and China trades.

In 1871 she was sold at San Francisco to S. L. Mastick to engage in the coastwise lumber service. Here she fell into competition with another of the famous old clippers, the *Dashing Wave*. The *Warhawk* set an all-time record in the trade, leaving San Francisco on February 19, 1872, and arriving at Port Discovery on February 23, four days out. The entire round-trip was made in 23 days, including the loading of 750,000 board feet of lumber, which itself required 15 days.

When one considers that her only motive power was sail, he can readily see the remarkable feats performed by this graceful square-rigger of old. Needless to say, she made considerable money for her owners throughout her career and had frequently showed her heels to steam-powered craft.

Shortly before World War II, the U. S. Maritime Commission launched a program of building modern freighters in an endeavor to bolster the sagging merchant marine. Most of the new ships were named for the fabulous clipper ships which in the mid-19th century had brought America to the fore as a maritime nation.

As a part of this far-sighted program, the 12,000-ton C-2 type cargo vessel *Warhawk* was built at Oakland, California, in 1943, to honor its predecessor. She went immediately into the war effort. After the armistice she took the banner of the Waterman Steamship Corporation and entered merchant service. On frequent occasions she steamed down the Strait of Juan de Fuca past the final resting place of her namesake at Port Discovery. No salute was given, however, as the years had slipped hastily by and nobody on the new ship was aware of the grave of the old clipper. The original *Warhawk* had faded away but the new counterpart left its silvery wake across the oceans of the world, carrying the American flag to far-flung ports.

R. K. HAM

One of the best known pioneer captains in the coastwise lumber trade of bygone days was Captain I. W. Gove, and one of the most widely known sailing vessels, was his command, the bark *R. K. Ham.* Together they had made more than 100 voyages between San Francisco and Puget Sound ports. No other shipmaster had commanded the *Ham.*

Captain Gove was accused of having salt in his veins. From boyhood he breathed the sea air. Born in Maine during the clipper ship era, he learned his trade at a tender age. Nobody knew how old he was when he first shipped out, but it was a certainty that he was on the high seas when most lads were hanging on to their mothers' apron strings. He came to the Pacific Coast in 1852 as a hand on the brig *Potomac.* A short time later he had his own command. Unlike most of the early ship masters, Gove remained with each ship for lengthy periods. He was an honest man, demanding the most of his crew but treating them squarely. He earned the respect of all who knew him.

In all of his career he had never lost a ship nor a man, a spotless record, and one with very few equals. He had been in command of the *R. K. Ham* for better than 20 years and was finishing a half century as a seafarer. Then tragedy struck.

The *R. K. Ham* was inbound for Puget Sound on a dismal August day in 1894. The Strait of Juan de Fuca was covered by a veil of fog. Countless times Captain Gove had sailed these waters and it was a popular saying that all he had to do was to sleep in his bunk and his ship would sail itself into port. But at this fateful hour in spite of his vigilance, the vessel strayed from its course, not much, but just enough. She crashed up on dread

84

Dungeness Spit, a narrow finger of sand stretching eight miles into the strait.

Here aforetime many splendid sailing vessels had met their doom. When the *R. K. Ham* came ashore there was no alternative for the saddened Captain Gove but to order abandonment of his beloved ship. All made it safely ashore. Shortly afterward the breakers rose to new heights, their liquid acclivities tearing at the ship and sucking her down into the sand.

When salvage was attempted the only recoverable item was part of the rigging which probably brought $50 on the open market.

The *R. K. Ham* was by no means a new ship and her tenderness lent to her falling to pieces so quickly. But it was more than just the loss of a ship, it was the parting of an aging mariner and the ship he had commanded for two decades.

Tears streamed down the old man's weathered face as he watched her break up in the surf. To him she was a home, a livelihood, a way of life. From the day of her completion at Port Blakely for the Port Blakely Mill Company she had been under his guiding hand. He had kept her immaculate in spite of the fact that her owners ran the heart out of her.

According to the oldtimers that yet remember, Captain Gove was broken in spirit as he stood gazing at the wreck. The wind whipped across the frenzied waters and into his face. He stood erect, his white beard swaying at the whims of the breeze. He removed his battered cap in memory of his ship, then slowly turned and walked away.

CLALLAM

There was panic and terror aboard the steamer *Clallam* on the 8th and 9th days of January 1904. En route to Victoria from Tacoma and Seattle, the perky little steamer, yet to pass a single year of service, ran head on into a driving gale of mixed snow and rain.

For some unexplained reason it has always been the general assumption that a new ship is invulnerable to the fury of the elements, They said that the *Titanic* was unsinkable and that the *Morro Castle* was fire-proof. How trivial such talk. Nothing made by man is indestructible. The *Clallam* was not without exception. A thorough buffeting by heavy seas and she opened up. The pumps became choked with coal dust and ashes; finally the fires went out. Now open to the gale's full thrust the ship was pummeled by crushing seas. The skylights were smashed, hatch covers knocked off. The water all seemed to come in but none went out. Ninety frenzied persons were aboard.

Then dissension broke out on board. Chief Engineer Scott DeLauncey was the center of it. He was accused of setting the two-way pump in the wrong way, allowing the water to be pumped in and not out. But as the threat of the sinking loomed, accusations gave way to outright fear, for there was a possible date with death for every soul aboard.

Nevertheless the chief engineer mulled over the events preceding the tragedy. Was he to be blamed? Had he not reported a sprung deadlight three months earlier to officials of the Black Ball Line and received not the slightest attention? And what about the pumps? He'd reported them too. The circulating pump was operating ineffectively and the plunger pumps were completely inoperative. He maintained that the trouble was not below decks but in the structural failure of the ship to withstand a severe winter gale. Why not let the shipbuilders take the blame? But they would maintain that the *Clallam* was built to the highest specifications.

Well, then, maybe it was the young Indian girl from Tatoosh Island who was to blame. Didn't she swing the traditional bottle of champagne at the steamer's launching, and miss? Then didn't the ship take to the water only to have her ensign hoisted upside down—an international signal of distress?

Maybe the old bell sheep which usually made the

round-trip on the *Clallam* had a premonition of what was to come. Repeatedly she had lured the flocks aboard at Seattle and off again at the Victoria dock. She had always fulfilled her mission cheerfully until this fatal voyage. Then for some strange reason she defiantly balked, the steamer being compelled to sail without her.

Now the *Clallam* was in the throes of a dilemma. The passengers were frantic. Down by the head, the ship rolled and pitched at unprecedented angles. All through the pitiless black night she floundered helplessly. Someone had forgotten to place distress flares aboard, thereby lessening any chance of aid from another ship. More negligence.

Then came Captain George Roberts' turn. Fearing that his ship was about to go down, he ordered the lifeboats lowered. The bucket brigade which had formed when the pumps quit, now dispersed, and readied themselves for evacuation. The first boat was filled to over-capacity with women and children. Nobody quite seemed to know what happened, but the craft had barely cleared when it was caught by a lunging sea and slammed against the side of the steamer, killing all of its occupants.

The second boat hit the water unceremoniously, careening wildly. Suddenly a fear-crazed man made a wild leap for it from the *Clallam's* hurricane deck, shouting "By God that boat don't go without me!" He landed squarely on the head of a woman, crushing her skull. His momentum carried him forward, causing the boat to overturn, and many were drowned.

A half-delirious young mother floated by the steamer, trying desperately to hold her baby above the raging tempest. A man at the ship's railing lowered himself by a rope in an attempt to snatch the infant, but a snarling wave beat him to it. The helpless babe became another grim statistic.

The third lifeboat also capsized and all in it were drowned. Not a woman or child remained alive.

All hands were occupied bailing water from the steamer until the forenoon. Then at long last the tug *Richard Holyoke* hove in sight. A feeble cheer rose from the weary band of survivors. Through the driving rain the tug came as near as possible and got a line on the floundering steamer. The perilous pull began. Midway between Smith and San Juan Islands, the tug skipper decided it wiser to take the *Clallam* to Port Townsend in order to get the aid of the outgoing tide. Like an ant pulling a dead beetle, the tug more than had her job cut out for her. She was experiencing great difficulty until

A short while later, the captain of the *Clallam*, fearing that his ship was going to go down, signalled the *Holyoke* to cut the hawser and stand by to pick up the survivors. In the murk, however, his signal was misinterpreted and the tug kept the strain on the hawser. A few minutes later the *Clallam* rolled over on her beam ends and settled beneath the waves, all aboard being forced to jump for their lives. The two tugs immediately cut the towlines and maneuvered about to pick up the struggling survivors. Some were sucked into the depths and those that were rescued were paralyzed with fear. Fifty-one lives were lost, mostly women and children.

Perhaps it was unfortunate that Captain Roberts and Chief Engineer DeLauncey lived to face the Board of Inquiry. The former lost his papers for a period of one year and the latter, after a severe reprimand, had his license revoked. The captain was criticized for launching the boats without placing competent ship's officers in charge. Not only was he the shipmaster but also a co-founder of the Black Ball Line, owner of the ill-fated vessel.

The entire Puget Sound area was in a state of shock over the disaster. Pressure was brought to bear on the officials of the Black Ball Line, from the president on down. The fact that the vessel carried no rockets or distress flares, slapped a healthy fine on her owners.

This punishment touched off the instituting of revised inspection laws. Thereafter, all Puget Sound steamers caught without foghorns, flares, fire axes, or lifeboat equipment, were subject to severe penalty. It took a costly lesson in disaster to enact the proper rules for safety.

Excepting for one other regrettable disaster, that of the steamer *Dix,* the Puget Sound inland waterways fleet, established an enviable record.

DIX

On the evening of Sunday, November 18, 1906, the little passenger steamer *Dix* put out from her Seattle pier with 77 persons aboard. Nearly all of them were homeward bound to Port Blakely on Bainbridge Island. It was a clear moonlit night and Puget Sound was like a mill pond. Captain Percy Lermond had gone below to collect the fares, leaving mate Charles Dennison at the wheel. A few moments later the freighter *Jeanie,* laden with iron ore for the Tacoma smelter, loomed up on the starboard quarter.

In some unaccountable manner never clarified, the *Dix* maneuvered dangerously close to the larger steamer. Captain P. H. Mason, skipper of the freighter, popped his head out of the pilot house door. "What in hell are you trying to do?" he bellowed across the narrowing gap of water separating the ships.

Dennison, his hands gripping the wheel, gaped wide-eyed. As a blatant whistle roared at him, he became confused. Instead of putting the wheel hard to port he swung it to starboard, directly across the bow of the other ship. The *Jeanie* crunched into the side of the *Dix* with such force as nearly to sever her in half.

Captain Lermond rushed toward the pilothouse, but was hurled against the bulkhead and knocked unconscious. As he tried to shake off the effects of the blow, the passengers, taken by complete surprise, were thrown into utter confusion. The *Dix* heeled slowly over, righted herself momentarily, and then began to sink stern first. There was no time to lower a boat or issue life jackets. There wasn't even time to think.

Those on the forward deck rallied frantically for a few precious seconds. Some leaped to the *Jeanie*. One man made a wild jump for her bowsprit and hung there until pulled to safety.

The steamer veered, sending passengers crashing into the cabin bulkheads and spilling others off into the chilling water. In the engine room the engineer and fireman never knew what hit them. Death was almost instantaneous.

Many remarkable escapes from certain death occurred. One young boy grabbed a rope from the *Jeanie* just as the *Dix* went under. It was the margin between life and death. Another young man managed to save his girl friend but lost his own life. Heroes all, but some posthumously.

After the *Dix* went down, the *Jeanie* patrolled the Sound for hours picking up survivors. But many of the dead were trapped in the *Dix's* cabin and the sea refused to give up its dead. After hours on death patrol the *Jeanie* returned to port with 38 survivors. Thirty-nine were dead or missing. Other accounts placed the toll at 45 dead, for among the passengers were an undetermined number of coolie millhands hired for employment at the Port Blakely Mill Company.

In the island mill town nearly every family had a loved one missing. The mill was shut down and flags stood at half mast. All of the ships lay idle in the harbor.

The *Dix* went down in 600 feet of water. Dragging operations proved futile. The bodies remained with the sunken ship—all except one, a bloated corpse found on the beach near Alki Point.

The Board of Inquiry convened and Captain Lermond, who had narrowly escaped with his life, described the last moments of the *Dix* as follows:

> The jib-boom of the *Jeanie* crushed through us just aft of amidships and heeled the *Dix* over on her port side. She lay there with water rushing in for almost two minutes and then heeled back to starboard.

I could hear the cries of men, women and children imprisoned below.

Though the mate, Charles Dennison, who had made the fatal navigation blunder at the *Dix's* helm, paid with his life, Captain Lermond came under severe criticism for not being in the wheelhouse when the crash occurred. The charge, however, was unjustifiable because it was common practice for skippers of small passenger boats to double as pursers when navigation was not considered hazardous. He was acting in this customary capacity collecting fares from the passengers when the collision took place.

Prior to the disaster, he had been on the Seattle-Port Blakely run 13 years without an accident. Despite insufficient evidence to the contrary, his papers were temporarily revoked, though his sympathizers far outnumbered his critics.

WINDWARD

If some dark night the reader strolls along Seattle's waterfront and hears the creaking of old rigging and the gurgling of bow wash, don't be alarmed, not even if there is no ship in sight. It is probably the rumblings of one of three ships resting uneasily in the fill—the *Windward,* the *Mississippi* or the *Idaho.* Landlocked and shackled by the works of man, these carcasses, once aristocrats of the sealanes, are doomed to the slow, tormenting process of decay.

Some port cities build their waterfronts on foundations of piling, concrete, dirt or brick. Though Seattle's waterfront has a little of each, it also contains the hulks of ships. How did they get there? Well, some ships are wrecked, some founder, and others are dismantled, but the passing of one of this trio, the clipper ship *Windward* was rather unusual. She lies under Western Avenue, sprawled out between Marion and Columbia streets.

The *Windward* was launched as a creation of man's great shipbuilding ability. Combining both grace and speed, she spread her wings after leaving the Trufant and Drummond Yard at Bath, Maine, in 1854. After making many splendid passages around the Horn, she was sold to west coast owners. Encountering trouble on the Columbia River Bar in her latter years, she was towed upriver and rerigged as a bark.

Under the command of Captain A. E. Williams, the *Windward,* with a crew of 15, sailed from Seattle on December 30, 1875, loaded with lumber for San Francisco. A heavy shroud of fog hung over Puget Sound. The vessel's canvas hung limp and only the sound of her hand-pumped foghorn penetrated the still air. Shortly before one o'clock in the afternoon, her forward movement suddenly ceased with a rude jolt that sent the crew sprawling. The beach at Useless Bay on Whidbey Island had been struck. As the tide ebbed, the ship was left high and dry.

The underwriters looked her over and, due to her age, considered her not worth salvage, except for her cargo of lumber. The owners disposed of her for a meagre sum. Eventually John Leary, John Collins, and J. M. Colman, three principals of the Seattle and Walla Walla Railroad Company, found it in their possession. The company owed Colman $800 and was unable to pay it, so persuaded him to accept the *Windward* as payment. This was done against his better judgment for by this time the wreck was half full of water.

In a novel salvage undertaking the vessel was raised by cutting holes through her hull, port and starboard, and running huge logs into the voids. Then on a high tide, barges were towed in and lashed to the protruding logs. On the following flood tide the wreck was raised from the bottom and towed to Seattle. It was beached just behind the present location of the Colman Building on Western Avenue, between Columbia and Marion streets. There, Colman had all the copper and usable metals stripped from the ship's hull. What remained was left for the children to play pirate with and the termites to fill their stomachs.

The old wreck became a landmark on the waterfront. During those early years the tide came up to First Avenue in many places and all the area between that and the present shoreline was later filled in and became premium property. The Seattle and Walla Walla Railroad Company claimed ownership of the adjacent land with agreement to purchase the riparian rights. These rights were in turn transferred to Colman in settlement of the debt and he became the sole owner. The property was worth a fortune. This land was to become the location of the Colman Building and the Colman Ferry Dock, presently the home of the Washington State Ferry System, the largest ferry line in the world. Little did Colman realize the good fortune the old *Windward* was to bring him.

As the old hulk drew her dying breaths, her masts disappeared and from them were made souvenir canes. In the 1880's, the Seattle Lake Shore and Eastern Railroad was built and, instead of removing the remains of the *Windward,* piling was driven through her stout timbers. Then came dirt, brick, concrete. Just to add a sweet note, a building was constructed over the wreck and became the home of the Society Candy Company.

Is it any wonder that the *Windward,* deep in her landlocked grave, moans in her death agonies?

A. J. FULLER

Fog hung over the waters of Seattle's Elliott Bay at 1 a.m. on the morning of October 30, 1918. The occasional blasting of a whistle or the clanging of a buoy were all that broke the silence. About 2000 feet off Harbor Island, the square-rigged ship *A. J. Fuller* lay at anchor, moored to a large steel buoy. She had arrived from Uyak, Kodiak Island, Alaska, her holds filled with 48,000 cases of salmon and 4000 barrels of salt fish, waiting to be discharged. All of her crew had gone ashore to see the bright lights, with pay checks in hand. Only the first mate and the watchman remained aboard.

Cutting through the thick strands of fog came the out-bound Japanese steamer *Mexico Maru*. She strayed into the anchorage area where lay the *Fuller*. Without warning she plowed directly into the sailing vessel, gashing a hole ten feet wide in her starboard bow. The mate and watchman rushed from their quarters and without surveying the damage immediately lowered a boat. Water rushed into the ship in a mad torrent and the escaping men had but one motive—to get as far away as possible.

It took but ten minutes for the 229-foot vessel to go under. She sank in 225 feet of water, dragging down with her the buoy to which she was moored.

When the *Fuller* arrived from Alaska she was carrying 100 cannery workers, plus her crew. Several of them had bunked near the spot where the collision occurred, but fortunately all had left the ship.

Captain Henry Finch, Seattle deep sea diver, investigated the wreck six months later. In a daring descent he went down into the black waters and managed to reach the topmasts of the sunken ship. There he perched himself in the rigging and with wire sweeps and grappling irons managed to recover the ship's compass, several blocks and chains, and part of the taffrail. His hooks actually pulled off the top of the wheelhouse and the compass came with it. Its extra-heavy glass had withstood the pressure of the water (pressure is one half pound per foot, making it 112 pounds where the wreck lay).

The *A. J. Fuller's* sanctuary was never again invaded. Henry Finch was of the opinion that the vessel could have been raised by use of sweep wires attached to barges, but the underwriters dismissed any such scheme as being too expensive for the valuation of the ship. Her cargo of salmon was a total loss without so much as the recovery of a single can.

Accordingly, the full loss claim was paid to Northwestern Fisheries Company of Seattle, owners of the *A. J. Fuller*. The captain and officers of the *Mexico Maru* were found negligent and the Osaka Shosen Kaisha Line paid $504,000 for the sustained loss.

ANDELANA

One might well expect a ship to be lost on the ocean coast in the fury of a gale, but it is unusual when a large ship at anchorage founders with all hands within the walls of a protected harbor.

The 2579-ton bark *Andelana* lay in Tacoma Harbor on the night of June 14, 1899. She had come to load a cargo of wheat for the United Kingdom. One of the largest and finest sailing vessels in the service, she had been built principally for the grain trade.

On the night of June 14, gusty winds whipped across the waters of the harbor. The *Andelana,* her masts almost touching the night clouds, rode high, kept on an even keel by chains strapped to logs on either side, at her waterline. All ballast had been removed preparatory to loading.

The wind increased until it blew a steady 38 miles per hour. All hands with but one exception were aboard. The absentee was a seaman who had gone ashore with a bad toothache. The shipmaster, Captain J. Gillis, had also planned on going ashore that evening but on feeling ill had decided to remain aboard. His decision was to cost him his life.

In a sudden moment of horror and without the slightest forewarning, the *Andelana* capsized in the wind, filled, and plunged to the bottom 200 feet down. She carried her entire crew of 17 with her. The catastrophe took place in a matter of seconds.

Tacoma's populace was stunned. Never before and never since has such an unusual tragedy occurred in the city's maritime annals.

An effort by four tugs to pull the submerged wreck into shallow water by her anchor chains proved futile. Underwriters paid the insurance to the ship's owners and the 17 bodies remained trapped within their steel domicile.

Many years later, a diver in attempting to locate the wreck, was himself claimed by the depths when his diving suit burst under pressure.

In March, 1935, while searching for a lost anchor off the City Waterway bell buoy, George Wayne, deep sea diver for the Olson Tugboat Company, quite by accident stumbled onto the remains of the *Andelana*. Thirty-six years on the bottom had caused havoc on the old ship, reducing it to a pile of rubble. Pressure, depths and darkness kept the diver from searching its deep recesses, though he did bring up pieces of the wreckage.

Wayne grimaced when he discovered the wreck, for he realized he was looking on the unhallowed grave of 17 seafarers.

Historic sidewheel steamer *Yosemite* aground in Orchard Narrows, near Bremerton, Washington, July 9, 1909. Total loss. In 1865 her boilers blew up in San Francisco Bay killing 50 persons.
(Joe Williamson collection)

Puget Sound steamer *Kitsap* raised from forty fathoms in Seattle's Elliott Bay after being rammed and sunk by the steamer *Indianapolis* December 14, 1910.

Fatally rammed on February 15, 1937 by the SS *Walter Luckenbach*, the Italian MS *Feltre* rests at the bottom of the Columbia River near Prescott, Oregon.

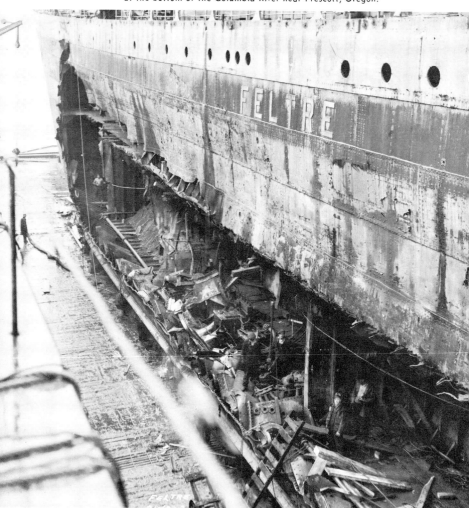

In drydock after major salvage work, the *Feltre* underwent a $300,000 rebuild. Note gash in her side.

From a thing of beauty to an object of regret. British bark *Peter Iredale* ashore on Clatsop Beach, Oregon, after stranding, October 25, 1906.

With only her mast protruding above water, U. S. Navy motor minesweeper *Nightingale* reposes uneasily after striking buoy off Columbia River bar December 26, 1941. Raised; sold surplus.
(courtesy Capt. Loring Hyde)

Eleven perished in the tragic fire which gutted the Danish passenger-cargo vessel *Erria*, just east of Astoria, December 20, 1951.

German bark *Mimi* ashore at the south entrance to Nehalem River, Oregon, February 13, 1913. Salvage attempts failed and 17 lives were lost when the ship rolled over.

Ashore on a clear, calm day with all sails set. British ship *Glenesslin*, October 1, 1913 at the base of Neah-Kah-Nie Mountain.

PART TWO

SHIPWRECKS OF THE
OREGON COAST

Chapter Five

COLUMBIA RIVER BAR TO TILLAMOOK BAY

DOWN through the years to the present time, the busiest maritime crossroads along the shores of the Pacific Coast have been Juan de Fuca Strait, the Golden Gate, and the entrance to the Columbia River. The latter, being the portal to a vast inland empire, has hosted a prosperous century of maritime commerce.

Tribute must be paid to those who pioneered the way, for there were numerous obstacles to be overcome. The principal one was making the Columbia Bar safe for navigation. Millions have been expended for this purpose, a far greater amount than for any other bar entrance in America. Acres of shoal waters have been eliminated by the construction of two tremendous rock jetties at the north and south entrances. Two former undependable channels have been roped and saddled into one deep bar passage.

Range markers, buoyage, light stations, lightships, radio, radio beacons, and radar are all in constant usage to guide ships in and out of the Columbia Bar. Yet, with all this progress, Oregonians are still not satisfied, and gallantly carry on their battle for more funds to rid forever the title of Pacific Graveyard, frequently applied to the Columbia River entrance.

Bar pilots and civic groups have agitated for congressional approval for a multi-million dollar dredging project that will maintain a depth over the bar of 48 feet. This would eliminate, once and for all, the danger of ships scraping over the bar in heavy swells. At present this giant undertaking is under way. It has been a great human battle against the elements, not won without costly sacrifice. Down through the past century since men first settled the lands of the Columbia, nearly 2000 vessels, from small fishing craft to deep-sea cargo vessels, have been wrecked or damaged around the Columbia River Bar, where that wide watercourse meets the ocean. More than 1500 lives have been lost.

Before the completion of the six-mile-long south jetty, the largest proportion of which was finished in 1885, ships entering the river from the southern approaches sailed dangerously near the shore. Sailing vessels frequently found themselves in jeopardy if the wind failed or if fog set in. The area was full of foul ground and strong currents to imperil ships time and time again.

SHARK

The U. S. Naval survey schooner *Shark* was wrecked on September 10, 1846, at the south entrance to the Columbia River. This same wreck was ultimately responsible for the naming of a town, plus the building of a ship which saved another community from starvation.

The *Shark,* in command of Captain Schenck and under the direction of Lieutenant Neil M. Howison, U. S. N., had been sent north by Commodore Sloat to make an examination of the coastal harbors, rivers, productions, climate and population of Oregon Territory. The schooner had been detached from the fleet and had arrived at the Columbia after a 25-day passage from Honolulu in the summer of 1846.

While feeling her way over the Columbia Bar, a lone negro in a small canoe came alongside and offered his services as a pilot. He claimed to be a survivor of the

98

Navy brig *Peacock* lost at the river entrance five years earlier. Though a ship's cook by profession he boasted sufficient knowledge of the bar to act as a pilot. The schooner's commander scrutinized the man carefully. He was dubious, but inasmuch as the ship's charts were extremely vague he put the colored man to work. With pride and frequent gestures, he assumed his duties. But his role as a pilot was indeed brief. Within an hour he had the schooner hung up on a sand bar. Fortunately the bar was calm and after considerable difficulty the schooner was worked free.

Unwilling to take further chances, Captain Schenck retired the colored man and sent word in for a more competent pilot. John Lattie, a pioneer, was the only man who could qualify. He brought the schooner in safely, but her arrival on the river was met with mixed emotions. True, the settlers had long demanded surveys of their contemptuous bar, and the *Shark* had been sent by the government to some degree for this purpose. Rumors, however, persisted that the ship's arrival was a war precaution in the face of the friction between Great Britain and the United States over the boundary question. It was assumed that the *Shark* stood ready for battle and that her survey mission was a mere cover-up. The *Shark's* officers and the British subjects at Fort George (Astoria) did what they could to allay this anxiety.

Then more trouble ensued. The *Shark's* crew, from long months at sea, began deserting and replacements were not to be had. Proclamations were issued for their arrest. For fear of further desertions, the survey of the river mouth was hastily conducted and the schooner was ready to make her final departure on September 10.

Without awaiting favorable tides for the outward crossing, the *Shark* weighed anchor. While in transit over the bar she struck the south shoals and was imperiled by the sands. The breakers began to slam against her sides and Captain Schenck feared for his ship. He ordered the three masts cut down and twelve cannon jettisoned. Still the schooner refused to budge from her perch and within a few hours gave signs of breaking up. Reluctantly the commander gave the order to abandon ship. There was no panic. All hands took their places at the oars in an orderly fashion and negotiated the bar to safety. They were taken in by the natives at the settlement and treated like members of the family. Their ship no longer constituted a danger to the peace.

During the bleak, stormy hours of that night the *Shark* broke up. A large portion drifted out over the bar and came ashore near Arch Cape.

Evidently the *Shark's* crew did not jettison all the cannon for among the wreckage was found one which ultimately resulted in the naming of Cannon Beach, Oregon. This ancient weapon, the ship's capstan, and some chain have been enshrined as a monument south of the town of Cannon Beach.

In the year of the wreck, John Hobson came down from Astoria to dismantle the ship's remains, but left much of it to the elements. Eight years later, the Indians told the early settlers of Tillamook County that part of the wreck still lay on the beach.

The men of Tillamook were isolated by mountain barriers on land and dangerous bar entrances by sea. Ship captains would not risk entrance into Tillamook Bay and the settlers had set about building their own supply ship in an effort to sustain existence. Their small schooner was being fashioned from materials at hand, but there was no iron or steel for bolts and fittings. The Indian story of the wreck started a rugged overland trek with pack horses to the site. From the bones of the *Shark* was extracted enough iron to supply all the needs of the blacksmith in pounding out the proper fittings for the little vessel. The finished result was the schooner *Morning Star*, first vessel constructed in Tillamook County. The impoverished pioneers gave thanks as she sailed for Astoria and returned with urgently needed food and supplies.

In Astoria today stands a boulder known as "Shark

Rock." The survivors of the wreck more than a century ago inscribed on it the date of her loss.

But the story does not end here, for the outstanding mission of the *Shark* has yet to be told. Following the wreck, Lieutenant Howison presented the ship's colors to the Provisional Government at Fort George (Astoria), accompanied by the following letter:

> To display this national emblem and cheer our citizens in this distant territory by its presence was a principal object of the *Shark's* visit to the Columbia; and it appears to me, therefore, highly proper that it should henceforth remain with you, as a memento of parental regard from the general government. With the fullest confidence that it will be received and appreciated as such by our countrymen here, I do myself the honor of transmitting the flags (an Ensign and Union Jack) to your address; nor can I omit the occasion to express my gratification and pride that this relic of my late command, should be emphatically the first United States flag to wave over the undisputed and purely American territory of Oregon.

Thus again the American flag waved over Fort George and from it grew the City of Astoria.

CITY OF DUBLIN

The British ship *City of Dublin*, 49 days at sea, bound for Portland, Oregon, from Port Chalmers, New Zealand, approached the Columbia River on October 18, 1878. Her master, Captain David Steven, was not familiar with the character of the bar, and without awaiting a pilot brought his ship in dangerously close. Suddenly the breeze died. Both anchors were dropped in an attempt to keep her off Clatsop Spit. Still the ship drifted. Frantically the Captain broke out a third auxiliary anchor and put it over the side. By now the ship was amidst the breakers, jerking on all three anchor cables. It began to drag again, the anchor flukes digging into the sand. The cables could no longer stand the strain and one after another parted.

After a valiant but fruitless effort, the vessel was dashed on the spit and immediately began taking water. A boat was lowered and the crew were forced to run the breakers to gain the beach. All made good their escape.

The *City of Dublin* valued at $40,000 was declared a total loss and sold on a where-is-as-is basis to the highest bidder. Salvage attempts began two weeks later. Despite herculean efforts by optimistic salvagers, the ship soon broke up, yielding little of value.

An interesting sidelight to the wreck revolved about its figurehead. She carried a carving of a red-painted Indian chief with a full headdress. As the breakers broke up the wreck, the figurehead was dislodged and drifted across the bar to Baker's Bay. There it was reputedly found by a resident of Ilwaco and promptly mounted on an old shed near the town. As the story goes, the shed eventually fell into a state of collapse and the figurehead was removed by an unnamed person. Fearing it might be claimed by another, he buried it on his Ilwaco acreage.

Some years later he died and nobody seemed to know exactly where the figurehead was buried.

Someday somebody may accidentally unearth the wooden image and wonder if he has discovered a mummified Indian. It is ironical that a ship named for an Irish city should carry the figurehead of an Indian. More interesting is that it ended up in Indian country, where once Chief Concomly, celebrated tribal leader, ruled with a powerful hand. Ilwaco was named for his son-in-law, Elowahka Jim.

PETER IREDALE

Rarely do the skeletal remains of a ship languish indefinitely in a shallow grave to form a pattern in the passing parade of time. The *Peter Iredale,* a huge creation of a sailing vessel, 278 feet from stem to stern, fashioned of steel plates on iron frames, was such a vessel. Though it saw but a decade and a half of service, it has remained on the sands of Clatsop Beach, half buried, for more than a half-century. Anybody familiar with the Oregon coast has doubtless seen the remains of the *Peter Iredale*.

This old wreck has become a tourist attraction, lying above most stages of the tide for the curious to examine. Each year it presents a different sight, sometimes nearly covered with sand, and again unearthed. Red with rust, succumbing bit by bit to the ravages of time, the *Peter Iredale* finishes out her days as a last reminder of the era of sail.

How did she get there? It was October 25, 1906, Captain H. Lawrence, master, picked up Tillamook Rock Light at 2 a. m., and called all hands.

They would stand off the Columbia to await a pilot.

A heavy southwest wind was in the making and sail was shortened. Before the faint glow of dawn the befuddled skipper found his ship amid a surging mass of breakers. Crunching over the bottom, the shock sent the mizzen top hamper crashing to the deck. The men scattered like frightened mice. The bark struck again. More sections of the masts, rigging, blocks and tackle, thundered to the deck. Again the crew scattered.

Captain Lawrence summoned all hands aft. The deck became a welter of wreckage.

The Point Adams Lifesaving crew, assisted by volunteers from Fort Stevens, hastened to the wreck. All of the survivors were landed safely, though shaky from their experiences.

The *Peter Iredale*, 28 days out from Salina Cruz, Mexico, was under charter to Balfour, Guthrie and Company, and was to have loaded wheat on the river. She was owned by Peter Iredale and Porter, large shipowners of Liverpool.

The vessel's hull was little damaged from stranding and an air of optimism brought high hopes of salvage. It was planned to tow the ship, stern first, through the breakers into deep water. Nature was, however, the superior force and finally the underwriters had to admit defeat. They paid the ship's full insurance value.

For a few more weeks the shipmaster stood by, hoping against hope for a miracle, but all salvage operations were soon abandoned and the ship, now on a severe starboard list and half imbedded in the sands, was deserted.

During World War II, the only enemy shells to strike Oregon soil landed near the *Peter Iredale*. They were shot by night from a Japanese submarine and soared directly over the wreck and into empty fields at Fort Stevens. No damage was done. The very next day the Army strung rolls of barbed-wire from Point Adams south, to thwart a would-be enemy invasion. The old *Peter Iredale* was entwined in it and remained so throughout the war.

Lying on a famous clam digger's beach, the old wreck has many visitors even today. They dig about her bones to unearth juicy bivalves.

Men have come and gone, lighthouses have been built and abandoned, military posts manned and closed down, wars fought and won, but still the wreck of the *Peter Iredale* lives on.

FRANCIS H. LEGGETT

Stark, terrible tragedy such as only shipwreck is capable of doling out was enacted on the tempestuous Pacific in the fall of 1914. The steamer *Francis H. Leggett* was outbound from Grays Harbor with a capacity load of railroad ties. San Francisco-bound, she carried a total of 67 passengers and crew members.

Proceeding down the coast, the steamer encountered strong winds from the southwest which began blowing with increasing fury. The ocean became a mass of great greybacks, raising their summits to unprecedented heights. The vessel's speed was reduced to a minimum but she pitched so furiously that none aboard could keep their feet. Green water came over the forecastle and smashed against the housing, every bolt in the ship turning in its socket. The wind velocity climbed rapidly on the Beaufort scale.

The ship's location was 60 miles southwest of the Columbia River.

Then came the shocking news. The chief engineer informed the bridge that water was pouring in below. Every pump was manned by crew and passenger alike. Tons of water were thrown back from where they had come but the outlet could not compare to the intake. The steamer dropped lower and lower with each boarding sea.

Terse calls of distress rattled over the wireless. Then the captain's hand gripped the whistle cord and several short blasts sent all hands scurrying to their lifeboat stations. The seas had not abated their fury one iota. Little chance existed for an open boat in that ocean. The captain had no solution.

In a few moments of horror it was all over. A hammering sea breached the entire ship. This time it failed to respond. Mournful cries, weeping and wild calls for help were the last human sounds uttered as the vessel went down.

Three ships intercepted the distress call and made full speed toward the scene. When they arrived all that remained was a floating mass of railroad ties and pieces of wreckage. Then, as if the hand of fate had intervened, two survivors were spotted clinging to bits of wreckage. Dazed and suffering from exposure, they were too weak to relate their frightful experiences.

The rescue ships continued to circle the area hour after hour and well into the next day, but only one body, that of a woman passenger, was recovered. Sixty-five persons perished, two survived. September 18, 1914, was listed as a black day in Pacific maritime history.

Grim reminders of the disaster were the large amounts of lumber and wreckage cast up on the Tillamook shores of Oregon. Beach combers took advantage of these gifts from the sea and one home at Manzanita was entirely constructed of ties from the wreck.

EARLY SPANISH AND ORIENTAL SHIPWRECKS OF THE NEHALEM SHORES

On Oregon's Nehalem beaches abound enough romance and mystery to capture the imagination of the wildest writer of fiction. Episodes of buried treasure; quantities of ancient beeswax; tales of redheaded, blue-eyed Indians; tribal chiefs with Negro blood and Oriental castaways, revolve about the ancient shipwrecks of this area. Unfortunately they occurred before the recorded coming of the white man and the only accounts were from the descendants of the early Nehalem Indians. The evidences have, however, remained to stir the imagination.

Just before the turn of the century, E. M. Cherry of Astoria found the last remnants of an age-old wreck unearthed by the shifting sands of Nehalem Spit. Still another unknown wreck has been located in deep water off Treasure Cove, below the towering cliffs of Mount Neah-Kah-Nie.

One legend handed down by the natives of Nehalem concerns an enterprising Oriental sailor. He was reputed to be a survivor of a wrecked junk carried across the Pacific by the Japanese Current about the time Columbus discovered America. Taken captive by the natives, he later gained his freedom through his talent for building small boats. Turning freebooter to exact tribute from the coastal tribes of Oregon, he organized a band of savages and pillaged villages from the Columbia River to Coos Bay via swift war canoes. He became a tyrannical figure among the Indians and one feared all along the coast.

Samuel A. Clarke, the Oregon poet, celebrated this "Nelson of the bays" with a ballad, of which the following lines give something of the flavor:

106

There was an ocean potentate
Who, all along the western shore,
  With war canoes of hemlock made,
Dashed through where noisy breakers pour,
  And battles won with gleaming blade—
With brazen gongs made great uproar,
  And all the coast in tribute laid.

It is a known fact that hundreds of Oriental junks were cast adrift in the Pacific, and it is not improbable that such a craft was cast ashore near the Nehalem River entrance more than 600 years ago. One record is still in existence of an early Chinese explorer who reputedly sailed along the Pacific Coast and made a landing on the west coast of Mexico in the fifth century A. D. In more recent years Oriental junks have been wrecked at Point Adams, at the mouth of the Columbia River (1820); at Cape Flattery (1833); and near Ocean Park, Wash., about the turn of this century. Hundreds more were lost from the Aleutians to the shores of Mexico, all victims of the Japanese Current.

Early white settlers of the Nehalem region found considerable quantities of teakwood on the beach, remnants of an ancient shipwreck. The wood showed considerable wear and deterioration which lends credence to the supposition that ships were wrecked on Nehalem's shores centuries before the land ever felt the footprint of a white man.

Then there is the story of a white survivor wrecked on the Nehalem shores about 1760. Reputed to be a Scot, with fiery red hair and beard, he was a rarity and something for the natives to behold. Marrying into the Indian family that had rescued him from the wreck, he made his home on the Clatsop Plains. His descendants were mentioned in the accounts of Lewis and Clark and also by John Minto.

In his *Manuscript Journals* (1813), Alexander Henry —clerk and fur trader with the North West Company— tells of an old Clatsop chief arriving with salmon and the meat of a large bitch. With him was a man about 30 years

107

of age with dark red hair, supposedly the offspring of a white man shipwrecked near the mouth of the Nehalem River many years earlier. He goes on to say that great quantities of beeswax were dug out of the sand near this spot and that the Indians would bring it to trade with the whites.

Henry further stated: "They bring us frequently lumps of beeswax fresh out of the sand which they collect on the coast to the south, where the Spanish ship was cast away some years ago and the crew all murdered by the natives."

The only place on the Pacific Coast where beeswax has been extracted from the beach in such tremendous quantities is from the sands around Nehalem Spit. The beeswax recovered has prompted the belief that more than one ship was wrecked there. Rotting hulls not visible to the eye, but buried deep in the offshore sands near Mount Neah-Kah-Nie, doubtless had much to do with the beeswax mystery.

Beeswax was an ordinary cargo for early Spanish vessels. Galleons plying the Pacific in trade between the Philippines and Mexico as early as 1565 returned frequently with beeswax among their cargo.

Spain's trade with the Philippines lasted 250 years. It is possible that a Manila galleon returning home was driven off her course and crashed ashore near Neah-Kah-Nie Mountain. Galleons frequently set their courses for giant headlands on the Northern California coast to gain their landfall. It is quite possible that stress of storm carried at least one of them northward, causing its stranding on Oregon's shores.

Then, too, tales have persisted of an English marauder or pirate ship in pursuit of a galleon. In its escape it was wrecked on the Oregon Coast. Golden goblets of Spanish origin have been brought up from the bottom of the sea near Yaquina Bay.

A century after Spain's trade with the Orient began, Spanish supply vessels sailed from lower California to the new missions in upper California with cargoes of beeswax. This wax was used in Catholic missions for tapers, candles, and images. Many times the supply vessels sailed northward to be lost without trace. Their doom was the rugged uncharted coastline.

One recognized theory as to the identity of the mysterious beeswax ship of Nehalem was suggested decades ago by historian Silas Smith. He believed it to be the Spanish supply ship or caravel *San Jose*. This vessel departed La Paz, Lower California, June 16, 1769 with mission supplies for San Diego. It was never again reported. Smith surmised that a storm at sea carried the ship far to the north and through inability to regain its course, the craft was cast ashore near the Nehalem River.

The fact that most of the wax was found about 200 yards from the sea would indicate that the crew attempted to save the cargo. They perhaps carried it to that spot where in later years much of it was covered by the shifting sands.

Some of the cakes of wax weighed several hundred pounds. The average was about ten. Some were inscribed IHS, a symbol for the Greek contraction of *Jesus*. Other pieces were inscribed with numerals and dates. One very large piece of beeswax, now in the Pioneer Museum in Tillamook, bears the date 1679 which might indicate that another vessel laden with wax preceded the *San Jose* by nearly a century.

Early scientists who studied the wax expressed disbelief that any one vessel could carry the tons of beeswax discovered in the area.

After the white man came to Oregon, this wax was brought by the Indians to Astoria where it was traded for, and shipped to California markets.

Some scientists in examining the substance, expressed doubt that it was actually beeswax. They insisted upon its being a product formed by nature known as ozocerite. These contrary theories, however, were quelled after Dr. J. S. Diller, one of the ablest field geologists of the United States Geological Survey, came to examine the Nehalem wax fields. His findings were that the wax was found in no other area and that a few generations earlier the tide had reached the place then occupied by the wax. He further stated that the substance was not derived from the adjacent land, chemical tests showing it to be beeswax and not ozocerite.

Another Spanish ship is reputed to have been lost on Clatsop Beach about 1725. A survivor whom the Indians called Konapee lived among them for many years, gaining his freedom by his skill in making knives.

Thus we find the evidences of maybe three Spanish vessels and a junk wrecked on the Oregon coast, all within a distance of perhaps 25 miles, long before the recorded coming of the white man.

And finally we come to another tale, the most captivating of all. This is the legend of the "Treasure ship," which has drawn hundreds to the slopes of Mt. Neah-Kah-Nie to seek a chest full of gold and jewels. The strongbox of Indian legend has, however, eluded the human grasp despite the fact that many have lost their lives in a vain search. Others have spent countless thousands of dollars seeking the treasure.

Because the stories of the "Treasure ship," like those of the "Beeswax ship" were handed down through generations of Nehalems, there are many conflicting versions. Some legends claim the two vessels were one and the same, but to all indications it would appear that they had no direct connection. Another debated version of the "Treasure ship" is whether it merely visited the place, left the treasure and sailed away, or whether it was wrecked as was the "Beeswax ship." The true account may never be known.

The generally accepted version is that a Spanish ship came to anchor off the Nehalem shores in the 17th century. A boat was lowered and sent ashore filled with men. After running the breakers, the craft was pulled above the highest stages of the tide. A ceremony took place on the beach. The natives, fearing the strangers, took refuge in the bracken, watching with aroused curiosity and noting the removal of a large chest from inside the boat.

110

Then began a long ceremonious march up the steep slopes of Neah-Kah-Nie.

On the southwest side the strangers began digging a deep hole and placed the chest inside, according to Indian tales of old. Before it was covered with earth again, a negro, probably a slave, was slain with a cutlass and his body laid over the chest. (The fact that the native word for a dead man and a crucifix were similar may have had some bearing as to what actually happened).

The Spaniards made sure that the natives watched the ceremony, as they knew that an Indian never disturbed the burial place of a dead man. The placing of a slave over the chest assured them that the grave would not be rifled. Their mission completed, the Spaniards returned to the beach.

At this point there are several conflicting avenues to the story. One is that the ship sailed out over the horizon and into oblivion. Another is that the ship's company remained among the natives for a considerable period. Homesick and with time on their hands, they aroused the anger of the natives by taking liberties with their women. Finally the tribe launched a savage attack. The castaways were forced to defend themselves with slingshots. A bloody hand-to-hand battle ensued but the superior native forces exacted their toll. Only one or two Spaniards escaped, they being taken as slaves.

It was considerable time after the white settlers came to Nehalem before they could win the confidence of the natives in divulging these age-old tales. Even then they feared reprisal.

Chief Kilchis, celebrated leader of the Tillamooks and friend of the whites, was said to have been a large man with African features, curly hair, a high forehead, flat nose, thick lips, and a long chin. Many believed him to be a descendant of a shipwreck survivor of Nehalem, though he himself insisted that he had nothing but Indian ancestry.

In conjunction with the buried treasure, several stones chiseled by crude instruments were unearthed around the

111

turn of the century. It was thought that these markings held the key to the location of the treasure chest. If so, however, no seeker ever found the correct interpretation.

The person most associated with the search was Pat Smith, to whom it became almost an obsession. He and his father before him located the marked stones, deeply imbedded in the ground, in the shape of a huge cross, 30 feet in length by 20 feet in width. The first boulder was discovered about 1878, but during the following two decades many would-be treasure hunters disfigured the rocks. Smith disregarded these stones, pinning his hopes on one buried to a depth of ten feet on the southwest slope of Neah-Kah-Nie. Later he found another which appeared to fit into his scheme, but his diggings were all to no avail. The rocks bore crude marks of arrows and dots, seemingly to indicate directions. The lure kept him searching until he became too old to carry on. Then and only then did he take another into his confidence. Charlie Pike was the man he chose, and, after Smith died, Pike became as absorbed in the quest as his deceased partner had been.

There were many humorous and tragic incidents in connection with the search. One divining-rod enthusiast labored for months on the high slopes of Neah-Kah-Nie where the swinging plumb bob had ceased vibrating. Through gale and wind he carried on until he had a minor excavation in the hillside. Like the others before him, tired and discouraged, he had to admit defeat.

Great holes were opened all over the mountainous terrain by treasure seekers who ebbed in and flowed out like the tide.

William Snyder, while digging a trench between two of the marked rocks, struck a boulder that gave forth a hollow sound. He was certain he had found the treasure and dug with the tenacity of a man 30 years his junior. Nearly winded and on the verge of collapse, he overturned the rock only to find that a ground hog had left a tunnel there, which had caused the sound.

In 1931, Charles Wood and his son Lynn sought the

treasure. A young grandson joined them and kept the camp while the elder men were off digging. The lad had been cautioned not to reveal the purpose of their venture but when they did not return for lunch or dinner, he became worried and started back to Nehalem to summon help. When the searching party arrived they found the two missing men buried in the hole in which they were digging, stone dead.

That the chest was buried on the hillside many generations ago is almost a certainty. Geologists claim that slides and erosion may have caused it to drop into the sea or to have been buried in tremendous depths within the mountain. A possible solution happened in recent years when an earthquake opened up a huge crevasse and swallowed some cattle that were grazing on the green slopes of the hill.

In 1938, a new link in coast highway, U. S. 101, was cut across the sheer face of the mountain, 500 feet above the roaring Pacific. Termed the million-dollar-mile, this marvel of roadway construction perhaps affords the most majestic seascape on the west coast. Yet with all of the excavating, chiseling and tunneling necessitated by its excavation, none of the laborers found any indication of the buried treasure.

Many tales concerning possible discovery of the treasure have sprung up through the years. Tom McKay, once an employee of the Hudson's Bay Company, reputedly dug for the chest. The company had a policy that anything found by its hired hands was Hudson's Bay property. McKay denied finding any trace of the treasure. Yet in later years when he settled at French Prairie, he always had an abundance of money and freely passed it around, starting the rumor that he had unearthed the chest.

Then there was a negro who made his way to The Dalles in the early 19th century, claiming to have been part of the crew of the treasure ship. He insisted that he was present when the treasure was buried. He told of chiseling into bedrock so that in case of a slide it would hold the chest fast. To get to The Dalles, he had eluded his Indian master to whom he was a slave and, for fear of his life, refused to go back with a search party. After being promised protection, he finally consented to return and reveal the whereabouts of the treasure. At the Astor colony he contracted smallpox and died. The authenticity of his claim could never be verified.

Even today, a beachcomber strolling Nehalem Beach can find an occasional piece of beeswax reputedly from an ancient shipwreck. If only that wax could speak what a story it might tell. But of such is the fabric woven into the most captivating of the stories of Oregon's seacoast.

GLENESSLIN

Not all of the mystery below the steep walls of Mt. Neah-Kah-Nie occurred in the days before the coming of the white man. The debated loss of the British full-rigged ship *Glenesslin* in 1913 culminated in a complex court of inquiry and investigation that commanded the attention of shipowners and insurance companies the world over.

On the first day of October, 1913, the *Glenesslin* bound for Portland, 176 days out of Santos, was sighted sailing unusually close to the Nehalem shores. It was a beautiful fall day, the ocean lay calm, and the sky was flecked with light clouds. Visibility was almost perfect and the gentle breeze should have been the delight of any deep water man. Suddenly and for no understandable reason the vessel pointed its bow directly for the devilish waters about the base of Neah-Kah-Nie, five miles north of the Nehalem River.

Those who observed the strange antics of the ship thought they were seeing an apparition. But this was no Flying Dutchman; it was a staunch iron ship with a crew of live men. All sails were set and she was coming in fast. At precisely 2:30 p.m. an underwater ledge of rock, ripped a hole in her bottom plates and the ship crashed head on against the precipitous base of the 1600-foot mountain.

Cresting breakers nipped at her stern with terrific force. With only a ballast of cement to keep her steady, she worked unceremoniously on the jagged teeth beneath her.

Captain Owen Williams, master of the stricken ship, was aware of his hazardous position. Little time was lost in shooting a line to the rocks, where willing shoreside dwellers had arrived to make it fast. All 21 crewmen reached the rocks safely. Those aiding in the rescue had plenty of questions, but Captain Williams remained silent as did the other officers. There was no mistaking the odor of liquor on many of the survivors. Some were actually said to have been drunk.

Even as some light gear and personal effects were removed, the ship, on a starboard list with all canvas set, gave indication of breaking up.

While photographers and painters captured her death struggles, the groundwork for legal procedure got under way.

Rocks having penetrated the hull, no hope existed of refloating the vessel. Lloyd's Insurance surveyor rushed down from Portland and found the tide ebbing and flowing through the bilge, and the sternpost started. He advised the immediate sale of the wreck. On October 7, A. Bremmer and John Caavinen of Astoria paid $560 for it, but a few days later gladly disposed of it to a Nehalem party for $100. The difficulty of getting anything of value to shore made it extremely problematical that the wreck was even worth the latter price.

A Court of Inquiry consisting of the British Consul; Captain Davidson of the British ship *Lord Templeton,* and Captain Dalton of the British steamer *British Knight,* met on October 11. After examining the officers and the crew of the wrecked ship, they revoked the master's certificate for three months and the second mate John Colefield's papers for six months. First mate F. W. Harwarth got off with a reprimand. The officers were also held responsible for the drunken behavior of their crew at the time of the stranding.

Because the wreck occurred in comparatively clear weather, Captain Williams was charged with being "negligent in his duty." The same charge was leveled against the second mate who was on watch when the ship struck the rocks. He had permitted the vessel to get too close inshore before calling the master. The reprimand was given the first mate because he failed to act immediately on being notified of the threatened danger. The charges were serious ones in the light of the obvious facts, and the scars were never erased from the records of the accused.

Navigators who knew the Oregon Coast at the point where the *Glenesslin* came to grief explained that a windless pocket existed inside Cape Falcon. Once a sailing vessel was in this bight, it became a virtual impossibility to bring it about.

The Liverpool-built *Glenesslin* became the primary target of crashing breakers which swept the length of her. Though she was quickly destroyed, the legal entanglement involving her loss was by no means rapid. Pages of testimony went on record and the insurance companies refused to pay claims. The cry sounded that the wrecking of the vessel was part of a nefarious scheme to collect her insured value in a day when the steamer was crowding the square-rigger off the high seas.

Settlement was reached only after volumes of paper work and exhaustive investigation. The insurance was finally paid, the loss being recorded as due to the inexperienced first and second officers who were only 22 years of age.

In pondering the wreck of the *Glenesslin,* the reader should understand existing conditions under which the latter-day sailing ships operated. Basil Lubbock, one of the best informed of British maritime writers, explains it thus:

> In the last half dozen years before World War I it was heart-breaking work for the masters of British sailing ships and many of them left their old love,

the square-rigger, for steam, simply because they could not get competent officers or men. Those who hung on usually had to put up with an old "has been" as a mate, who either drank or was such a poor sailorman that he had either lost his ship in disgraceful circumstances or had never been trusted with one. And for second mate, the windjammer "old man" had to be satisfied with a boy just out of his time. More than three-quarters of the crew, also, were likely to be useless steamboat men or crooks and invalids, who were of no use aloft.

In such conditions sail could not be carried safely, for the skipper was certain to be let down by his watch officers or his crew at the first emergency. The former could only handle the ship in the clumsiest fashion and the latter could not take in sail in any wind. There were, of course, any number of good officers and men afloat, but they preferred the easier conditions and greater opportunities of steam. Thus in her old age we find the *Glenesslin* sailing without her royal yards and with two boys as mates.

And so the loss of the *Glenesslin,* one of the most discussed shipwrecks on the Pacific, passed into history, but in the memory of many salts, the ship lived on. In 1901 she had won a trans-ocean sweepstakes race over a field of eight square-riggers by some 17 days. In 1902, the *Glenesslin* covered 1000 miles in four days running. She also held a record never equaled by any other sailing vessel—Portland, Oregon, to Port Elizabeth, South Africa in 74 days. This exceedingly handsome ship, built in 1885, once the pride of the DeWolf fleet, had left her mark but was stricken from the records by human failings.

LIFE-LINE

"Go ye into all the world and preach the Gospel," was the Lord's command. This is the story of a Gospel mission boat and of saints who became fishers of men.

This small boat carried the Gospel to almost isolated people along the ocean stretches, coves and inlets of the Oregon Coast. Commanded by a faithful few who served a great cause, the craft braved the severest conditions of weather against a backdrop of inhospitable shores.

The *Life-Line* was built on Coos Bay in 1912 through the farsightedness of her originator, the Reverend G. L. Hall, a Baptist missionary. Noting the difficulties of transportation when he arrived in the Coos Country and also the fact that most of its citizenry dwelled along rivers, inlets, and ocean frontage, he conceived the idea of ministering to his flock by boat. Thus came about the birth of a motor launch adequately christened *Life-Line,* and built through subscription.

Hall's venture met with great success and the craft gained world-wide recognition as a means of bringing the church to the people. The Reverend Hall also acted as skipper and only carried one assistant crew member. When the boat reached a landing on its scheduled run, the pastor would shed his overalls and don his Sunday-go-to-meeting clothes. Nor was lack of a baptistry a problem. The entire Pacific surrounded the craft wherever it went and many were immersed in natural surroundings.

Congregations anxiously awaited the arrival of the vessel and, once it was secured to dockside, the services would promptly proceed in the main cabin. Though only 45 feet long, the *Life-Line* was an institution. She had to be rugged to cross cantankerous bars and to brave the rigors of the ocean. Sometimes services were delayed by weather but the Reverend Hall was a good sailor and with God as his captain feared not the wrath of the sea.

The boat's only propulsion was a 25-horsepower gasoline engine which proved as dependable as Paul after his conversion. Though the *Life-Line* frequently piled up on sand bars in heavy fogs, the damage was always negligible and the next day she would be under way again. Weddings, funerals, religious coffee breaks, as well as the regular evangelistic services, were a part of the monthly routine.

With the advent of new coast roads superseding water transportation, after the First World War, the silver wake of the *Life-Line* was terminated and the craft was sold in order to equip the Reverend Hall with a new highway cruiser. He continued to preach to the pastorless and isolated until age forced his retirement.

Following a brief lay-up, the *Life-Line* continued its missionary role. The Reverend Lund became her ecclesiastical skipper and piloted her northward to serve other out-of-the-way communities.

In May of 1923 the *Life-Line* departed Coos Bay bound for Kelso, Washington. About midnight she was skirting Mt. Neah-Kah-Nie in a restless sea when she scraped over a ledge of rock near the shore and developed a serious leak. Her luck had run out. Captain Lund and his one-man crew had no alternative but to leap overboard. In pitch darkness, through frigid water they prayed and swam. The Lord must have heard them, for He spared their lives.

The half-sunken wreck washed ashore and was swallowed in the sea sands. It had been almost forgotten when at low tide 26 years later, a bulldozer accidentally uncovered its skeleton.

And so ended the story of a boat with a heart and a soul.

MIMI

The wreck of the German bark *Mimi* actually involved two shipwrecks in one. The first was a relatively harmless occurrence, but the second claimed 17 lives.

The German square-rigger in command of Captain Westphal, ran aground at the south entrance to the Nehalem River on February 13, 1913. The shipmaster had lost his position in thick weather and had mistaken the Nehalem for the Columbia River. The *Mimi*, formerly the British bark *Glencova*, remained on an even keel and at ebb tide was partly out of water. There was nothing fatal about the stranding, but the problem rested in salvage.

119

Captain Robert Farley, keeper of the lifesaving station on Tillamook Bay, learning of the distressed ship, brought a surf boat ten miles down the beach. But his efforts were all in vain. The tide was such that the crew could walk ashore if they so desired.

Members from the Board of Underwriters visited the wreck and decided that it could be refloated. Captain E. C. Genereaux and several other prominent marine surveyors examined the vessel as well, and were of similar opinion. The German owners were willing to abandon her to the underwriters unless they obtained a good price for her. The bark was insured for $60,000, and carried no cargo.

The salvage plan recommended by the underwriters was to place two 8000-pound mushroom anchors three-quarters of a mile offshore. Two donkey engines placed on barges held secure by the anchors would pull on cables from the ship in an effort to free her from the sands. Bids were asked, with the stipulation that the vessel be delivered to Astoria before salvage money could be collected. Salvagers were required to post bond to relieve owners from responsibility of men and gear.

Bids and counter-bids were made, ranging between $14,000 and $48,000. One of $24,850 was accepted.

Against the advice of many, 1300 tons of ballast were removed from the *Mimi*. She stood in seven feet of water between tides and was sand-banked on the shoreward side.

Plans proceeded satisfactorily for nearly three months and the salvage prospects in general took on a rosy hue. As salvage preparations continued, the *Mimi's* crew, composed mainly of young Germans, the oldest 28 years of age, integrated themselves into the German families residing in the Nehalem area.

April 6 was the date set for the attempt at towing the *Mimi* off the beach. On this day an extreme flood tide was anticipated. There was much speculation on the outcome. Keeper Farley and others maintained that too much ballast had been removed for the safety of the ship.

The entire Tillamook area was excited over the forthcoming event. Lumber mills closed, canneries locked their doors, loggers laid down their axes.

On the Friday night preceding the undertaking, the *Mimi's* mate, Frederick Flagg, had a dream that the vessel was a dead man's hotel at the bottom of the ocean and all the crew except two of the men and the captain wore seaweed on their heads and a cloud covered their faces. So real was this nightmare that it prompted Flagg and the other mates to come ashore hand-over-hand on the cable between the ship and the shore.

On Saturday, Farley returned to the scene again to warn Captain Westphal of the danger of taking so big a ship, minus its ballast, out through the breakers. "She'll capsize, I warn you!" he protested. But his warning fell on deaf ears.

The boss of the wrecking engineers overheard the conversation and, with his face wrapped in a scowl, walked over to the captain. Farley saw them go into consultation. Then suddenly the shipmaster grabbed the megaphone and hollered down to Farley.

"When we need you, sir, we'll let you know."

There was no feeling of thanks for the keeper's solicitude and he wearily trudged back toward his station, muttering of the trouble for which they were heading.

The operation got under way early Sunday morning. Half of the regular crew were on shore leave. Fourteen were aboard, plus a dozen wreckers. A constant watch was kept at the lifesaving station when word was received that a storm was approaching. Up went the hurricane flags with their ominous squares of red and black.

Farley phoned the headquarters of the wrecking company at Brighton to warn them of the approaching bad weather. "You'll risk the lives of all those aboard," he said, "and probably force me to risk the lives of my men."

The reply was a rude one and keeper Farley hung up the phone greatly angered.

In spite of all warnings and protests, the operation proceeded. The shore cables were cut and the donkey engines roared and rattled. The offshore cables grew taut as fiddle strings and the giant anchors dug into the underwater sands. The flood tide inundated the exposed beach; and the tall ship, its masts reaching 200 feet into the air, began to inch its way over the sandy bottom. The surf was running high and the wind was already mounting strongly. As the vessel hit deeper water it began to roll in a fashion that skilled eyes knew spelled disaster. Then with terrifying rapidity she rolled over on her side.

Following were 24 hours of intense drama. At the center of it was Captain Robert Farley. The question was: did he do all in his power to save the lives of the unfortunates trapped inside the ship. It was on its side, with its deck exposed to landward, hatches wide open.

The lifesaving boat under Farley's direction was immediately launched against a strong wind and a towering surf, all hands being thoroughly soaked before their oars cut into the foaming maelstrom. When they finally got near the wreck they found her well on her starboard side down by the stern. Masts, yards, and rigging had been knocked free, forming a welter of entangled flotsam, rising and falling with the pulsation of the sea. Farley got his craft within 50 yards of the *Mimi* and was then encompassed by an impenetrable mass of wreckage. He tried to steer his boat this way and that but the oarsmen had no solid water into which to dig their oars. There was no channel through the debris. Two of the masts from the wreck were whacking against each other like a pair of shears. Spars were up-ended on the bar, amid planks, rope, and rigging.

As the lifeboat rolled and pitched, the bowman suddenly sprang to life with a boat hook. He stretched it out over the frenzied waters and plucked out the denim-clad lifeless body of one of the wrecking crew.

Farley then got his craft to the seaward side of the *Mimi* but the breakers were coming in with such fury that boarding was impossible. If only there were some way to get a line to shore thought Farley, but the distance was far too great and he had yet to see a sign of life aboard the bark. Could all hands have drowned, he wondered.

When the boat came back in through the surf, an agitated crowd met Farley and urged him to go back again. The situation was further tensed when from the bilge boards the body of the wrecker was removed.

By now walls of water sometimes 30 feet high were bashing the wreck, frequently obscuring it from the view of those on the shore.

The surfmen, chilled to the bone, were warming themselves against a fire made by local fishermen in a nearby sandy pit. Suddenly outbursts of excitement revived the crowd of spectators. Someone had reportedly seen one of the after portholes on the wreck thrown open and the waving of hands and white rags. Men cheered, women wept, and dogs barked in response.

Again all eyes were on Farley. But to him the barrier of reaching the wreck still existed. Slightly after 4:30 p.m. on that dismal Sabbath, Farley and his boys put out through the surf once again. The tide was ebbing but the breakers were equally as bad if not worse than before. The surf boat ran the gauntlet and, as it neared the wreck, nearly stood on end. The strong currents swept the craft well past the *Mimi*. Massive seas thwarted further attempts, forcing the lifeboat to return.

This in no way quieted the crowd who openly intimated that Farley and his crew were cowards. Some of the surfmen became extremely hostile toward their tormenters. They had gone since early morning without food and their nerves were on edge. The mass of humanity on the beach was about equally divided in its sentiments, which only made the situation more explosive.

Before darkness the surfmen tried again, but the attempt ended in failure. Many of the friends of those aboard the ill-fated ship wanted to go to their aid and the three mates who had "jumped ship" asked permission of Farley to take out his surfboat. Their request was refused, which set the crowd to the boiling point.

Night finally dispersed the spectators and there was nothing for the lifesaving crew to do but await the dawning of a new day. Farley stood alone in the dark, ponder-

123

ing the preceding hectic hours. Well trained in his occupation, he had done all that he thought feasible, but there was misery at having an uninformed public digging at him constantly. Reporters from one of the local newspapers were on his side but those on the rival sheet were about to label him as unfit for his job. Tomorrow's headlines were in the making. He had risked the lives of his men repeatedly and had used the line-throwing gun from the beach and from the surf without success. The distance and the wind were against him and so were half of the people.

On Monday morning, Captain Farley and his nearly-spent crew put out into the surf again and succeeded in reaching the *Mimi* under considerably improved conditions. Captain Westphal and three others were yet alive, struggling for their very existence. The surfboat, now able to navigate underneath the *Mimi's* bulwarks, came in between an up-ended spar wedged in the bottom sands at one end and a set of empty davits at the other. With but ten feet of working space in a pulsating sea, skillful seamanship was essential.

The first survivor, a young German lad, unconscious, was lowered by the heels through an after porthole to the waiting hands of the surfmen. The second survivor was the *Mimi's* cabin boy who managed to leap into the boat under his own power.

"How many more are there?" called Farley from the lifeboat.

"Just me and the president," retorted Captain Westphal from the dark recesses.

"President of what?" asked Farley.

"The wrecking company."

The two remaining men were pulled into the rescue craft. Then began the ticklish course back to the beach. Again the boat almost capsized but finally reached safety.

Captain Westphal informed Farley that he knew at least two of his crew had been dead since the first night but could not account for any of the others. The two corpses he could account for were lashed to spars under the bulwarks.

The survivors gulped down hot whiskey and wrapped themselves in blankets until ushered off to homes of nearby residents. The young boy who had remained unconscious was taken to a nearby cabin and given first aid. His legs were numb and his skin blue, but after an application of hot water and mustard, he revived.

While Farley and his men were at the cabin with the boy, one of the German mates who had abandoned the *Mimi*, entered. He demanded that the surfmen go back to the wreck and pick up the missing bodies and find the ship's papers. Farley, however, declined to order his exhausted crew out again until low tide, and the intruder left in a huff. True to his word, Farley put out to the wreck at slack tide to do the mate's bidding.

After a long sleep and a hot meal, Captain Westphal told of his miserable experience:

> Shortly after three p.m. Sunday morning as I was walking forward to tell the donkey engine man not to pull the *Mimi* further seaward, but to anchor her where she was, a sudden lurch took the vessel and I was pinned to the forward deckhouse by a fallen top spar. This lurch immediately preceded the capsizing of the *Mimi*. I distinctly remember hearing Captain Crowe (of the wrecking crew) speaking, but when we reached there, no one was to be seen nor were there any signs of life on the forward part of the ship at all. The donkey engine, mounted there, had slid into the sea. After a two hour endeavor to prevent sailors from leaping overboard and telling them that their best course was to stay by the ship, my efforts proved all for naught by their plunging overboard. Had it not been for the seven-foot board that ran around the vessel we would all have been carried away. To this alone we owe our escape.
>
> Until we reached the extreme after part of the ship, no sign of life was to be seen, although we

searched all that part of the vessel that was out of water. Here, clinging to the lifeboat lashed to the afterdeck, we found Captain Fisher and Tom Koen. Grasping for a lifeboat which was lashed round to the afterdeck, we discovered that one had slipped down into the water and was nearly submerged. Here we heard Koen call for help. We hastened to pass a line under his arms, with the assistance of Captain Fisher, and were able to raise him about two feet, but owing to his weight we were unable to get him higher. Koen with a final effort that seemed to sap his remaining vitality, threw his legs up over a spar that was lashed on deck near the rear starboard bulwark. Two minutes after this, a peaceful expression came over his face and he fell limp and passed to his God.

The other sailors died during the course of Sunday night. One man went crazy early Sunday morning after the first lurch and before she capsized. We called for three hours before an effort was made by the lifesaving crew to launch their boat. I guess they could not hear us and it was then that we undertook the dangerous efforts to attract attention by climbing up in the scupper and waving to those on shore. With the coming of darkness we gave ourselves up for goners, as we knew the tide was higher than that of the night before—and that almost covered the boat.

All night long we cheered each other by telling of other wrecks and situations worse than ours, where men had been rescued. With the coming day and the sighting of the lifesaving crew standing by out toward us on the way to our rescue, our hopes rose higher. The most sickening feeling anyone could have was experienced when the last attempt at rescue failed Sunday night. It looked as though our lives were to sink out with the dying sun. But we held fast and prayed. My God how we prayed and hoped and clung. It is too horrible to relate the horrors of that second night in our danger. We were paralyzed from

126

the cold, sickened by exposure and faint from hunger and thirst. The smell of the sea was horrible. Young Ludwig (the unconscious boy) stood to his waist in water almost Arctic in temperature for 28 hours. That we survived is a wonder. I want to forget it all.

Another survivor, Captain Charles Fisher, president of the Fisher Engineering Company in charge of salvage operations, thus related his experiences:

My whole life put together did not seem as long as the hours between sunset Sunday and daybreak this morning (Monday). It seemed years. All we could do was wait. Often during the long hours I thought I would give up my hold and fall into the water to join the others we knew had gone before us. Several times I lost heart but something seemed to cause me to cling. I was frozen with the cold of the water, was sickened by the cries of the people about us and was faint from hunger and thirst. I cannot see how I held on as long as I did. I shall return to my home and attempt to recover from the shock and horror of it all.

A different light on the situation was shed in the testimony of young Fritz Ludwig, following his recuperation.

We wanted to come ashore before the attempt to pull the *Mimi* off, but we were held back by the captain at the point of a gun. He threatened to shoot the first man that left the ship. We boys saved the captain's life when he was pinned down by the fallen forward yard. We felt no ill will toward him, as it was his duty to prevent desertion and it was our duty to help him.

In accordance with Fritz Ludwig's statement concerning the desertion of the ship, many of the crew, despite the captain's warnings, disobeyed his commands and jumped overboard. They attempted to swim ashore but one by one were drowned or crushed amid the wreckage. Most of them died grim deaths. Some tried vainly to right a smashed lifeboat which had overturned. Others perished of exposure after beating their arms and legs throughout the night to keep up circulation.

After the facts had been revealed, Captain Westphal was satisfied that Farley had done all that was within the realm of common sense to save the shipwrecked mariners.

But even at that hour a Tillamook newspaper was screaming Farley's incompetence, charging cowardice and drunkenness. Weak-minded people who had seen the surfmen stumbling about a beach fire nearly exhausted, labeled it drunkenness.

The only persons on the beach qualified to know the condition of the surf, besides the lifesaving crew, were the local commercial fishermen who had backed the rescuers to a man. Public sentiment and the press can, however, be sharper than a two-edged sword when they take prejudiced sides.

When the federal investigator arrived, as was always the case when loss of life was incurred, affidavits were taken. The fishermen vowed that Farley and his men were justified in their every decision.

Persons in all capacities present on the beach at the time of the tragedy were interviewed. The investigator's report as received at headquarters in Washington, D.C., read:

> The charges of drunkenness were unfounded and the major portion of the blame seems to have been voiced by the head of the wrecking firm who must recognize there had been criminal carelessness on his own part, or the bark would not have capsized. Had Farley listened to the clamor of the crowd and tried to put out through the wreckage another tragedy would have occurred.

According to the most reliable reports—of the 21

SS *Minnie E. Kelton* being towed to Astoria after becoming waterlogged off Yaquina Head, May, 1908. Eleven died. (Woodfield Photo)

Rusted boiler from wreck of the steam schooner *J. Marhoffer*. For this old boiler, Boiler Bay, Oregon, was named. The wreck occurred in 1910.

Tug **L. H. Coolidge** totally wrecked at the entrance to Coquille River, Oregon, August 20, 1951.
(courtesy Carl Christensen)

Four crew members succumbed when the Corps of Engineers' dredge **Wm. T. Rossell** was rammed and sunk by the Norwegian MS **Thorshall** off Coos Bay bar September 10, 1957.
Tug **Salvage Chief** standing by. (courtesy Marine Digest)

Wreck of the steam schooner *Fort Bragg*, torn asunder by incessant breakers on Coos Bay bar. Lost September 7, 1932. (courtesy Carl Christensen)

Passenger steamer *Santa Clara* hopelessly aground on Coos Bay bar November 2, 1915. Rescue is under way here. 21 lives were lost.

Smoke and fire pour out of the liner *Congress* afire off Coos Bay, Oregon September 15, 1916. The first lifeboat is being lowered. (Rehfeld Photo)

Thoroughly swept by fire, the *Congress* is seen several days after the conflagration. All passengers and crewmen made an orderly escape.

persons aboard the *Mimi* when she rolled over, 17 lost their lives. Four were saved. Had not the three German officers quit the ship, the death toll might have been higher. The much debated loss of the ship is still spoken of in hushed tones, though it happened half a century ago.

Chapter Six

TILLAMOOK BAY TO COOS BAY

THE coast of Oregon has never been a pilot's dream. The people of the Tillamook country faced near starvation in the early years because sailing ship masters refused to run Tillamook Bar. It was narrow and treacherous and death to many mariners.

Jetties have improved it in recent years but it is still very narrow and a place with which only seasoned pilots should flirt.

South to Coos Bay, the coast is very rugged and the limited number of passable bars are shallow and marred by shoals. High government maintenance costs have left many of these passages neglected.

Coos Bay Bar, on the other hand, has received every attention to be one of the major bar entrances on the west coast. The greater Coos Bay area has become the largest lumber export center in the world. Until recent decades, however, Tillamook and Coos bars held high mortality rates where loss of life and commerce were concerned.

ARGO

On November 26, 1909, the little passenger-cargo steamer *Argo* stood off Tillamook Bar. Breakers, white ridged, obscured the entrance, preventing her crossing. The vessel was more than four days at sea since leaving the Columbia River. Twelve passengers were aboard, two women, two children, and eight men. It had been an extremely rough voyage and most of the passengers were violently seasick. Some had remained in their berths the entire time.

About three that afternoon, the ship's captain decided to test the bar, but while in transit struck a sandy finger with a frightening jolt. The vessel's timbers were strained

130

from stem to stern. Passengers rushed to the boat deck only to see some of the ship's planks and a section of her keel drift by in the frenzied water below. The blow had been a fatal one and Captain Snyder informed all hands to prepare for the water.

Five or six times the *Argo* thumped against the ledge of sand. Suddenly she was turned broadside and nearly rolled over on her side. The engineer emerged on deck to inform the skipper that the engine was out of commission, and that several of the steam pipes had burst. Suddenly the steamer swung into the trough of the sea, drifting by the whistling buoy which was giving out its ominous warnings. Water poured into the ship. Some of the passengers were clad only in their bedclothes and life jackets. No panic ensued but on the faces of the saltiest seadog to the daintiest passenger, fear was evident. Many were wrapping towels about their heads and ears to keep out the sand, should they be tumbled over the sandy bottom by the breakers. Others were so seasick that it was all they could do to hang onto the railing.

At last, hope. Nine minutes after the *Argo* had struck, the surfboat from the Tillamook Bay Station was under way, battling the bar against towering breakers. With extreme difficulty the lifesaving crew led by Captain Farley (the same man later involved in the *Mimi* tragedy) reached the side of the foundering vessel.

The crushing seas banged the boat against the side of the wreck with a sickening thud. Frantic passengers jumped blindly into its confines. It was a heart-rending moment as the craft pulled away. It had taken all the women and children and four of the male passengers. There were feeble hand waving and tears at the sight of those left behind. But there were even more tears when the surfboat was forced to return, because of sustaining such damage by striking the wreck as to place the safety of the survivors in jeopardy. The male passengers were put back aboard the *Argo,* and the lifeboat put out again for the shore. The breakers, however, were now almost insurmountable and Captain Farley elected to row northward and attempt landing on the beach. The craft was leaking bady and all not engaged at the oars bailed with their hands. At a point one-half mile north of Twin Rocks, Farley ordered a run for the beach.

All held fast as the surfboat dug its nose into the first comber. The drag was out, but as the tremendous avalanche of water struck, the boat was lifted endwise. The fastenings of the drag tore loose and the craft became air-borne, doing a complete flip and throwing its occupants into the surf. Breaker after breaker emptied its contents upon them. After each wall of liquid fury, the life-jacketed survivors gasped. They would try to rub the salt sting from their eyes to catch sight of those about them. The unrelenting seas had no mercy, driving, twisting, curling. Lungs were at the breaking point. Captain Farley tried to shout directions while himself floundering about, but was suffering the pain of a broken arm and internal injuries. He and three others finally succeeded in reaching the overturned boat but another breaker struck and scattered them.

Next the despairing souls struck out for the shore but the strain was beginning to tell. One of the young girls drowned before the eyes of the others, floating head down in her life jacket.

Along the beach, people gathered to form a human chain into the surf to bring in the struggling souls. Already three had perished before these saving hands could reach them.

Back on the *Argo* the situation was equally as bad. Some of the remaining hands were employed jettisoning cargo in a last-ditch effort to keep the ship afloat. The others worked frantically at the pumps until their endurance was spent. The *Argo* was but a plaything in the clutches of the breakers. The skipper despairingly ordered his men to abandon, at once.

Captain Snyder took one boat and Johnson, the first officer, the other. Two passengers and the better part of the crew were in the first boat and six passengers and four crew members in the second. One fireman and a passenger did not answer the call to abandon. They could be found nowhere and were believed to have been swept overboard and drowned.

The ordeal was far from over. Johnson's boat was jostled about so as to take water continuously until midnight. At last, lights were seen coming toward them. As they approached, the weary souls were warmed, for these were the lights of the motor vessel *Oshkosh* in search of the survivors. All were taken safely aboard. (Two years later the *Oshkosh* was wrecked on the Columbia River Bar under similar circumstances, with the loss of six of her seven crew members.)

The captain's lifeboat could be found nowhere and it was feared that it had foundered. The next day, however, it was sighted off the Columbia River. The survivors were picked up by the steamer *Coronado* which was relieving the lightship off the Columbia Bar.

The *Argo* was reduced to rubble within a few days, while amidst scenes of gloom the dead were laid away.

CARMARTHAN CASTLE

On December 2, 1886, the full-rigged British ship *Carmarthan Castle* was beating her way up the coast to Portland from San Pedro. The course was set well out from the teeth of the Oregon Coast. Because of obscured visibility Captain William Richards had charted his course 30 miles offshore. Dead reckoning told him he was 80 miles from Tillamook Bay when suddenly the ship was engulfed by breakers. He had been navigating with a defective compass.

It was a wind-filled night. Massive breakers pounded incessantly against the steel ship until it ground to a halt. All hands were mustered aft and given orders by Captain Richards. The situation appeared hopeless to them, so far were they away from any means of communication.

The ship lay just south of the Nestucca Bar and was exposed on three sides to the fury of the storm. The sands

133

were already building up around her hull and the hammering of the surf left the decks flooded with water. All hands hung on till morning. Then they lowered all four boats, and ran the surf at ebb tide.

On reaching shore, the captain was more at sea than he had been aboard ship. The virgin countryside posed a question as to just which way to start out in search of help. Including the captain, there were 28 survivors—a lot of hungry mouths to feed. After moments of indecision as to the best course to follow, some white settlers, alerted by Indians from a nearby village, arrived with horses.

To these men of the sea, horse riding was a new experience and one which proved trying. Captain Richards pulled so hard on the saddle horn while going up a steep grade that he pulled the horse over on him and nearly drowned in a creek. In spite of the misfortune to his ship he proved a better sailor than he did a horseman.

When he finally reached civilization, tired, wet, and with a very sore posterior, he swore he'd never ride another horse. "If I ever lose another ship," he said indignantly, "I'll walk to the nearest shelter if it's a thousand miles away."

J. MARHOFFER

What's in a name? Usually a great deal, should one take the time to find out. Every year thousands of tourists thrilling to the scenic delights of Oregon's fascinating seacoast, will in all probability stop at Boiler Bay. At this eye-catching gap in the coastline, the ocean puts on a splendid show, boiling and hissing among the rocks like a thousand whales on a rampage.

Just how this place got its name might not enter the casual observer's cranium. He would assume that the title was derived from the appearance of the disturbed waters that abound there.

Such, however, was not the case. Strange to say, of all the beautiful, charming and intriguing names that could have been attached to this bay, it was named for the rusty boiler from the wreck of an ignominious steam schooner with the unromantic handle of *J. Marhoffer*.

Why then not Marhoffer Bay or Wreck Bay? No, not these, for it was that old rusty boiler that stuck around long after the wreck had disappeared. Season after season, dating from the time of the disaster in 1910, the boiler stood the gaff of winter storms and the towering breakers. It stood out like a sore thumb and anyone who visited the bay could not deny that there was something about that old boiler. Just an old scrap of iron but enough to catch the fancy, so much so that for it Boiler Bay was officially named and none has attempted to change it.

Recorded here are the last days of the steam schooner *J. Marhoffer*.

In the afternoon of May 18, 1910, the Portland-bound vessel was moving along at a nine-knot clip with the aid of tail winds off Yaquina Head. She was running light, having discharged her cargo at San Francisco. Burly Captain Gustave Peterson poked his head out of the pilot house window, satisfied that all was going well with the weather and with his crew.

The first engineer was dozing in his cabin. His assistant was in the engine room fiddling with a newfangled gas torch. Unfortunately he had no book of instructions and was trusting to his mental ingenuity in an effort to get it to burn. The inevitable happened. The thing exploded and threw a path of fire over the confines of the oil-soaked engine room. Even before the scorched assistant could get topside, the deep recesses of the steamer were a mass of flames eating and ripping through everything in their way.

In spite of the intense heat which the flames radiated, the engine continued to turn over. The boss of the black gang was rousted out and Captain Peterson was hot on his heels.

The Old Man asked for volunteers to go below to open the sea-cocks and flood the engine room.

But who'd volunteer to turn the red-hot valves?

The ship soon was an inferno and Captain Peterson,

seeing the futility of it all, gave out with the terse announcement, "Abandon ship!"

He had already altered his course for the rock-infested shore which lay three miles off.

The skipper glanced at his wife who stood by his side. "You must go in the first boat," he informed her.

"I don't go without you," she answered.

"There's no time to argue," asserted the captain. "You will go in the first boat."

She reluctantly joined the crew members in the first boat as flames crackled all about them. The first mate reached out from the lifeboat for the ship's canine mascot, and pushed it overboard. The boat hit the water, picked up the dog and pulled away for the shore. Captain Peterson's wife glanced back with tear-filled eyes and prayed that she might be reunited with her husband.

Shortly afterward the *Marhoffer* drifted among the rocks just beyond the breakers. By this time the flames were leaping into the air and the entire amidship section of the steamer was enveloped. There was nothing further to do. Captain Peterson had done all that any shipmaster could do.

There was the danger of explosion if the fire ate through the fuel tanks. The only course for the few still aboard was escape. They lowered the only remaining boat, and set out for Fogerty Creek.

"Grandma" Wisniewski observed their plight from her hillside home. She hastened to the beach near the sandy creek mouth and attempted to signal the sailors that they might make a safe landing. She waved her red sweater but they interpreted her signal as a warning of danger and rowed on to Whale Cove, south of Depoe Bay. The first boat and the second boat fell in together and both stood into the cove. One craft capsized in the surf and the ship's cook who had already suffered burns from the fire, was drowned. All of the others gained the shore.

The following day Captain Wellander and his men from the Yaquina Bay Lifesaving Station arrived with food and first aid for the survivors. They also inspected the burned-out wreck.

From the bowels of the ship, the scorched boiler broke free in shallow water. It remained there to bestow its name upon the little bay.

The *J. Marhoffer* was valued at $80,000 but was insured for only $26,000 by her owners, Olson & Mahony. She was built only three years prior to her destruction.

And so it was that the ignominious boiler of a shipwreck has been perpetuated while the name of the steamer from which it came has all but been forgotten in the passing parade of time. Yes, Boiler Bay, 14 miles north of Yaquina Bay, was named for just what the name implies —a ship's boiler.

MINNIE E. KELTON

At precisely 12:15 p.m., May 3, 1908, the U. S. Lifesaving Station at Yaquina Bay, Oregon, was alerted of a steamer in distress 10 miles northwest of the station and a mile offshore. Her distress flags were flying and her deck load of lumber was washing ashore.

The keeper of the station immediately rounded up his men and readied the surfboat for a long, hard pull through adverse seas. It was flood tide on the reefs and the breakers were roaring. The lifesaving crew pulled hard, riding the crest of one and dropping into the pitiless chasm before the next. Numbed by the wind-driven sting of salt spray, they rowed like mechanical men. Once clear of the reef, they took a momentary rest and set a sail to use the favorable southerly winds to move up the coast.

A few hours later the wreck was sighted dead ahead, wallowing badly. Her deck houses, boats, and deck load had been carried away by boarding seas and she had taken a dangerous list.

At first it was feared that the steamer had been abandoned but, as the surfboat pulled closer, frantic calls were heard over the troubled waters. The rescuers gripped their oars even tighter for the tricky maneuvering. By pulling in and moving out at the opportune moments all nine persons aboard were rescued.

The survivors told a frightening story of how 12 of their shipmates had been carried overboard the previous day by gigantic seas.

The disabled lumber carrier, drifting inevitably toward the shore, was slowed only by her three dragging anchors.

Following the rescue, the wind increased and the seas followed suit. This quelled any chances of returning to the lifeboat station. So the keeper in charge of the boat shaped a course for Siletz Bay. It was the only chance of getting the survivors ashore. The need was urgent, as they had been without food or water since the previous day.

It was 5:30 p.m. when the lifeboat arrived at a point south of the bay entrance. A narrow hole in the reef was found and it was decided to enter. The weight of seven surfmen, plus nine survivors, decidedly reduced the boat's reserve buoyancy. To give her additional freeboard, all surplus gear, mast, sail and rigging were jettisoned. The crew exerted all of their skill as they brought the craft through the opening and landed the survivors safely on the beach.

Meanwhile another of the *Kelton's* crew, believed drowned, was found cast up on the beach with a broken leg. Some children found him sitting atop a box of corned beef nursing his wounds. They took him to their home on an improvised sled. A young girl at the home had to go on horseback to Newport to fetch a doctor to set the sailor's broken leg. The survivor must have liked his adopted home, as he remained for two months.

With this sailor had been three other shipmates, all clinging to the same piece of wreckage, but one by one they were swept into the cruel sea. One body was found in a pile of lumber and another in the bottom of a metallic lifeboat that had been torn from the steamer's davits.

All that first night by the eerie glow of torches, surf-men had plodded the beach searching for other possible survivors. None was found. Five bodies were later recovered and buried under simple crosses at the Eureka Cemetery in Newport. The grim total showed 11 dead or missing. Ten were saved, including the sailor with the broken leg.

The day following the tragedy, the surf was still running high, so much so that there was no possibility of returning to the station. Instead, the surfboat was pulled up high on the beach to await more favorable conditions. The situation was no better on May 5. So the lifesaving crew and the survivors carried the bodies of the dead overland to the station.

The waterlogged *Kelton* was later retrieved by a tug and towed to the Columbia River. One report claimed that the vessel had struck Otter Rock while her anchors were out. One look at her would have left little doubt that she was a near total loss. Appearances are sometimes deceiving, however, for many months later the *Minnie Kelton*, shorn of her housing, was back at work. She was used as a barge to haul rock for the Columbia River jetty.

When war broke out in Europe, ships were in demand and the barge was completely rebuilt, emerging as the steamer *Rochelle*, a lumber vessel with accommodations for passengers. On October 21, 1914, she struck Clatsop Spit at the Columbia River entrance. Her crew of 19 were rescued by the Coast Guard but her cargo of coal caught fire, speeding her total destruction. This time there was no restitution.

SEA OTTER

All but lost in the dim past is a scant account of the wreck of the British trading ship *Sea Otter*. Driven ashore on August 22, 1808, she became Oregon's first recorded shipwreck. Had it not have been for a remarkable overland trek by the survivors, this ship, like so many others in early western history, would have faded into obscurity.

Generally speaking, the year 1808 is not an ancient date. The Thirteen Colonies were already very old. But out in the Pacific Northwest it was still all Indian country and miles wide. Just 16 years had passed since the intrepid Robert Gray discovered the entrance to the Columbia River. Most of the bays and inlets along the west coast, however, had yet to be entered by white men.

Those familiar with the Oregon Coast of today label it rugged and treacherous. So imagine it 150 years ago, void of lighthouses, buoys, settlements.

The *Sea Otter,* a ship of 120 tons from London, was on a fur-trading venture with the natives of Northwest America. Furs were in demand in world markets and the most bountiful caches, especially of otter, were along these shores. Captain Niles was commander of the ship and had high expectations for a successful voyage.

But tragedy struck. Under stress of stormy weather the vessel was wrecked near the mouth of the Umpqua River. All but six of the crew perished. The pitiful band of survivors stood mournfully on the beach on that fateful day of August 22, 1808, wondering if they would ever again see civilization.

Since no civilization existed anywhere near the vicinity, they salvaged what supplies they could. Then they elected to set out on foot, traveling over half of the continent to Red River, Louisiana. They had long been given up as dead. Enduring terrible hardships, they fought snow, rain, and wind; traveled over deserts, high mountains and through unfriendly Indian country. Gaunt, weary, and worn, they survived the ordeal to tell of their fantastic escape.

BLANCO, UNCLE SAM, AND FEARLESS

Three Oregon shipwrecks long open to speculation have remained cloaked in a veil of mystery. They occurred between 1864 and 1889. Each of these vessels was found cast ashore. In each case there were no survivors; dead men tell no tales.

The first in this unusual sequence of events was the brig *Blanco* lost in the year 1864. The primary question here is whether her crew was lost through stress of storm or was murdered by coast Indians.

The battered hull of the *Blanco,* split from deck to keel, was washed ashore near the mouth of the Siletz River, leaving no trace of those who manned her. The Indians made sure there was no metal left by ransacking the remains.

One day some white settlers visited an Indian village in the vicinity and found two kegs of nails, five sheets of zinc, one oil coat, eight pairs of gaiters, two pairs of boots, a calico dress, rope, and sail cloth. This led to immediate supposition that the brig had been plundered at the hands of the Indians and the crew all murdered.

But the Indians wouldn't talk except to say that they found the wreck lying abandoned on the beach. No visual proof that the crew had been murdered was ever brought to light and the case was closed, unsolved.

The ill-fated *Blanco,* first vessel built on Coos Bay, was a brig of 284 tons launched at North Bend, Oregon, in 1859 for A. M. Simpson. His brother Elbridge had come west from Maine expressly to construct the vessel. It cost $15,000 and was designed for use in the coastwise lumber trade.

The second in the sequence of unsolved sea mysteries was the loss of the schooner *Uncle Sam.* This 113-ton vessel came drifting ashore at Cape Foulweather near Yaquina Bay in early March of 1876. It was the same case as that of the *Blanco*—there was no sign of her crew. It was assumed that she had been badly mauled in a severe storm on February 7 of that year, while on a voyage from Wilmington, California, to Coos Bay. The supposition was that she had rolled over, drowning all hands before they could escape. But again it was mere speculation and to this day the whereabouts of her complement remains unknown. The *Uncle Sam* was built at

Big River on the Mendocino Coast of California in 1873 by a man named Peterson.

The last in this weird entanglement occurred on November 20, 1889. The steam tug *Fearless,* in command of Captain James Hill, was dashed up on the north spit of the Umpqua River entrance while bound for Coos Bay from Astoria.

At 3:00 p.m., however, on the day of the wreck she was sighted steaming down the coast off Upper Ten Mile just outside the fringe of breakers. The sea was rough and she was under a slow bell. At 6 p.m. her whistle was heard off the mouth of the Umpqua. At 6:45 p.m. she gave three sharp blasts in rapid succession. No more was seen or heard of the vessel until her broken pilothouse, the stern section, one side of the hull, and numerous pieces of wreckage came floating up the river with the incoming tide.

Again the theories flew fast and furious. Most agreed that the tug was old and tender, that she had probably sprung a leak and was attempting to enter the river. This theory gained impetus, as the vessel had been off the Umpqua for over an hour before the accident occurred. The captain would have had no other reason for entering the river with his destination at Coos Bay a short distance away. Captain Hill was known as a competent master, having skippered the tug at intervals for 15 years. He was thoroughly conversant with the dangers attendant on entering the Umpqua on an ebbing tide. Thus his actions could only be accounted for as a last resort.

The missing included the captain, the engineer, a fireman, two deckhands, a Chinese cook, and George Marshall, a passenger and proprietor of the Empire City Cannery. Marshall's body was later found on the beach clad in a life preserver. It lay several feet above the tide line, indicating that he may have reached shore alive but had perhaps perished from exposure before being found.

Had he remained alive, he alone could have broken the jinx of three mysterious shipwrecks without a survivor.

TACOMA

Take a steamship, new, well built, and seaworthy above all required standards. Put the most competent captain aboard as master and give him an excellent crew. Give the ship accurate charts, a good rudder, wheel, and a dependable engine. Your end result should be a money earner.

But take that same steamer with all the above requirements and give her a defective compass and what have you got? Trouble.

The striking new steamship *Tacoma* built in 1882 especially for the Pacific Coast coal trade between Tacoma and San Francisco had just arrived from her builders' yard on the east coast. A scant month later, January 29, 1883, having never earned a thin dime for her owners, she was written off the books as a total loss.

Riding well below her marks, on her fatal voyage, the vessel pointed her bow for San Francisco, laboring under 3500 tons of coal. Fuel was poured into the boilers and the taffrail log showed a steady 14 knots.

Captain George D. Kortz had in mind some kind of a record. But take 14 knots, coupled with 3500 tons of coal, and you have the equivalent of a battering ram. Yet a battering ram made of steel is like putty in the hands of a molder when it strikes solid rock.

At 9:00 p.m. the steamer crashed up on a sharp reef four miles north of the Umpqua. The shock was terrific, throwing the sleepers from their berths and sending all loose gear sliding across the deck. The wheel spun like a windmill, the helmsman's arms almost being torn out of their sockets in the effort to control it.

When a ship gets herself in such a position something's got to give. Despite the superior qualities of the *Tacoma*, she began to quake from keel to masthead.

All through the night she lay on the rocks. The men huddled below decks with premonitions of being sealed in their great steel coffin.

By morning all but one of the lifeboats had been stove

143

by the seas and still no aid was in sight. The men ventured forth from their close confinement and with great difficulty got the one remaining lifeboat over the side. Into it went the captain and four of his men, to seek aid.

After several hair-raising moments the lifeboat got away and battled its way through a high surf to the beach. The captain found his way to the nearest settlement and made immediate plans for tugboats to rush to the scene of the stricken freighter.

Answering the call were the *Sol Thomas, Escort,* and *Fearless.* Each tried to maneuver in close enough to get a line on the wreck but the rocky tentacles poking out of the water thwarted all efforts.

When Captain Kortz learned of their failure he attempted to take his lifeboat back out through the breakers to save those on the ship. The boat capsized en route and he and his shipmates, wet and bedraggled, struggled back to the beach.

The *Tacoma's* situation grew worse by the hour and grave concern was expressed for the despairing souls aboard.

All attention was focused on the lifesaving crew from nearby Gardiner. "Launch your boat and save the perishing," demanded the irate public.

"No," said the keeper, "I'll not risk my men or my boat in that surf."

Those who heard his remark were worked up to such a pitch that it was a wonder they did not hang him from the nearest tree.

Captain Kortz was frantic. He felt deeply responsible for the lives of his men. His only alternative was to try again with his bulky lifeboat. This time, amid many cheers, he and his crew negotiated the breakers and fought valiantly to the side of the wreck. The best they could do was to save two others before being driven back by vicious seas.

Then, as in most calamities, a hero was born. A German sailor, John Bergman, organized a volunteer crew and, with a surfboat, sturdy oars, strong backs and stout hearts, got alongside the wreck. In and out, up and down, pitching, rolling and dipping, they made one trip after another.

All the while the *Tacoma* was being pummeled. Her back was broken and it was a question of time as to when she would fall to pieces.

The desperate men still aboard the wreck were apprehensive. The surfboat was returning for what would be her last trip. In fear of being left behind they panicked. First assistant engineer Grant drew his revolver and warned he would shoot the first man who got out of line. Only then did the melee cease. In orderly fashion the men jumped into the craft.

Then the unexpected happened. A plunging breaker caught the boat in the stern quarter and hoisted it skyward. Every man was thrown into the churning water, fighting, gasping, choking. Some didn't come back up. The others swam toward a fallen mast and clung desperately. One by one they were swept off and drowned. Others found wreckage and clung till rescue came.

Grant made an effort to swim ashore through the surf. He exerted his last ounce of strength and died on the inner fringe of sand. His death raised the toll to ten. Bergman, on the other hand, was saved.

The *Tacoma* immediately broke up and by the following morning only her cylinder head remained above the surface.

Bergman and his associates received gold medals from the United States Government for their heroic acts in saving lives at the risk of their own.

Bergman later became keeper of the Lifesaving Station at Gardiner, Oregon, rendering splendid service, unlike his cowardly predecessor.

CAPTAIN LINCOLN

The all too apparent need of protection for the early pioneers against hostile acts by the Indians, prompted the government to dispatch the U.S. transport schooner *Captain Lincoln* to Port Orford in 1851.

In December of that year the vessel departed San Francisco with a contingent of 36 dragoons. On nearing her destination, a storm of considerable magnitude prevented her entrance, and she was swept to the northward.

As the gale grew in intensity, a serious leak was reported below the waterline. The pumps were manned around the clock, but on January 3 a fog set in with the gale, and the schooner piled up on the beach two miles north of Coos Bay.

All had anticipated the worst but in the morning the vessel lay high on the beach, surrounded by acres of sand. Neither the captain, crew nor the dragoons knew just where they were. One thing was certain—it was the end of the line as far as the voyage was concerned.

All hands abandoned the schooner. Supplies and equipment were salvaged and temporary lodging was set up on the beach. The little settlement was affectionately named "Camp Castaway." This was the first settlement of whites in what is now Coos County. But the camp was short lived, for the party were already mapping plans for an overland trip to Port Orford.

Meanwhile they traded freely with the Indians, receiving ducks, geese, venison, and fish for articles of clothing, hardtack, rice and trinkets.

Within four months Camp Castaway had completely folded and the last of the men took their supplies across the sand spit to Coos Bay, to make their way thence on foot down the coast to Port Orford.

White men had previously settled on the Umpqua and at Port Orford, but until the wreck of the *Captain Lincoln,* Coos Bay had never been considered as a site for settlement. Strange that the wreck of a ship should open a new area with such a promising future.

The survivors of the shipwreck told many vivid tales of the country surrounding Coos Bay. One of the surviving dragoons, H. H. Baldwin, penned a poem forty years after the wreck of the *Captain Lincoln,* of which the following is a small part:

> Come listen to my shipwreck tale, a deep and dismal one,
> Which happened to thirty-five dragoons, close to the wild Cowan.
> The morning of the thirty-first, and last of the old year,
> It filled all hands with joy, for each knew the port was near.
> Alas! How short is human bliss, the wind commenced to blow,
> Which forced our poor, short-handed crew, all canvas safely stow.
> For three long days and dismal nights the tempest blew its best;
> The water broke into our hold, the pumpers saw no rest.
> At five a.m., "Great God; she's struck," the morning of the third;
> Then fore and aft and either side were roaring breakers heard.
> Again she struck with giant force, the mad waves leaped her deck,
> Another giant, parley blow, "Then *Lincoln* lay a wreck."

C. W. WETMORE

Maritime history was made in 1891 when the *C. W. Wetmore,* an extreme innovation in cargo ships, arrived in the Pacific Northwest. She was built on the Great Lakes, hundreds of miles from salt water. After completion, she loaded 100,000 bushels of wheat for Liverpool, England. The *Wetmore* was so extreme that she was the center of attraction wherever she went. Appropriately called a whaleback, she could well have been

147

mistaken for the fantastic *Nautilus* immortalized by Jules Verne in his *Twenty Thousand Leagues Under the Sea.* The only difference was that she sailed on top of the water or at least was supposed to. As time passed, the ship became associated with a wry joke. It was said that she was "wet more" than she was dry.

Should such a craft be sighted on the high seas today it doubtless would be reported to naval intelligence as some kind of a super submarine of the U. S. S. R.

Except for stingy pieces of superstructure fore and aft connected by a catwalk, the rounded back of the 265-foot brute resembled that of a whale. When fully loaded (3000 ton capacity), the greater share of her was beneath the water.

Her builders had great expectations. The ship started out by making a successful maiden voyage from Duluth to England, under the capable hands of Captain Joseph Hastings. Though the *Wetmore* attracted crowds, she was not greatly at variance from other seagoing vessels in her underwater lines, nor were her engines and big Scotch boilers out of the ordinary. The rest, however, was a remarkable departure from the commonplace.

From England the *Wetmore* loaded materials for the construction of other vessels of her breed, and then started for the Horn. She made it around "Cape Stiff" through the roaring forties and up the coast of South America. Then her luck ran out.

Perhaps no vessel that ever came west was so ill-fated. Off the California coast in heavy seas her rudder slipped its fastenings and she went adrift, completely unmanageable. Nor was there a suitable mast from which to rig a sail. For days she drifted at the mercy of the wind, tide, and current until abreast of the mouth of the Columbia.

Gradually, but surely, she was carried toward destruction when the British steamer *Zambesi* arrived and got a line on her. While under tow over the bar the hawser parted and the *Wetmore* narrowly missed going to her doom amid the shoal-infested breakers. Bar pilot George

Wood then left the *Zambesi* and boarded the whaleback to help pilot her over the bar to Astoria.

There the rudder was repaired and she steamed out for Puget Sound. The cargo, discharged at Everett, formed the nucleus for another whaleback steamer, the *City of Everett,* destined to be the largest commercially constructed vessel in the Pacific Northwest up to that time.

Meanwhile the *Zambesi's* crew was awarded nearly $50,000 salvage money for services rendered in saving the *Wetmore.*

The jinx continued. The whaleback was placed in the coal trade between Puget Sound and San Francisco but on her first voyage the cargo shifted. They finally got her into port and then there followed a rash of collisions, dock smashings, strandings, and crew troubles, the like of which has never been seen before or since.

On September 8, 1892, the ghost was finally given up. In command of Captain Johnny "Dynamite" O'Brien she crashed ashore in a heavy fog on the north spit of Coos Bay Bar, one mile from the entrance.

A steady succession of distress blasts echoed across the surf but the shroud was so dense that it was 24 hours before aid arrived. By then the coal-burdened steamer was lying parallel with the beach, vehemently beaten by the seas. All hands were removed by the lifesaving crew. O'Brien and one of his men remained behind. The following day they too were forced to evacuate.

O'Brien kept returning to the scene in hopes of saving his ship, but the elements were working against him. Due to the ship's peculiar construction it remained intact but settled deep in the sands, eliminating hopes of salvage.

It was there that the old whaleback ended her short but lively existence. Her destruction, however, was not mourned by other shipowners in the same trade. Competition was rough in the year 1892 and coal was valued at but $1.35 per ton.

149

Chapter Seven

COOS BAY TO THE CALIFORNIA BORDER

Fᴿᴼᴹ Coos Bay south to the California border the coastline is very irregular, with a variety of great headlands, rocky promontories, rock-ribbed and sandy beaches.

Good harbors are few. But in this area abounds a wild beauty and grandeur as the silver surf pounds incessantly against mighty ramparts.

Many years ago, fast passenger liners plied the coastwise route connecting the principal ports of Washington, Oregon and California. For the most part these were pleasant experiences for the tourists but on every seaway trouble is sometimes unavoidable.

CONGRESS

There were all the markings of a terrible marine tragedy on that 14th day of September 1916. The $2,000,000 liner *Congress* of the Pacific Coast Steamship Company was afire three miles off Coos Bay, with 423 souls aboard.

The liner was out of San Francisco, Seattle-bound, in command of Captain N. E. Cousins, when the fire was reported in the ship's after hold.

It grew in intensity, spread among the general cargo, and ate its way through the hatch covers. The officers attempted to play down the situation until it was seen whether the fire could be brought under control. But on shipboard nothing remains a secret for long. Passengers began evacuating their cabins, the saloon was emptied, the deck games ceased, and conversation became low and whispering in all sections of the ship.

Each person was asking the other what he knew about the extent of the fire. The purser was hounded as were the stewards. A mask of grave concern had now come over the captain's face and he conveniently avoided the passengers.

Fire at sea can be a terrible thing. If allowed to go unchecked it can result in a terrible ordeal. Thus no stone was left unturned by the shipmaster.

When all reports were in, he was convinced that the fire was out of control. He headed directly for the wireless room.

"Sparks!" he exclaimed, pulling open the door, "Get out an urgent call for assistance."

The wireless operator didn't have to be told a second time, and his message was soon being relayed from shore station to shore station.

The anxious passengers under the all-seeing eye of the crew were herded to their lifeboat stations, clad in life jackets. As they went, the ship's whistle blasted its weird warnings. Outside of some emotional women, the operation went like clockwork.

As the passengers huddled like sheep before a storm, smoke billowed high from the after holds, black, choking smoke fanned by a steady breeze.

Both excitement and fear prevailed among the passengers. None among them had ever been forced to take to lifeboats while on the high seas. Fortunately the water was calm. One after another the boats were lowered from the davits until a sizable fleet hovered about the liner like ducklings turned away from their sick mother.

The fire blazed hotter and hotter as the breeze fanned it. Those in the lifeboats did not even need their coats out on the usually cold Pacific. The liner was like a blast furnace. So enthralled were the survivors with the fire that many were unaware of the arrival of the rescue lifeboat from Coos Bay.

Other ships including the government dredge *Col. P. S. Mitchie,* arrived on the scene. The lifesaving craft flitted about like a waterbug transferring survivors to the larger vessels. Soon all of the passengers and crew of the *Congress* had been evacuated from the lifeboats.

Now the *Congress* was aflame from stem to stern. The salvage tug *Salvor* arrived and tried to get near the liner. The heat raised paint blisters on the tug and she retreated, content to let the fire run its course.

And run its course it did. Never did a ship burn more thoroughly and not sink. Everything above the waterline was completely consumed except the steel hull and superstructure which were seared and scorched into a smutty black. The liner got so hot that witnesses said it actually glowed red through its steel plates. At night it appeared like a glass ship with a massive red light on the inside. No living thing could get within 50 feet of it.

To all intents and purposes the 7985 ton steamer was a complete loss. Yet she was still afloat. For days after the flames had subsided she smoked and smoldered.

When finally there was nothing else for the fire to consume, the gutted wreck commenced to cool, at the same time taking a decided list. She looked for all the world like a subject for Dante's inferno.

The blackened ghost was towed to Seattle and rebuilt for the China Mail Steamship Co., at a cost of $2,000,000, the amount for which she was originally constructed. It required 14 months to complete the job. It was as if the vessel had been raised from the dead.

Renamed *Nanking* she entered service to the Orient. But shadows of opium smuggling and white slavery crept into the life of the liner. Several times on arrival at San Francisco she was libeled for $1,000,000. For this and other reasons her owners folded financially.

Next the ship reverted to her original owners as the *Emma Alexander* and again entered coastwise passenger service. She was laid up in the late 30's, and not restored to service until World War II. The British took her over as the transport *Empire Woodlarks,* and she weathered the ravages of the hostilities. In a half century of service the fire off the Oregon coast in 1916 was her only serious setback.

CZARINA

The most disastrous shipwreck from the standpoint of loss of life in the Coos Bay area occurred in 1910. On November 13 of that year the cargo steamship *Czarina* crossed out over the Coos Bay Bar, bound for San Francisco with coal, cement, and lumber.

As she crossed the bar tremendous breakers mounted to great summits, crashing and foaming. Pitching like a pump handle, the ship poked its nose into one, hoisted it aside and tackled the next. It was a touchy game and one that might have been victorious for the steamer had not its steering apparatus become disabled.

It took only seconds for the seas to move in for the kill. The *Czarina* was literally thrown on the north spit, an open target for the laughing tempest. The steamer scraped over the shelves of sand, each breaker wedging her tighter than the last. When she became immobile the seas really settled down to business. Gray, gruesome, liquid acclivities bore down on the imperiled ship. Holes were opened in her decks, the boats torn from their davits, the cowls, railings and fittings carried overboard. Water scudded through the superstructure, down the passageways, into the holds. The onslaught was indescribable.

The nearby lifesaving station was alerted, but the seas were so savage that rescue was a virtual impossibility. Beach equipment was rushed to the scene but even as it was assembled the desperate men on the *Czarina* were already in the rigging of the foremast trying desperately to escape. The 220-foot iron vessel was foundering amidst the breakers and her heavy cargo fastened her to the bottom.

By this time hundreds had gathered on the beach. All wanted to render aid but were completely helpless. In the sea mist far out in the breakers, beyond the reach of the line-throwing gun, they could see the helpless seamen clinging for their very existence. Few can imagine their agony in their last precious minutes. Numbed by the chill air and soaked by driving salt spray, their cries for help froze in their mouths. One by one they were swept from their perch. After each rolling sea, the numbers would lessen. They appeared like spiders being sprung from a web. Before the brief but terrible ordeal had ended, the rigging was void of all life—24 men were carried to their deaths. There was but one survivor, the chief engineer who miraculously reached shore.

The *Czarina* wreck became a silent one. People had little desire to discuss it. It is torment to watch men die before one's very eyes and yet be unable to do anything about it.

The *Czarina* was valued at $75,000 and was a staunch iron-hulled vessel, an 1883 product of Sunderland, England.

SANTA CLARA

Another very black day in the annals of transportation was November 2, 1915. The SS *Santa Clara* of the North Pacific Steamship Company, inbound from Portland, struck an uncharted shoal, stranding at the south entrance of Coos Bay Bar.

A gale was blowing and the seas were unusually rough. Captain August Lofstedt glanced at the ship's clock. It read 4:28 p. m. He rubbed his eyes nervously, at the same time ringing the telegraph to full astern. The liner trembled violently but there was no reverse thrust from the propeller. Nearly 60 souls were aboard. The pernicious sea was not conducive to lowering the boats and fear filled those who waited.

The engineer grabbed the speaking tube and informed the captain that water was coming into the engine room. All hands huddled on the boat deck awaiting the skipper's decision. The passengers were extremely nervous. Finally with a set jaw, and with certain misgivings, Captain Lofstedt gave the command to lower away. Six boats in all were put over the side. Fangs of white spume leaped all around them. They were tossed violent-

ly about. Suddenly one boat flipped over and all in it
struggled frantically in the water. The other lifeboats
with inexperienced men at the oars bumped into each
other trying to save the drowning. Many were lost, a few
saved. For hours the lifeboats were jostled about but
finally gained the beach. Sixteen lives had been lost.

The wreck was short for this world. The breakers combined their devilish tendencies and pulverized it beyond
recognition.

The *Santa Clara* had not the same resisting powers as
on April, 1910, when she got snagged on Humboldt Bar.
On that occasion she emerged triumphant, but not so
now on Coos Bar. She struck a shoal not marked on the
charts, one believed raised by earlier storms.

This ended the steamer's career which began at
Everett, Washington, in 1900, when as the *John S. Kimball* she was the largest steam schooner on the coast. She
had another alias too, the *James Dollar,* and during her
checkered 15 years of service had no less than seven different owners.

Though the wreck of the *Santa Clara* has long since
vanished it has left behind its whistle. Salvaged by the
late Louis J. Simpson and installed at the Old Town
Mill in North Bend, it called the employees to work
faithfully every day that the mill operated. When the old
mill was torn down and the site sold to the Weyerhaeuser
Timber Company, William Vaughn, operating manager
of the Coos Bay Logging Company, offered the whistle
to the new mill on condition that it be used. The offer
was accepted and the whistle is still in use—the last
remembrance of a tragic shipwreck.

YMS—133

Sometimes it is better if names are not mentioned.
One for instance—the master of the 135-foot U. S. Navy
motor minesweeper *YMS—133.* The vessel was involved
in a disaster that might have been avoided by one more
familiar with the temperament of the Coos Bay Bar.

The *YMS—133* had its birth amid the dark days at the beginning of World War II. She was launched by the Western Boat Building Company at Tacoma, Washington, on December 18, 1941. Of 260-tons, this minesweeper was a twin screw vessel of 1200 horsepower developing 16 knots.

America's total unpreparedness at the time of the attack on Pearl Harbor demanded every available ship for military service. Not an hour was lost in getting the *YMS—133* completed and into the patrol units of the Pacific Coast fleet. Her services were urgently needed and she fulfilled a worthy purpose both as a patrol craft and a sweeper. But her days were unfortunately limited.

On February 22, 1943, while in transit of Coos Bay Bar, she was struck by tremendous wind-lashed seas. The craft pitched so furiously that her propellers spun in the air as her nose went under green water. Then she would raise her forefoot in the air and bury her stern. Fearing that the bar breakers were no match for his ship, the skipper made the fatal blunder of ordering his helmsman to put the wheel hard over, and head back into safer waters. Such an order under the circumstances might have afforded an incentive for a second "Caine Mutiny." But the command was obeyed. When the vessel came broadside to the watery onslaught it was struck with such force that it rolled over, not once but time after time according to the few witnesses who watched from the murky shores. Smashed, pummeled, filled with sand and water it succumbed to the elements. There were 29 fear-crazed men aboard.

As rescue boats rushed to the scene, they plucked 16 injured, bleeding and half-drowned men from the water. Thirteen others never knew what struck them. Their nearest of kin were notified that they were lost in action with the U. S. Navy on the 22nd day of February, 1943.

OLIVER OLSON

The story of the wreck of the *Oliver Olson* on November 2, 1953, had a very unusual ending. When salvage efforts were abandoned it was decided that the wreck would remain as part of Coquille River's south jetty.

The 307-foot *Oliver Olson* was crossing over the Coquille River Bar to load lumber at Bandon when she was caught in a strong cross current and struck the jetty rocks on the south side of the harbor entrance. Three gaping holes were torn in her starboard side below the waterline, flooding two holds and the engine room. The rudder became jammed and the propeller would not turn over. Aboard were 29 men, including the shipmaster, Carl Hubner.

The Coast Guard cutter *Bonham* and the tug *Port of Bandon* rushed to the scene, awaiting an opportunity to pull the vessel off the rocks. A breeches buoy was rigged between the end of the jetty and the stranded ship as a precaution, should the crew have to be removed.

Only three days after the stranding, the decision to abandon the vessel was made. E. Whitney Olson, president of Oliver J. Olson & Company, announced from his plush San Francisco offices that the wreck belonged to the underwriters, principally Lloyd's of London. "The decision whether or not to attempt salvage rests with the insurance companies," he asserted.

Since large holes were ripped in the ship's steel plates, fears were expressed that she might capsize and block the harbor entrance should an attempt be made to free her from the rocks. Even with the decision to abandon her, a storm was in the making. Twenty-seven crew members were evacuated by breeches buoy and, before the storm struck, Captain Hubner and his chief engineer also came ashore.

William W. Jewett, Portland representative for Lloyd's, had inspected the wreck and declared it would cost more to salvage than it was worth and that the cost would be in excess of the insurance. The freighter's 35 years were also against her. She was valued at $250,000.

The tug *Port of Bandon* had meanwhile made several futile efforts to budge the freighter. This was prompted by the fact that the Olson Line freighter *Cynthia Olson* aground at the Coquille Bar north entrance a year earlier had been successfully refloated.

Another problem arose. The Port of Bandon Commission had been trying to get a $250,000 federal appropriation for maintenance of its south jetty. Congressman Harris Ellsworth had visited the wreck scene and promised to work toward immediate restoration of the south jetty where the wreck lay.

On November 21, sealed bids were called for, to purchase the wreck on an as-is-where-is basis. They were to be opened not later than November 30, 1953. Berry & Lane Company of Napa, California, submitted the winning one of five bids at $11,500, and after closing the deal, immediately put their plans into effect.

The Olson Company had meanwhile received full payment by the insurers and had retained the hull with the right to dispose of it.

Toward the end of December, 11 members of the wrecking crew while working on the *Oliver Olson* were faced with a dangerous situation. The catwalk by which they reached the ship was partly destroyed by lashing winds which reached a velocity of 80 miles an hour.

Oara Walker, foreman, made five trips across the 75-foot bridge, untangling the ropes and cables, taking off loosened boards and assisting in rigging up a boatswain's chair as a means of evacuation. One man while riding the boatswain's chair became entangled in the ropes midway between the ship and the jetty. He was freed in a delicate breath-catching operation. By the time the second man had been removed, Ernest Lane of the salvage firm arrived with a high-line crew. Eleven additional men were then taken off the wreck in a cargo net.

After the storm had run its course, salvage operations were resumed. Later two public auctions of salable materials were held. Last items removed from the *Oliver Olson* were the condenser and the propeller which contained nine tons of brass; various pumps, the steam engine, and about 80 tons of boiler tubes. The radio room equipment was disassembled as a unit.

In spite of the pounding storms, the wreck remained on the rocks in its original position. The next step was to cut away the upper part of her hull, for the Army Engineers had now received the green light for the extension of the jetty by 450 feet.

Why not incorporate the wreck as part of the jetty? It all fitted into a perfect pattern. The sub-contracting firm of Stoen, Stoen and Frazier, who were awarded the job, did just that. Cutting torches burned away all but the lower section of the *Oliver Olson's* hull and this in turn was filled with rock from the nearby Tupper Quarry and incorporated into the jetty.

Before the end of the summer of 1954, the entire job was completed. The wreck now served a worthy purpose and Bandon had the improved jetty for which its merchants had so long agitated.

ALASKAN

The entire Pacific Coast was shocked in 1889 by the terse news of the foundering of the sidewheel steamer *Alaskan* with a loss of 31 lives off Cape Blanco, Oregon.

The story of the terrible disaster is told here directly out of the pages of the ship's logbook. Captain R. E. Howes was master of the ill-starred steamer.

> Steamer *Alaskan* left Portland, Oregon, Friday, May 10, at midnight, arriving at Astoria, Saturday May 11th, at 8:00 a.m. Left the Oregon Railway & Navigation Company dock at 11:30 a.m., crossed out over the bar, which was very smooth, wind light from the westward. Took our departure from the whistling buoy at 1 p.m., set the patent log, everything working well, ship making nine miles an hour, and shaped our course south by east. At 11:30 p.m. Foulweather Light (Yaquina Light) bore east northeast, fourteen miles distant, wind light, south

159

southeast, passing rain showers, barometer 29:85 steady. Sunday, May 12th; Longitude by observation 43° 5', eighteen miles offshore; wind increasing, sea getting rough, ship laboring heavily and commencing to make water; slowed the ship down dead slow. At 3:00 p.m. set main trysail to keep ship's head to wind and sea. At 4:00 p.m. port guard began to break up, and afterhouse began to work so that water came in freely; tried to stop the leaks with bedding. At 6:00 p.m. port guard went, just forward of the wheel, carrying away the covering board and bursting one of the upper plates.

Up to this time had kept the ship free; pumps reported as doing well, and by stuffing the rents with blankets we had great hopes of saving the ship, if it moderated at all, but it did not, wind and sea increased and the ship's upper works gradually went to pieces, water pouring in on all sides, pumps working to their fullest capacity but the water increasing rapidly. Put the ship before the wind and sea at 11:00 p.m. and made preparations to save life. Launched all four boats successfully, but one got stove in before we could get anyone in her. The fires were out before we undertook to launch the boats, and, before the first boat was launched, the ship had stopped turning her wheel; all hands obeyed orders and doing well.

The boats were astern and the men still aboard ship were ordered to put on life preservers and go on a line to them, but were afraid to go, preferring to stay by the ship rather than take the chance of being picked up by the boats. At 1:00 o'clock Monday morning saw a vessel's lights to the northward, sent up rockets and burned torches, and at 2:15 a.m. our ship went down stern first and broke in two, the captain, engineer and about ten others on board.

The brevity of Captain Howes' report camouflaged

Death raised its ugly head in the fall of 1910, and 24 of the 25 men seen here clinging to the rigging of the *Czarina* were carried to a watery grave. (courtesy Charles Fitzpatrick)

Schooner *Advent* totally and completely demolished after wrecking on the south spit of Coos Bay bar, February 18, 1913.

Veteran freighter *Oliver Olson* hard aground on Coquille River bar south jetty
Nov. 2, 1953 (courtesy Carl Christensen)

British bark *Baroda* aground near Bandon, Oregon in 1894. She was refloated many months later.

Steam schooner *Phyllis* ended her lumber carrying days near Humbug Mountain on Oregon's yeasty coast March 10, 1936. (Sawyer Photo)

On February 10, 1937, the steam schooner *Cottoneva* crashed ashore near the *Phyllis* and also became a total loss. (Sawyer Photo)

Near Rogue River, Oregon, the *Joan de Arc* is battered to pieces after stranding November 15, 1920.

A mass of wreckage is all that remains of the steam schooner *Willapa* after crashing ashore near Port Orford, Oregon December 2, 1941.

those frightening last minutes before the ship sank. Fortunately the steamer was not carrying her usual passenger list, else the toll might have been considerably greater. Not on her scheduled run, the ship was en route to San Francisco for dry docking and repairs.

Al Rahles, veteran steward, bowed down by the weight of years, refused to leave the wreck in spite of persuasion by the captain. "It's no use," he told Captain Howes, "I'm too old. I can't make it. I'll have to go down with the ship."

And go down with the ship he did, completely resigned to his fate.

The chief engineer, the second officer and several others also refused to leave the steamer, preferring to take their chances aboard. Little could they be blamed for their decision as the seas were dark and perilous and it appeared that each of the drifting lifeboats would be swallowed up before daybreak.

It wasn't long after the last boat had left the *Alaskan* that she began sinking. The master and the second officer were on the bridge. Suddenly the latter went below to check the engine room. He was never seen again. The steamer raised her bow in one final gasp for air and then was completely covered by a gray film of gyrating ocean water.

In a last-second desperation leap, Captain Howes jumped clear of his ship to avoid being sucked down. When he rose to the surface the steamer had vanished. He swam toward a portion of the deck and succeeded in squirming up on it where he floated around for an hour. Then he spotted the chief engineer also clinging to a piece of wreckage. The two paddled toward each other and combined rafts until sighting the pilothouse drifting by with three additional survivors perched atop of it. The engineer determined to reach it against the captain's advice. Again they parted company but the chief, unable to overtake the pilothouse, was swept off his raft and drowned.

The tug *Vigilant,* Captain Edward McCoy, later crossed

over the debris-laden sea. Handicapped by the dredge it was towing, it worked in the grip of the heavy seas, circling the scene of the sinking. After hours of searching, only Captain Howes, the three survivors from the pilot-house, and one dead man, were picked up.

The following morning, the *Alaskan's* first officer was sighted from the tug's masthead, clinging to a piece of wreckage hardly buoyant enough to keep him afloat. He had held on for 33 hours, the last 12 being compelled to remain on his hands and knees to keep from being drowned. In this position, without food or water the entire time, he was almost unconscious when rescued. The same morning, the quartermaster was also picked up from a hunk of wreckage. His leg had been caught in the propeller just before the ship went down and he had lost so much blood that he died shortly afterwards. He and the other dead were given a proper sea burial from the tug. The survivors were taken to the mouth of the Columbia River and transferred to the steamboat *Columbia* which took them to Portland.

The second lifeboat containing 10 men came ashore at Siuslaw but the other boats foundered in the heavy seas, drowning all of their occupants. Of the 47 men aboard the *Alaskan,* 31 were officially listed as dead.

The *Alaskan,* though intended mainly for inland water transportation, was an iron-hulled vessel. She and her sistership, the *Olympian,* had come around the Horn from the east for passenger service on the Columbia River and Puget Sound.

J. A. CHANSLOR

Most of the victims of the perils of Cape Blanco were doomed from the start. Take for instance the Associated Oil Company tanker *J. A. Chanslor*. She was wrecked on December 18, 1919 with a loss of 36 lives. Only three escaped.

The *Chanslor* was the victim of fog and strong ocean currents which carried her out of her course onto the

162

jagged rocks within view of the Cape Blanco Lighthouse. Titanic breakers scudded entirely over her. The fore part of the tanker was viciously driven on the rock ledge and the strain caused her to crack amidships. Captain A. A. Sawyer and his 38 man crew were swept overboard like sitting ducks. Thirty-six perished but the captain and two seamen emerged from the churning depths and clung desperately to pieces of wreckage. The water around the wreck ranged from 60 to 150 feet in depth and was a mass of white fury. The three survivors lived to tell their harrowing tale.

The fore part of the 4900-ton tanker remained fast on the rocks for several weeks, marking the mass grave. Ultimately the last remnants were swept into the depths to end a tragic chapter in the history of petroleum transportation. Lost also was the cargo of 30,000 barrels of oil in bulk which the tanker was taking up the coast from California ports.

The wreckage of the *Chanslor* promoted demands for coastwise vessels to set their courses farther offshore to allow for compass deviations in fog and current.

T. W. LUCAS

Off Port Orford on October 24, 1894, a driving southeast gale was blowing out its lungs. For nearly a week it had heaped devastation along the shipping lanes, and many ships had taken terrific punishment.

One of the hardest hit was the brig *T. W. Lucas,* laden with lumber from Hoodsport for San Francisco. She had sprung a bad leak and was taking water rapidly. After fighting the storm from its outset, she appeared to be coming out the loser. Almost waterlogged, seas careening over her deck load, her master, Captain Bose, decided to make a desperate run for Port Orford to save his ship and crew. Sail was run up the naked masts as the vessel swung abruptly about.

It was morning of the 24th day of October, 1894, as the old brig pointed her bow shoreward. Within a few hours she had become unmanageable, and her pumps clogged with debris. Distress signals went up.

The steamer *Homer* sighted her and came alongside to perfect a rescue. With great difficulty all hands were removed and the abandoned brig left to her fate.

Captain Bose figured that his ship would immediately sink, but instead it set out on its own. At the mercy of the wind and currents it drifted up and down the coast, sighted here and there, always eluding the salvage minded. Finally her masts went overboard and her decks were entangled with rigging and torn sails. Part of her bowsprit was missing. Her cargo of lumber was scattered about like tenpins. Like a legendary ghost ship she drifted mile after mile, defying would-be salvagers until she became a worthless derelict. Another gale and she was at last whipped into submission, ending her cruise to nowhere.

Not many lamented her loss. But despite her 37 years, she put up a gallant fight before bowing to the elements.

WILLAPA

The decade of the 1940's marked the end of an era for a type of vessel developed exclusively on the West Coast. The wooden steam schooner, small, maneuverable and highly efficient, was the lifeblood of the Pacific coastwise lumber trade from 1884 until recent times. The greater share left their gnarled bones to whiten on perilous stretches of the Pacific Coast.

These stalwart steamers traveled dangerously near the coast, skirting breakers, rocks, and reefs, loading where there were no ports, darting in and out of dog holes, shoal-infested bays, or wherever somebody set up a loading chute to send lumber down to their hungry holds.

It is safe to say that of a fleet of over 200 wooden steam schooners built from 1884, seventy-five percent were wrecked along the Pacific Coast. This is a staggering percentage probably never surpassed, but one must remember that they did their business under the most hazardous of conditions, hugging the coast so close as to scare the whiskers off deep water sailors.

One of the last of the little wooden steam schooners was the *Willapa,* wrecked 20 miles south of Port Orford on December 2, 1941. The lumber-laden vessel was bound for San Francisco from Marshfield. Storm-swept seas opened her seams and she began filling with water. Captain Oscar Peterson ordered flares shot. One after another they lighted up the sky like a 4th of July celebration. But there was no celebration aboard ship. The black, rain-filled skies were unloading a barrage of rain and wind. The Coast Guard lookout spotted the flares and, shortly after, a motor lifeboat launched out in the storm. By this time the flares were all gone and the lifeboat was unable to find the wreck in the inky blackness, groping blindly about throughout the night.

Not until morning broke could the derelict be found. Her bridge had washed away and her deck cargo had become a sea of lumber. The main deck was completely awash. All hands, including Captain Oscar Peterson, were struggling for their very existence when the lifeboat came alongside.

All 24 were taken aboard the 32-foot craft, filling it like a can of sardines. Though crowded to the gunwales, it was then or never, for even as the last survivor was rescued the *Willapa* was on her side almost wholly under water.

First mate of the *Willapa,* E. Stahlbaum, was getting a complex. He had been wrecked on the steam schooner *Cottoneva* four years earlier within a few miles of where the *Willapa* now met her fate.

The survivors were taken to Port Orford but the seas were so high that the motor lifeboat could not make a landing. It was then that James Combs, a local fisherman with a dory, made a dozen trips through 800 yards of choppy water to remove the survivors, two at a time. His skill in maneuvering his boat was uncanny. He

165

handled it like a row boat in a mill pond until every survivor was safely ashore.

The *Willapa,* owned by the Hart-Wood Lumber Company, was reduced to a tangled mass of wreckage in quick order.

Chapter Eight

SHIPWRECK—UP COLUMBIA

A MIGHTY river with a mighty mission is the Columbia. From time immemorial it has sent its torrent seaward from a vast area. Second only to the Mississippi, it winds through 2000 miles of the Pacific Northwest, the largest fresh water portal on the Pacific Coast, navigable for 400 miles. No other river in the world is the source of so much water power and with its tributaries, the Willamette and the Snake Rivers, it forms the backbone and lifeblood of a fabulous empire.

From the pioneer villages down to our present concrete and steel jungles, the Columbia has been frequented by an endless parade of maritime traffic. Unlike other great river systems where water transportation abounds, the Columbia and its tributaries have been the scene of relatively few serious marine disasters.

SILVIE DE GRACE

Probably the first shipwreck of any major consequence exclusive of the treacherous river bar, was the stranding of the American packet ship *Silvie de Grace* (frequently called *Sylvia de Grasse*) on a rock ledge near Astoria in the year 1849.

The vessel was at anchor awaiting a bar pilot, having earlier loaded a full cargo of lumber at upriver ports. As soon as the pilot arrived, preparations were made to weigh anchor and get underway for San Francisco. The crew chantied as they catted the anchor. Then they scurried aloft to make sail. The ship was free now, but was suddenly caught in the freshets and carried upon a rocky ledge only a stone's throw from her anchorage. And there she remained. All hands thought it was a matter of hours, or at longest the next flood tide, till she

167

would float free. Complications then set in—her deck cargo shifted, wedging her tighter on the rocks. Unfortunately the packet had been grossly overloaded, her owner William Gray being bent on making a one-voyage killing on the overly-ripe San Francisco market.

With each passing day the situation appeared more hopeless. Gray who had voyaged on his ship from New York was now desperate. He attempted to line up other ships on the river that could carry the cargo to San Francisco before the inflationary Gold Rush prices took a plunge.

Boarding the ship *Walpole* lying at anchor nearby, Gray offered her skipper a cool $10,000 to make the voyage. He met with an abrupt refusal because the *Walpole* was already under charter to the U. S. Government.

Finally in desperation Gray secured the services of three small schooners. Days and weeks dragged on while the lumber was lightered from the *Silvie de Grace* and divided among the smaller carriers.

Finally they sailed out over the bar but when they reached San Francisco the lumber market had taken a drastic drop. What might have been a successful venture ended in financial failure for the disheartened Mr. Gray.

The *Silvie de Grace,* reputedly fashioned in France, was of ancient vintage. She bore the distinction of bringing the first news of the French Revolution to the United States.

A half century after the vessel was wrecked, an Astoria boat builder visited the scene at slack tide and found some of her old timbers. He salvaged and reused them in the construction of a new vessel. And good lumber it was, unharmed by the ravaging effects of nature. The durable wood was mainly live oak and locust, unsurpassed for ship construction.

Parts of her ancient anchor chain are still in the possession of the Oregon Historical Society.

For many years a buoy marked the wreck of the *Silvie*

de Grace and three times before the turn of the century it was carried away by ice in the river.

GAZELLE

The worst steamboat explosion on Oregon's rivers involved the pretty little sidewheeler *Gazelle* more than a century ago. The *Gazelle* was built at the peaceful little Willamette River town of Canemah, in the spring of 1854. On her maiden trip to Corvallis she carried an excited group of passengers and a quantity of cargo. That it was a pleasant voyage was borne out by the words of an Oregon City newspaper editor:

> The fine weather and good music tended not a little to enhance the pleasure of the ladies and gentlemen on board, and all were highly entertained and pleased. Her tables are laden with Oregon's choicest productions, together with a select variety of imported fruits, etc. Who wishes for better accommodations, even in this "tyee" day of Oregon refinement.

The owners of the *Gazelle* had also purchased the sidewheeler *Oregon* to run opposite the new paddler.

While the *Gazelle* was on her maiden trip, her running mate snagged herself just below Salem, and settled to the bottom in eight feet of muddy river water. Promptly the *Gazelle* was ordered downstream to assist. This didn't interrupt the revelry aboard but only incited more riotous actions among the passengers. The *Gazelle* lost no time in reaching the *Oregon's* side and divesting her of her cargo. Suddenly the wrecked steamer popped back up from the bottom like a cork and took off merrily downstream on her own. Before the *Gazelle* could muster sufficient steam to give chase, the elusive wreck struck a sand bar and heeled over, sustaining such damage that her owners let her go for junk.

So the *Gazelle* left her cousin to rest and continued on

her way. But a short way downstream huge amounts of drift appeared everywhere and, grinding over some half submerged logs, she knocked several of the buckets from her paddle wheels.

Replacing the buckets was no chore but on April 8, of the same year 1854, while preparing to depart from the wharf at Canemah, it happened. Captain Robert Hereford was anxiously awaiting to get underway and was summoning lingering passengers aboard with a final whistle signal. It was a moment of horror that wasn't soon forgotten. It was as if all hell broke loose. The *Gazelle's* boiler exploded, sending her sky high, along with the mangled limbs of some 28 persons. Amid the hiss of steam, the upper works burst apart and boxes of cargo were found far above the banks on either side of the river. The steamer *Wallamet*, berthed nearby, also sustained considerable damage from the blast.

Within moments the entire town of Canemah was on the scene, stunned at what they saw. Among the dead were many notables, including David Page, superintendent of the Willamette Falls Company, owners of the *Gazelle*. The pilots of the *Gazelle* and *Wallamet* were also killed. Captain Hereford, though seriously injured, lived to continue steamboating on the river.

Skiffs were immediately launched to pick up the injured and the dead floating among the debris. Such a tragic scene has seldom been witnessed on Oregon's waterways. There was wailing and moaning from the 32 injured persons, many of whom hovered between life and death.

Just before the terrible blast, a very unusual bit of drama was staged which may have held the key to the disaster. The *Gazelle's* chief engineer, Moses Toner, ran down the gangplank and disappeared through the fringes of the gathering crowd just seconds before the boiler let go. He was never seen in Oregon again. Some said he was heard of up on Puget Sound at a later date but he kept a wide range from the locale of the disaster. Why? That was the question asked of the coroner's jury at the inquest. No help came from the assistant engineer either; he had been killed in the explosion.

Captain Hereford was exonerated. Some experts testified that the *Gazelle's* boiler was constructed of a brittle, poor grade metal which might have given way under any sudden strain. But Moses Toner held the answer and they never found him. He doubtless had carried more steam than was safe and had neglected to carry sufficient water in the boilers. Had they caught him, they would have slapped a charge of gross and culpable negligence on him and probably linched him on the corner apple tree with no questions asked.

Nothing remained of the *Gazelle* but her bare hull. In the debris within were found a few detached arms and legs. The town of Canemah and, for that matter, all of Oregon were shocked.

Every river port where the *Gazelle* had stopped, temporarily shut down to mourn the dead. The clatter of the lumber mills was silenced; the iron works ceased operating; blinds blanked store windows.

Strange indeed that the *Gazelle's* gutted hull should live again. Rebuilt completely and christened with the lyrical title *Senorita,* she was dropped over the falls and placed on the Astoria run. Outside of losing her hurricane deck in a gale near the Cascades, she overcame the jinx and operated until 1859 when she gave up and had her engine transferred to a spanking new river boat.

ELK

The explosion of the small sternwheeler *Elk* has gone down in Willamette folklore. She was built in 1857 by a group of enterprising pioneers. While methodically steaming along just below the mouth of the Yamhill at Davidsons Landing shortly after her entry into service, her boiler got overly hot. Whoosh! Up went her cabin, stack, and pilothouse, with the skipper still inside. The captain, George Jerome by name, was blown up in the air to such an elevation that it is averred that he could peer through the opening in the stack and see his old friend and passenger Captain Miller sitting on the river bank. On the downward part of his air flight Captain Jerome landed unceremoniously in the top of a cottonwoood tree and sure enough there below him was Captain Miller, who had been tossed gently to the river bank by the explosion. And for 20 years thereafter every river boat skipper pointed out that fabulous tree to tourists.

Without dignity Captain Jerome climbed from his perch and sat next to his friend to discuss the aspects of human flight.

Some of the passengers were injured but in no case so seriously that gauze and tape could not mend them. One group of passengers in the *Elk's* cabin had a stove explode beside them and the bulwarks around them blown far and wide, but they themselves received not so much as a scratch.

The old *Elk* bore the brunt of the destruction and but for the fickle hand of fate the death toll could have been equally as bad as that of the *Gazelle* three years earlier.

SENATOR

Again, the scene was on the Willamette and the vessel involved was the sternwheeler *Senator,* a 298-tonner on the Portland-Oregon City run. On the afternoon of May 6, 1875, the *Senator* ran down to the Oregon Steamship Dock to take on freight and passengers. Then she darted back to her Alder Street pier, last stop before shoving off for Oregon City. As she pulled in alongside the steamer *Vancouver* her engines were shut down and her wheel idling. Without warning her boiler gave way. The tremendous explosion deafened Portlanders. Window glass in waterfront establishments was shattered, bottles were knocked from shelves. And on the steamer, the main cabin and all above it were hurled sky high. Everything forward of the king post was pulverized.

The *Senator,* or what was left of her, drifted downriver out of control. The perplexed captain of the *Vancouver*

172

pulled in his gangplank and got underway in hot pursuit of the naked hull. Like a greyhound the steamer overtook its prey. The captain pushed his gangplank across, and rigged lines to hold it tight while every available hand searched the floating coffin. Toward the bow, scattered among the wreckage were several dead and wounded, but aft the king post where the greater share of the passengers had congregated, few were seriously hurt, just badly stunned.

While the *Vancouver's* crew collected the unfortunates, the waterfront became blackened with curious crowds. When the last person was removed from the ill-fated steamer, the *Vancouver* cut her loose and hastened back to the landing to seek care for the injured. The count stood at seven dead and eight seriously scalded, maimed, or bruised.

Captain Dan McGill, who had been at the wheel when the boiler blew, was instantly killed. A marine engineer standing next to him survived, but lost his leg.

Meanwhile the drifting *Senator* came ashore at Albina where she was secured to the river bank. A thorough inspection revealed that only the forward end of her boiler remained, so completely had it been ripped apart.

Again the coroner's jury; the inevitable verdict: carelessness. The blame fell on the engineer J. V. Smith who let the water fall low in the boilers, so that when the engine was stopped the pressure rose too rapidly for the safety valve.

Witnesses had him dead to rights on criminal negligence. Subsequently he was arrested on a charge of manslaughter but must have known the right people for he was ultimately acquitted. The episode, however, weighed heavily on him, as jobs on steamers didn't come easily for him thereafter. Such a blunder, when others' lives are at stake, will wreck a man one way or the other.

TELEPHONE

Devastating fires on Columbia River steamboats were

fortunately few. The one that stands out above all others was the conflagration on the sternwheeler *Telephone* on November 20, 1887. The *Telephone* was advertised as the fastest sternwheeler in the world, and never existed the boat that could prove differently. She was the speed queen of the river and could show her heels to her gamest

On this certain day in the fall of 1887, with her venerable skipper U. B. Scott at the wheel, she was skimming over the water en route to Astoria from Portland with 140 passengers and 32 crewmen.

Fire suddenly broke out below deck and even before the general alarm could be sounded flames were sweeping through the craft. Captain Scott who had experienced steamboat fires on the Ohio River, was all too familiar with the agonizing cries of people being consumed by flames. He had one objective, to put his ship ashore fast. He spun the wheel full left rudder, at the same time signalling the engineer for full throttle. The boss of the engine room held on tight as the long, slim princess heeled over. He opened her wide and with the rest of the black gang stormed topside to mingle with the frantic, coughing passengers groping about in the smoke and flames.

There was great risk in running the burning steamer at full speed. The breeze fanned the flames to sweep them the length of the ship. Captain Scott was aware of this but every moment was precious. He gambled, and on that gamble lay the lives of 172 persons. The floating inferno, like an express to Hades, doing better than 20 miles an hour slammed into the shore just east of Astoria. The shock knocked the passengers to the heated decks. But bruises were secondary to survival, and men, women and children scrambled over the guards like frightened sheep. It was a wild rush but except for the captain's long gamble the loss of life might have been enormous.

Up in the pilothouse Captain Scott, who had remained at the wheel, glanced aft to sight the progress of the fire. To his horror he found that it had already consumed the pilothouse steps. Without delay he did a swan dive out of the window and escaped just before the entire upperworks caved in.

A count of the survivors was made on the river banks. Though seared around the edges, all were accounted for with the exception of one man, an inebriate, who, befuddled by the fire, had groped about blindly until overcome by suffocation.

The horse-drawn fire wagons were already on the scene, pumping long streams of water into the charred remains. The eerie flames, burning well into the night, cast weird reflections over the waters. To quote a dull statement, "The *Telephone* was out of order." She was gutted down to the waterline and her smoldering hull was left to die on the river bank.

But somebody decided that the *Telephone* should be connected again, and like many of the other disregarded hulls of the steamboat era she was rebuilt from the waterline up. In a new and gaudy role she returned to the river and kept her original name. More lavish and more ornamented than before, she was an even greater favorite with the passengers. About the only thing she didn't surpass was her former speed. Though still mighty fast, she couldn't better her record between Portland and Astoria, nor in sober truth could any other river boat.

In 1892, the *Telephone* got out of order again. She left Astoria on a foggy night and felt her way cautiously all the way up the Columbia until she reached the confluence with the Willamette. There the fog obscured all navigation lights and the *Telephone* punched her prow into a revetment and sank until only her upperworks protruded from the surface. Again she was raised and patched to grind out a wage for her owners for another two decades, finishing her days down California way.

CLAN MACKENZIE

A disastrous collision occurred at 1 a. m. on December 28, 1889. The crack steamship *Oregon,* river pilot George

Pease in command, knifed into the side of the British ship *Clan MacKenzie* lying at anchor in the river. The wounded Britisher a few hours earlier had been in tow of the sternwheeler *Ocklahama,* bound upriver to Portland. But en route the towing steamer had run low on fuel and had been compelled to ditch the *MacKenzie* for the purpose of wooding up. The anchored vessel was a sitting duck.

The heavily-laden *Oregon* raised its sharp bow to strike the sailing ship between her stem and the cathead on the port bow, cutting her cleanly down to the keel. The *Oregon* was nearly 30 feet into her victim.

As the *Ocklahama* came clanking back to pick up her tow, her master was horrified to find it sitting on the bottom of the river. Already her crew had been taken aboard the *Oregon* and a search was underway for two members of the crew reported missing. Their bodies could not be found.

The survivors offered a solution; that the men may have taken advantage of the situation and deserted ship. If so, their whereabouts were to remain a mystery, but then discontented sailors before the mast frequently found berths on other wanting sailing ships with few questions asked.

The sunken wreck, as a barrier to river traffic, had to be removed. The reputable salvage master, T. P. H. Whitelaw of San Francisco, was awarded the job. He knew his trade well and raised the 260-foot square-rigger on January 27, 1890. She was towed to Portland for urgent repairs. The job was given priority and by June 2 she was completely mended in time to carry a full load of grain to Liverpool.

WELSH PRINCE AND IOWAN

Collision prevention in any river is difficult. A fog settling over any restricted channel makes navigation hazardous at best. In open water there is room to navigate but in a river hemmed in by banks it is frequently

176

a case of the right whistle signal, a pilot's sixth sense, or a prayer.

It was night, fog-filled and clammy. The time was 11:10 p. m., May 28, 1922. Inside the mouth of the Columbia off Altoona Head, two sizable freighters were feeling their way, the British steamer *Welsh Prince* and the American freighter *Iowan*.

Except for the eerie drone of foghorns, the night was disturbingly still. Suddenly two whistle signals stood out above the others. The rapid succession of blasts warned of impending danger. Then came an ear-rending crash of steel against steel, a tearing, grinding, sickening crash. The Britisher had cut across the *Iowan's* bow and in turn had received a mortal blow which nearly sliced her in half. For a minute after the collision there were human cries and then for a brief moment silence. The river was so black and foggy that neither ship could identify the other despite the fact that they were interlocked. Then from out of the night came a cry, "We're afire!"

Fire hose from both ships were trained on the dancing flames aboard the Britisher, caused by the terrific friction of the crash. The battle with the fire was ultimately won. Then all efforts were concentrated on the water-filled fo'c'sle of the *Welsh Prince* which had been directly in the path of the crushing stem of the *Iowan*.

Seven had perished, bodies mangled and lungs filled with water. Five were dragged out, but the remaining two could not be recovered until slack tide.

A call of distress brought out the tug *Oneonta* from Astoria but other vessels nearby, fearful of a similar fate, were slow in coming. As the tug untangled the two freighters, the *Welsh Prince* settled on the river bottom and the *Iowan* with a badly crumpled bow was ushered off to Portland.

The captain of the *Iowan* cried, "foul," that the *Welsh Prince* had cut across his bow. This of course was true, but neither captain nor pilot could be excused from the near nine-knot clip he was making under a veil of night

177

fog. The American skipper claimed that the accident could have been averted after a frantic exchange of signals at 2000 feet, provided the British vessel had kept a straight course. But sharp words could not bring back the seven men who had died on that regrettable night.

Most vessels sunk in a river area can be salvaged, due to the fact that divers can work in protected waters. But the mortal wound suffered by the *Welsh Prince* placed her future in jeopardy.

An obstruction to navigation, it was all too apparent that she would have to be removed. Every salvage attempt to raise her proved an outright failure despite the fact that her upperworks extended above the water at most stages of the tide.

The agents for the ship informed her owners, Furness, Withy & Company (Prince Line Ltd.) that she must be considered a total loss. And a hard shock it was for Lloyd's of London when their inspectors arrived at the same conclusion. The ship was relatively new and heavily insured. Seldom did the underwriters ever abandon a ship sunk in a river but there was no alternative in this case. The mud, silt, and sand deposits had built up around the shattered hull below the waterline. Every conceivable means was devised to get her off the bottom but she held fast. Now it was in the hands of the government.

When all else failed, the only answer lay in dynamite. It was evident that the ship would have to be removed in sections. M. Barde & Sons were the successful bidders for the removal of the wreck. The dynamiters they employed ordered ten tons of super power gelatin dynamite. (Too bad the atom bomb hadn't been invented.) The deck of the freighter was blown off and the cargo of steel inside, removed. Then with a thundering report the hull was ripped asunder in a blast that rocked the river area for miles around. When the water regained its normal flow the hazard to navigation was non-existent.

FELTRE AND EDWARD LUCKENBACH

A remarkably similar collision to that of the *Welsh Prince* and *Iowan* took place on February 17, 1937. In a heavy fog on the Columbia River near Prescott, Oregon, the Italian motor ship *Feltre* was rammed by the freighter *Edward Luckenbach.*

The Italian vessel in the Mediterranean-Pacific Coast service, was a trim 450-foot cargo-passenger vessel. Her 10,000-ton opponent was a stout steel freighter engaged in intercoastal operation. When the two collided it was the *Edward Luckenbach* that rammed her bow into the side of the *Feltre,* almost amidships. She opened a massive hole large enough to drive two locomotives through. Scores of steel plates crumpled like egg shells right down to the keel plates. Within a few minutes the *Feltre* was sitting on the river bottom. Fortunately all hands aboard the Italian vessel escaped the death-dealing blow, though many were thrown to the deck by the impact.

The *Edward Luckenbach* suffered a battered nose but nothing that couldn't be repaired. As for *Feltre,* her situation was a desperate one.

The pilots of the respective ships differed on the cause of the collision. Other factors, not necessarily concerned about who was to blame, enlisted divers to remove the most valuable portion of the cargo from the sunken vessel—365 bars of silver, valued at $185,000. That was on February 22. Two days later it was decided to attempt raising the ship.

On March 18, in a remarkable job of salvage, they had the *Feltre* pumped out and floating. The great optimism of the salvagers was short-lived, however, when the *Feltre* suddenly sank again in virtually the same spot. On March 21, they went at it again with a host of pumps and got her off the bottom for a second time. With a crash mat over her wound and several tugs at her side, she was brought up river to Portland the following day.

After the usual inspections and official red tape, the

Feltre was moved to drydock on the 18th of April for the big survey to find the complete extent of damage and to decide her disposition. Time marched on and then on May 13 the salvage firm filed a $200,000 libel action against the vessel. Then came June 1 and the *Feltre* was placed on the block to be sold the following week to the highest bidder. The successful bidder was announced on June 9 as the Pacific American Fisheries Company of Bellingham. The price, a mere $55,000, a fraction of her original cost. The new owners planned to use her in the Alaskan service far from her sunny Mediterranean home.

Then came the big news for the Portland maritime industry.—A $300,000 rebuilding and overhaul contract on the *Feltre,* the largest marine repair job in the city's history, to that date. A year and one week later this fugitive from the river bottom was like a brand-new ship. She was easily without equal on the Alaska run.

And so began the second chapter in her life, only now her old name had been given the "deep six" in favor of *Clevedon.* After three and a half years of service she came to her untimely end in the role of an Army transport during World War II. The details of her destruction were not made public until hostilities had been terminated. The *Clevedon* had been taken over by the Army early in the war and operated under strict military secrecy. On January 13, 1942, while loaded with ammunition at Yakutat, Alaska, a mysterious fire broke out. In a dramatic moment, the freighter *Taku* steamed in and got a line on her. The blazing vessel was beached a safe distance away and shortly after blew herself into thousands of pieces.

ERRIA

The most recent addenda in the fire chapters of Columbia River's maritime annals occurred off Tongue Point, east of Astoria, on December 20, 1951. The sleek, all-white Danish passenger-cargo liner *Erria* was lying

at anchor awaiting a favorable tide for crossing the
Columbia River Bar.

The hands of the clock had slipped around to 2:30
a.m. and the lights aboard the vessel made shimmering
paths across the dark river. Then from that peaceful
scene a curling wisp of smoke rose, followed by great
fingers of orange flame. The *Erria*, toast of the European-
Pacific Coast trade lanes, was afire.

Aboard were 114 souls, most of them asleep when the
alarm rang. Captain Niels Agge, aroused and confused,
was at a loss to do anything but to order immediate
abandonment of his ship to save the passengers. Overpowering fumes and choking billows of smoke had
already filled the passageways. Crew members with gas
masks or towels about their grim faces beat a hasty trail
down the lengthy corridors pounding on stateroom
doors. The passengers, shocked by the reality of fire,
were led down the passageways away from the intense
heat. Eleven didn't make it. Three crew members and
eight passengers amidships were hemmed in by flames
and blinding, suffocating smoke.

The charred bodies of the eight passengers were later
found sitting in chairs in the lounge as if waiting to be
led away from the inferno.

As the boats were swung over the side, Coast Guard
and other rescue craft hovered about to pick up the
survivors. The fire raged furiously. Pillars of flame leaped
high into the cold night air. Coast Guard cutters wrestled
with the liner and finally managed to get her aground
a few hundred yards from shore where steady streams of
water played on her all night. So much water was poured
into her that she took a decided port list. Still she burned.
The bridge melted away and some of her plates became
so hot they popped their rivets. Coastguardmen cut
holes in her steel sides and pumped in carbon dioxide
but several days later the ship was still smoldering. The
No. 2 hold, loaded with lumber, had constantly fed the

flames and the engine room was saturated with oil from leaking tanks.

While still hot, the underwriters wrote the vessel off the books as a total loss. Cause of the fire was believed to have been due to a shorted wire in an electric cable. On two occasions before the fire broke out, the electricity had faltered momentarily.

Some days later the gutted ship was pulled off the mud and taken to Portland, a 17-hour tow. The object of a thousand curious eyes, the former pride of the Danish merchant fleet awaited her fate. Salvage was meagre but what remained of the cargo of lumber, pulp, wheat, steel and miscellaneous freight was removed from her dank inwards. The scuttlebutt was that she would be torn apart for scrap, but with the high costs of shipbuilding her owners decided that they might yet rebuild her, a gigantic, costly job, though far from the price of a new replacement. After months of debating one way and the other, her owners, the Danish East Asiatic Company Ltd., of Copenhagen, engaged the powerful Dutch tug *Zwarte Zee*, one of the heftiest towing craft afloat, to make a most unusual and lengthy tow—from Portland to Rotterdam, 8900 miles. There the *Erria* was to be rebuilt from her bare hull up. The tug knocked off 170 nautical miles a day with her unwieldy 8700-ton charge. She departed Portland on May 16, 1952, and plodded faithfully through two oceans for 51 days.

A million and a half went into the reconstruction of the *Erria* which emerged as a splendid counterpart to her old self. All she lacked was her lavish passenger accommodations. She was strictly a freighter now. But her rakish lines like those of a royal yacht were still preserved.

PART THREE

SHIPWRECKS OF THE

CALIFORNIA COAST

Chapter Nine

ST. GEORGE REEF TO CAPE MENDOCINO

CALIFORNIA'S ocean coast, equal to that of Oregon and Washington combined, is a long stretch, pock-marked with good and bad harbors, changeable seas, rich lands, and wastelands. Along its extent are some of the largest seaports on the Pacific Coast where a constant flow of maritime traffic arrives and departs from every port in the world. From the timber-rich redwood country of Humboldt to the Silver Gate at San Diego, California combines a seacoast delightful to the eye but a trap for ships that get snagged on its sharp teeth.

BROTHER JONATHAN

Northern California's most gripping and tragic shipwreck was the loss of the steamer *Brother Jonathan* on St. George Reef, July 30, 1865. Of some 185 persons aboard only 19 survived to tell the harrowing tale. Only two disasters on the American side of the Pacific have surpassed the *Brother Jonathan* in loss of life. The steamer *Pacific* off Cape Flattery in 1875 (275 lost) and the SS *Princess Sophia* on Vanderbilt Reef, Alaska, in 1918 (343 lost).

The *Brother Jonathan* was a 1359-ton sidewheel steamer built at New York in 1851 for the Long Island Sound trade. She, however, was sold on completion and sent to the Pacific Coast. On reaching San Francisco she was placed in the service of Vanderbilt's Nicaragua Line, but shortly afterward was sold for a handsome price to John T. Wright. He renamed her *Commodore* and made a financial go until 1858 when the ship narrowly averted foundering off the Washington Coast with 350 passengers aboard.

Perhaps Wright saw the handwriting on the wall and figured that he wanted no part of a disaster. Accordingly he sold his ship to the California Steam Navigation Company. They spent several thousand dollars on the badly-shaken vessel, rebuilding and refitting her in nearly every department.

Back she went in the coastwise trade, and made a small fortune for her owners. For several months prior to her fatal voyage, cargo bookings had been exceedingly heavy. Most of the California Steam Navigation Company vessels were having to leave freight on the dock for lack of space. Even then, they were sailing over-burdened. This was the existing situation on July 27, 1865, before the *Brother Jonathan* sailed for Victoria from San Francisco. Captain Samuel De Wolf, master, endeavored to induce the ship's agent to stop receiving cargo because the vessel was grossly overloaded. De Wolf asserted that his ship could not run safely under such conditions. A hot argument ensued and the agent informed the captain that he would be relieved of command if he didn't follow orders.

Unfortunately the agent was acting for the regular agent who was also vice-president of the company. The captain was furious, but held his temper, finally turning his back on his superior and boarding his ship. As it turned out, overloading may well have been the cause behind the impending disaster.

The arrogant agent was probably haunted to his dying day by the thought of the 166 souls who had perished in the catastrophe.

At the stroke of noon on July 28, the *Brother Jonathan* cast off her lines and slipped through the Golden Gate. A persistent headwind and a heavy sea, plus the overburdened condition of the steamer, made progress difficult. Many passengers were confined to their state-rooms and much of the gaiety usually attendant on the early coastwise passenger steamers was noticeably absent. It wasn't until July 30 that the vessel passed Crescent City, barely holding her own against adverse headwinds.

Captain De Wolf doggedly kept his course until 1 p.m. when the vessel gained a point 16 miles northwest of Crescent City. The gale had reached full proportions. Here all forward progress was thwarted and the skipper's only alternative was to come about and seek shelter until the storm blew itself out. The vessel had logged about six miles in the opposite direction when suddenly she struck something with a fearful jolt. The passengers stood frozen in their tracks. The steamer was hung up on inundated Northwest Seal Rock, part of the dreaded St. George Reef, eight miles from the mainland. The initial impact was fatal. Pieces of broken keel came floating to the surface and pandemonium broke loose in a scramble for the boats.

The only survivor on duty at the precise moment of the crash was quartermaster Jacob Yates. Following was his testimony:

> I took the wheel at twelve o'clock. A northwest gale was blowing and we were four miles above Point St. George. The sea was running mountain high and the ship was not making headway. The captain thought it best to turn back to Crescent City and wait until the storm had ceased. He ordered the helm hard aport. I obeyed, and it steadied her. I kept due east. This was about 12:45. When we made Seal Rock the captain said, "South-east by south." It was clear where we were, but foggy and smoky inshore. We ran till 1:50 when she struck with great force, knocking the passengers down and starting the deck planks. The captain stopped and backed her, but could not move the vessel an inch. She rolled about five minutes, then

gave a tremendous thump and part of the keel came up alongside. By that time the wind and sea had slewed her around until her head came to the sea, and she worked off a little. Then the foremast went through the bottom until the yard rested on the deck. Captain De Wolf ordered everyone to look to his own safety, and said that he would do the best he could for all.

From that moment confusion reigned. The lifesaving apparatus was unfortunately in bad need of repair. Great holes had been opened in the ship's hull. The gale-whipped seas slammed at the port quarter veering the vessel around until it came head to the wind. The wedge-shaped pinnacles holding her captive, ripped open the bottom of the ship and the foremast virtually dropped out of sight.

The pushing, screaming crowd gathered about the lifeboats as harassed crewmen tried desperately to get them lowered. One boat was finally cleared away but so many of the hysterical passengers piled into it that it capsized. All were drowned. This made it difficult to get passengers into the second boat. When it was almost filled, the steamer took a severe lurch and the craft, still dangling in the falls, plummeted into the water and swamped.

The third mate, James Patterson, who had been asleep when the ship struck, was now on deck attempting to get still another lifeboat over the side. He succeeded in placing five women and three children in it, but before he could round up additional passengers, ten members of the crew leaped in. Patterson was now in the stern sheets and against his orders, the crewmen lowered the boat. Either by miracle or the capabilities of officer Patterson, this boat carrying 19 occupants was the only craft that reached shore and in it were the sole survivors of the wreck.

None could ever know the grim and horrible moments as the *Brother Jonathan* was swept from the reef, taking down with her those 166 souls. All but 55 were passengers, many of them women and children. They didn't have a chance.

The steamer *Del Norte,* Captain Henry Johnson, was dispatched to the scene after receiving word of the sinking. He succeeded in rescuing the 19 survivors but an extended search of the area produced only numerous bloated bodies, many of which washed up on surrounding beaches.

The handful of survivors were not anxious to tell of their harrowing experiences. They remembered all too clearly those last terrifying moments, with passengers gathered about Captain De Wolf pleading for help it was beyond his power to give. The captain's last words were like the voice from the tomb. "Tell them," he said, "that if they had not overloaded us we would have got through all right, and this never would have happened."

One of the stories that pulled at the heart strings concerned journalist James Nesbitt, who, awaiting his death, sat down on the ship's forward hatch cover to write his will in his litttle notebook. He then wrapped it neatly and tied it about his waist. After the steamer went down his body was cast up on the beach, the notebook still secured about him.

And there was Brigadier General Wright, U.S. Army, who made such an inspiring tableau as he placed his coat about his wife. She was to have gone into the one boat which gained the shore but her devotion to her husband was a binding tie. They sank beneath the waves, with arms wrapped about each other.

Before many weeks had passed 75 bodies were washed ashore, many mutilated beyond recognition. The others were never recovered.

Down through the years, fabulous tales have been told about the treasures aboard the *Brother Jonathan* on her fatal voyage. Many accounts claimed that she carried in excess of $1,000,000. According to reliable sources the money she carried was the payroll for Army troops in the Pacific Northwest, and totaled only $250,000. Nevertheless the treasure hunters have preferred the exaggerated account and for decades have been making dangerous descents into the depths in a search for the lost money. Many claimed to have found the location of the wreck but nothing has ever substantiated their claim. To the most reliable intelligence the position of the vessel still remains a mystery and none of her loot has actually been recovered.

More than two decades after the loss of the *Brother Jonathan* the lantern in the St. George Reef Lighthouse was put into operation. This masterpiece of lighthouse construction, ten years in its creation, cost the government nearly a million dollars, the most expensive beacon in America. Somewhere below its probing beam lie the remains of the *Brother Jonathan,* her crew of dead, and a large payroll that has never been recovered.

SUBMARINE H-3 AND USS MILWAUKEE

Call it a Navy fiasco. The facts presented here have been more or less secret down through the years for obvious reasons. The Navy pulled a boner and no matter how hard they tried to hide it there was no denying the evidence. The first part of the episode might have been the story of any stranded vessel, but the latter part resulted in the wreck of the 10,000-ton cruiser USS *Milwaukee,* one of the Navy's greatest peace time losses.

It all began on the Morning of December 14, 1916, when the United States submarine *H-3* en route to Eureka, California, from Astoria, Oregon, went ashore in a dense fog at Samoa Beach, four miles north of the entrance to Humboldt Bay. Indefinite information reached the Humboldt Coast Guard Station at 9:20 a.m., less than a half hour after the stranding. Making a toilsome tramp along the beach and over sand dunes, with the assistance of a two-horse team, the Coast Guard lifesaving crew arrived with their beach apparatus.

The *H-3* was broadside to, about 200 yards from shore and in the thick of the pounding surf. The seas were breaking entirely over her and she was rolling so heavily

188

that her superstructure was dipping in the water from side to side. Trapped inside her steel belly was her complement of 27 men. The only visible sign of life was an occasional blast of her whistle.

Coastguardmen promptly rigged up a Lyle gun and shot a line to the submarine but nobody emerged from the conning tower to secure it. This left no alternative but for a boat to go out to the wreck.

The keeper sent several of his men back to the Coast Guard Station to bring the surfboat. Meanwhile, as the tide ebbed, the seas began to moderate somewhat. By 3 p. m. another line was shot across the submarine. This time some of the crew broke loose from their stuffy confines, hauled in the shot line and made fast the tail-block and hawser. For some reason they were unable to clear the gear. Within 20 minutes their efforts were abandoned and all disappeared below, locking the hatch cover behind them.

It was then that the surfmen launched their boat, weathered the breakers, and reached the side of the stricken vessel. The submarine was rolling heavily and, to avoid being smashed underneath it, a volunteer jumped to her deck to clear the fouled lines. This daring errand was accomplished without accident and the surfboat promptly returned to shore, leaving the volunteer behind to manipulate the gear. He hung on precariously with one hand and worked the lines with the other. The submarine rolled like a rocking horse. The men inside were not even aware that he was on deck.

From that point it seemed but a routine matter except for one hitch. A crowd of several hundred had gathered on the beach to watch the rescue operation. They were well-intentioned but difficult to control. As is natural in such a situation, several insisted on lending a hand. When the gear was ready, somebody in the crowd, doubtless well meaning, gave the hawser a turn around a large tree stump. A moment later the stranded craft took an outward roll. As the rope failed to give, it grew taut and the pull of the vessel caused it to snap. Fortunately the whipline remained intact, and another length of hawser was sent out and set up. The work now went along without mishap, and the crew of the submarine were rousted out, surprised and slightly embarrassed by the work accomplished by the lifesaving crew while they were huddled inside their submersible.

They were brought ashore one by one via the breeches buoy. Despite the rock-and-roll actions of the submarine, all hands were landed uninjured.

The submarine itself was left to the mercy of the surf. Between December 15 and 20, ineffectual efforts to free her were made by the Coast Guard cutter *McCulloch,* the U. S. monitor *Cheyenne,* and the Navy tug *Arapahoe.* The situation grew more complex. The Navy, however, had no intention of abandoning the *H-3.* The craft had been built at the Moran Yard in Seattle only three years prior to the mishap. With a surface speed in excess of 14 knots it was one of the fastest submarines in the Navy.

The government then asked for bids from private concerns for refloating the vessel. Several were submitted but all were rejected as being excessively high. Then came the blunder. A group of high ranking naval officers came to the conclusion that it was merely a matter of getting a vessel with superior power to pull the *H-3* free from the sands. Their choice was the 9700-ton armored cruiser *Milwaukee.* She had power equal to all the largest tugs on the Pacific Coast combined—24,504 horsepower.

An enemy could not have done a neater job of sabotage, but, despite everything, the deep-drafted giant was dispatched to the scene.

A heavy hawser was placed between the *Milwaukee* and the *H-3* and another line from the *Milwaukee* to the 1000-horsepower Navy tug *Iroquois* which stood out beyond the breakers to keep the cruiser from drifting into shallow water.

Then began the mighty pull. The line between the battle wagon and the submarine grew fiddle-string tight and in turn, the hawser from the cruiser to the tug. It was one of the greatest displays of horsepower ever put into a sal-

190

vage job. With lightning rapidity the inevitable went
wrong. The line between the *Iroquois* and the *Milwaukee* parted under the strain. The cruiser veered
sharply and went hard aground. The savage breakers
slashed angrily about her thick-armored hull. It was a
dramatic moment for which there have been few counter-
parts. Hundreds of blue-clads were aboard, including
several high navy officers.

The Coast Guard stood ever ready and lost little time
in getting a line to the helpless monstrosity. There was
indecision on the cruiser among the officers as to what
to do next. The primary goal they finally agreed to, was
to get all hands ashore. Every effort was bent to that purpose.

Coastguardmen soon had a breeches buoy rigged and
men began coming ashore. A total of 438 souls were
aboard the cruiser, which meant that the evacuation process would be a long and trying undertaking. It lasted
throughout the night and all of the next day. Over 150
came ashore on the breeches buoy and the remainder by
boat while townspeople stood on the beach with piles of
blankets to bundle each sailor as he arrived. The survivors stood around big beach fires warming themselves
while coffee and stronger stimulants were served.

Despite the arduous task in rescuing all hands, not
a single life was lost — a tribute to the valor of Coast
Guard and Navy personnel.

Ultimately a channel was cut through the sands of
Samoa Peninsula and in an unusual salvage operation
the stranded submarine was relaunched into the calm
waters of Humboldt Bay. She was repaired and returned
to service.

The *Milwaukee*, however, was a hopeless loss and a
severe blow to Navy pride, not to mention the multi-
million dollar setback to Uncle Sam's Pacific fleet.

The cruiser's superior construction permitted her to
brave the elements for many months. She stood in the
breakers like some prehistoric monster, the seas knocking

her away bit by bit to afford beachcombers treasured souvenirs.

So went the Navy's greatest peace-time fiasco.

MERRIMAC

A sorrowful tug with a mighty name was the *Merrimac*. Her presence on Humboldt Bay came about because of the stranding of the existing bar tug during the winter season of 1862-1863.

Humboldt Bay was dangerous, to say the least. In those early years there were no jetties, and pilots had only their personal knowledge to forewarn them of changing shoals.

The tug *Mary Ann,* Captain H. H. Buhne, skipper and pilot, was the only means of getting lumber schooners in and out of the bay. After the tug got fouled in the lines of a vessel which it was towing, it was driven on the spit and held fast. They couldn't get it off and the industry of Humboldt was imperiled until a replacement could be found.

The powers-to-be therefore lined up the tug *Merrimac* —still building on the ways at San Francisco. She was fitted up for immediate service and arrived off Humboldt Bay on February 21, 1863. Though the bar was passable, the tug for some reason did not attempt to enter. She was signaled by the steamer *Panama;* there was an exchange of information after which the larger ship sailed northward.

The following day—Sunday morning—the *Merrimac* was still circling off the bar when again the *Panama* hove in sight. Limited communication took place between the two vessels, though it was believed that the liner was engaging the tug to take her mail and passengers over the bar.

Then, as seen through the keeper's telescope at the Humboldt Lighthouse and the guard's at Fort Humboldt, the tug with a full head of steam approached the bar from a northwesterly direction.

In the twinkling of an eye a great sea erupted under-

Navy's big fiasco—USS *Milwaukee*, a total loss, stranded while trying to save the submarine *H-3* aground at Samoa Beach, California, January 1917.

Navy submarine *H-3* hard aground off Samoa Beach, December 1916. The H-3 was later refloated in Humboldt Bay after a channel was cut through the sand. (courtesy Carl Christensen)

Death ship! Twisted remains of the steam schooner *Brooklyn* battered into submission off Humboldt Bay, California in 1930. All but one of the crew perished.

Another victim of Humboldt Bay bar—passenger ship *Corona*, stranded March 1, 1907. One life was lost.

Grim tombstone. Mast of sunken SS *Alaska* off Blunts Reef, California, August 6, 1921. Forty-two lives were lost. (courtesy Carl Christensen)

British freighter *Orteric* aground on Fish Rocks, near Point Arena, California, December 11, 1922. She soon broke up.

Steamer *Argo* ashore at Eel River, California. Refloated, she was totally wrecked off Tillamook Bay bar, Oregon in 1909. (courtesy Carl Christensen)

British four-masted barkentine *Collaroy* wrecked near Humboldt Bay in 1889.
(Freese & Fetour photo)

Tragic loss of the liner *Bear* near Cape Mendocino, California, June 14, 1916.
Five were drowned. Salvage failed.

neath her. Over she flipped, end for end. Water smoth-
ered the craft with each succeeding sea.

The *Panama* stood helplessly by. The keeper at the
lighthouse, alerted by the stark tragedy, started down
the beach to enlist help. As he ran he was surprised to see
the liner steam away to the southward. It was feared that
aboard the tug were passengers and mail earlier transferred from the big ship. Now it had sailed away bearing
the secret and the landsmen had no way of knowing how
many were aboard the tug when it capsized.

It was believed the *Merrimac* had gone down, until its
watersoaked hull was cast up on Humboldt's north spit,
bottom up. Getting a line to her proved to no avail. So
three small boats went out to investigate. They too were
unsuccessful in reaching the wreck.

During that night the stranded tug refloated itself and
drifted over the bar, grounding again, near Bucksport.

At daybreak the sloops *Sam Slick* and *Glide* came
alongside and made her fast. Eventually they succeeded
in wrestling her into Jones' Wharf, where she was righted. She had been severely mauled by the seas. Her masts
were broken off near the deck, much of her deckhouse
was missing, part of her boiler was smashed, the engine
was gone, and the stern was stove above the waterline.
The propeller, pumps, and much of the heavy gear were
still intact.

Sleuthing went on to learn how many lives had actually been lost. Kin of the missing swarmed aboard the
wreck to search for bodies or personal belongings that
might identify the dead. A man's foot was sighted protruding from the smashed housing. His body was hauled
out and identified as that of the tug's fireman. Later
the body of a 12-year-old Indian boy was uncovered from
a pile of wreckage. Initialed shirts, letters, and suitcases
were also found scattered about.

Nearly two months passed before word was received
on Humboldt Bay concerning the *Panama's* role in the
disaster. All of the passengers debarking for Humboldt
Bay had desired to go in aboard the tug, as the bar was

not considered passable for the liner. Captain Johnson, master of the steamer, would not permit this, however, but instead asked the tug to cross the bar so his ship could follow her in if conditions were favorable. If not, she was to lay off the bar until the following day when Captain Buhne could come out and pilot her in. This was agreeable with Captain Hatch of the *Merrimac* but the fatal crossing was not attempted until the following day after the two vessels rendezvoused off the harbor entrance. The reason for the tug's delay was due to her boiler flues being clogged and the fear that she could not raise sufficient steam to make the crossing. The *Panama,* on the other hand, had been going from port to port but was always prevented from entering by impassable bar conditions.

The capsizing of the *Merrimac* shocked the passengers of the *Panama,* many of whom were eye-witnesses. The tug capsized at 12:30 p. m. on that fateful February 22 just as the chimes for the midday meal were being tolled on the liner.

The *Merrimac's* entire crew of seven were lost as well as an undetermined number of others aboard the tug. Final figures ranged between 13 and 18 dead, though an absolute figure was never reached. Among the victims were three prominent business men and a sportsman. It was indeed a black day in the Humboldt country when the *Merrimac* fell victim to the bar swells, but the toll might have been far greater had Captain Johnson allowed his passengers to transfer to the tug for the fatal crossing.

After being completely rebuilt, the ill-fated craft was put back in commission the following summer and for many years afterwards negotiated Humboldt Bar. She never again capsized but the sorrowful saga of her past was never forgotten.

MENDOCINO

From the yellowed records of the old Humboldt Lifesaving Station comes the story of the wreck of the steam schooner *Mendocino*. Only a few months out of her builder's yard on San Francisco Bay, this steamer was wrecked on December 2, 1888.

At the time, the telephone was a brand new apparatus in the area and it was somewhat of an historic occasion when a phone was used to pass along news of the wreck. The stricken ship was first sighted from Captain H. H. Buhne's farm overlooking Humboldt Bay. The news was telephoned to Buhne's Store in Eureka. From there it went from mouth to ear until the whole town knew.

Meanwhile Captain Buhne's bar tug headed for the scene of the wreck to render assistance. At this stage of the story the reader is perhaps wondering who this fellow Buhne was. To be brief, he was the mainspring of the Humboldt County business enterprises. He was not only a pilot, captain, and ship owner, but also a merchant and farmer in his off hours. There were also a few other pastimes he indulged in, but space doesn't allow.

On the way out to the wreck the tug stopped at the Humboldt Lighthouse wharf and found some of the survivors had already been landed there by the lifesaving crew—the chief engineer, his wife, and five crewmen. Along with them was the body of a small child.

The tug proceeded to the wreck. It was lying a half mile from the bay entrance and 75 yards from the channel, in the south breakers. While Captain Buhne surveyed the situation the lifeboat again came out from the lifesaving station to stand by. Captain Jensen, the first mate, and six crewmen still aboard the wreck, expressed their willingness to accept assistance from the tug. The lifeboat relayed the message but the tug could do nothing until high tide.

Meanwhile back at the lighthouse, reporters were getting the story from chief engineer Frank Bragg. He told it with tear-filled eyes, for he and his wife had suffered the loss of their child. Said Bragg:

Due to uncertain bar conditions it was decided that the steam schooner *Tillamook* would go over the bar first and that the *Mendocino* would follow. When the *Tillamook* got to the bar, her captain felt it was too rough to chance and turned back. He signaled Captain Jensen to follow but he kept his course and continued over the bar. Shortly after, she struck, swinging violently around and losing all steerageway. She was completely at the mercy of the seas. Water boarded, flooding the engine room and putting out the fires in the boiler while the steamer was yet full astern. She remained fast on the south spit.

A boat was immediately lowered into which went Bragg, his wife and child, as well as the assistant engineer, a fireman, and the messboy. The lifeboat had barely drifted free of the *Mendocino* when a breaker turned it over end for end. All floundered about in the water for nearly thirty minutes before the lifesaving crew plucked them to safety. The child drowned because his lifejacket was secured about him improperly and he was unable to keep his face out of the water. On sighting the child, one of the lifesavers dived overboard to get him into the boat but resuscitation failed to revive him. For the following 48 hours the lifesaving boat made run after run out to the wreck, waiting to see if her captain was ready to abandon ship. The lifeboat was tossed about like a cork and its crew grew hungry and cold. During this period they had rescued two additional crewmen from the wreck by tossing them a line which was made fast about their bodies. They jumped off the ship's forecastle and were pulled through the water to the lifeboat. But as they were taking the men aboard, a huge crested breaker slopped over into the boat, thoroughly dousing all within and nearly swamping the craft. As the two men were pulled in over the gunwales another huge sea lunged at the boat, turning it around and slamming it down on the sands, wrenching the oars from the hands of the surfmen. Four oar blades were snapped off. The others were hauled back by the cranelines.

The lifeboat then retreated and its lifesaving equipment was put aboard the tug which was standing by. The line-throwing gun was assembled on the forward deck. After it was correctly sighted it was fired. The iron shot soared gracefully to the wreck, but the charge had severed the line and it dropped into the depths unattached. A second shot missed the mark, falling astern of the vessel. The third try was rewarded, the shot passing squarely between the *Mendocino's* masts.

For 30 minutes the *Mendocino's* crew hauled in on it. Suddenly they ceased their efforts, worn out and discouraged by the flooding tide which had carried the line inshore.

After some encouragement from the tug's crew they resumed their back-breaking chore and finally got the block aboard, followed by the heavier lines. Then came the shocker. The strain on the line caused it to break, ending any present hopes of pulling the wreck off the shoal.

With the chips down, the lifeboat craft went into action once again, and through an uncanny job of boat handling allowed all but Captain Jensen to jump into its confines. The skipper of the *Mendocino* got entangled in a welter of loose lines and could not be rescued. He finally worked his way free and struggled back onto the wreck to await a favorable turn of the tide when the boat could return. After several hours the surfboat did return and Captain Jensen was saved.

By December 24 the surf had moderated and Captain Hennig and his lifesaving crew made a run out to the wreck to remove personal property and navigation instruments. The incoming tide, however, soon put a halt to the operation and the surfboat was forced to return to its station.

Nor did Christmas Day deter the indomitable surfmen from their task. They again rowed out at slack tide, and ran a line to the wreck, the channel end of which was anchored and buoyed.

Then under the shield of night, away from the watchful eye of the would-be tugboat salvagers, the *Mendocino* decided to escape. Snapping the buoyed line she drifted free with the ebb tide, across the channel entrance and stranded on the north spit. At dawn the lifeboat was under way again, Hennig intent on boarding the wreck and dropping her anchors to keep her from drifting farther up on the beach. But, contrary to expectations, the steamer began settling in the sands.

Captain Buhne's tug was on the scene pulling with its every ounce of horsepower, but the ocean sands had a firm grip on the wreck and it refused to budge.

By January 7, 1889, the vessel had to be abandoned. The entry in the "Wreck Book," at the lifesaving station read: "All efforts to save the vessel were, for the present, abandoned."

During the interim Captain Jensen received orders from John S. Kimball of San Francisco, owner of the wreck, to make every effort to remove the cargo of lumber valued at $17,000. It was consigned to San Pedro interests. The steamer itself was valued at $40,000.

H. D. Bendixsen was commissioned to handle the discharge of the lumber and under the vigilance of the keeper of the lifesaving station, operations got under way immediately. The lumber was laboriously transported on tramways across the spit to the bay.

Before the *Mendocino's* holds were emptied, heavy lines were rigged to make her secure. If it was feasible to bring her broadside to the beach there still existed the possibility of blocking her up on the sands. Since it appeared impossible to re-launch her through the surf, there was a remote chance of moving her across the spit and into the calmer waters of Humboldt Bay. The possibility of such a salvage undertaking was by no means a shot in the dark for it had been tried with success in the same area when the tug *Mary Ann* was wrecked on Humboldt's south spit in January of 1863.

St. George Reef to Cape Mendocino

On the 21st day of February efforts to jack up the *Mendocino* from the sands were commenced. Her bow was raised four feet between tides and it was expected soon to start her on the epic journey across the spit to the bay. But the rising optimism died when soft sands halted the forward progress. The vessel had been moved but a few hundred feet when the operations bogged down.

In March, the wreck was sold at auction in San Francisco. Bids started at $500 and rose to $1950, the successful bidder being James Townsend who was rumored to have had a part interest in the vessel. He also purchased the ship's loose gear for $157.50, bringing his total investment to $2107.50.

That he got a suitable return on his gamble is highly problematical, for despite his all-out efforts the *Mendocino* ended her days where she lay. A few years back, one of the old timers of the Humboldt region revisited the salvage scene and reported seeing only a small section of the ship's keel protruding from the sands.

CORONA

Men who sailed on the steamer *Corona* as crew members referred to her as a "good luck" ship. Since her building at Philadelphia in 1888, she had performed admirably and was popular with passengers in the Pacific coastwise service. Many looked upon her as one of those fortunate ships that always escaped serious mishap. They based their opinion on an incident that occurred in Alaska off Lewis Island in 1898. Even when the cards were stacked heavily against the ship, she came through. She piled up on the rocks and, when she backed off, the gaping hole in her hull gave every indication that she would go down. Temporary repairs and crash mats could not hold out the water. Then when it appeared that she was doomed, the inrush of water came to an abrupt halt.

The confused skipper ordered an immediate investigation. It was discovered that a sizable blackfish had been sucked into the hole and become wedged so securely that fire axes had to be used to free it, when the ship reached the dry dock.

But, as it must be with all ships—the *Corona* came up with the low card on March 1, 1907. The liner was entering Humboldt Bay, Eureka-bound, when, according to the accepted version, Captain Boyd gave an order to the helmsman who misunderstood and turned the wheel the wrong way, driving the vessel aground. Not all shared in this intelligence, including a member of the Humboldt lifesaving crew, the late Gustav (Gus) Christensen. He recalled the Humboldt Bar of yesteryear as a very treacherous place. He remembered that ships used to come in by way of the north channel with breakers on either side. When the *Corona* made its turn at the north jetty, Christensen was of the opinion that a big sea caught her and took her out of control and landed her on the wrong side of the jetty.

Be that as it may, the *Corona* piled up off the jetty amid the pounding breakers with some 154 persons aboard. The frantic passengers crowded to the afterdeck as the ship listed. Life jackets were distributed but some of the passengers and crew members got panicky and tried to launch one of the lifeboats. It hit the water, capsized, and one life was lost. The survivors were hauled back aboard and willingly awaited the arrival of the Humboldt Lifesaving crew.

Probably no shipwreck in Northern California has had a larger audience on hand to watch rescue operations. An estimated 5000 persons gathered on Samoa Beach. People from just about every walk of life from miles around stood wide-eyed as if watching a tense, staged drama. There was stark drama all right but it was far from staged. The spectators wanted to see a show and they weren't disappointed. The lifesaving crew put on a spectacular death-defying display, making repeated runs through mountain-high breakers. At times their boat almost stood on end. With fantastic agility and skill, those at the oars came alongside the liner, rescuing survivors again and again. Not one did they lose nor an error did they make in handling their craft, despite terrific odds. If those on the *Corona* had not insisted on lowering the one lifeboat, there would have been no loss of life.

With all survivors safely landed on the beach, efforts were turned toward saving the liner. There was much speculation over the undertaking. Owners of the *Corona*, the Pacific Coast Steamship Company, were not optimistic. After a few days of incessant pounding by the bar breakers all hopes of salvage waned.

But C. P. Dow of San Francisco was certain of ultimate success, so much so that he is alleged to have expended $40,000 in an effort to free the *Corona*. His tenacity, however, went unrewarded and the ship settled deeper in the sands.

Today, a half-century later, the sands have shifted. One of the masts of the ill-fated steamer still marks the spot where the ship went aground. Like a lone sentinel, it juts high above the jetty sands which have completely swallowed the ship. The mast is a jutting tombstone over one of Humboldt's most famous shipwrecks—the SS *Corona*.

NORTHERNER

To those of us who live in the age of radar, radio, and automatic navigation aids, it is difficult to picture the hazards which confronted the early mariner.

Without ship-to-shore communications, vessels, disabled at sea, drifted at the mercy of the storm. All that stood between them and the hope of rescue was an inverted ensign, a flare or a barrel of burning oil. In such a situation was the Panama Mail Steamship Company's sidewheel steamer *Northerner*, wrecked more than a century ago.

The *Northerner*, in command of Captain W. L. Dall, left San Francisco on her final voyage January 4, 1860, at 4:30 a. m. Her destination was the Columbia River and Puget Sound. While steaming up the coast the following day at a near 12-knot clip she ran afoul of Blunts Reef, off Cape Mendocino. The encounter with the inundated rocks did not cause a severe shock and none of the crew or passengers were aware of the resulting damage.

As a precautionary measure Captain Dall sent his first officer below to make a survey of the damages, and his pilot Captain Thomas Gladwell to take bearings on the reef which was unmarked on the navigation charts. While the first officer was below, the steamer swung off the rocks and drifted free. It was then that water began pouring in between her started planking at an alarming rate. All pumps were immediately placed in operation and worked to capacity. In spite of the fact that they were throwing out water at a rate of 12,000 gallons per minute, it gained rapidly. The steamer was three and a half miles north of Cape Fortunas when the engineer informed the captain that the fire in the boilers would soon be extinguished by the rising water.

Captain Dall, his brow furrowed with concern, realized the impossibility of reaching Humboldt Bay and instead elected to steer his ship for the nearest beach. A titanic effort was made to keep the water from disabling the boilers but by the time the steamer hit the offshore shoals her sputtering engine was turning at a mere 20 revolutions.

The seas were so extremely heavy that it was impossible to cut the masts away. All of the passengers were kept in their cabins, as the breakers swept entirely over the decks. When there appeared a brief lull between seas the crew succeeded in readying a lifeboat on the leeward side. Most of the women and children passengers were herded topside and seated in it.

First officer A. French was given the responsibility of getting them ashore. One woman refused to enter the craft because her brother was not permitted to join her.

The boat was lowered away and took to the heaving bosom of a great swell with a terrible splash. The women screamed and the infants quaked with fear. French was a handy man with a small boat, however, and succeeded in bringing the craft's nose to the wind. As if master over the sea he took the boat on a hectic surf ride and kept his strong arms locked about the steering oar until the beach was reached.

The next boat, in charge of the second mate, carried all of the elderly male passengers and the woman who had earlier refused to disembark. Fear and persuasion had changed her mind. Perhaps she made the wrong decision. The boat capsized and all in it perished except the officer in charge and one of the oarsmen.

Captain Gladwell took charge of the third boat but it too was rudely upended and most of its occupants were sacrificed to the merciless sea. The first and only boat to reach shore made a daring run back to the wreck but, owing to the carelessness of the oarsmen, it was sucked under the *Northerner's* quarter, drowning first officer French.

From that moment there was disorganization aboard the wreck.

Thomas O'Neil, the chief engineer, was perhaps the sustaining factor in the saving of many lives. Without hesitation he removed his shoes, coat and pants, made a line fast, grabbed the working end, and plunged overboard. With powerful strokes the intrepid seafarer surmounted the irascible breakers. Courageously he carried the line to shore, offering an escape route for the despairing passengers.

It was a black night and the seas so threatening that most of the passengers could not be persuaded to leave the steamer.

Unable to talk them into evacuation, by 1:30 a. m., Captain Dall, Pilot Rogers, and Purser Breck started ashore via the line. The cowering passengers watched wide-eyed. The fact that one man had already been swept from the rope and drowned did little to convince the timid.

In another section of the ship, a despairing seaman entered the cargo hold and managed to get a horse up on deck. Few noticed his struggle with the balking animal. He whipped it, pushed it, poked it and tugged on it until at last he got it to the railing. When the ship took a sharp list he shoved it overboard and jumped in after it, clinging tightly to its tail. The horse instinctively headed for the shore and the sailor hung on with such tenacity that he almost pulled the beast's tail off. Both reached the shore.

In those terrible and final hours the steamer began to fall apart. Those remaining on her slanting decks clung desperately, hoping and praying. Then as if the hand of God were present, a large piece of the deck detached itself and began drifting toward shore, crowded with life. With naught but a tormented sea to guide it, the wreckage drifted onto the beach and those who had managed to keep from being swept off, were saved.

In all, 38 persons perished and many others suffered from injuries and exposure. The list of passengers and crew at sailing time had numbered 108 and it was a small wonder that death lurking over those darkened waters did not wrap its clammy arms around many more.

From the outset it was claimed that the *Northerner* was old and tender and ripe for a hasty departure from this world. Actually the New York-built steamer had seen but 13 years of service which in those times was not considered ancient for a ship. More suspect than age and tenderness were the relaxed inspection laws and poor navigation charts. The *Northerner's* owners, the Pacific Mail Line, had an appalling record of ship disasters. Between 1853 and 1915, a total of 31 steamers under their ownership was wrecked—with the loss of nearly 2000 lives. All but two of these ships were lost in the Pacific Ocean.

BROOKLYN

The wreck of the steam schooner *Brooklyn* was brief and terrible. A lone survivor escaped the indescribable mass of wreckage.

The vessel stood out from Humboldt Bay, down to her marks with lumber, on the afternoon of November 8,

1931. There was a heavy swell on the bar and a driving offshore wind that had everything well riled up. Captain Johansen, raised with the steam schooner fleet, was an old hand at navigating rough seas. He didn't give the gale a second thought. Perhaps he was overconfident and bore no fear of nature's forces.

Suddenly a series of great breakers broke in sequence. His ship straddled the bar in such fashion as to break her back and leave her vulnerable to an ocean gone mad. There was no chance to lower a boat, not even time to don life jackets. Coastguardmen were unable to surmount the bar in a rescue attempt. Even a Coast Guard plane was turned back due to fog and rain squalls which prevented all contact. Nothing but the wild ocean fury and the crashing of runaway lumber and wreckage, could shore lookouts pick up with their telescopes.

When the seas had calmed sufficiently to allow the motor lifeboat to cross the bar, the Coast Guard found not a single sign of life, only the mangled ribs of what 24 hours earlier had been a lumber steamer. After days of futile searching, the incident was logged as a major disaster.

Then, several days later, a coastwise steamer picked up a man draped over a half-submerged hatch cover many miles from the entrance to Humboldt Bay. After being revived, the survivor revealed himself as the second mate of the *Brooklyn*.

He was the sole survivor of the tragedy. Eighteen perished.

Few ships die with a parting tribute, but the *Brooklyn* did. At her birthplace at Aberdeen, Washington, following the disaster these words appeared in the *Aberdeen Daily World*:

> Strewn on the California shore near Humboldt Bay are the bones of a once fine ship. A scattering of planking, sections of her frames, ribs and odds and ends are all that remain of the little steamer *Brooklyn*, which so proudly slid down a Grays Harbor ways

in the summer of 1901. The *Brooklyn* was built by John Lindstrom after his own design and was one of the first vessels to be turned out in the shipbuilder's yards in Aberdeen.

The vessel lived for almost 30 years, full evidence of extreme care in her construction. That she would have lived many years more is unquestioned had not fate sent her to death in a Humboldt storm. Steamboat inspectors had passed her as seaworthy no longer ago than last April. With the meticulous care characteristic of the old school of wooden ship fashioners, the Brooklyn was built during the early part of the century. She was the forerunner of many ships to be built of Grays Harbor timber. Hand labor contributed to the excellence of her construction. Bit by bit she was built up, the old timers say, worked out by hand with the aid of a band saw and a steam box. Her trun'ls were driven by hand sledge and her works smoothed by block plane. Her launching was a holiday event.

Few persons ever get an obituary of such elegance.

TRICOLOR

Captain Wold, master of the Norwegian freighter *Tricolor*, was in the chart room going cautiously over his charts. Not since departing Ladysmith, British Columbia, had his ship run into such a wall of fog. Dead-reckoning told him he was near Cape Mendocino, but how near was anyone's guess. He was certain that ponderous headland had been passed and accordingly altered course. It was yet the wee hours of morning. Besides being foggy, it was black, very black, and, try as they might, those on watch could not pick up the mournful cry of the fog signal at Mendocino Light Station. It was as if all the foghorns for hundreds of miles in every direction had been permanently muzzled.

Speed had been reduced to half. Captain Wold and

first officer Iveson discussed their situation at length in the dim glare from the binnacle lamp. The ship's clock struck six bells. At that precise moment on July 26, 1905, the vessel crashed. There was a murderous grinding of steel against rock. The two men were knocked against the telegraph. The wheel spun wildly, completely out of the helmsman's grip.

The ship's whistle wailed out its ominous tones but the sound fell on an empty sea. The blasts, however, were heard by occupants at the distant Ocean House near Cape Mendocino. The shore people could see nothing but a wall of white but some among them had heard vessels sounding their death calls on previous occasions and immediately made phone connections with Eureka, reporting the possibility of a ship in distress.

Within an hour the tug *Ranger,* with lifesaving boat in tow, crossed out over Humboldt Bar and groped its way down the coast. Cutting through great strands of fog, it was 10 a.m. before the tug managed to reach *Blunts Reef Lightship.* It was discovered that the survivors of the *Tricolor* were already there. In desperation they had lowered three lifeboats and made a daring trip along the rock-studded coast until they picked up the lightship's fog signal.

The distraught Captain Wold was noticeably worried over the loss of his ship. He told the lifesaving crew that he had encountered thick weather the night prior to the stranding and had made a mistake in dead reckoning of 15 or 20 miles. He was certain the ship had rounded Cape Mendocino and had pursued a southeasterly course when it brought up on the outreaching tentacles of the cape.

Instead of being south of the cape, Captain Wold's course led the *Tricolor* in behind the reefs. There was the faint sound of surf and the call from the bow watch, "breakers ahead!" Then the ship plowed into the rocks. The engines were thrown into reverse with no response. Full ahead gave the same results. Her propeller fanned the air, the ship shaking violently. Suddenly her stern swung abruptly around and caught on another patch of rock. Now she rose and fell with the ground swell scraping her steel plates dangerously both forward and aft on the wave-sharpened prongs.

For hours the chief engineer employed all his cunning and know-how in an effort to get sufficient response from the engine to lift the ship from her perch, but already holes were being ripped in the ship's bottom. Finally the water rose in the engine room and put out the boiler fires, driving all hands up on deck. Boarding breakers ripped off hatch covers and water slopped into the holds where tons of coal were stowed. Even if the *Tricolor* had freed herself she would have been swept on other rocks, the area being likened to a marine pin cushion.

Realizing the hopelessness of the situation, Captain Wold had ordered the boats cleared away at 7 a.m. Already one of the lifeboats on the weather side was filled with sea water. Three other boats took all hands. Instead of risking a quarter-mile run through massive breakers, it was decided to seek out the lightship five miles away.

The perilous position of the *Tricolor* left virtually no hope of refloating her. The best the salvage tug could do without risking its own destruction was to get within a mile and a half of the wreck. Thus were all efforts of saving the freighter abandoned.

On the day following the wreck, three of the *Tricolor's* crew were taken as near the freighter as possible by the *Ranger* and put over the side in a lifeboat. They succeeded in reboarding the ship and removing personal effects, and navigation instruments. The vessel's position had not changed but it was working hard on the rocks and gave every indication of breaking its back at any moment. The crew members hastily left the wreck and were later picked up by the tug.

Two days afterward, all of the survivors were taken into Eureka. There, Captain Wold telegraphed the loss of the ship to its owners, the Wilhelmsen Steamship Company of Hunsberg, Norway. It came as a blow to them, as the 6950-ton freighter had seen but 11 months of service since being launched at Shields, England.

Meanwhile great throngs of people gathered on the slopes of Cape Mendocino to watch the watery destruction of the writhing giant. Murderous seas soon reduced her to a twisted mass of rusted steel. Her cargo of coal was spread generously along the ocean floor, a veritable coal mine for zealous divers. The *Tricolor* had joined a fleet of vanquished vessels that had been riddled to pieces off Mendocino's great cape.

BEAR

The wreck of the passenger steamer *Bear* was listed as a million-dollar tragedy and one of the most discussed shipwrecks to occur on the Pacific Coast. It created some of the hottest legal controversies of that decade. Charges and countercharges of negligence, faulty navigation, and nefarious scheming were openly made. The persistent claim that the wreck was deliberate, was nullified by experts. They testified that the *Bear* could not have been brought into its position with the best of navigation, for to get through such a network of rocks as infested the Cape Mendocino area was a masterful machination, described as an "act of God."

Captain Louis Nopander, commander of the *Bear,* did not know until the daybreak before the stranding that he had blundered as to his position. He assumed he was several miles at sea when his ship crashed ashore on a sharp reef about 300 feet from the beach. He had mistaken Sugar Loaf Rock for Cape Mendocino in the prevailing fog.

The wreck occurred while the liner was running down the coast toward San Francisco from Portland. The date was June 14, 1916, and the hour was 11:30 p.m. when she went on the rocks. Aboard were more than 100 passengers and a crew numbering 82. The vessel, valued at $1,000,000, had for six years been on the coastwise run. It had long been under the capable hands of Captain Nopander who was considered a splendid navigator by the ship's owner, the San Francisco and Portland Steamship Company. Both the *Bear* and her sister steamship the *Beaver*, 4057-ton vessels, were considered the ultimate in coastwise passenger service.

After the *Bear* ran aground, confusion reigned. The fog was so dense that neither passengers nor ship's officers could ascertain their position. The ship's whistle signals had been heard by some of the ranchers in the upper valleys but it was not until the following day that any of them reached the wreck. Some phone calls were exchanged and finally hitching wagons and buckboards, laden with warm clothing, blankets and brandy, appeared on the beach. The fog by now had lifted a trifle, revealing the silhouette of the stranded steamer and the outline of Sugar Loaf Rock, a quarter-mile away.

Twenty-nine survivors were found congregated on the beach. Five others were drowned when the lifeboats in which they had left the steamer capsized in the surf. In addition, ten had received injuries, two of whom were on the critical list. They were taken up to Capetown and hospitalized at the old Country Hotel. All were suffering from shock and exposure and told of their harrowing experiences in muffled tones.

All agreed that the *Bear* was running at slow speed through the dense fog and that there was no decided impact when she struck. No panic was evident among the passengers. At the order of the captain, who feared his ship might immediately break up, the boats were lowered. Two of them capsized and their occupants were thrown into the boiling surf to fight for their survival.

After a hectic battle, one boat was righted but when all had regained their seats, it was upended a second time. Five perished; the others struggled up on the beach, blue with the cold and suffering from exposure.

The other lifeboats, rather than chancing the surf, rowed toward the *Blunts Reef Lightship*, guided through the fog by its foghorn. One after another they arrived much to the amazement of the lightship crew. Men, women and children, 155 strong, crowded into the little vessel until it bulged at the seams. Every blanket was utilized. Coffee and stimulants ran out. Later the tug *Relief* arrived with additional passengers from a lifeboat that had strayed from the fold.

What to do with all the survivors? Neither the lightship nor the tug could accommodate them. After some spirited wireless exchanges, the steamer *Grace Dollar* hove to off the lightship. Like a commuter ferry service, boat after boat was rowed to her side and emptied of its passengers. The seas remained calm and all of the survivors were placed aboard the steamer without incident. Then with a prolonged blast of her whistle she made a beeline for Eureka.

Now that lightship procedure was reinstated, all concern was turned to the stranded steamer. Would she be floated or was she to become a total loss? Last to leave the wreck were the boatswain, quartermaster, winch driver and Captain Nopander. One of their number came ashore on a raft at daybreak after a draw-line between the ship and shore failed. The others came ashore via the repaired draw-line the following afternoon.

Captain Nopander was met by members of the press, anxiously awaiting his story. In a defensive phrase he told them, "I realize that this is the worst thing that can happen to me. I feel that it would be an injustice to myself or employers to make an extended statement. The proper time will come when I appear before the federal inspectors." And with that the disgruntled reporters departed the wreck scene.

Following the abandonment of the liner a delicate situation arose concerning a $7000 thoroughbred horse held prisoner in the hold of the steamer. It was the property of the president of the steamship company and was being shipped to San Francisco to take part in a Preparedness Day Parade there.

An attempt was made to rescue him. They got him out of the hold and over the side but an endeavor to induce him to swim with a halter and a rope tightly drawn, resulted in his drowning. The would-be horse rescuers were openly accused of not having good horse sense, for the animal would have been fully capable of maneuvering for itself had it been left alone to manage its own escape.

After several days it became obvious that the *Bear* was not going to break up. She was holding fast in her exact position. At extreme low tide one could get within a stone's throw of her.

While the owners and the insurance companies studied the situation, orchids of gratitude were handed out to those instrumental in the rescue of survivors. The battleship *Oregon,* Commander George Williams, was the first vessel to answer the *Bear's* distress message. In the thick of the fog she was navigated among the myriad of dangerous rocks in a vain attempt to rescue passengers. Also praised were the alert crews of the tug *Relief,* the *Blunts Reef Lightship,* the steamer *Grace Dollar,* and the Coast Guard lifeboat *Liberator.*

Salvage attempts were commenced almost immediately in an effort to refloat the *Bear.* A paper cargo valued at $50,000, one thousand cases of condensed milk, and hundreds of sacks of flour, had to be jettisoned. Even after this was accomplished the vessel would not budge from her cradle.

As the cargo washed ashore local residents swarmed to the beach to haul it away. Many succeeded but others ran into opposition with company officials and several hot words and a few wild fists were thrown over rights to the goods.

Things then got worse. Looting was reported. Members of the salvage crew were reported going through the personal baggage of the passengers. Some of the luggage drifted ashore and was rifled by beachcombers. Most of it was later landed, assorted, and sent to its owners, but the missing articles were never accounted for.

After the *Bear* was free of all cargo and freight, the owners and underwriters settled down to the serious business of refloating the liner. The salvage steamer *Iaqua* arrived but after several futile attemps to pry the *Bear* loose, was forced to withdraw without success.

St. George Reef to Cape Mendocino

Then Lloyd's of London, principal insurers, dispatched the Canadian steamer *Salvor* to the scene—the largest and most powerful salvage vessel on the Pacific Coast. Despite her full output of power she had no better success.

Finally a contract was entered into with Way and Coggeshall of Eureka, who were commissioned to transport the beached cargo over the rugged hills and rough roads to Eureka.

On June 24, ten days after the wreck, the owners of the *Bear* abandoned all hope of salvaging the steamer, leaving any further efforts to Lloyd's and the other insurers.

Week after week, as the surf pounded away at the vessel, great mounds of sand built up until she was completely surrounded. It was then that an attempt was made to sell her as she lay. But there were no buyers. All types of novel salvage innovations were suggested but most were fringed with futility. By October, the underwriters were ready to give up.

On November 11, a contract was negotiated with the Porter Wrecking Company who, for a fraction of the value of the ship, prepared to refloat her by digging a canal. On November 14, sands were washed out from under the hull. This succeeded only in breaking the ship's back.

From then on it was a case of salvaging what materials could be cut free. What couldn't be removed was left. The winter storms had already begun to kick up their heels and claimed a generous share of the loot.

Through the years, time and nature have removed most of the evidence. Only a few of the local old-timers can still remember that fatal day that one of Humboldt's most costly shipwrecks was enacted below the rocky cliffs of Cape Mendocino.

ALASKA

The dance band was playing the lively strains of Dardanella. The merry-making passengers danced lightheartedly. Honeymooners strolled the promenade deck.

The evening was warm and jolly inside the liner *Alaska*

as it moved down the coast on that memorable night of August 6, 1921. Outside, a heavy pall of fog had draped its veil about the steamer. The ocean was calm but a sharp lookout was maintained. Captain Harry Hobey was always cautious when his ship was near Blunts Reef off Humboldt's notorious coast.

It was 9 p.m. The shadowy liner slipped inevitably toward beckoning doom. Suddenly the band music ceased as the vessel trembled violently. In a few scant seconds the human mask of joy was transformed into terror. There were 211 persons on the liner, and the realization of pending disaster put fear into every heart.

The ship reeled from the impact and then plunged forward for a second contact with the rocky obstruction. Down crashed her foretopmast, splitting the deck and sending human forms scattering like ants under the foot of man. The *Alaska* had tangled with the dreaded fangs of Blunts Reef and was in immediate danger of going down. The melodious orchestral strains were now interchanged for the strident commands of officers ordering the 131 passengers to don lifejackets and rush to their lifeboat stations.

In the radio shack the wireless operator hammered out a frantic SOS. Water was reported pouring into the deep recesses of the steamer. As the teeth of the reef gashed new holes in the ship's hull the mournful crescendos of the ship's whistle echoed across fog-laden waters with dread finality.

First to pick up the urgent message was the Canadian steamer *Anyox,* some 15 miles away. The nearby Table Bluff Radio Station was unable to intercept the call, as it was handling another message. But the station at North Head, Washington, several hundred miles away rather miraculously intercepted the message and relayed it to Eureka.

The *Anyox* by then was proceeding at full speed toward the foundering liner. The bar tug *Ranger* of Eureka put out in search of the wreck at daybreak. But her services were not needed. The *Anyox* had radioed Table Bluff these terse final words:

> Steamer *Alaska* ashore on Blunts Reef, listed heavily to starboard and sank in deep water within 15 minutes of striking. The loss of life is heavy. . .

The last words emitted from the radio shack on the *Alaska* before the end, were:

> We are sinking!

Then there was an ominous silence. Ships converged on the disaster scene from every direction.

A moment before the *Alaska* struck, Captain Hobey was in his quarters. Immediately after the crash he rushed out on deck and began directing the passengers. He ordered all those asleep to be rousted from their bunks and those at the dance to stand by to evacuate the ship. After ascertaining the nature of the damage, not a moment was lost in lowering the boats. The first boat creaked down the falls half-filled with passengers and almost as soon as it took to the water a breaking sea capsized it and all within were crushed to death against the steamer's side.

The second and third boats got away safely but the fourth one turned turtle and most of its occupants were drowned. The lifeboats were all under-manned in the hastiness of getting away from the sinking ship.

The waves dashing over the hidden reef, struck broadside and made it difficult to row away from the wreck. In desperation, several of the women grabbed unmanned oars and pulled mightily to gain open water.

The despairing souls in the open boats looked back at the liner. Its lights were blinking off and on, like those of a haunted mansion on a lonely island. The running lamps grew dimmer and finally went out. The surf roared like a cage of angry lions turned loose as the ship worked hard on the reef. Then every light on the ship was eclipsed. The entire area for miles in every direction lay in total darkness.

To those still aboard it was a nightmare come true. The engine room was now completely flooded and the ship was listing dangerously. Then it slipped from the reef and took its final plunge, the whistle still blasting. Those awaiting the bitter end threw themselves blindly into the vortex. As the frigid ocean water covered the boilers there was a muffled explosion, the ignited oil throwing a thick, hot film over everything and everyone.

The *Alaska* went down hissing and twisting. A great cavity was opened. Then only bits of flotsam and a scattered lifeboat here and there remained. Now and then a faint cry broke the terrible silence. Dazed and oil-smeared human forms struggled to the lifeboats, coughing, gagging. Misery was all about. Children had been drowned, families separated.

In those terrifying moments before the *Alaska* sank, passengers and crew members had urged Captain Hobey to get into the last lifeboat or to at least don a life jacket. He refused to do either.

"I prefer to go down with my ship," he said. "My place is on this bridge until the last man and woman are safely afloat."

A few minutes later the ship took a severe list. The stack crashed to the deck, pinning the captain beneath it. Death came suddenly.

The steamer *Anyox*, first to pick up the distress call, made a daring run to the scene, handicapped by a cumbersome barge tow. Despite the fog, the ship barreled through. It was about 10 p.m. when the lookout located the first lifeboat nearly swamped. It was laden with oil-soaked passengers groaning in agony. They were promptly rescued, each managing feeble smiles through their tears.

Meanwhile volunteers from the *Anyox's* crew emptied the lifeboat of water and with their skipper's permission rowed about the shrouded sea in search of others. Like angels of mercy they pulled on the oars hour after hour without thought of food or rest. They picked up 30 persons from makeshift rafts and pieces of wreckage.

Other boats were also sent out from the *Anyox*. Before the night was over 96 passengers and 70 crew members answered the survivors' roll call. Some were burned or injured and nearly all were soaked with oil. Among the survivors was a five-year-old girl who had clung to a piece of wreckage for eight hours. Another survivor, an 18-year-old girl who had been crushed between the lifeboat and the liner, had somehow remained afloat until the rescue boat arrived.

Eventually the tug *Ranger* arrived from Eureka to pilot the *Anyox* over Humboldt Bar. Red Cross teams and city volunteers were waiting to care for the survivors. The city opened its heart. Hospitals, charitable institutions and churches threw open their doors.

On August 9, 1921, a coroner's jury was convened and a study of the disaster undertaken. At that time, 17 bodies lay in the morgue awaiting identification. Scores were as yet unaccounted for. The jury returned a verdict that death was caused by drowning, because the *Alaska* struck Blunts Reef and sank, "precipitating passengers and crew into the sea . . ."

Testimony from many survivors was bitter, placing much of the blame on the ship's officers. Charges of negligence were intermingled with accolades of heroism. The case rested pretty much the same way it began.

The day following the jury's adjournment most of the passengers left for their homes. At the scene of the wreck only the tip of one of the *Alaska's* masts broke the water's surface. Below, in the glowering depths was the grim shadow of the ship.

The remainder of the story was statistics only. The 327-foot liner was on the bottom, beyond all hope of salvage. The final tally—166 survivors; 42 dead and missing.

Chapter Ten

CAPE MENDOCINO TO POINT BONITA

FROM Cape Mendocino south, offshore maritime traffic is heavy, for it is the main sea road to and from San Francisco and other major ports. Fog is all too frequent in this area and has caused the destruction of many fine ships.

COLUMBIA AND SAN PEDRO

On the night of July 20, 1907, the passenger liner *Columbia* was bound for Puget Sound from San Francisco. Off Shelter Cove, south of Mendocino Cape, a ship's whistle was heard off the starboard bow. The night was black and filtered with patches of fog so that a constant watch had been kept on the bridge. Captain Peter Moran stood intently next to the quartermaster, listening. Suddenly the running lights of the nearby ship came into view and immediately the engines were thrown in reverse. The ship trembled violently, as she was full ahead at the time the ship's telegraph made its arc. The frantic exchange of whistle signals and the hasty maneuvering on the part of both ships could not prevent disaster. The other vessel plunged squarely into the side of the *Columbia*. Captain Moran scurried down the bridge ladder to learn that he had been rammed by the steam schooner *San Pedro*, fully laden with lumber. The collision was no brush, but a mortal wound, a gash 30 feet abaft the *Columbia's* stem on the starboard side. Water poured in unchecked. The liner was going down. As the boats were being lowered the steamer careened sharply and within five perilous minutes she slid beneath the surface. It was a nightmare for the 200 passengers. Few of the boats had hit the water when the ship went down. The *Columbia* was carrying a total of 249 persons. So quickly did the sinking occur that many of the ship's company were carried down with the ship without ever stepping foot on deck. The terrible agonizing cries were wafted over the black stretches of sea like a cloud of living death. Only Satan could know the suffering and anguish enacted as the *Columbia* dropped into the depths. Overturned lifeboats; bleeding, shattered corpses; stumbling, fighting, clawing persons grabbing life jackets or attempting to reach their loved ones as the decks beneath their feet were flooded with the inrushing water. Passageways were jammed; lifeboats swung in their davits; furniture, dishes and silverware went scudding across the dining salon. Then the ship's final plunge and the sea bespeckled with the black forms of men, women and children fighting to keep their faces above the eternal maelstrom.

A little girl of 12, a brave heroine, kept another small girl from drowning and helped an injured man remain afloat for an hour before rescue came. Some of the men removed their life jackets in the water and passed them to women and children while others fought for a grip on an overturned lifeboat or a hunk of wreckage.

Nor were things well aboard the *San Pedro*. She had lost her mainmast, the cutwater was battered, and her seams were letting in a generous portion of the Pacific. Her deck load of railroad ties and fence posts were swathed with a green film of sea water. She was that low and to all intents and purposes was kept afloat only by the buoyancy of her cargo.

As the *San Pedro* struggled to keep from sinking, swarms of survivors from the *Columbia* descended on her atop anything that would float. Never was there such a hodgepodge of maritime miscellany as drifted about above the grave of the *Columbia*. As the disabled *San Pedro* floundered about, some 70 survivors of the liner were taken aboard, adding more weight and more grief to a small 400-ton lumber carrier. As she drifted away from the scene of the wreck, the SS *George W. Elder*, answering the calls of distress, searched the scene and picked up 88 survivors. Other ships also arrived but, though they searched far and wide and checked every floating object, no other survivors were located. Company officials dejectedly set the grim list of dead and missing at 87, one of the most tragic shipwrecks ever recorded along the California coast.

The *San Pedro* was ultimately towed into port, but the *Columbia* had gone down in deep water beyond any chance of salvage. She had long been a popular passenger liner on the coast and carried the proud distinction of having been the first ship (1880) to be equipped with electric lights.

As in every major disaster, the decision of the Board of Inquiry was awaited with anxiety. The outcome was no surprise. A final ruling placed blame on the masters of both vessels, but more so on the mate of the steam schooner, who was accused of following an erratic course. He was deprived of his license for five years. The master of the *San Pedro* was charged with not being on the bridge during dangerous weather, despite having been summoned by the watch officer. Captain Moran of the *Columbia* was charged with operating his vessel at excess speed during poor visibility but he could not attend the hearing, having gone down with his ship.

DONNA MARIA

It was fog, thick and unyielding, that plagued the entire coast of northern California on that weary 23rd day of May, 1854. The Swedish brig *Donna Maria* plodded her way southward laden with 17,000 feet of piles for San Francisco. She was six days out of her port of departure, Sooke, B. C., and for three days Captain Sampson had been unable to get an observation, let alone tell the mainmast from the foremast, so thick was the shroud. Each helmsman held to the prescribed course which even the master admitted was a guess.

Until the fog had closed in on the *Donna Maria,* she had logged a creditable run but now speed was no longer a factor.

"Breakers ahead!" shouted the watch in his Swedish tongue. Before the wheel could be put hard over, the brig scraped over a ledge of rocks and heaved crazily.

The captain's predicament was a fearful one. It was shocking to him to drive men to such extreme lengths. Yet he had no choice. He had to get his ship free or it would be a total loss and maybe the end of each of them. The ship was pounding itself to death. There was seepage everywhere. At each crash of the liquid whips, the crew felt as if their nerves would snap. They were glad to be busily occupied jettisoning deck gear and dumping the deck load of piling. Finally the masts had to be chopped away.

The brig lifted itself momentarily and was carried over the ledge of rock further inshore. There was nothing more the crew could do. Hope of saving the vessel was gone. They must now think only of saving themselves. The *Donna Maria* had been hurled into the inner breakers and was in a position where all hands had an even break of gaining the shore. But just where the shore was and what it looked like was unknown to them, for the fog had not lifted its heavy veil one iota.

At Captain Sampson's command, a boat was swung over the lee side and after a hectic surf ride all hands, well immersed, staggered up on the beach.

By morning the seas had thoroughly demolished the wreck. Captain Sampson and his men stood on the beach still enveloped in fog. It was a lonely beach, void of all habitation. There was only one alternative—to start walking. And that is just what they did. For more than 30 hours, almost non-stop, they tramped over dunes, rocks, and hills, till weary and footsore they reached the little settlement of Bodega. Here they fell in with Captain Fitch of the schooner *Sovereign,* who gave them transportation back to San Francisco.

So thick had the fog been at the time of the wreck that Captain Sampson did not learn of the exact spot where he lost his command until nearly a year later. Forty miles south of Cape Mendocino was the location, a place where numerous ships came to grief in the following decades.

ALLIANCE No. 2

An old Gloucester power schooner, several times removed, transferred, sold, and seized for poaching, came to a dismal ending on Malpass Rock, six miles north of Point Arena on October 17, 1915.

The vessel in question passed into oblivion almost unnoticed, for the name gracing her bows was not the one by which she had so long been known. Her last given title, of perhaps a few weeks' standing, was *Alliance No. 2*. Her maiden name, *Charles Levi Woodbury*, bequeathed at her launching in Essex, Massachusetts, in 1889, had stuck until just before her fatal voyage.

After ten years in the codfishing business on the east coast, the 105-ton vessel came to the Pacific and operated out of San Francisco, Honolulu, and Seattle, carrying so many fish that her timbers were well seasoned with rock salt.

After being seized on many occasions for poaching, she was kicked around like an old man's shoe. In 1914 we find her at Port Townsend, being sold to satisfy creditors by the U. S. Marshal. Next she turned up at Victoria, B. C., where her new owners found a profitable source for a resale to Jean Abila of Mexico. He lined up a crew and departed the Canadian port for Mexico in early October 1915. Captain Delouchry was in command and, including the owner, ten persons were aboard. Destination was Guaymas, Mexico, where the *Alliance No. 2* was to return to the fishing banks. But the tired old gas schooner never reached her goal. At 2 a.m. in the bleak hours of October 17, she fell into a persistent wall of fog. She piled up on Malpass Rock near Point Arena, and every timber in her was started. Her years told on her as the sea combers made a clean breach of her sodden decks.

There was no time for organized escape. Not even the sound of a command. The lifeboat broke loose and plummeted crazily into the seething mass of fury. Every man was left to fight for his life. The odds were stacked mightily against them and only two managed to see the dawn of a new day. Eight, including the captain and the new owner, went down, and the meanderings and vicissitudes of the old wooden, two-master, ended abruptly.

DUNKERQUE

The foremost thing in this episode is not the shipwreck but rather the story of the biggest white elephant fleet that ever sailed the seas. The shipwreck is secondary, but a typical example of the waste of millions of dollars in ships that were never worth their salt.

It was the frantic years of World War I. Tonnage had been depleted by German U-boats and the United States as well as her allies were crying for cargo ships to replace those already sunk or pressed into direct war service. It had to be a ship that could be turned out in assembly line production at a modest cost. For this reason one of the outstanding marine phenomena of World War I was the construction on the West Coast of wooden sailing vessels and low-powered auxiliaries. The story of this fleet was an unfortunate one, a fleet that virtually passed into oblivion within a few years after the Armistice. Only a handful of the wooden vessels turned out between 1916 and 1920, were able to survive as factors in ocean trade after 1922, and in their brief and hectic existence they left a sour taste on the tongues of their owners.

One of the most profitable of the wooden shipbuilders of that period was the Foundation Yard, a corporation specializing in the construction of bridge piers, factory foundations, and mine shafts. When they entered shipbuilding early in the war it came through their contacts for construction ways at existing shipyards. This led to a contract with the Emergency Fleet Corporation in 1917 for ten wooden Ferris-type hulls which they built at a yard in Kearney, New Jersey. They next landed orders for twenty 3000-ton and five 2800-ton wooden steamers for the British and French governments which were built at Point Hope and Point Ellice, British Columbia. An additional contract with the French Government was also secured for forty 3000-ton steam auxiliary five-masted wooden schooners, divided between yards established at Tacoma, Wash., and at Portland, Oregon, for better insurance against fire or labor difficulties. In other yards spread throughout the United States, the Foundation Company built barges, minesweepers, and small auxiliaries, the total sum of their wartime contracts amounting to over $200,000,000.

Like the Portland yard, the Tacoma yard was actually owned by the French Government and operated by the corporation under the direction of Cox & Stevens, naval architects of New York. The 20 vessels built at the Tacoma yard, of which the *Dunkerque* was one, were nearly all named for French battlefields. They were 260-foot, five-masted schooners with a pair of triple expansion coal-burning steam engines, driving twin screws. They carried two smoke stacks, one on either side of the fifth mast. The engine contracts were divided between three sizable East Coast shipbuilding companies and machine works.

Inasmuch as these ships, for the main part, were to relieve the North Atlantic tonnage situation, they sailed for France immediately on completion. The record of their voyages was a continuous series of engine and boiler troubles, storm damage, leaks. Added to this they carried inexperienced officers and crew members. Faulty navigation and poor ship handling added to an already hopeless situation.

Such a vast fleet was never dispersed with such rapidity. Within a year or two of the Armistice most of those that still remained afloat had already had their worthless engines removed and were ultimately relegated to the junkyard. Even their yield of scrap was negative and the flaming torch was set to many of them without so much as a tear-filled eye.

The *Dunkerque* was the sixth schooner turned out at

A plaything in the breakers ten miles north of Point Arena, California.
Steam schooner *Alcatraz* wrecked May 2, 1917.

Port of no return. Steam schooner *Merced* aground at Point Gorda, California, October 15, 1913.

Tanker *Lyman Stewart* battered by the surf off Point Lobos, near the Golden Gate in 1922. She was left there to die.

Tanker *Frank H. Buck* which came home to die alongside her sister ship the *Lyman Stewart*, at Point Lobos (near San Francisco's Cliff House) in 1937.

SS *Ohioan* broke in three sections after stranding near Point Lobos at Land's End, California in October 1936. (Fred Meyer Photo)

Sinister scene—dim outline of sunken Navy hospital ship *Benevolence* off the Golden Gate. Sunk in collision with SS *Mary Luckenbach*. Twenty-three lives lost, August 25, 1950.

Steam schooner *Flavel* ashore off Point Carmel, on the Monterey Coast, December 15, 1923.
She sailed no more. (collection of Roy Graves)

Total loss at Point Gorda, California—SS *St. Paul*, October 5, 1905. Sixty-one were rescued.

the Tacoma yard. She was launched on July 4, 1918. After completion, she cleared for San Francisco en route to Peru and then Europe. But after leaving Puget Sound her record became vague, for next we find her dashed up on the beach near Point Arena, California. That's as far as she got on her maiden voyage. War secrecy clouded all of the details of the wreck but one can fill in between the lines. An awkward five-masted schooner, with a faulty engine, an inexperienced crew, and green lumber in her hull.

It was indeed a sad day for the French Government when it ordered those 40 white elephants.

KLAMATH

It was just plain black fury on the night of February 4, 1921. A driving gale born in the Arctic wastes had swept down the entire Pacific Coast carrying with it terrific winds of mixed snow and rain. Distress calls were heard at regular intervals from positions off the Washington, Oregon, and California coasts. The Coast Guard was being run ragged. It was on this storm-swept night that the steam schooner *Klamath* was battling terrific seas while en route to Portland from San Francisco. She was riding in ballast which made her light and susceptible to the wild ocean.

Captain Thomas Jamieson had turned the watch over to third mate A. Arneson and had gone below to catch a wink of badly-needed sleep. When he left the bridge, the wind was blowing about 25 knots and the glass was dropping steadily. The captain knew he would be aroused within a few hours and accordingly took advantage of the interval for some shuteye.

The helmsman peered out through the pilothouse windows into a blanket of driving rain and pitch darkness. He looked over at the mate but received little more than a perceptible lowering of the eyebrows.

Within two hours the wind was scudding over the Pacific at a 75-knot clip and the buffeted *Klamath* was slowed to a crawl to keep her from hammering herself to pieces.

Suddenly the lookout yelled, "Breakers ahead!" Even before the wheel could be spun hard over, the steam schooner smashed into a rock off Del Mar Landing, south of Point Arena, and reeled from the shock.

Captain Jamieson made a wild dash to the bridge and ordered full astern. The engine ground out its reverse spiral but the ship had lodged itself on another rock, knocking out the propeller and tail shaft. An SOS was promptly sent out by the wireless operator and the captain mustered the passengers and crew members on deck to prepare for the worst.

Then came a breath of good news. The frantic key punching of the wirelessman had brought results. The steamships *Curacao,* and the *Everett,* sistership to the *Klamath,* had altered course and were coming at top speed. The Coast Guard motor lifeboat was also battling her way through tremendous seas to reach the stricken ship.

Yes, help was coming from every direction but could the *Klamath* hold together until aid arrived? Lowering her boats in such a sea would be suicidal.

The situation grew more desperate and the rescue ships had yet to be sighted. The *Klamath* trembled violently from stem to stern with each plunging sea. It was a touch-and-go situation on which the odds were lengthening. Then like an angel sent from heaven, a volunteer, a sea-man named Charles Svenson, with a lifejacket and a line, swam ashore against almost insurmountable odds and succeeded with the help of others in setting up a breeches buoy.

It was then that the evacuation of the passengers got under way. Some were hesitant, but finally decided there was no other way out. Then a problem arose—an 18-month-old child. How could they get it ashore? Finally one of the ship's crew came up with a brilliant but strange solution. This inventive-minded seaman tied a gar-bage can to his back, placed the infant within and rode the breeches buoy ashore. The small lad was deposited on the beach asleep, undisturbed by the commotion about him.

Meanwhile the *Curacao* and the *Everett* hove to, but were kept well away from the wreck for fear of joining her in her death agonies. Then, too, the wireless operator on the wreck had been ordered ashore by Captain Jamieson and there was no communication between the ships.

After all hands had gained the shore, via breeches buoy, the *Klamath* was left to ride out the gale. When at last the wind subsided she appeared to be holding her own. Would-be salvagers little knew that her back was ready to snap. Then came another big blow to raise still more lunging seas. The *Klamath* broke in two, but her stern, still intact, remained impaled on the rock. Her forward section drifted in behind the rocks. There's not much more to tell. Within a short time all that remained of either section was a mass of strewn timbers and unrelated bits of marine miscellany.

There was one casualty—Snookums, the ship's cat, which had taken the order of abandonment too seriously and had gone over the seaward rail never to come up again.

SAN AGUSTIN

The first recorded shipwreck on the Pacific Coast, north of the Mexican border, was that of the Spanish galleon *San Agustin*, under the shadow of California's Point Reyes north of San Francisco, in 1595.

Near the close of the sixteenth century, Spain became greatly disturbed for the safety of her rich galleons plying the Manila trade. Within a decade of Sir Francis Drake's fabulous voyage, Thomas Cavendish, intent on plunder, hove to off Cabo de San Lucas in the *Desire*. The large galleon *Santa Ana*, the most treasure-laden ship ever to depart the Philippines, was captured and plundered by the Englishman after a furious five-hour battle. The loss of thousands of marcos of gold; 22 arrobas of musk; an abundance of civet; many priceless

227

pearls; and the finest silks and brocades, brought the strongest protests from merchants in Manila, Acapulco, and Cadiz. A persistent plea arose for Spain at all costs to establish harbors and anchorages where galleons might find refuge from the ruthless attacks of the ships and men of piratical intent.

In response to this plea, Captain Sebastian Cermenon was issued orders in 1594 to "chart all harbors homeward." After a passage across the Pacific, Cermenon brought his command, the *San Agustin,* to anchorage in Drakes Bay under the shadow of Point Reyes. Most of the ship's complement had gone ashore to begin work on a small boat with which to chart the indentations and bays along the coast. Then, with a frightening suddenness a flash southwester struck the coast, preventing the men from returning to their ship. Only a few still remained aboard the galleon. The storm blew with unabating fury and, despite her several anchors, the unwieldy vessel began dragging toward the rocky shore. The frantic souls aboard were helpless and could only hang on and await the crash.

In the *San Agustin*'s holds was a precious cargo of porcelain, silks, and beeswax. As night came on she straddled a reef of rocks. Her bottom was ripped out and she was brutally twisted and gnarled by the roaring surf. The cargo was a total loss, and most of those aboard perished.

Cermenon was greatly depressed , but he rallied his men to finish building the small open survey boat and then sailed south. Before he departed, however, several of his crew deserted and sought escape overland. They reached Mexico with the fabulous story of the great landlocked harbor heretofore undiscovered and capable of holding all the ships in the world in protective surroundings. They listed their discovery at 38 degrees and in all probability had discovered San Francisco Bay. Their claim was not generally accepted, however, and considerable time elapsed before the renowned bay was "officially" discovered.

Meanwhile Cermenon continued south after giving the name *La Bahia de San Francisco* to the bight that arched from Point Reyes to low-lying Point San Pedro. He sailed by the Farallon Islands, but failed to find the key to the Golden Gate which for so long defied the navigators and explorers.

In the wake of the loss of the *San Agustin*, the King of Spain decreed that all cargo-laden galleons returning from the Philippines should refrain from engaging in exploration and survey missions. Thereafter the smaller caravels and carracks performed these duties. Carlos III of Spain was determined to build a great stronghold in the western world, north of Mexico, for everywhere the supremacy of Spain was being both challenged and threatened.

LABOUCHERE

In early April 1866 the sidewheel steamer *Labouchere* owned by the Hudson's Bay Company, departed San Francisco for Victoria, B. C., with about 85 passengers and a crew of 15. In addition, she carried the mails and general cargo. In command of Captain William Mouatt, she passed through the Golden Gate, heaving and rolling at a snail's pace in a dense fog that had blanketed the entire California Coast. The *Labouchere* had just completed a $30,000 major overhaul and drydocking at the Bay City and was considered shipshape in every way.

The fog continued thick and shadowy. The steamer's course became erratic and, unbeknown to Captain Mouatt, the ship was drifting into hazardous Drakes Bay. It was on the evening of April 3 that she struck a ledge of rock near Point Reyes. After a few frantic moments she backed off and steamed out toward open water. Keeping ahead of a resultant leak, she floundered about like a lost sheep until 5 the following morning when the captain was informed that another leak had developed. The pumps had been going around the clock, but by 5:30 a.m. two feet of water was reported in the engine room. A few minutes later all hands were summoned topside and efforts to save the steamer abandoned.

In orderly fashion Captain Mouatt ordered the boats

lowered away with strict command that women and children be placed in the first boats. While this was being carried out a frantic male passenger standing on the fringe of the waiting passengers panicked and made a dash for the lifeboat.

"Stop where you are or I'll shoot!" shouted the captain. The man refused to yield and the gun was fired point blank. Several of the crew grabbed the wounded man and flung him aside until the women and children could get their proper places.

The evacuation procedure continued until eight boats had been lowered away. The last boat to clear capsized near the steamer and the ship's cook and a passenger were drowned. The other boats all reached shore safely.

Twenty-three remained aboard the wreck, including Captain Mouatt. Toward evening the situation became serious due to the pounding breakers. The steamer gave signs of breaking up. As if it were a wishful apparition, an Italian fishing smack suddenly appeared from out of nowhere and removed all hands just 30 minutes before the entire upper deck cabin was swept into the sea.

At 8:15 the following morning the steamer rolled sharply to one side, crushing her sidewheel and paddlebox. Then she gave a mighty thrust forward and went to the bottom bow first. Down with her went the mails and her general cargo.

As the passengers were transported back to the Bay City, the story of the *Labouchere* was being told far and wide, for here was a steamer which in the space of eight years had made Pacific Coast history. She came to the coast from London, England, where after her construction at Green's, Blackwall, in 1858, she entered the service of the Hudson's Bay Company. The cumbersome 202-foot vessel was fitted with two giant sidewheels with oscillating engines of about 180 horsepower, and had two giant smokestacks which gave her the appearance of being top-heavy. She was bark-rigged, in addition to her steam power. Immediately after arriving at Victoria in 1859 she was pressed into the coasting service, trading mainly with the Indians. During the next few years she had some very narrow escapes at the hands of hostile natives. Here is a page from her logbook of Saturday, August 2, 1862, while she was anchored at Hoonah, Alaska:

> Crew employed tending the gangways and trading. Indians very troublesome and numerous. From appearances expected a disturbance. At 10:30 a.m. Indians refused to trade sea otter skins under a very exorbitant figure. At 11:00 a.m. lit fires and prepared to get underway. At 1:00 p.m. the chief of the lower village came on board, and all Indian women left the ship. After much discussion and anger, from the Sitka Indians especially, they refused to trade and forced the gangway. Captain John Swanson (master of the *Labouchere*) and Mr. Compton each being seized by about thirty Indians armed with knives, guns and clubs, were instantly disarmed, about three-hundred savages rushing on deck. By order of the captain, the chief officer placed the men under arms with rifles, revolvers and swords, and succeeded in keeping the Indians aft at the point of the bayonets, but dared not fire as it would be the signal for the instant death of the captain and the trader. Ordered the crew forward and trained two cannon aft loaded with grape and cannister which enabled us, after much discussion and with great forbearance on the part of the crew, to effect a parley, and both sides agreed to discharge arms in the air, our men on the bridge and the Indians on the quarterdeck. On the Indians giving two sea otter skins and the chiefs expressing their contrition, many of them departed, taking the revolvers of the captain and Mr. Compton and retaining possession of them. To please the natives the captain and the trader entered the chief's canoe and paddled around the harbor amidst singing etc. At 10:00 p.m. succeeded in getting rid of all of the Indians without violence by

allowing the interpreter to go ashore with them for two or three hours . . ."

On receiving a hint that the Hoonah chief was planning a resumption of hostilities the following day, the vessel stole away under full steam at 3 a.m. the following morning, thus averting a bloody battle.

The *Labouchere* continued in the trade until the end of 1865 when a grant of a subsidy of $1500 a trip was made by the Crown Colony. The steamer was to carry the mails between Victoria and San Francisco, which began her brief role in the coastwise passenger service. The rest has been told, for on her first voyage north she came to grief on the jagged fangs of Point Reyes.

BREMEN

The Farallon Islands off the entrance to the Golden Gate are a desolate group of isolationists. Few Californians have ever seen them, let alone walked over their rocky contour. Their destructive qualities as far as commerce is concerned have kept ships at a safe distance since the beginning. These offshore monoliths, less than 10 miles from the mainland, were responsible for the delayed discovery of the Golden Gate by early mariners.

Most important of this useless sprinkling of rocky bastions is the Southeast Farallon. It is honored by having a lighthouse crowning its summit—Farallon Light. It's the only man-made object thereabouts that has weathered the test of time. But there's a reason for the light. Ships have frequently fouled themselves on the Farallons in the pea-soup fogs that abound there. The ship *Lucas* was lost on the Island on November 9, 1858, with her entire crew of 23. In 1882, the ship *Franconia* was lost at Breaker Cove and her crew escaped by the skin of their teeth. The ship *Bremen* struck the south shore directly under the fog whistle in 1883, and thereby hangs a tale. This was not an unusual shipwreck nor was loss of life sustained. But there was one outstanding factor involved—she was carrying a full cargo of Scotch whiskey. The crew took to the boats until the fog lifted. It lifted all right, but when it did the *Bremen* had vanished.

It had slipped off the rocky ledge and gone down in deep water.

Since liquor could not be purchased on the open market in those years the estimated value of the cargo reached staggering figures. The loss of the Scotch on the rocks was mourned far more than the loss of the ship. It was as though a bolt of lightning had struck San Francisco. The Barbary Coast went dry.

Word of the whiskey disaster reached every grog shop and saloon from San Diego to Eureka within the week. The bottom of the sea was full of "firewater." The ultimate outcome was a hovering of small craft of many sizes and descriptions about the Southeast Farallon waiting for something to pop to the surface. Nor did the anxiety die out with the passing years. In 1929, T. H. P. Whitelaw, one of the coast's top salvage masters, got interested in the case after reading the ship's manifests. He engaged a San Francisco diver to make an underwater search but before negotiations were completed the men seemed to have lost their "spirits." Maybe it was because Uncle Sam got wind of the scheme—remember those prohibition days?

The temperance groups were happy about the whole thing, but it is often said that mariners, when they pass the grave of the *Bremen,* still lick their lips at the thought of a cask of 80-year old whiskey bobbing to the surface.

PRINCE ALFRED

When the steamship *Prince Alfred* departed her San Francisco pier for Victoria in June of 1874, she had among her cargo $25,623 in gold being shipped by Wells Fargo, the property of several banks. The ship also carried 94 tons of hides and various general cargo. Then of course there were passengers. The Rosenfeld & Bermingham Line ship, an English built iron bottom, ran into a dense fog as she threaded her way through the

Golden Gate. Captain Sholl, in command of the steamer, was traveling at excessive speed. The ship drifted too close to the inshore and crashed on dreaded Duxbury Reef, near Potato Cove, six miles north of the Bay City. That was on June 14. She slid off the reef but would have been better off to have remained fast. A gaping hole had been torn in her hull and water poured in. In spite of the maximum output of all the pumps, the water within 28 minutes had risen to such a degree that there was three feet in the engine room. A sail was broken out of the locker and placed over the hole, but it proved worthless. Captain Sholl then ordered Chief Engineer McDermott to give her every last ounce of steam in a frantic dash for the shore. The passengers hung on like frightened sheep as the vessel made its desperate run at speeds it had never before exceeded. As the water reached up to the boiler door the old *Prince* struck the rocks in a cove about 300 yards from the beach with a mighty impact which did no damage to the rock but went far in polishing off the veteran steamer once and for all.

All hands were very orderly in their abandonment of the ship, but the priority item appeared to be the removal of the gold. As in so many wrecks, in the hasty departure, the gold is left to go down with the ship. But not so with the *Prince Alfred's* gold. It was the very first thing removed. Next came the passengers, the mail, the crew, and finally the captain. And the steamer—well, she had reached her last port. But she was auctioned off and the gavel went down on the sum total of $350. When the lucky bidder went out to see his prize he found her over on her beam ends, shorn of everything useful.

Prince Alfred's face would have been red if he could have seen the way his namesake ended it all. And it's also too bad for the treasure divers. Not much use searching for the wreck unless one should be in the market for several tons of slightly watersoaked hides, three-quarters of a century old, plus the age of the cows from which they originated.

HANALEI

A ghostly stillness surrounds the remains of the wreck of any ship. Discarded and teredo-eaten planks, rusted fittings, sodden decking and dank caverns, all instill a quietude in the curious examiner. There were such remains that came ashore near Duxbury Reef, California, many years ago. They held the riddle to the loss of the steam schooner *Hanalei*.

This ship, her decks laden with lumber, was steaming down to San Francisco from Eureka on the morning of November 23, 1914. There was considerable activity aboard the 600-ton steamer, for in addition to her complement of 26, she carried 34 passengers, several head of cattle, some sheep, and a couple of porkers.

The vessel was five miles offshore, fighting a choppy sea through patches of fog and rain. Shortly before eight bells, the ship's captain, J. J. Carey, found a clear spot and had a good landfall on Point Reyes. The watches were set and all appeared to be routine.

Then came the fog, thick, heavy, billowy. In accordance with the captain's instructions, the vessel should have been well on her course, nor was there any reason that the helmsman should have altered the course. But for some undetermined reason the steam schooner was attracted to the shore. No indication was given until the bow watch shouted, "Breakers!" Instantly the ship responded to the order of full astern and warily backed away from the shallow water just a moment before running up on a reef.

The vibrating ship, struggling for another chance, brought the skipper and the mate running to the bridge, but this time there was no hole in the fog and no way to take a sight on the shore. By dead reckoning Captain Carey believed he was near the Golden Gate.

The *Hanalei* steamed about in aimless circles as eyes peered and ears listened for something familiar. Occasionally the awesome sound of the breakers would find the helmsman spinning the wheel about to start the

235

steamer out toward deep water again. Her whistle was sounded as a warning to other vessels. There was such fear and anxiety aboard that nobody remembered to take any soundings. Suddenly the skipper ordered the vessel to stop dead in the water and everybody just listened. It was as if the ship had drifted off the edge of the world. It was silent. Not even the sound of another foghorn. Then as the steamer drifted in the eerie pall, once again the roar of breakers filled listening ears. The engines came to life quickly with a reverse thrust of the propeller.

Around and around went the steamer like a bewildered lamb that had strayed from the fold. It was like a game of blindman's buff, but even in a game there must be a conclusion. That conclusion was not a kind one. The *Hanalei* finally rammed into a reef off Duxbury Point, nine miles north of San Francisco. She was hung up by the stern and down by the head with the breakers performing their usual malicious acts. The *Hanalei* was finished, her shadowy silhouette now dimly visible to the men with the earphones at the nearby Marconi Wireless Station on Duxbury Point.

The news of a ship in distress reached San Francisco in the twinkling of an eye and the tugs *Defiance* and *Hercules* were immediately dispatched. Other ships picked up the message and altered their courses. The USS *Rainbow* and the steamer *Richmond* and the Coast Guard lifeboat from Fort Point were parting the seas in a mad dash to the vessel's side. The mere mention of a wreck on Duxbury Reef brought any and every ship within miles around, for the notorious reputation of this barrier was well established as a man killer.

A relief party was set up on the beach opposite the wreck with medical aid, food and coffee. A plane took off in search of the wreck with newsmen anxious to get a first hand story of the battle against the seas.

There was tense drama aboard the *Hanalei*. Captain Carey had all the crew and passengers huddled aft and each issued a life jacket. The line-throwing gun was broken out. With a heavy shot it soared toward the shore but fell short of the mark. With its one shot gone it rendered the gun useless. Then two seamen stepped forth and volunteered to swim ashore with a line. Heroes both—for no man hath greater love than to lay down his life for others. They were both drowned in the seething surf.

Because of the persistent fog, the tugs in search of the wreck were compelled to return to port. The airplane was no more successful and went back to the airport. The larger rescue ships stalled by the fog were prevented from getting anywhere near the *Hanalei* for fear of being ground on the rocks. Two big fish boats with shallow drafts attempted to run in close to the wreck but were thwarted by savage seas. The Coast Guard lifesaving crews did all in their power to get a line on the wreck even to the point of damaging their craft, taking the lives of two.

That the situation was beyond the ultimate in lifesaving know-how left little doubt. For more than 16 hours the *Hanalei* was torn apart piece by piece by the demanding ocean. Wreckage of all kinds and descriptions began washing ashore in the reflection of the strange glow of the fires burning on the beach. The flames issued a faint ray of hope to the despairing souls on the wreck.

But in the hopelessness of the situation landsmen wouldn't give up. A large Lyle gun with 2000 pounds of gear and a nine-man crew were rushed out to the scene from San Francisco. They were set up for action by 1:30 a.m. the following morning. The gun was fired from atop the 200-foot cliffs above the beach but line after line fell short of the mark. In a last-ditch effort, a line gun was placed on a raft and after suicidal attempts on the part of the lifesaving crews a line was finally landed on the wreck. It was hastily made fast and was the means of bringing the remaining survivors to safety.

Twenty-three lives were lost. Among the dead were 18 passengers, including several women and a baby girl. At the convening Board of Inquiry, Captain Carey assumed the blame and lost his license. The Board, however, showed leniency inasmuch as he had performed heroically in an attempt to save the lives of those aboard his vessel. The chilling aftermath of the wreck was not soon forgotten and Duxbury Reef was declared a no man's land in the book of every mariner who skirted its dreaded fangs.

Chapter Eleven

SAN FRANCISCO BAY AND THE GOLDEN GATE

C ALIFORNIANS have always done things in a big way even in the golden days of steamboat racing. But doing things in a big way unfortunately does not always mean using good sense along with it. As California highways today usually lead the nation in grim fatality statistics, so did their waterways once claim an overabundance of casualties due to neglect and carelessness.

Let us look back to the beginning of the golden era of steamboating between San Francisco and Sacramento. It was the spritely river steamer *New World* that opened the gates of rapid water transportation between the two ports in the spring of 1850 by astounding Californians with a run of five hours and 35 minutes. From that day forth it was a question of speed. Every boat was a competitor and when two met on any given course a race would ensue with no holds barred. Anything was allowed without regard for safety. It was winner take all.

In rapid sequence following the *New World's* triumph on the Sacramento River, the *Fawn* trying to fly over the water blew up on August 18, 1850, injuring many; the *Sagamore* was blown apart on October 29, killing 50 persons off the Stockton pier. On January 23, 1851, the steamer *Major Tompkins* exploded with dire results. Even the *New World,* trying to outdo herself, popped a steam line in Steamboat Slough, killing seven.

The following years brought a rash of needless killings and scaldings, all for the love of speed. Over a wager of a few moldy cigars the engineer of the steamer *R. K. Page* tossed a cask of oil into an overheated boiler in a contest with the challenging steamer *Governor Dana.* He got his increased steam all right and a resounding ex-

239

plosion that blew the insides out of the *Page,* taking three passengers along for the death ride.

The sidewheeler *Jenny Lind* on the San Francisco-Alviso Creek route shot skyward in 1853 with a loss of 31 lives. Then in the same year, with total disregard for safety rules, which were in truth non-existent, the river steamers *American Eagle, Stockton, Ranger,* and *Helen Hensley* all suffered major explosions with prodigal, nonchalant losses of lives.

SECRETARY

Since narratives of the numerous steamboat explosions on the rivers around San Francisco would in themselves fill a book. let the telling be limited to one of the more disastrous episodes.

On April 15, 1854, the steamboat *Secretary,* which had been fitted out with the engines from the ill-fated *Sagamore,* was involved in a dockside wager of a race before leaving San Francisco.

The captains of the respective steamers each claimed that his was the faster vessel. They agreed that there was only one way to settle it—full steam ahead.

The *Secretary* and her rival both pulled out of the dock at the precise moment and pointed their bows toward Sacramento. Their paddle wheels slapped at the water like the hands of an angry father spanking a naughty child. The *Secretary* was more than holding her own when between Brothers and Sisters Rocks in upper San Francisco Bay her boilers let go with a resounding blast. Sixteen passengers were killed outright and nearly everybody else aboard was seriously scalded. All of the hospitals in San Francisco were taxed to the limit. One after another the hospitalized succumbed to their burns and abrasions until the list of dead rose to 47.

At the inquiry following, it was learned that the *Secretary's* engineer, when the boiler could stand no more, grabbed an oar and, finding a fulcrum point, held the safety valve down with the blade end. That the man went free could only be attributed to a smart young lawyer who attested that the boiler was made of faulty iron . . . and certainly in those wild frontier years when it took months to get to the east coast, nobody was interested in tracing down the manufacturer.

Nor did the *Secretary* disaster teach the rivermen a lesson. The explosions, fires, and strandings continued at the same rapid pace. The river paddlers, *Chrysopolis, Contra Costa, J. A. McClelland, Yosemite, Julia,* and scores of others all blew themselves skyward on the Sacramento and San Joaquin rivers. But, then, if man disobeys the rules in any game he must pay the consequences. The consequences, in these instances, were a tombstone for many and the loss of limbs, sight and speech for countless others.

SAN RAFAEL

The sinking of the trim San Francisco Bay passenger steamer *San Rafael* is destined to live as long as people read books about the sea. It was this episode in the fall of 1901 that led to the opening of Jack London's celebrated novel, *The Sea Wolf*. He described it thus:

> The fog seemed to break away as if split by a wedge, and the bow of a steamboat emerged, trailing fog-wreaths on either side like seaweed on the snout of a leviathan. The vessels crashed!

When Jack jotted down these words he was passing through one of the quick phases of his life as an oyster pirate on San Francisco Bay.

It was on November 30, 1901, that the *San Rafael,* ferrying between Sausalito and San Francisco departed her Lombard Street Wharf. She pulled out into the stream 12 minutes late, loaded with commuters. A dense fog was draped over the bay. The entire waterway was like a spirit cloud haunted by the weird intonations of ship whistles. The *San Rafael* felt her way cautiously along, those in the pilothouse listening intently for a blast that might not have that faraway sound. They heard one all right, off Alcatraz Island, close by and deep throated. Nor was it an unfamiliar sound. There was no mistaking it as that of the commuter steamer *Sausalito*. There was no time for last-minute, course changes. The *San Rafael* took a punishing punch broadside. The *Sausalito's* bow ended up in her dining salon sending the surprised passengers scurrying like bees about a disturbed hive. The human mass scattered in disorganized retreat.

Both vessels were now in the process of going full astern but it would have been better if the *Sausalito* had kept her affixed position, for the gaping hole left in the *San Rafael's* side made her short for this world. As the hysterical passengers felt the ship settling beneath their feet they leaped frantically to the deck of the other steamer.

But there were brave souls on the sinking ship concerned about others than themselves. For instance the *San Rafael's* heroic fireman who dived into six feet of water in the engine room to bleed the boiler, averting an explosion which could have claimed many lives.

Topside it was all confusion. The passengers paid little attention to the ship's officers who were vainly attempting an orderly abandonment. Fortunately only four lost their lives. One survivor, a preacher of the Gospel, leaped aboard the *Sausalito*, ran up the ladder to her pilothouse, flung open the door, and began lecturing her skipper. "Why don't you blow your whistle oftener in this fog?" he indignantly demanded.

At that moment he was as welcome as Satan at the gates of St. Peter. "Save your sermon for Sunday morning," snapped the irate master of the *Sausalito*. "Right now we've got a rescue to perform."

Amid a few words of profanity the preacher beat a hasty retreat.

It took just 20 minutes for the *San Rafael* to go down. Twenty fathoms covered her grave. For two decades she was left to her repose. Then, on a July morning in 1921, the anchor of the liner *Matsonia* was raised from the bottom silt and there hanging to its fluke was part of the *San Rafael's* walking beam and the ornamented brass eagle that was mounted above her engine. For a brief moment the tragic event was revived.

PERALTA

Recently a visitor returning to San Francisco after a lapse of many years looked over the bay. "My God!" he exclaimed, "Look at those bridges." Then there was a moment of silence as he scanned the growing metropolis around the harbor. He shook his head. "What a shame," he continued, "Nearly all the ferryboats are gone. San Francisco will never be the same."

Though the fantastic bridges have speeded transportation and given San Francisco and environs twentieth century streamlining there are many of the more nostalgic variety of people who mourn the ending of one of San Francisco's romantic attributes.

Most ferries of the vast San Francisco fleet, once the largest in the world, were successfully operated but there was one that ran into a jinx and didn't overcome it until its gutted hull was sold and ushered away from the bay.

The vessel in question was the *Peralta*. Built by the Moore Shipbuilding Company at Oakland, she and her sister ferry the *Yerba Buena* were the dream of the Key System to revolutionize commuter traffic on San Francisco Bay. They pioneered these fast turbo-electric type ferries, which almost crowded the old walking-beam paddle-wheel shuttlers from the bay. Key System officials had embarked on a progressive note with their latest creations in offering unexcelled fast transportation.

One of these so-called dream boats was the *Peralta*, delivered March 15, 1927. Her sister ferry was turned out a month later. Big, and awesome with her blinding coat of orange paint, the 287-footer was powered with a 2600-horsepower engine. She was a double-ender; everything at one end had a duplicate at the opposite end. The only distinguishing marks between her fore and after parts were legends scrolled inside the pilothouse: Oakland End and San Francisco End. Those opposite ends were like prohibitive aliens. The Oakland end never touched the San Francisco wharf and the San Francisco end never felt the auto ramp on the Oakland side.

When the *Peralta* entered service in the late spring of 1927 she was a real innovation in bay travel. She was tops in her commuter role until a jinx descended on her. The designers of the *Peralta* and *Yerba Buena* had gone overboard in their desire to make them the best, even to the point of outguessing passengers by placing large salt-water ballast tanks at each end of the vessels. The after tank always remained in ballast to trim the ship when the surge of commuters pushed to the forward end to disembark. A sizable centrifugal pump in the engine room transferred the ballast while the ferry was lying in its slip at each terminal.

Somebody pulled a boner on February 17, 1928, and left the forward tank in ballast. The crowd surged forward anticipating the landing. The bow dipped deep into the brine and 30 persons were washed overboard, five of them drowning.

Needless to say, it was bad publicity and no time was lost in ripping out the ballast tanks. The ingenious invention of the ferry's creators turned out to be an article of calamity.

Following this unfortunate incident all went well with the *Peralta* until May 6, 1933, when a disastrous fire broke out at the Key System Terminals at Oakland. The flames leaped sky-high and every fire rig for miles around hurried to fight the conflagration. The *Peralta* was tied up at the slip and within minutes was completely engulfed. Those aboard had dispersed like frightened gazelles. There was no time nor manpower to get her away from the dock. She burned furiously. When at last the charred terminals and the *Peralta* cooled, the inspectors

244

waded about in the welter of wreckage to survey the damage. The pier was temporarily patched within four days but the *Peralta* had been gutted beyond recognition. Only her hull remained intact.

So it was goodby to San Francisco for the ill-fated *Peralta*. In a way the Key System hated to see her go. They disposed of her to the Puget Sound Navigation Company of Seattle, a little over a year later. The hull was towed to Puget Sound, and taken through the locks to Lake Washington where far-sighted P. S. N. officials had her rebuilt from the bare hull up. Renamed *Kalakala* (Chinook for Flying Bird) she became queen of the Black Ball Line, and the world's first streamlined ferry. Tourists found her name a tongue-twister but by any name the *Kalakala* was the most remarkable departure in ship design in a century, and it was a one-ferry publicity agent for the Puget Sound Country. Superstitious San Franciscans said that her jinx would continue. Granted—on the shake-down cruise her massive Busch-Sulzer diesels capable of 18 knots, broke just about every piece of glass in the ferry. The steel in her superstructure could have been heavier to eliminate vibration which has always been somewhat of a problem on the *Kalakala*. But the silver-painted shuttler more than proved herself. At this writing she has completed over two decades of operation on Puget Sound, on long runs, Seattle to Bremerton and across the open waters of Juan de Fuca Strait between Port Angeles and Victoria. She has given a remarkable account of herself and, except for a few minor bruises, has gone unscathed. The second phase of her life brought about her escape from a jinx. Now operated by the Washington State Ferries, she has been restored to much of her original splendor. She attracts the tourists but many of her daily clientele still prefer the conventional type of ferry.

Thanks to the building of the San Francisco Bay Bridges, Seattle became the recipient of many of its ferries. The State of Washington a few years back purchased the Puget Sound Navigation Company which is now the largest ferry line in the world. The *Kalakala* is still going strong, a unit of a fleet which through the years has had an unexcelled record without a single major accident.

BLAIRMORE

The British ship *Blairmore* arrived on San Francisco Bay in February of 1896, laden with coal. After discharging she lay idle at anchor, empty except for 260 tons of standing ballast. Because the bottom fell out of the charter market, the *Blairmore* tugged at her chains well into the spring of the year. On April 9, the big square-rigger was greeted by a squall driven on the wings of a southwest wind. Lying in an east-west direction, the flood tide caught her broadside and worked on her iron hull. Drawing little water and with her towering masts touching the clouds, conditions were just right to roll her over on her side. And that is precisely what happened. She heeled dangerously, and the nearby tug *Active* inbound with another sailing vessel, saw her dilemma, dropped her own charge, and hurried to the *Blairmore*'s side.

The assistance of the tug was flatly refused by Captain John Caw, master of the *Blairmore,* probably because he was afraid of salvage claims. While the tug stood by, the ship's fore, main and crossjack yardarms were dipping into the water, and then she went over, filling through her hatches.

Even as the *Blairmore* was careening over, the mate Thomas Ludgate and several seamen were in one of the holds, cleaning. They made a wild scramble for the hatch but in the process Ludgate was struck on the head by a floating capstan bar which was carried over the hatch coaming by the inrushing water. Another apprentice was struck by a flying plank and instantly killed.

Air imprisoned in the *Blairmore*'s hull kept her partly afloat, with only her bilge above water. Nobody knew in the suddenness of the accident how many were trapped in her hull nor how many had escaped. Boats from all ships in the harbor hurried to the scene. The men who had jumped free of the *Blairmore* were plucked from the water by boats from the British, Italian and American ships.

Imprisoned crew members still inside the hull could be heard hammering against her sides. This grotesque message brought men out from the Union Iron Works to cut a hole in her bottom plates. It was unfortunately assumed that the vessel was resting on the bottom. The workmen marked an 18-inch square on the *Blairmore's* hull and began swinging sledge hammers and chisels to cut almost through the iron plate. Then after repeated blows the lightly held plate was knocked in.

Immediately the massive hulk gave a decided lurch and a geyser of water shot several feet into the air. Water poured into the opening and came head-on with the escaping air. The workmen were rudely knocked from their perches. The ship settled deeper and the hammering of those still inside was silenced.

The smell of death hung over the wreck. Those who perished within the iron prison were the first mate, the sailmaker, two seamen, an apprentice, and a steward. The latter was trapped in the galley and drowned before he could unlatch the door on the upper side. Captain Caw, the second and third mates, and five crewmen escaped.

Even if the wreck had been considered not worth raising it would have been raised anyway. It constituted a hazard to navigation and as such was the object of a major salvage endeavor. After being refloated and patched in a costly undertaking, it was ushered to a nearby dock, pumps going constantly. As it rested at dockside idle and rusting, impetus was given to the weird tales that usually become synonymous with a death ship. The *Blairmore* was labeled a haunted vessel. Lights were reported moving about its sodden decks and clanking noises emanating from its hull like those of the trapped men hammering on its sides.

One story is told of the dock watchman who on hearing these weird noises from the *Blairmore's* hold went aboard to investigate. As he lowered his lantern into the open hatch the flame suddenly went out. He scrambled over the gunwales like a man 25 years his junior and was never seen about the dock again.

To put the casual reader at ease, the bodies were recovered and given proper burial, but of course this did not lay the ghostly wraiths rumored to be haunting the vessel.

The ghosts, however, were to have company. The haunted *Blairmore* was given a new lease on life. Accepted under American registry and completely renovated, she returned to the sealanes as the *Abby Palmer* and later as the Alaska Packers' *Star of England*. She continued to carry evidences of her alias as inscribed on her capstan and bell. And what eventually became of her? Well, like many of the old square-riggers, she was reduced in the age of steam and diesel to the ignominious role of a sawdust barge in British Columbia waters.

PARALLEL

On January 14, 1887, the schooner *Parallel* weighed anchor in San Francisco Bay. Her destination was Astoria, but she didn't make it. She didn't even get out of the Golden Gate.

In her holds, in addition to her general cargo, she carried 100,000 pounds of giant powder. Need it be said that fifty tons of super dynamite packs a mighty punch should one ever be so foolish as to touch it off.

As the 148-ton vessel reached the Pacific she was met at once by strong headwinds, which forced her return. The captain had no desire to take any chances with his load of dynamite. While he lay in wait off Point Lobos, the wind suddenly subsided and the swift currents began carrying the schooner toward shore. The anchors were let out but too late and the schooner was carried ashore at the south end of Point Lobos near Seal Rocks.

The wreck was in full view of tourists at the Cliff House. They could even see the captain and crew abandon in the ship's boat. Little did they know that the vessel was in imminent danger of exploding due to the wave action. The survivors tried to land on a nearby beach to warn others of the peril, but the breakers were too high, forcing them to row into the bay. They landed at Sausalito.

Word did not travel fast in those days, and nobody at the Cliff House yet knew the contents of the *Parallel's* cargo.

In the interim lifesaving crews came out to examine the wreck but the surf had grown in magnitude and they made no attempt to reach it, since nobody was aboard.

Unaware of the danger of exploding dynamite, three members of the lifesaving crew took posts on the beach to prevent looting of the abandoned ship. Night came on and toward midnight there was a slight rumble aboard the schooner and then a mighty explosion. The *Parallel* was blown into a million pieces with such a concussion that windows for miles around were shattered.

The guards who had remained at their posts were painfully injured. The props were knocked out from under the Cliff House and one side of it torn wide open. Pieces of the cliff slid into the ocean. Other buildings, including the signal station and the concert hall, were demolished. Pieces of the schooner were found nearly a mile from the scene of the explosion. Many persons were injured but none fatally, which was nothing short of a miracle.

CITY OF RIO DE JANEIRO

San Francisco's most appalling shipwreck was that of the Pacific Mail steamer *City of Rio de Janeiro*. For many decades the people of the bay area had been aware of the maritime hazards at their front door. Pea soup fogs and strong currents were all too apparent in their otherwise unsurpassed landlocked harbor. Yes, they had been aware of these hazards but it took the wreck of the *Rio de Janeiro* to shock them into the reality of better guarding their waterways. Nothing, with the exception of

249

the San Francisco earthquake of 1906, has so left its mark on the city by the Golden Gate.

The *Rio de Janeiro* was feeling her way toward San Francisco on the morning of February 22, 1901. The fog was wool thick. Visibility was zero. Captain William Ward paced the bridge, the quartermaster gripped the wheel, and lookouts were spaced generously about staring blindly into a blank wall. Shortly after five o'clock, the liner, filled with passengers, neared the Golden Gate. Somewhere out there in the murk were the jagged rocks of Fort Point. The steamer was a little too far south on her course, and a few yards can be costly. They were now. As those on watch kept eyes and ears alert, some of the crew—anticipating docking at San Francisco—got out the hoses for the morning wash-down while passengers snoozed soundly after the gaiety of the frolic-filled night preceding.

Suddenly the shrouded images of Mile Rock, Land's End, and Fort Point loomed up blurred and eerie. With a terrific jolt the liner struck. It was a hard blow, a crippling, devastating blow. She backed slowly off as 200 half-clad passengers rushed up on deck, pushing and screaming. The steamer was going down fast amid the terse wail of her sonorous whistle and the sound of escaping steam.

There were 18 minutes to live. The screams of the panic-stricken women drowned out the orders of the officers who were trying desperately to restore a semblance of order and evacuate some of the passengers. Those boats that could be lowered, were overcrowded, smashed or crushed. The slanting decks were like insurmountable inclines. In the wild stampede men ran roughshod over women whose night clothes had been torn from their bodies. Children were screaming frantically for their parents. Fist fights broke out over life jackets. Some were peacefully praying, others hysterical on the threshold of death, scratching, clawing, weeping.

Then, as though the flood gates had been opened, torrents of water swept over the decks, dashing droves of humanity against the bulkheads. Then it was all over.

The *Rio de Janeiro* went down and, in the vortex, debris and bodies were spun around in a massive whirlpool.

At last, but almost too late came help. Boats moved in to pluck both struggling and still figures from the fog-filled acres. At Lands-End and on Point Lobos men waded waist deep into the water to grab mutilated bodies. At the final count there were but 81 survivors; 129 had perished, among them Captain William Ward who had bravely gone down with his ship.

Just why nobody knew, but for years after the sinking, the survivors met each February 22 to recall the horror of that disastrous occasion. Better they should have forgotten it, but San Francisco never has, to this day.

In the aftermath of the tragedy, fabulous reports of quantities of gold and silver estimated as high as $3,000,000 were reputed to have been lost with the liner. Though her manifests listed no treasure, the reports have persisted and numerous companies have sent divers down to find the ship's location. The quest has gone on through the years but not only has the treasure eluded the grasping hands of men, so also has the ship. It has never been found unless the report of diver Bill Wood can be considered authentic. He claims to have found her location by accident in 1937 while looking for another vessel. He said he identified her by a plate pried from one of her lifeboats which read, *"Rio de Janeiro,* capacity 20 persons."* He further said he had no intention of going back because he had seen her manifests, and knew there was nothing worth searching for.

And so, as the *Rio de Janeiro* is slowly reduced to a rusted mass, over her pass the ships of another era, the lifeblood of San Francisco.

LYMAN STEWART AND FRANK H. BUCK

This is the story of indisputable proof of the old proverb "truth is stranger than fiction." Though these incidents may be viewed retrospectively in the calm of in-

tervening years, none can deny that their outcome was almost uncanny.

The life cycle of the salmon is mysterious. They spawn in the upper reaches of some inland stream, and then swim out to the open sea, live their widely dispersed lives and—no matter how many miles distant in a vast ocean—they swim back, fighting every obstacle of the depths. They will enter the very same stream and buck insur mountable rapids, currents and even waterfalls to get back to the precise spot from which they originated; there to spawn. Similar to this wonder of nature was the tale of two oil tankers, one the *Lyman Stewart* and the other the *Frank H. Buck*. They were launched side by side at the Bethlehem Shipyards in San Francisco in 1914, and were similar in every respect. Built to the same specifications, they slid down the ways within a few days of each other and both entered their respective routes in the same business—petroleum transportation. The *Stewart* was owned by the Union Oil Company and the *Frank H. Buck* by the Associated Oil Company.

Both went their respective ways and served their owners well without major consequences until October 7, 1922, when the *Lyman Stewart* locked horns with the SS *Walter A. Luckenbach* in a fog off Point Lobos. Half submerged, she crashed ashore on the rocks just below the Cliff House. Her crew was rescued but the ship was abandoned where she lay—a total loss. Thus the first of the twin tankers had come home to die at the doorstep of the port where she had been launched eight years earlier.

The astounding part of the story is yet to come. The *Frank H. Buck* continued on her way transporting oil coastwise, transpacific, to South America and to the East Coast. She pursued her nomadic wanderings until the year 1937. Twice during the intervening period she suffered strandings—at Point Montara in 1919 and at Point Pinos in 1925. On one occasion she was refloated in spectacular touch-and-go salvage operations. . . . There seemed to be a reason. Then on March 3, 1937, without warning, she was struck in the fog off Point Lobos by the liner *President Coolidge,* at almost the identical spot where her sister tanker had been struck 15 years earlier. The tanker's crew were forced to take to the lifeboats. Efforts were made to tow the battered vessel to port but she refused to obey and drifted aimlessly toward shore. Finally she grounded, breaking in two and settling down within less than 50 feet of the *Lyman Stewart,* part of whose steel frames still were visible at low tide.

And there they were together in death as they had been at birth: built in the same yard in the same year and both going their diverse routes, one for eight years and the other for 23. Then each met the same fate 15 years apart and came to rest in the same watery plot in the shadow of their birthplace less than a stone's throw apart—the exact distance they had been separated by their launching cradles.

To be sure there were many vessels wrecked along the awesome cliffs between Seal Rocks and Point Lobos, before and after the *Lyman Stewart* and *Frank H. Buck,* but no two ships on the seven seas could ever boast of such human homing qualities.

Chapter Twelve

POINT MONTARA TO THE MEXICAN BORDER

YP-636

MOST shipwrecks of notoriety occurred in ages past but we do have atomic age wrecks also. For instance, take the case of the United States naval patrol vessel *YP-636* which left bomb-blasted Bikini Atoll on August 19, 1946. She was on the special assignment of bringing back to the United States radio-active fish for study. Prior to returning she had cruised in among the waters of what had once been an undisturbed Pacific paradise to pick up the specimens. The titanic blast had pulverized the atoll.

The *YP-636*, converted from a tuna clipper, stored the radioactive fish in its special frozen lockers. When fully stocked she left the scene of devastation and set her course for San Francisco where her atomic cargo was to be transported to the research laboratory of Stanford University.

The voyage was without incident until the craft approached the California Coast. There, as the reader might guess on such a date as September 12, fog abounded. The vessel groped about off the bizarre and barren cliffs south of the Golden Gate. Just south of Half Moon Bay she straddled a ledge of rock, her radio instantly screaming of the crew's misfortune. The vessel was badly holed and two officers and 25 enlisted men were forced to brave the surf to gain the shore. There were no casualties but the *YP-636* and her atomic specimens were swallowed up by the surging breakers. There was no salvage, not even a radioactive fish.

But some possible consequences are suggested to the imagination. The seas must have ripped apart the deep

254

freeze compartments to empty its contents and to allow fish swimming about the wreck to devour the frozen assets—their atomic cousins. Then again maybe a fisherman has hooked one of the live fish that swallowed radio active morsels and himself been poisoned.

SAN JUAN

A log of shipwrecks off the California Coast would not be complete without mention of one of the most shocking disasters—the sinking of the liner *San Juan* which carried 87 unsuspecting souls to a hasty grave. Words cannot describe the anguish, frustration, and hopelessness of the situation. There was an 18-minute struggle for survival by those who went down on the *Rio de Janeiro* as previously told, but the *San Juan* after being struck by another ship vanished from the face of the sea in a mere five minutes.

It happened on August 29, 1929, out in the steamer lanes off Pigeon Point, 50 miles south of San Francisco. The Standard Oil Company tanker *S. C. T. Dodd* was coming from one direction and the *San Juan,* a veteran liner in the service of the Los Angeles-San Francisco Navigation Company, from the other. Fog prevailed. Navigation was hazardous. Whistle signals were misunderstood. Then there was a terrible crash. The heavy bow of the tanker knifed into the side of the *San Juan,* inflicting a gash that a locomotive could pass through. Her iron plates withered as if they were tin. The old liner nearing a half century of service, was nearly severed in half. The tanker backed off, her bow badly crumpled.

From that moment it was just five minutes until the *San Juan* went down. There was no time to lower boats or issue lifejackets. It was every man, woman and child for themselves. The liner filled rapidly. There was barely time to get out a call of distress. Fortunately the tanker, though badly damaged, was still afloat and standing by to pick up survivors.

The steamer *Munami,* sailing close to the scene of the

collision, picked up the call of distress and hurried to the location, but the heavy fog clung to the water to render aid difficult.

The pathetic thing about the *San Juan* tragedy was that most of the passengers never had a chance. They were asleep in their bunks or trapped in the lower compartments of the vessel which filled so rapidly there was no passage of escape. One of the most phenomenal escapes was that of the steamer's boatswain. He was asleep in his bunk when the tanker struck. The bow smashed directly through his stateroom, knocked him from his bunk and pinned the door shut to trap him inside. The lights went out and he lay there stunned and wide-eyed as the clammy fingers of death reached out for him. As the bow of the tanker backed away from the giant hole in the *San Juan's* side, water poured into his quarters like a rushing river. He began his final prayers when suddenly he felt a rope brush across his face. As fate would have it, it was dangling from the bow of the tanker. With the most determined grip of his maritime career he grabbed it and hung on tenaciously. Hand over hand he bodily pulled himself upward until to his great surprise he reached the tanker's forecastle. He lived to tell his tale.

As the *San Juan* sank, the water was a mass of pleading, struggling humanity clinging to bits of wreckage and overturned lifeboats. Anything large enough to float had people attached to it. There was terrible frustration in their struggle for existence. Wailing, shouting, pleading, swearing, all mixed in one chilling chorus.

Eighty-seven souls—passengers and crew members were sucked down by the *San Juan's* death plunge. Forty-two were saved, 31 of whom were picked up by the tanker and 11 by the *Munami*. The rescue vessels steamed about the area all through the night and well into the next day looking for other possible survivors.

The last man to get off the *San Juan* was chief officer Charles Tulee. Numbed by his brush with death, he recovered sufficiently to go back to sea as master of both sailing vessels and steamships.

Explosion-racked tanker *Markay* which blew up with disastrous results in Wilmington, Los Angeles Harbor, July 23, 1947. Eleven lost their lives.

Survivor's eye-witness photo of the Norwegian MS *Fernstream* sinking in San Francisco Bay after colliding with the *Hawaiian Rancher*, December 11, 1952.

(Photographed by Dr. Willard L. Strode)

Uncle Sam's greatest peace-time naval loss. Some of the seven destroyers ashore in the fog off the Honda, near Point Arguello, California, September 1923.

The destroyers *Delphi, Fuller, Woodbury, Young, S. P. Lee, Nicholas* and *Chauncey* were all wrecked with a total loss of 22 lives on that foggy fall day in 1923.

The short duration of this regrettable episode precluded the usual sweep and drama attendant in a shipwreck—one of the most terrible disasters to mark California's coastal waterways.

LA NATALIE

On the shores of beautiful Monterey Bay, which Robert Louis Stevenson once described as the most fascinating seascape in the world, there hangs a tale of a famous shipwreck.

It is famous because the ship involved is alleged to have been the same one on which Napoleon escaped from the Isle of Elba, when he returned to France in 1815, for the 100-days' war which ended in the Battle of Waterloo. The name of this famous vessel was the *Inconstant,* a French sloop of war.

Back in port following Napoleon's epic escape, the *Inconstant* was seized by the allied European powers and eventually passed into the hands of a company seeking to colonize California.

Next the notorious vessel turned up at Monterey Bay, California, where she was allegedly engaged in illegal smuggling trades. Her name by this time had been changed to *La Natalie.* She was rigged as a five-masted schooner and flew the flag of Mexico.

One night in the year 1831, the ship lay off the foot of Figueroa Street. There was an ominous quiet hanging over Monterey Bay. The surf rolled lazily in, while scattered clouds drifted overhead like flocks of sheep. Night dropped its canopy over the schooner and with it came Captain Jose Abrego's good news that all hands would be granted shore leave to attend the grand "Cascarone Ball," one of the celebrated Spanish hoedowns of yesteryear.

Only a couple of hands were left aboard. While the ball was in full swing, with all the revelry of old world splendor, Captain Abrego and his men were unaware of a rising storm. The fleecy clouds quickly vanished and a

257

black mantle covered the half-moon. The quiet surf suddenly was angered into roaring acclivities. The waves caused *La Natalie* to drag her anchors, placing her in jeopardy. The few men aboard were powerless in the face of the gale. Dragging across the bay, the schooner was dashed on a shallow bottom where the wanton surf began ripping her apart.

As the spirits of wine clouding the brain of Captain Abrego cleared slowly away, he became aware of the driving winds outside the ballroom. He rounded up his men and all ran out into the storm. But it was too late. *La Natalie* was finished.

The very next morning he and his men labored about in the dangerous waters off the beach, dismantling what they could from the storm-racked ship. The lumber and fittings they extracted were used to construct the "Abrego House," an old-world domicile on the shores of Monterey, an ancient landmark still viewed by tourists.

Three times in a century the remaining portions of the old French man o' war have come above the surface of the tide, due to shifting sands. On the night of September 12, 1924, Henry Leppert of Monterey risked his life in the undertow to rescue relics of the ship. A few years later, Ernest Doelter and his sons salvaged a small portion of the vessel, together with copper and brass bolts, spikes, and other fittings.

La Natalie was officially identified as the French sloop of war *Inconstant* by a French Naval officer who visited Monterey in 1846. Part of her bow salvaged long before the turn of the century, was for many years housed in the De Young Museum in Golden Gate Park, San Francisco.

Most of the wood taken from the wreck was teak, and many decades in salt water and sand had not erased the marks of the adz and saw. This wood came from Australia and most of it was cut from the natural outcroppings—the tree trunk forming one angle and the limb the other. When the builders fashioned the *Inconstant* they built her to last. But, like Napoleon himself, nothing can endure all the rigors of life, and the old ship met her Waterloo on the shores of Monterey Bay halfway around the world from where the little emperor made his last stand. Napoleon died of cancer in 1821 and just a decade later, some say on that exact day, the ship on which he escaped from Elba, was wrecked at Monterey.

MONTEBELLO

The North Atlantic, the rich hunting grounds of the German U-boat through two world wars, left an almost irreparable scar on American and allied shipping. The toll in lives, ships, and cargoes was both staggering and disastrous. No instrument of the enemy came so close to knocking the Allies out of action.

Throughout World War I, the Pacific Coast, due to the great distances between the Atlantic and the Pacific, was not menaced by the U-boat. When America got embroiled in World War II, however, Japan was the enemy and for the first time American shipping on the Pacific got a sampling of the devilish destruction caused by submarine torpedoes.

Main targets of marauding long-range Japanese submarines were petroleum carriers, for they were the lifeblood of the nation's war machine. America's total unpreparedness when the Pearl Harbor attack occurred, left merchant ships on the Pacific like sitting ducks— no escort, convoys, or protective armament.

The *Montebello,* an 8272-ton tanker owned by the Union Oil Company, was proceeding out of Oleum, northward toward Vancouver, B. C. with a cargo of gasoline. On the afternoon of December 23, 1941, about six miles off Piedras Blancas Point at 4 p.m., a submarine's periscope was sighted. Captain Olaf W. Eckstrom, master of the *Montebello,* immediately ordered a zig-zag course. The loaded tanker swung slowly this way and that but the submarine was in hot pursuit. It was a losing race for the tanker. At 5:20 p.m. a torpedo was loosed and slithered along under the surface, catching the tankship at the forward hold. The well-aimed missile struck the only tanks in the vessel *not* filled with gasoline. Even so, one of the crewmen described it as "a hell of an explosion." The tanker folded like a tired accordion, the blast being heard for miles in every direction. Several houses along the shore reported broken windows from the concussion. Only to the fact that the torpedo struck the empty compartments did the crew owe their lives.

There wasn't much time to clear the boats away. And even as the tanker, reduced to a twisted mass of wreckage, was going down, Captain Eckstrom made an attempt to open the ship's safe containing an undetermined amount of money. He was unable to accomplish his mission because the lighting system was completely knocked out. Barely did he get to the boat deck as the last lifeboat was being put over the side.

When all the lifeboats were safely in the water the marauding submarine surfaced and began firing on the survivors with machine guns and rifles, an act of the most inhuman character. It was fortunate that the shots went wild and perhaps the only reason that the Japanese did not complete the job was the fear of a bomber flying out from the mainland. It was but two weeks after Pearl Harbor and the Nipponese had not yet tested America's coastal defenses. The lifeboats took out for the shore with the determination of a boy being chased by an angry bear.

Several persons along the shore who had witnessed the distant explosion, were on the lookout for survivors. The surf was high and the problem of landing in a lifeboat, difficult. There were four boats in all. The one in which Captain Eckstrom rode was upset in the breakers and all in it had to be helped ashore. They were so cold and numbed by the time they got their feet on dry land that they could hardly speak. The other boats came ashore at various spots, all encountering trouble but none sustaining loss of life.

After the war ended, one of the strangest legal cases involving the loss of a tanker was held. The Union Oil Company of California, owner of the ill-fated *Monte-*

bello, brought suit against the War Damage Corporation to the tune of $1,600,000 to recover loss of their ship. After a long, controversial hearing, the U. S. District Court decided against the claim. Following is a statement of the facts and the decision as taken from the official records:

> Action brought by plaintiff to recover the full value of its tanker steamship *Montebello,* and her cargo. The vessel was torpedoed and sunk by a Japanese submarine December 23, 1941 off the coast of California in the vicinity of Point Piedras Blancas, while en route from a California port to Vancouver, B. C.
>
> The defendant, War Damage Corporation, was a government corporation and a wholly owned subsidiary of the Reconstruction Finance Corporation.
>
> The action was brought pursuant to a public announcement by Mr. Jesse Jones, as Federal Loan Administrator, on December 13, 1941, to the effect that loss or damage of property within the United States by enemy action would be covered by the newly-formed War Damage Corporation (then the War Insurance Corporation). The action was also founded on Section 58 of the Reconstruction Finance Corporation Act, as amended—March 27, 1942 (5 U. S. Code 606 b-2). Under Section 5g, the War Damage Corporation was authorized to compensate for losses by enemy action in the United States occurring between December 6, 1941 and July 1, 1942, without requiring a premium to be paid. After July 1, 1942, premiums were required and by specific regulation vessels (with a few minor exceptions) were excluded from the coverage.
>
> The case was tried before a jury. The sole issue submitted by the jury was whether the vessel was lost within the United States; that is, whether it was

within three miles of the coast when lost. The officers and members of the crew produced by both parties disagreed in their estimates of the distance from the shore. Defendant produced evidence which located and identified the position of the vessel at the time of trial. The original location of the wreck by defendants was accomplished by the same method which was used in locating the wreck of the *Lusitania*. Transit bearings were obtained from shore witnesses and by means of cross bearings an estimated position of the sinking was obtained. The area was searched with a fathometer and an object which appeared to be the steamship *Montebello* was located in 850 feet of water, six miles off the shore. Subsequently, the object was definitely identified as the steamship *Montebello*, by means of undersea photography. A special type of camera and equipment which was developed during the war was used. A photograph was obtained showing valves on the main deck which when compared to the sister ship of the steamship *Montebello* established its identity. This is reputed to be the greatest depth at which a photograph of a wreck has been obtained. Oceanographers testified that currents along the ocean floor at such depth are slight and that because the wreck was located in a submarine canyon, it could not have shifted from any position nearer to the shoreline to its present position.

The verdict was for the defendant, finding that the vessel had been lost outside the United States.

After the survivors of the *Montebello* reached shore they were told that supposedly the same submarine had torpedoed and shelled the General Petroleum tanker *Emidio* near Blunts Reef two days earlier. Five of her crew of 36 were missing and some of the shells had injured the survivors in the lifeboats. Just a few hours before the *Emidio* was blasted, the submarine had molested the Richfield Oil tanker *Agwiworld*. Her submarine-wise skipper out-foxed it, however, with a zig-zag course in the vicinity of Cypress Point. Eight shells were shot from the submarine's deck gun but the tanker escaped after a 30 minute chase. On reaching San Francisco the crew's single reaction was: "If we'd only had a gun."

Though Japanese submarines succeeded in sinking many American ships in the Pacific, their action along the Pacific Coast was held to a minimum by the vast distances from refueling bases.

In the fall of 1942, the Japanese again sent a fleet of long-range submarines across the ocean to feed on Pacific Coast shipping. At that time they knocked out such well-known freighters as the Coastwise Line's *Coast Trader* off Cape Flattery and sank the tankers *Camden* off Willapa Bay and the *Larry Doheny* off Southern Oregon. There were others torpedoed also but the raids subsided after 1942, and most of the enemy submarine fleets were pressed into action in the South Pacific area or in the Aleutian Islands. The allied forces drove them steadily back, destroying them in droves until they were no longer a menace. The *Sakuri* sunk off Palos Verdes, California by U. S. forces in December, 1941, was the first Japanese submarine casualty.

And so an added danger along the shipping lanes, one not produced by weather and nature, was at last conquered.

SEVEN U. S. NAVY DESTROYERS

As long as men go down to the sea in ships they will never forget what was perhaps the greatest peace-time loss in the history of the United States Navy. Seven destroyers crashed on the rocks off Honda, north of Point Arguello, California on September 9, 1923, and 22 lives were lost.

On the same date American newspapers told in brief of a wreck that occurred on San Miguel Island off the coast of California. The victim was the steamship *Cuba*. As no lives were lost on the *Cuba* the brevity of the article can be readily understood. Indirectly, however, that wreck is believed to have contributed, just four hours later, to the loss of a destroyer flotilla and 22 of its men—a disaster that grayed the hair of the Navy's most boastful admiral.

The frantic exchange of radio messages that followed in the wake of the *Cuba* wreck, so interfered with reception on the squadron of 18 navy vessels of the United States Battle Fleet maneuvering in the same vicinity that they were unable to secure adequate guidance from the shore stations.

Enveloped by a steep bank of fog, the naval squadron was steaming in formation at a speed of 20 knots, and, what was worse, as it later developed, 30 miles off course. Off the Honda, 75 miles north of Santa Barbara, the flagship destroyer *Delphy* scraped bottom, and then heaved crazily on a rocky promontory that jutted 500 yards into the ocean. There was no time for the vessels immediately following to alter course and, even if there had been, the commander of any destroyer so disposed could have faced a general court martial. One after another the six destroyers following the *Delphy* piled up—the *S. P. Lee, Young, Nicholas, Woodbury, Chauncey,* and the *Fuller.* The seven destroyers were lying at intervals of about 250 feet along the rock-rimmed coast—irretrievably lost.

Boiler fires were extinguished immediately on the destroyers to prevent a conflagration, and with darkness about them the scores of sailors were left to fend for themselves with the use of hand flashlights. The Honda was a stretch of coast that had claimed many ships and was a notorious killer of seafarers. The slim lines of the destroyers were like fodder for the boarding seas. Had it not been for the heroism of men like Chief Engineer Erckenburg of the *Delphy,* the loss of life might well have risen to a far greater proportion than it did. Twice he plunged into the hammering surf and like a possessed man carried lifelines ashore, the means by which many made their way to safety.

The weird display of moving flashlights like fireflies on a summer night, attracted the attention of an unknown woman who stood on the shore gazing out beyond the reef. Even as she summoned help, the navy personnel were clambering over jagged rocks in an effort to reach shore. When help did come, lines were properly rigged and some 630 men were brought to the beach where they were conveyed to the nearest railroad station, given first aid, and provided with transportation to naval district headquarters.

As the survivors landed, the rest of the squadron, some 11 ships of various categories, stood helplessly by at sea, unable to render assistance because of the fog, swift running tides, jagged rocks, and total lack of communication with the wrecked ships.

Navy men are proud of their ships, and there were many wet eyes as the castaway crews watched the watery destruction of their craft. Nor was Uncle Sam any happier, financially, for the loss ran into millions. All seven destroyers were first-line fighting ships, 310-foot, four-stacked vessels built between 1918 and 1920 to the latest specifications. There were many questions and accusations at the ultimate hearings behind closed doors. There was much testimony that the Navy did not wish to reach the ears and eyes of John Q. Public. It was as though they had come out the loser in a major naval battle. In one sense they did. They flirted with the elements of weather and hostile shores, an unbeatable combination.

And yet the entire story of disaster might have read differently and the destroyers have been spared from the merciless fury of the pounding surf if the steamship *Cuba* had kept her course on that foggy September day in 1923.

YANKEE BLADE

Somewhere in the shadowy depths off Point Arguello, lies the wreck of the steam packet *Yankee Blade*. No ship loss on the Pacific Coast has been the target of so many wild tales. Her cargo of gold has been estimated at anywhere from $153,000 to $7 million; her loss of life from 15 up into the hundreds.

The *Yankee Blade* operated between San Francisco

and Panama under the flag of the Independent Vanderbilt Line and, on September 30, 1854, cleared from San Francisco on what proved to be her last voyage. Several hours later and at top speed, she rammed hard ashore between Points Arguello and Conception in a blanket of thick fog. She filled rapidly as the sharp rocks punctured her timbers.

Aboard were 819 passengers, 63 women and children among them; 120 crew members and an unknown number of stowaways. Records say she had aboard $153,000 in treasure—nuggets and gold dust, mostly from the rich fields of California, and all fortunately insured. Just how much uninsured loot was aboard the ship will perhaps never be known.

Immediately after the ship struck, there was panic aboard. Captain Henry Randall ordered a boat over the side. In this, he and a handful of crewmen made their way through the fog to shore to find a landing place for survivors. This proved a fatal error.

Aboard the wreck, mayhem had broken loose. Stowaways had come out of their hiding places and joined the seamen in a raid on the liquor cabinets. Passengers, filled with fear of impending disaster, became the targets of the drunken men, who beat and robbed them and even committed murder. They then tried for the gold, but it was deep in the bowels of the ship, which were well inundated by water. All the while the fate of the wreck grew graver. She was beginning to break up. Many of the panic-stricken passengers went over the side on improvised life rafts, or anything buoyant enough to hold them above the pounding surf. More than 200 tried such methods and, according to records, fewer than half of them gained the beach.

On the next day, the steamer *Goliah* happened on the scene and removed all she could take, some 600 from the wreck. These were taken to San Diego. The *Goliah* returned to the wreck a few days later to rescue the others, but found that most of the so-called "shoulder striker" stowaways, who had helped cause the riot, were ashore in complete control of the situation. They had set up a separate camp on the beach and were selling the ship's provisions that had washed ashore.

Two of the many reasons for the wreck that were presented to the court of inquiry were more dramatic than others. One held that the *Yankee Blade* was racing south against the steamer *Sonora*, a ship that cleared on the same day from San Francisco. According to this account, a considerable amount of money had been placed on the outcome and, in order to gain advantage, the *Yankee Blade* had cut too close to shore, causing the stranding. The other reason held that "shoulder strikers" deliberately planned the mishap in order to loot the ship and claim salvage. The question of tampering with the compass was also suggested.

One authority brought up an interesting sidelight— there was no light in the Point Conception lighthouse . . . the government was awaiting delivery of a long-over-due lens and lighting apparatus from Paris, France.

The dead from the wreck were buried in a mass grave on the cliffs above Point Pedernal, commonly known as Saddle Rocks.

Within the last three decades, scores of divers have claimed to have found the wreck of the *Yankee Blade,* but none of these claims has been verified. It must be remembered that the Point Arguello area is full of the hulks of rotting and broken ships, any of which might be mistaken for the wreck of the *Yankee Blade.* Pieces of ships have been raised which have had little monetary value, but the irascible ocean displays its ugly temper in this area much of the year and, even under the most favorable conditions, salvage work is difficult. Yet, stories of great treasure aboard the *Yankee Blade* are more prevalent today than when the ship went down well over a century ago.

Los Angeles's vast oil industry is without parallel. Any time day or night in Los Angeles Harbor the odor of petroleum is prevalent. Tankers, great mammoth 40,000-tonners down to the wee coastal variety, buzz in and out of the Harbor like bees around a honeycomb. Black gold is a multi-billion dollar enterprise. Tankers carry it far and wide. Massive storage tanks, refineries, petroleum by-products, all are housed in rambling firms rimming the waterfront area. Petroleum is the backbone of industry but working with it demands the ultimate in precautionary efforts, for oil and fire is one of the most dangerous combinations known.

For the most part, safety rules have been strictly adhered to, which has given the Los Angeles area a good record. When something gets out of line, however, watch out! There's no stopping it once it gets started.

Something got out of line in the summer of 1947, and such an inferno has seldom been seen. About the best words to describe the holocaust would be the screaming newspaper headlines — "Devastating Tanker Explosion Rocks Los Angeles Harbor." The victim was the 11,085-ton T-2 tanker *Markay* operated by the Keystone Shipping Company of Philadelphia. The big tanker was to have sailed for Puget Sound with its petroleum cargo. She had already taken on 2,940,000 gallons of fuel, at Berth 168, the Shell Oil Company. Then at 2:06 a.m. on Sunday morning, June 22, 1947, it happened. Tank No. 7 with a capacity of 17,408 barrels, along with tank No. 3 about the same size, appeared to be the origin of the blast. But nobody really knew, as evidence and key personnel were destroyed.

Since the terrible Texas City disaster a few months earlier, Los Angeles Harbor had been alerted for just such a blast. It came, all right, and with devastating results. When the explosion erupted it was so powerful that it folded back the *Markay's* deck plating as though it were rubber belting. The sides of the ship were split wide open and she sank at once, spilling a flaming cargo of gasoline, oil, and butane gas on the channel waters and firing the American President Line's docks 1000 feet to the west. A 15-ton section of the tanker's deck was hurled ashore by the blast, landing perilously near the Shell Oil storage tanks holding 6,000,000 gallons of high-test fuels. Eleven men were lost and 22 injured. Two of the dead were found in the channel waters, two in the upper deck of the crew's quarters on the mutilated tanker, one among the wreck-littered waters beneath the burned dock. Six were completely missing.

The Shell Oil Company lost all of its port facilities except a portion of Berth 169. American President Lines across the channel lost one dock and had another seriously damaged. The docks were fired when burning oil from the wreck drifted across the waterway and ignited the pilings beneath the structures.

As the white-hot flames leaped to fantastic heights there was fear that the entire Wilmington waterfront would be razed by chain reaction. Except for a favorable wind, the entire waterfront would have been torn asunder to make it one of the most costly fires known to man. The raging heat blistered paint on several huge tanks on the Shell farm on 30-acre Mormon Island. Waterspouts atop the tanks—20 of which on the Shell property alone contained 325,000 barrels of fuel—were credited with saving an explosion which would have brought tremendous devastation in the entire Los Angeles-Long Beach area.

Blaze-defying attempts of a boarding party to recover additional bodies from the burning hulk of the tanker were beaten back several hours after the explosion. Every piece of fire-fighting equipment in the entire area, both engines and fireboats, was pouring its capacity of water into the conflagration. The tanker was twisted almost like a pretzel. Part of its bow and stern rose at peculiar angles from the water and the entire midships were shattered into a tangled mass of scrap iron. The dead and missing probably never knew what struck them, so complete and terrible was the explosion.

The ship's bridge was but a pile of melted metal. Fortunately the *Markay's* master, Captain John P. Torrance, was not aboard or he may well have been underneath that scene of devastation. While he was spared, Shell's port captain, Carl Hogstrom, was among the missing, along with the ship's third mate.

Even as the boarding party surveyed the damage long after the flames had cooled, gasoline fumes, oil, and other volatile fuels were almost overwhelming. Los Angeles fireboats hugged the side of the tanker for several days after the explosion, keeping a weather eye for new outbreaks of fire.

As the investigation immediately got under way, special praise was heaped upon the Coast Guard's Admiral Frank Higbee, retired warden of the Port of Los Angeles, for the efficient functioning of the security-safety personnel he had organized a short time before the explosion to cope with just such a disaster. A favorable wind and a well-organized team of firefighters prevented another Texas City disaster which started in the same way just two months earlier. In that catastrophe, following the explosion of the French steamer *Grandcamp*, most of the dock area was destroyed and there were 510 known dead.

The quick thinking of second mate William Thomson and the crew of the Union Oil tanker *L. P. St. Clair*, berthed dangerously near the exploding *Markay*, saved that ship from destruction and a second explosion which could have spread the fire and loss of life to much greater proportions. In the absence of both their captain and port captain, these unsung heroes disconnected loading rigs, cut the hawsers, got up steam, manned the wheel, and within 15 minutes had their ship en route for safe anchorage four miles distant.

It was many months before Wilmington Harbor and greater Los Angeles shook off the effects of the terrible conflagration which, except for intervening circumstances, might have eclipsed the Texas City disaster.

Marine disasters resulting from explosion on the Pacific Coast have taken many lives but the unfortunate incident in Wilmington Harbor was surpassed only by two other catastrophes in loss of life. At San Diego on July 21, 1905, a boiler explosion on the USS *Bennington* claimed the lives of 65. Then at Port Chicago, California, on July 17, 1944, two war-built ships loading ammunition, the *Quinault Victory* and the *E. A. Bryan*, were blown sky-high, demolishing the docks and nearby installations and claiming more than 300 lives.

The ways of the sea are pitiless but there are many means of destruction for which it is not responsible. For certain, the behavior of the sea does not change with the passing parade of time. Now or 1000 years ago, in mad debauch it is vicious and merciless and marked by authority—yet its destructive powers are far surpassed by man's own carelessness along the shore.

APPENDIX

MAJOR SHIPWRECKS ON THE COASTAL, OFFSHORE AND INLAND WATERS OF THE PACIFIC COAST WASHINGTON, OREGON AND CALIFORNIA (*CIRCA* 1550-1962)

This list for the most part is restricted to vessels of 50 tons and over except in isolated cases where unusual loss of life is involved—or to preserve an important segment in maritime history. The wrecks listed here have occurred from all causes: strandings, founderings, fire, explosion, war action and disappearance.

*—Removed, rebuilt or salvaged.

SHIPWRECKS—1500-1849

Spanish vessel (name unknown) —about 1550—Near Quinault R., Wash. (Indian legend)
San Agustin—1594—Drakes Bay, Cal.
Spanish vessel (name unknown) —about 1679—Nehalem Beach, Ore.
Santa Rosa—1717—Reefs off Bishop Rock, SSE Cortez Bank, Calif.
Spanish vessel (name unknown) —1725—Clatsop Beach, Ore.
San Sebastian—1754—Santa Barbara, Calif.
San Jose—1769—Nehalem Beach, Ore.
Boat from Sonora—July 14, 1775—Near Pt. Grenville, Wash.
Boat from Imperial Eagle—1787—Near Pt. Grenville, Wash.
Sally—Sept. 2, 1796—Johnsons Island, Columbia River, Ore.
San Carlos—Mar. 23, 1797—San Francisco Bay, Calif.
Sea Otter—Aug. 22, 1808—Near mouth, Umpqua River, Ore.
St. Nicholas—Nov. 1, 1808—Near Quillayute River, Wash.
*Tonquin—Mar. 22, 1811—Columbia River Bar.
*Raccoon—1813—Columbia River Bar.
Junk (name unknown) —Mar. 24, 1815—W. S. W. Pt. Conception, Calif.
Junk (name unknown) —1820—Clatsop Spit, Ore.
*John Begg—Sept. 20, 1824—Begg Rk., Calif.
*Blossom—1826—Off California Coast.
William & Ann—Mar. 10, 1829—Clatsop Spit, Ore.
Isabella—May 23, 1830—Sand Island, Ore.
Russian Whaler (name unknown) —1830—Near Port Orford, Ore.
La Natalie—1831—Monterey Bay, Calif.
Junk (name unknown) —1833—Cape Flattery, Wash.
Peor Es Nada—1835—Off Golden Gate, Calif.
Commodore Rogers—1837—Monterey, Calif.
*Sulphur—1839—Columbia River Bar.
Peacock—July 18, 1841—Peacock Spit, Wash.
*Toulon—Aug. 23, 1841—Near Fort Vancouver, Wash.
Shark—Sept. 10, 1846—Clatsop Spit, Ore.
Elizabeth—winter 1847—Near Santa Barbara, Calif.
*Sitka—Feb. 12, 1848—San Francisco Bay, Calif.
Vancouver—May 8, 1848—Columbia River Bar.
Maine—Aug. 25, 1848—Clatsop Spit, Ore.
Flora—May, 1849—San Francisco, Calif.
Aurora—June, 1849—Columbia River Bar.
Morning Star—July 11, 1849—Sand Island, Ore.
Tonquin—Nov., 1849—Tonquin Shoal (Golden Gate, Calif.)

Shipwrecks of the Pacific Coast

Silvie de Grace or Silvie de Grasse—1849—Near Astoria, Ore.
Josephine—1849—Clatsop Spit, Ore.
Pioneer No. 1—1849—Sacramento River, Calif.
Edward Everett Jr.—1849—Sacramento River, Calif.
Helena—1849—Near Bodega Bay, Calif.
Hackstaff—about 1849—Near Rogue River, Ore.

SHIPWRECKS — 1850-1859

*Orbit—Mar., 1850—Sand Island, Ore.
Flagstaff—Spring 1850—Rogue River, Ore.
Bostonian—Oct. 1, 1850—Umpqua Bar, Ore.
*Mariposa—Oct., 1850—San Joaquin River, Calif.
Sagamore—Oct. 29, 1850—Sacramento River, Calif.
Colonel Cross—Jan. 29, 1850—San Francisco, Calif.
Eclipse—1850—Humboldt Coast, Calif.
Susan (or Sarah) Wardwell—1850—Humboldt Coast, Calif.
*Major Tompkins—Jan. 23, 1851—Sacramento River, Calif.
Commodore Preble—May 6, 1851—Humboldt Bay, Calif.
Jane—1851—Humboldt Coast, Calif.
Robt. Bruce—Dec. 16, 1851—Willapa Bay, Wash.
Santa Clara—1851—San Joaquin River, Calif.
Una—Dec. 26, 1851—Near Cape Flattery, Wash.
Lawrence—1851—Off Golden Gate, Calif.
Caleb Curtis—1851—Umpqua Bar, Ore.
Miner—Oct 8, 1851—Sacramento, Calif.
Capt. Lincoln—Jan. 2, 1852—North of Coos Bay, Ore.
Almira—Jan. 9, 1852—Near Umpqua River, Ore.
Anita—Jan., 1852—Port Orford, Ore.
Oxford—Jan., 1852—Tomales Bay, Calif.
Sea Gull—Jan. 26, 1852—Humboldt Bar, Calif.
General Warren—Jan. 28, 1852—Clatsop Beach, Ore.
Juliet—March, 1852—South of Yaquina Bay, Ore.
Potomac—May, 1852—Columbia River Bar.
Nassau—July 22, 1852—Umpqua Bar, Ore.
Pioneer—Aug. 15, 1852—San Simeon Bay, Calif.
*James P. Flint—Sept. 22, 1852—Cape Horn, Columbia River, Ore.
Machigone—Nov. 20, 1852—Off Columbia River.
Marie—Nov. 29, 1852—North Head, Wash.
Lord Raglan—1852—Off Cape Flattery, Wash.
*Willimantic—Sept., 1852—Grays Harbor Bar, Wash.
Dolphin—1852—Clatsop Spit, Ore.
Samoset—Dec. 1, 1852—Fort Point, San Francisco, Calif.
Bordeaux—Dec. 13, 1852—Clatsop Beach, Ore.
Cornwallis—1852—Humboldt Coast, Calif.
Home—1852—Humboldt Coast, Calif.
John Clifford—1852—Humboldt Coast, Calif.
Santa Cecilia—1852—Three miles off Ship's Rock, Calif.
*Comanche—Jan. 3, 1853—Suisun Bay, Calif.
Vandalia—Jan. 9, 1853—Columbia River Bar.
Mindora—Jan. 12, 1853—Sand Island, Ore.
I. Merrithew—Jan. 12, 1853—Clatsop Spit, Ore.
Roanoke—Feb. 2, 1853—Umpqua Bar, Ore.
Tennessee—Mar. 6, 1853—Near Pt. Bonita, Calif.
R.K. Page—Mar. 23, 1853—Sacramento River, Calif.
*James P. Flint—Mar., 1853—Upper Columbia River.
Tennessee—March 6, 1853—San Francisco, Calif.
S. S. Lewis—April 9, 1853—Duxbury Reef, Calif.
Jenny Lind—April 10, 1853—Las Pulgas Ranch, Calif.

Major Shipwrecks on Coastal, Offshore and Inland Waters

Carrier Pigeon—June 6, 1853—Near Pigeon Pt., Calif.
Willamette—Sept., 1853—Grays Harbor Bar, Wash.
Oriole—Sept. 19, 1853—Columbia River Bar.
American Eagle—Oct. 18, 1853—San Joaquin River, Calif.
*Stockton—Oct. 18, 1853—San Joaquin River, Calif.
Palos—Nov., 1853—Pt. Leadbetter, Wash.
Joseph Warren—Nov. 25, 1853—Yaquina Bay, Ore.
Ancon—1853—Pt. Wilson, Wash.
El Dorado—1853—Pt. Reyes, Calif.
Sir John Franklin—1853—Pigeon Pt., Calif.
Hoosier—1853—Sacramento River, Calif.
Winfield Scott—Dec. 2, 1853—Anacapa Isl., Calif.
Mexican—1853—Humboldt Coast, Calif.
Ranger—Jan. 8, 1854—Sacramento River, Calif.
*Helen Hensley—Jan. 19, 1854—San Francisco Bay, Calif.
San Francisco—Feb. 8, 1854—Near Point Bonita, Calif.
Firefly—Feb. 24, 1854—Near Astoria.
Duchess San Lorenzo—March, 1854—Off Cape Flattery, Wash.
*Gazelle—Apr. 8, 1854—Canemah, Ore.
Secretary—April 15, 1854—San Francisco Bay, Calif.
Gabriel Winter—April 15, 1854—San Pablo Bay, Calif.
Golden Fleece—April 22, 1854—Fort Point, San Francisco Bay, Calif.
Donna Maria—May 23, 1854—Near Cape Mendocino, Calif.
Arispe—May, 1854—Haven Anchorage, Calif.
Yankee Blade—Sept. 1, 1854—Off Pt. Arguello, Calif.
Southerner—Dec. 26, 1854—South of Cape Flattery, Wash.
*Water Lilly—Dec. 1854—Duwamish River, Wash.
Castle—1854—Tongue Pt., Ore.
W. T. Wheaton—1854—So. of Pt. Sur, Calif.
Empire—1854—Willapa Bar, Wash.
Oregon—1854—Umpqua River, Ore.
Plumas—1854—Sacramento River, Calif.
Chansey—1854—Coos Bar, Ore.
Pearl—Jan. 27, 1855—American River, Calif.
America—June 24, 1855—Crescent City, Calif.
Loo Choo—July 15, 1855—Umpqua River Bar, Ore.
Louika—July, 1855—San Juan Is., Wash.
*Georgiana—Nov. 23, 1855—Near San Francisco, Calif.
Detroit—Dec. 25, 1855—Columbia River Bar.
*Stilwell S. Bishop—1855—Bishop Rk., Calif.
Hodgdon—1855—Off Cape Flattery, Wash.
Sea Witch—1855—Arch Rk., Golden Gate, Calif.
Piedmonte—1855—Humboldt Coast, Calif.
Sierra Nevada—1855 or 1856—Humboldt Coast, Calif.
Isabelita Hyne—Jan 8, 1856—Near Golden Gate, Calif.
*Decatur—Jan., 1856—Blakely Rocks, Wash.
Charlotte—Feb. 5, 1856—Klamath River, Calif.
Belle—Feb. 5, 1856—Sacramento River, Calif.
Quadratus—1856—Coos Bay Bar, Ore.
Gold Beach—Feb., 1856—Near Klamath River, Calif.
Fawn—Nov. 21, 1856—Cape Perpetua, Ore.
Iowa—1856—Port Orford, Ore.
Francisco—1856—Port Orford, Ore.
Desdemona—Jan. 1, 1857—Desdemona Sands, Ore.
Jackson—Jan., 1857—So. Spit Coos Bar, Ore.
Fairy—Oct. 22, 1857—Near Steilacoom, Wash.
J. B. Brown—Oct. 30, 1857—Mouth Noyo River, Calif.
Washington—Dec. 12, 1857—Scottsburg, Ore.
Portland—1857—Willamette River, Ore.

Underwriter—1857—Sacramento River, Calif.
New World—1857—Coos Bay Bar, Ore.
Emily Packard—Feb. 21, 1858—Willapa Bar, Wash.
Traveler—March 3, 1858—Off Foulweather Bluff, Wash.
Zenobia—April, 1858—Point Bonita, Calif.
Lucas—Nov., 1858—Farallon Isl., Calif.
Enterprise—1858—Columbia River Bar, Astoria, Ore.
John Stevens—Dec. 4, 1858—East of Dungeness Spit, Wash.
Cyclops—1858—Coos Bay, Ore.
*Oregon—1858—Pt. Reyes, Calif.
Toronto—1858—Humboldt County, Calif.
A. Y. Trask—1858—Protection Isl., Wash.
Blue Wing—Jan., 1859—No. end Vashon Isl., Wash.
Ellen Maria—Jan., 1859—No. end Vashon Isl., Wash.
Rose of Langley—Feb. 22, 1859—Strait of Juan de Fuca.
Exact—Mar. 21, 1859—Crescent Bay Bar, Calif.
*Contra Costa—April 3, 1859—San Francisco Bay, Calif.
Mary F. Slade—Sept. 6, 1859—Near Cape Mendocino, Calif.
Rambler—Dec., 1859—Columbia Beach, Ore.
*Gomelza—1859—Hood Canal, Wash.
Caroline—1859—Lummi Isl., Wash.
Forest Monarch—1859—Off No. Calif. Coast.
Palestine—April, 1859—South of Cape Flattery, Wash.
J. W. Ryerson—1859—Humboldt County, Calif.

SHIPWRECKS—1860-1869

Northerner—Jan. 5, 1860—Blunts Reef, Calif.
Friendship—Apr. 14, 1860—N. of Sixes River, Ore.
Granada—Oct. 13, 1860—Fort Point, Calif.
John Marshall—Nov. 10, 1860—60 Mi. off C. Flattery, Wash.
Morning Star—Nov. 10, 1860—Juan de Fuca Strait.
D. L. Clinch—Nov., 1860—Juan de Fuca Strait.
Florencia—Dec. 8, 1860—Off C. Flattery, Wash.
Leonese—Dec. 27, 1860—Clatsop Spit, Ore.
Ann Perry—Dec., 1860—Appletree Pt., Wash.
H. C. Page—1860—Pt. Hudson, Wash.
Calamet—1860—Off Willapa Bar, Wash.
*Lolita—1860—Pt. Hudson, Wash.
Henrietta—1860—Near Astoria, Ore.
Lily—1860—Tacoma Narrows, Wash.
Success—1860 or 1861—Humboldt County, Calif.
*Syren—Apr. 25, 1861—Mile Rk., S. F. Bay, Calif.
Sea Nymph—May 4, 1861—Pt. Reyes, Calif.
Woodpecker—May 10, 1861—Clatsop Spit, Ore.
Cleopatra—July 1, 1861—Off So. Calif. Coast.
Persevere—Sept., 1861—40 mi. off C. Flattery, Wash.
*Pacific—1861—Coffin Rock, Columbia R.
Baltimore—1861—Baltimore Rocks, Ore.
Marmon—1861—Off Cape Flattery, Wash.
Willamette—1861—Willapa Bay Bar, Wash.
Kossuth—1862—Off Dungeness Spit, Wash.
*Coquimbo—Jan. 22, 1862—East of Dungeness Spit, Wash.
Flying Dragon—Jan. 29, 1862—Near Arch Rock, Calif.
Polynesia—Mar. 1, 1862—San Francisco, Calif.
Tolo—Feb. 23, 1862—San Juan Isl., Wash.
Carrie Ladd—June 3, 1862—Upper Columbia R.
*Mary Woodruff—July 31, 1862—Camano Is., Wash.

Major Shipwrecks on Coastal, Offshore and Inland Waters

Cadboro—Oct., 1862—Near Port Angeles, Wash.
*Brandt—1862—Off Tillamook Bay, Ore.
T. H. Allen—1862—Humboldt Coast, Calif.
Noonday—Jan. 1, 1863—Uncharted Rk. near Golden Gate, Calif.
F. W. Bailey—Jan. 8, 1863—3 mi. So., Pt. Lobos, Calif.
*Mary Ann—Jan. 28, 1863—Humboldt Bar, Calif.
Aeolus—Jan. 28, 1863—Humboldt Bar, Calif.
*Merrimac—Feb. 28, 1863—Humboldt Bar, Calif.
Ada Hancock—Apr. 27, 1863—Sacramento River, Calif.
Dashaway—1863 or 1864—Humboldt Coast, Calif.
Nevada—1863—Cache Slough, Calif.
*Frigate Bird—1863—Appletree Cove, Wash.
Milton Willis—April 27, 1863—San Pedro, Calif.
Jennie Ford—Jan. 29, 1864—North Head, Wash.
Ocean Bird—Mar. 19, 1864—S. W. of Cape Flattery, Wash.
*Jenny Jones—May 14, 1864—Peacock Spit, Wash.
*Washoe—Sept. 5, 1864—Sacramento River, Calif.
Cornelia Terry—Oct. 19, 1864—Yaquina Bay, Ore.
Sophie McLean—Oct. 26, 1864—Suisun Bay, Calif.
Ork—Nov. 24, 1864—Umpqua R. Bar, Ore.
Iwanowa—Nov. 24, 1864—Off C. Flattery, Wash.
Fanny—1864—Off Willapa Bay, Wash.
Brandt—Nov. 26, 1864—Off Ediz Hook, Wash.
Blanco—1864—Off Siletz Bay, Ore.
Enterprise—1864—Pt. Chehalis, Wash.
Hartford—1864—Humboldt Coast, Calif.
Young America—Jan. 13, 1865—Marysville, Calif.
Sir John Franklin—Jan. 17, 1865—Franklin Point, Calif.
Doyle—Mar. 11, 1865—Yaquina Bay, Ore.
Industry—Mar. 15, 1865—Columbia R. Bar.
S. D. Lewis—Mar. 16, 1865—Clatsop Spit, Ore.
Susan Abigal—July, 1865—Off Cape Flattery, Wash.
Brother Jonathan—July 30, 1865—St. George Reef, Calif.
*Yosemite—Oct. 12, 1865—Rio Vista, Calif.
Ann Perry—1865—So. of Golden Gate, Calif.
Novick—1865—2 mi. No. of Pt. Reyes, Calif.
Decatur—1865—Off Grays Harbor, Wash.
Ella Francis—Feb. 1866—Off Calif. Coast.
Fremont—Feb. 2, 1866—Dungeness Spit, Wash.
La Bouchere—Apr. 4, 1866—No. of S. F., Calif.
W. B. Scranton—May 5, 1866—Clatsop Spit, Ore.
Susie Merrill—1866—Near Noyo, Calif.
Coya—Nov., 1866—Franklin Point, Calif.
Mauna Kea—Nov., 1866—200 mi. off Columbia R.
Kiyus—1866—Upper Columbia River, Ore.
*Mary Glover—Mar. 1, 1867—Near Port Discovery, Wash.
*Iconium—Mar. 1, 1867—Near Dungeness Spit, Wash.
George Washington—Mar. 3, 1867—Dungeness Spit, Wash.
Northern Light—Mar. 31, 1867—Lime Kiln, Wash.
Oroville—April 11, 1867—Petaluma Creek, Calif.
Nahumkeag—Apr., 1867—Drakes Bay, Calif.
Lizzie Boggs—Sept., 1867—10 mi. So., Cape Flattery, Wash.
O. K.—Oct. 13, 1867—Sacramento, Calif.
Autocrat—Nov., 1867—Arch Rock, S. F. Bay, Calif.
Ellen Foster—Dec. 22, 1867—Near Neah Bay, Wash.
*Shubrick—1867—30 mi. So., Cape Mendocino, Calif.
*Montana—1867—Duxbury Reef, Calif.
Western Belle—1867—Out of Eureka, Calif.
H. L. Rutgers—Jan. 1, 1868—Potato Patch near S. F., Calif.

Shipwrecks of the Pacific Coast

Resolute—Sept. 19, 1868—Near Olympia, Wash.
D. M. Hall—Oct. 3, 1868—Coos Bay Bar, Ore.
Ocean—Oct., 1868—Dungeness Spit, Wash.
Nightingale—about 1868—Grays Harbor, Wash.
Oliver Cutts—1868—Alcatraz Is., Calif.
Noyo—1868—Coos Bay Bar, Ore.
Hellespont—Nov 21, 1868—Off Franklin Point, Calif.
Ann—Apr., 1869—Near Harrisburg, Ore.
Harlech Castle—Aug., 1869—Harlech Castle Rock near Piedras Blancas Pt., C.
Ranger—Sept. 4, 1869—Sauvies Is., Columbia River.
Lark—Oct. 6, 1869—Sacramento River, Calif.
Sierra Nevada—Oct. 7, 1869—3 mi. No. Piedras Blancas, Calif.
W. A. Banks—Nov. 10, 1869—Near Clallam Bay, Wash.
Ida D. Rodgers—Dec. 15, 1869—Coos Bay Bar, Ore.
Alaska—Dec., 1869—Coquille River Bar, Ore.
*Oriflamme—1869--Coquille Point, Ore.
Anna C. Anderson—1869—Off Willapa Bay, Wash.
Ranger—1869—Portland, Ore.
Enterprise— (1860's) —Near Port Madison, Wash.

SHIPWRECKS—1870-1879

Chas. Devens—Feb. 1870—Coos Bay Bar, Ore.
Champion (or Joe Champion) —Apr. 15, 1870—Columbia R. Bar.
Ellen—Apr. 20, 1870—Willapa Bay Bar, Wash.
Occident—May 3, 1870—Coos Bay Bar, Ore.
Active—June 5, 1870—22 mi. So. C. Mendocino, Calif.
Pet—June, 1870—Sacramento, Calif.
Bunkalation—June, 1870—Cape Blanco, Ore.
Goldhunter—June 5, 1870—Cape Mendocino, Calif.
Belle—Oct. 18, 1870—Sacramento R., Calif.
Commodore—Oct. 22, 1870—Coquille R. Bar, Ore.
Litta— (1870's) —No. of Shelter Cove, Calif.
Emily Harris—Aug., 1871—Strait of Georgia, Wash.
Hattie Besse—Nov. 20, 1871—20 mi. So. of Cape Flattery, Wash.
U. S. Grant—Dec. 19, 1871—Sand Is., Ore.
*Shooting Star—Dec. 23, 1871—James Is., Wash.
*Windward—Dec. 23, 1871—Sand Is., Ore.
*Nanaimo—1871—Cypress Is., Wash.
Reindeer—Feb. 24, 1872—Near Port Townsend, Wash.
Resolute—Apr. 12, 1872—Portland, Ore.
Rose Perry—Sept., 1872—So. Spit, Willapa Bar, Wash.
Walter Raleigh—1872—Off Cape Flattery, Wash.
*Jane A. Falkenberg—1872—Clatsop Spit, Ore.
Live Yankee—1872—Portland for San Francisco, Calif.
Sacramento—1872—Point Antonio (Sacramento Reef) , Calif.
Enterprise—Feb. 20, 1873—Umpqua R. Bar, Ore.
Meldon—Mar. 16, 1873—Umpqua R. Bar, Ore.
Sedalia—July 1, 1873—Near Kalama, Wash.
Bobolink—Oct., 1873—Umpqua River Bar, Ore.
Aculeo—1873—Near Pt. Montara, Calif.
*Almatia—Nov., 1873—Near Skip Jack Is., Wash.
Millie Bond—about 1873—Tillamook Bar, Ore.
*Eliza—Jan., 1874—So. of Cape Flattery, Wash.
Diana—Jan. 7, 1874—So. of Cape Flattery, Wash.
*Jennie Thelin—Mar., 1874—No. Spit, Coos Bar, Ore.
*Sidi—Mar. 1, 1874—Sand Is., Ore.
Christopher Mitchell—Mar. 2, 1874—Dungeness Spit, Wash.
Prince Alfred—June 14, 1874—Duxbury Reef, Calif.

Major Shipwrecks on Coastal, Offshore and Inland Waters

Rescue—Oct. 3, 1874—Authorities differ. Both North Head, Wash., and San Francisco given.
Shoshone—Nov., 1874—Near Salem, Ore.
Edwin—Dec., 1874—Strait of Juan de Fuca (hull drifted to Hesquiet, B. C.)
*Fannie Troop—1874—Cowlitz R., Wash.
Junk— (name unknown) —1874—Near Pt. Loma, Calif.
Laura May—1874—6 mi. No. of Coos Bay, Ore.
*Elida—1874—Off Coos Bay, Ore.
Northwestern—Jan. 3, 1875—Rogue River Bar, Ore.
Albany—Jan. 6, 1875—Long Tom R., Ore.
Pelicano—Jan. 19, 1875—Near Neah Bay, Wash.
Ontario—Mar. 25, 1875—San Juan Is., Wash.
Architect—Mar. 28, 1875—Clatsop Spit, Ore.
Ventura—Apr. 20, 1875—Pt. Sur, Calif.
Senator—May 6, 1875—Portland, Ore.
Union—May 7, 1875—Clark Is., Rosario Strait, Wash.
Orient—May 7, 1875—Pt. Leadbetter, Wash.
Eastport—July 23, 1875—Near Pt. Arena Lt., Calif.
Clara R. Sutil—July 25, 1875—Off No. Calif. Coast.
Milan—Aug. 17, 1875—Mission Bay, S. F., Calif.
Liguria—Oct. 11, 1875—Off Pacific Coast.
Camille Cavour—Oct. 1875—North Pacific (ship remains washed ashore at Manzanillo, Mexico)
Willimantic—Nov. 3, 1875—off Humboldt Bay, Calif. (abandoned ship remains washed up at Gold Beach, Oregon)
Pacific—Nov. 4, 1875—Off Cape Flattery, Wash.
Florence—Oct. 9, 1875—20 mi. off Umpqua R., Ore.
Emily Farnum—Nov. 18, 1875—Destruction Is., Wash.
Milo Bond—Nov. 21, 1875—Rogue River Bar, Ore.
Mary—1875—Coquille R., Ore.
Sparrow—Dec. 4, 1875—Near Umpqua R., Ore.
Rebecca—1875—S. W. of Columbia R., Ore.
*Windward—Dec. 30, 1875—Useless Bay, Whidbey Is., Wash.
   (hull towed to Seattle—beached)
Isaac Jeans—1875—Near Golden Gate, Calif.
Sunshine—Nov., 1875—North Beach, Wash.
Star King—1875—Off Coos Bay, Ore.
Harriet Rowe—Jan. 28, 1876—Port Orford, Ore.
Lizzie—Feb. 16, 1876—Yaquina Bay Bar, Ore.
Dreadnaught—Feb., 1876—Clatsop Beach, Ore.
Nabob—Mar. 4, 1876—Off Columbia River.
Uncle Sam—Feb. 7, 1876—Off Cape Foulweather, Ore.
Caroline Medeau—Apr. 5, 1876—Yaquina Bay Bar, Ore.
Perpetua—Oct. 24, 1876—Off Coos Bay Bar, Ore.
Daisey Ainsworth—Nov., 1876—Near The Dalles, Ore.
Messenger—1876—Coos Bay, Ore.
*General Harney—1876—Appletree Cove, Wash.
Yakima—1876—John Day River Rapids, Ore.
Albert & Edward—1876—Humboldt Bay area, Calif.
Commodore—Jan. 10, 1877—2 mi. So. Cape Flattery, Wash.
Oregonian—Jan. 16, 1877—Coquille River Bar, Ore.
Frank Jones—Mar. 30, 1877—Near Pt. Bonita, Calif.
Albert and Edward—April 18, 1877—Humboldt Bay Bar, Calif.
Cambridge—June 13, 1877—15 mi. So. Cape Flattery, Wash.
W. C. Parke—Aug., 1877—Off Cape Flattery, Wash.
Clinton—Oct 27, 1877—San Francisco, Calif.
Continental—Dec. 14, 1877—North of Eel River, Calif.
Nimbus—Dec. 29, 1877—25 mi. N. W. Columbia River
Continental—1877—Near Table Bluff, Calif.

Shipwrecks of the Pacific Coast

Marietta—1877—Humboldt Bay Bar, Calif.
Osmyn—Jan. 10, 1878—Marrowstone Pt., Wash.
Susan A. Owen—Jan. 21, 1878—Mouth Big R., Calif.
King Philip—Jan. 25, 1878—Near Pt. Lobos, Calif.
Pacific—Jan. 30, 1878—Off No. Calif. Coast.
Grace Darling—Jan., 1878—Off Cape Flattery, Wash.
Cordelia—Jan., 1878—Off Golden Gate, Calif.
  (remains of hull washed up on Vancouver Is. in March, 1878)
Johanna Brock—Feb. 17, 1878—Off Rogue R., Ore.
  (hull drifted ashore 15 miles north of Rogue River, Ore.)
Twin Sisters—Feb.,.1878—Trinidad, Calif.
Lola—Feb., 1878—Trinidad, Calif.
Wenant—Mar., 1878—Skagit R., Wash.
Western Shore—July 11, 1878—Duxbury Reef, Calif.
Phil Sheridan—Sept. 15, 1878—15 mi. off Umpqua River, Ore.
City of Dublin—Oct. 18, 1878—Clatsop Spit, Ore.
Free Trade—Oct. 21, 1878—Off Quillayute Rocks, Wash.
*Laura Pike—1878—Humboldt Bar, Calif.
Ocean Pearl—1878—Off Humboldt Coast, Calif.
Great Republic—Apr. 19, 1879—Sand Is., Ore.
*Allegiance—May, 1879—Sand Is., Ore.
Washington Libby—July 23, 1879—Near Port Angeles, Wash.
*Alaska—Sept., 1879—Noonday Rk., Farallons, Calif.
Esther Colos—Oct. 21, 1879—Rogue River Bar, Ore.
Annie Stoffin—Oct., 1879—Caspar, Calif.
Marmion—Nov. 8, 1879—Off Cape Flattery, Wash.
Mary D. Pomeroy—1879—Off Pt. Reyes, Calif.
Sara—1879—Humboldt Bay area, Calif.

SHIPWRECKS—1880-1889

General Harney—Mar. 4, 1880—San Juan Is., Wash.
Dilharree—Mar. 10, 1880—Peacock Spit, Wash.
Oliva Schultze—Apr. 28, 1880—Siuslaw R. Bar, Ore.
Fishing Fleet— (numerous small vessels from Columbia River and Willapa River fleets capsized off Cape Disappointment in a storm May 4, 1880, with a loss of 200 lives.)
Gussie Telfair—Sept. 25, 1880—Rocky Pt., Coos Bay, Ore.
W. H. Gawley—Oct. 23, 1880—Golden Gate, Calif
David Hoadley—Dec. 15, 1880—Pt. Williams, Wash.
Jessie Nickerson—1880—Willapa Bay Bar, Wash.
*Augusta—1880—Port Madison, Wash.
Red Bluff—1880—Near San Francisco, Calif.
*Edward Parke—1880—Humboldt Bar, Calif.
Washington—1880—San Francisco, Calif.
Lupatia—Jan. 3, 1881—Tillamook Head, Ore.
*Emily Stevens—Feb. 8, 1881—Clatsop Spit, Ore.
Clatsop Chief—Feb. 28, 1881—Willow Bar, Columbia River.
Kate L. Heron—Apr. 27, 1881—Tillamook Bay Bar, Ore.
Pilots Bride—Aug. 1, 1881—Nestucca Bay Bar, Ore.
Rival—Sept. 13, 1881—Peacock Spit, Wash.
Olympus—Sept. 14, 1881—Off Wash. Coast.
Fern Glen—Oct. 16, 1881—Clatsop Spit, Ore.
Lammerlaw—Oct. 31, 1881—Pt. Leadbetter, Wash.
G. Broughton—Nov. 1, 1881—Pt. Leadbetter, Wash.
Edith Lorne—Nov. 17, 1881—Columbia River Bar.
Mary Zephyr—1881—Near Pt. Arena, Calif.
*Seventy-Six—1881—Near Neah Bay, Wash.
Rainier—Jan. 5, 1882—100 mi. off No. Calif. Coast.

Major Shipwrecks on Coastal, Offshore and Inland Waters

Harvest Home—Jan. 18, 1882—North Beach Pen., Wash.
Corsica—Feb. 21, 1882—12 mi. S. W. Columbia River.
Bulwark—Feb. 27, 1882—300 mi. off Oregon Coast.
*Eliza Anderson—May, 1882—Dock, Seattle, Wash.
*Roswell Sprague—June 25, 1882—Off Golden Gate, Calif.
Lammermoor—June, 1882—Bodega Reef, Calif.
Chehalis—Nov. 9, 1882—Snohomish River, Wash.
*Humboldt—Dec. 17, 1882—Humboldt Bay Bar, Calif.
Primrose—1882—Clatsop Spit, Ore.
Franconia—1882—Southeast Farallon Is., Calif.
Escambia—1882—Off Golden Gate, Calif.
*Newbern—1882—Folsom Wharf, San Francisco, Calif.
*Josephine—Jan. 16, 1883—Near Tulalip, Wash.
Tacoma—Jan. 29, 1883—4 mi. No. Umpqua River, Ore.
Gem—Feb. 7, 1883—Off Appletree Cove, Wash.
C. L. Taylor—Feb. 20, 1883—25 mi. S. W. Cape Flattery, Wash.
Victoria—Mar. 28, 1883—Cape Blanco, Ore.
War Hawk—Apr. 12, 1883—Port Discovery, Wash.
Phoebe Fay—Apr. 16, 1883—Cape Foulweather, Ore.
Mississippi—May 13, 1883—Seattle, Wash.
*Ferndale—July, 1883—Saunders Reef, Calif.
*Queen of the Pacific—Sept. 5, 1883—Clatsop Beach, Ore.
Windemere—Sept. 7, 1883—Fort Ross, Calif.
Cairnsmore—Sept. 26, 1883—Clatsop Spit, Ore.
Ona—Sept. 26, 1883—Near Yaquina Bay, Ore.
Willamette—Sept., 1883—Grays Harbor Bar, Wash.
J. C. Cousins—Oct. 7, 1883—Clatsop Spit, Ore.
Whistler—Oct. 27, 1883—North Beach Pen., Wash.
Caroline Medan—Oct., 1883—Russian Gulch, Calif.
*California—1883—Hueneme, Calif.
Bremen—1883—Southeast Farallon Is., Calif.
Saucelito—1884—San Quentin Wharf, Calif.
C. G. White—1884—Bridgeport, Calif.
*Umatilla—Feb. 9, 1884—Umatilla Reef, Wash.
    (sank after being towed to port—later raised)
Mose—May 25, 1884—Near Port Orford, Ore.
Napa City—Sept. 27, 1884—So. of Coquille River, Ore.
Devonshire (or Dovenshire) —1884—Clatsop Spit, Ore.
Maria—1884—Tacoma, Wash.
Agnes Nicholayson—1884—Little River, Calif.
Cora—1884—Calif. Coast.
Edith—1884—Mouth of Eel River, Calif.
Sol Thomas Jr.—Jan. 4, 1885—Empire City, Ore.
Abbey Cowper—Jan. 4, 1885—Pt. Leadbetter, Wash.
Dewa Gungadhar—Jan. 18, 1885—Pt. Leadbetter, Wash.
Gazelle—Mar. 12, 1885—Snohomish River, Wash.
*Wildwood—July 21, 1885—Near Olympia, Wash.
Haddingtonshire—Aug. 20, 1885—So. of Golden Gate, Calif.
Alexander Duncan—Sept. 9, 1885—Fort Point, Calif.
Humboldt—Sept., 1885—Navarro, Calif.
Sea Foam—1885—Off Westport, Calif.
Lizzie Merrill—1885—Off Cape Flattery, Wash.
Carrie B. Lake—Jan. 3, 1886—North Beach Pen., Wash.
John Rosenfeld—Feb. 19, 1886—Saturna Is., San Juans.
A. A. McCully—May 22, 1886—Lower Cascades, Ore.
Beda—Mar. 17, 1886—40 mi. W. of Cape Perpetua, Ore.
Trustee—Apr. 24, 1886—Grays Harbor Bar, Wash.
W. H. Besse—July 23, 1886—Peacock Spit, Wash.
Sierra Nevada—Sept., 1886—Off Cape Flattery, Wash.

Shipwrecks of the Pacific Coast

Anna Hormme—Oct. 22, 1886—Pt. Blacklock, Ore.
Webfoot—Nov. 12, 1886—Juan de Fuca Strait, Wash.
Sir Jamsetjee Family—Dec. 1, 1886—Near Quinault River, Wash.
Carmarthan Castle—Dec. 2, 1886—Near Nestucca Bay, Ore.
Atlantic—Dec. 16, 1886—Near Pt. Lobos, Calif.
Ella S. Thayer—Dec. 16, 1886—15 mi. off Cape Flattery, Wash.
Westport—Dec. 18, 1886—Westport, Ore.
Lilly Grace—Dec. 20, 1886—Off Grays Harbor, Wash.
Escort—Dec. 22, 1886—Empire City, Ore.
Lief Erickson—Dec. 24, 1886—Off Alki Pt., Wash.
Hyde—Dec., 1886—Pt. Arena, Calif.
Mary and Ellen—Dec., 1886—San Francisco, Calif.
Verson—Dec., 1886—Pt. Arena, Calif.
Phantom—1886—Lopez Rks., Wash.
Aurora—1886—Off Cape Flattery, Wash.
Ariel—1886—Clatsop Spit, Ore.
Irene—Jan. 2, 1887—30 mi. W. S. W. Cape Flattery, Wash.
Parallel—Jan. 15, 1887—Pt. Lobos, Calif.
Austria—Jan. 21, 1887—Off Cape Alava, Wash. (Flattery Rks.)
*Kennebec—Feb. 4, 1887—San Pedro, Calif.
Lottie—Feb., 1887—Near Deception Pass, Wash.
St. Stephen—Apr. 1, 1887—Off Cape Flattery, Wash.
Active—Apr. 1, 1887—30 mi. off Cape Flattery, Wash.
Eldorado—Apr. 1, 1887—Off Cape Flattery, Wash.
North Star—Apr., 1887—Off Cape Flattery, Wash. (drifted to Vancouver Island)
Ocean King—Apr., 1887—40 mi. No. Cape Blanco, Ore.
Veto No. 1—Sept. 9, 1887—Sellwood, Ore.
Queen of the Bay—Sept. 11, 1887—Nehalem River Bar, Ore.
Phil Sheridan—Sept. 15, 1887—Off Umpqua River, Ore.
Telephone—Nov. 20, 1887—Near Astoria, Ore.
Yaquina City—Dec. 4, 1887—Yaquina Bay Bar, Ore.
Gray Hound—Dec. 4, 1887—Near Port Orford, Ore.
Grace Roberts—Dec. 8, 1887—2 mi. So. Leadbetter Pt., Wash.
Harvey Mills—Dec. 14, 1887—60 mi. off Cape Flattery, Wash.
San Vincente—1887—Off Pigeon Pt., Calif.
Abercorn—Jan. 12, 1888—10 mi. No. Grays Harbor, Wash.
Gleaner—Jan 28, 1888—Tongue Pt., Ore.
Z. B. Heywood—Jan., 1888—Navarro, Calif.
Julia—Feb. 27, 1888—So. of Vallejo, Calif.
Salisbury—Feb., 1888—200 mi. S. W. Cape Flattery, Wash.
Bob Irving—Apr. 1, 1888—Skagit River, Wash.
Otago—July 28, 1888—4 mi. No. Pt. Reyes, Calif.
Cassandra Adams—Aug. 16, 1888—Off Destruction Island, Wash.
City of Chester—Aug. 22, 1888—Off Golden Gate, Calif.
Hermina—Aug. 23, 1888—Willow Bar, Columbia River.
Respigadera—Sept., 1888—Pt. Fernin, Calif.
Makah—Oct. 24, 1888—Off Tillamook Head, Ore.
Bonanza—Nov. 11, 1888—Wallings, Willamette River, Ore.
Mendocino—Dec. 2, 1888—Humboldt Bar, Calif.
Yaquina Bay—Dec. 9, 1888—Yaquina Bay Bar, Ore.
Lief Erickson—Dec., 1888—Off Alki Pt., Wash.
Antelope—1888—Near San Francisco, Calif.
C. D. Murray—1888—Redondo Beach, Calif.
Leo—1888—Lake Wash., Wash.
Julia H. Ray—Jan. 26, 1889—Coos Bay Bar, Ore.
*Thistle—Jan. 13, 1889—Rogue River Bar, Ore.
Port Gordon—Feb. 27, 1889—40 mi. So. Cape Flattery, Wash.
North Bay—Mar. 5, 1889—Near San Juan Is., Wash.
Bee—Apr. 6, 1889—Duwamish River, Wash.

Major Shipwrecks on Coastal, Offshore and Inland Waters

Alaskan—May 13, 1889—Cape Blanco, Ore.
Dispatch—May 22, 1889—Seattle, Wash.
Emerald—May 26, 1889—Port Gamble, Wash.
Bee—June 2, 1889—Seattle, Wash.
Neptune—June 6, 1889— (drydock) Seattle, Wash.
Collaroy—June, 1889—Near Humboldt Bar, Calif.
Fearless—Nov. 20, 1889—No. Spit Umpqua Bar.
Wide West—Dec. 27, 1889—Destruction Island, Wash.
*Clan McKenzie—Dec. 28, 1889—Near Kalama, Columbia River, Wash.
Idaho—Dec. 1889—Port Angeles, Wash.
General Harney—1889—Goose Is. (San Juans, Wash.)
Artemisia—1889—North Beach Pen., Wash.
Erial—1889—Near Salt Pt., Calif.
Fidelity—1889—Humboldt Bar, Calif.
*J. B. Libby—1889—Ebey's Landing, Wash.

SHIPWRECKS—1890-1899

*Douglas Dearborn—Jan. 4, 1890—Off Columbia River.
*J. Ordway—Jan. 8, 1890—Portland, Ore.
Isabel—Jan. 22, 1890—Sellwood, Ore.
Nellie May—Jan. 24, 1890—Off Cape Flattery, Wash.
Little Anne—Feb. 3, 1890—Coquille River, Ore.
Otter—Feb. 17, 1890—Off Des Moines, Wash.
Rosalind—Feb. 18, 1890—3 mi. No. Rogue River, Ore.
Granger—Apr. 15, 1890—Strait of Juan de Fuca.
Dispatch—May 22, 1890—Seattle, Wash.
Edith—May, 1890—Bellingham Bay, Wash.
Ajax—Sept. 18, 1890—Near Shelter Cove, Calif.
Gov. Moody—Sept. 20, 1890—North Head, Wash.
August—Oct. 2, 1890—Off Port Angeles, Wash.
*Michigan—Nov. 1, 1890—Off Oregon Coast.
*Virgil T. Price—Dec. 6, 1890—Dock, Seattle, Wash.
Ferndale—Dec. 15, 1890—Off Lopez Is., Wash.
Atlanta—Dec. 16, 1890—50 mi. W. Cape Flattery, Wash.
Pioneer—Dec. 17, 1890—Cape Kiwanda, Ore.
Squak—Dec. 25, 1890—Lake Wash., Wash.
Straun—Dec., 1890—Off Nestucca, Ore.
Savona—1890—Dungeness Spit, Wash.
E. N. Cook—1890—Clackamas Rapids, Ore.
Napa City—1890—Off Pt. Reyes, Calif.
Sunbeam—about 1890—Siletz Bay, Ore.
Alida—1890—Gig Harbor, Wash.
Welcome—1890—Gig Harbor, Wash.
Union—Feb. 10, 1891—Near Anacortes, Wash.
Elizabeth—Feb. 21, 1891—4 mi. No. Pt. Bonita, Calif.
Marion—May 20, 1891—Upper Columbia River.
Palestine—June 26, 1891—San Francisco Bar, Calif.
Express—Sept. 7, 1891—Coos Bay, Ore.
Mary—Sept. 8, 1891—Lake Wash, Wash. (Seattle)
*Evangel—Oct. 15, 1891—Sehome (Bellingham), Wash.
Strathblane—Nov. 3, 1891—North Beach Pen., Wash.
General Butler—Nov. 28, 1891—100 mi. S. W. Coos Bay, Ore.
*Maggie Ross—Dec. 8, 1891—Off Oregon Coast (wreck towed into Yaquina Bay)
General Butler—Dec. 11, 1891—100 mi. S. W. Cape Arago, Ore. (parts of hull drifted to Yaquina Bay)
*Eastern Oregon—Dec., 1891—Olympia, Wash.
Lucia Mason—1891—Lewis River, Wash.
Union—1891—Off Hat Is., Wash.

Shipwrecks of the Pacific Coast

Dominion—1891—Off Cape Flattery, Wash.
Ferndale—Jan. 29, 1892—15 mi. No. Grays Harbor, Wash.
Cowlitz—Jan. 29, 1892—Off Cape Flattery, Wash.
Big River—Jan., 1892—Off Grays Harbor, Wash.
Josephine—Feb. 2, 1892—Allyn, Wash.
*Humboldt—Feb. 3, 1892—Humboldt Bay Bar, Calif.
Lucy Lowe—Apr. 4, 1892—Deception Pass, Wash.
Lottie—Apr. 17, 1892—Off Tillamook Bay, Ore.
Lena—Apr. 18, 1892—Colby, Wash.
St. Charles—May 17, 1892—100 mi. N. W. Cape Foulweather, Ore.
R. C. Young—July 22, 1892—Doves Landing (Willamette River), Ore.
C. W. Wetmore—Sept. 8, 1892—No. Spit, Coos Bay Bar, Ore.
E. M. Gill—Sept. 29, 1892—Case Inlet, Wash.
*Premier—Oct. 8, 1892—Off Marrowstone Pt., Wash.
Mary Parker—Oct. 25, 1892—Port Townsend Bay, Wash.
Margey—Nov. 9, 1892—Deception Pass, Wash.
Bonita—Dec. 7, 1892—Fashion Reef, Ore.
Forsaken—Dec. 16, 1892—Snohomish River Flats, Wash.
Majestic—Dec., 1892—Near Humboldt Bay, Calif.
Cornelius—Dec., 1892—Off Cascade Head, Ore.
*General Miles—1892—Coos Bay Bar, Ore.
Lens—1892—Puget Sound, Wash.
Venture—1892—Rockport, Calif.
*Lottie—1892—Off Tillamook Bay, Ore.
Courser—1892—Off Oregon Coast.
Rustler—1892—Willamette River, Ore.
Majestic—Jan., 1893—Off Cape Flattery, Wash.
Wilmington—Feb. 5, 1893—Linnton, Ore.
J. C. Ford—Feb. 17, 1893—Off Grays Harbor, Wash.
Mystic—Feb. 17, 1893—Elliott Bay, Seattle, Wash.
Fanny Lake—Apr., 1893—Skagit Bay, Wash.
E. W. Purdy—Apr., 1893—Near LaConner, Wash.
J. C. Brittain—May 10, 1893—Bell Rock, Wash.
Emily—July 17, 1893—So. Spit, Coos Bay Bar, Ore.
Eritrea—Aug. 4, 1893—Dungeness Spit, Wash.
Milton—Aug. 8, 1893—Near Dash Pt., Wash.
Annie Faxon—Aug. 14, 1893—Snake River, Wash.
Lenore—Oct. 4, 1893—3 mi. No. Quillayute River, Wash.
Garcia—Dec. 12, 1893—Cape Meares, Ore.
Senegal—1893—Off So. Calif. Coast.
*South Coast—1893—Near Tillamook Bar, Ore.
Albion—1893—Mendocino Coast, Calif.
City of New York—1893—Pt. Bonita, Calif.
*Whitelaw—1893—Russian Gulch, Calif.
Edna—1893—Off Cape Flattery, Wash.
George Thompson—1893—32 mi. off Cape Flattery, Wash.
*J. R. McDonald—1893—Prevost Is., Wash.
Virgil T. Price—Jan. 11, 1894—Port Gamble, Wash.
Norway—Jan. 11, 1894—Off Clallam Bay, Wash.
City of Stanwood—Jan. 21, 1894—Near Tulalip, Wash.
*Archer—Mar. 18, 1894—Off Cape Flattery, Wash.
Los Angeles—Apr. 21, 1894—Pt. Sur, Calif.
*Alcalde—April 29, 1894—Smith Is., Wash.
Dispatch—May 24, 1894—Near Friday Harbor, Wn.
Messenger—May 28, 1894—Tacoma, Wn.
*Henry Bailey—May 31, 1894—Mouth Skagit River, Wn.
Columbia—Aug. 2, 1894—Upper Columbia River (Little Dalles, Wash.)
R. K. Ham—Aug., 1894—Dungeness Spit, Wash.
Ivanhoe—Sept. 28, 1894—Off Cape Flattery, Wash.

284

Major Shipwrecks on Coastal, Offshore and Inland Waters

Willamette Chief—Sept., 1894—Portland, Oregon.
Newbern—Oct. 14, 1894—North of San Pedro Light, Calif.
Nora Harkins—Oct. 16, 1894—Grays Harbor Bar, Wash.
T. W. Lucas—Oct. 24, 1894—Off Port Orford, Ore.
Crown of England—Nov., 1894—Santa Rosa Is., Calif.
Anasha—Dec. 6, 1894—Fort Mason, Calif.
Montserrat—Dec. 7, 1894—Off Cape Flattery, Wash.
Keweenah—Dec. 7, 1894—Off Cape Flattery, Wash.
William L. Beebe—Dec. 10, 1894—3 mi. So. Pt. Lobos, Calif.
John Worcester—Dec. 11, 1894—40 mi. off Grays Harbor, Wash.
*Southern Chief—Dec., 1894—50 mi. S. W. Cape Flattery, Wash.
*Evangel—1894—Port Angeles, Wash.
Juanita—1894—Black River, Wash.
Mallory—1894—Near Neah Bay, Wash.
*Baroda—1894—Near Bandon, Ore.
Samson—Jan. 4, 1895—Pt. Bonita, Calif.
*Buckeye—April, 1895—Off Eliza Is., Wash.
Mogul—May 12, 1895—2 mi. E. Tatoosh Is., Wash.
*Anna M. Pence—June, 1895—Camano Is., Wash.
Bawnmore—Aug. 28, 1895—So. of Coquille River, Ore.
Humboldt—Sept., 1895—Pt. Gorda, Calif.
Bandorille—Nov. 21, 1895—Near Umpqua River, Ore.
Ella Laurena—Dec. 23, 1895—Off Cape Blanco, Ore.
Bering Sea—1895—Off Cape Flattery, Wash.
*Lily and Maude—1895—Off Deception Pass, Wash.
Cadzow Forest—Jan., 1896—Off Columbia River Bar.
Cricket—Feb. 5, 1896—Near Everett, Wash.
Point Loma—Feb. 28, 1896—Seaview, Wash.
*Kilbrannan—Feb., 1896—Near Pt. Wilson, Wash.
Glenmorag—March 18, 1896—North Beach Pen., Wash.
*Blairmore—Apr. 9, 1896—San Francisco Bay, Calif.
St. Paul—Aug. 18, 1896—Off Pt. Joe, Calif.
Maid of Oregon—Sept. 9, 1896—Southern Oregon coast.
Arago—Oct. 20, 1896—Coos Bay Bar, Ore.
Potrimpos—Dec. 19, 1896—North Beach Pen., Wash.
Corvallis—1896—Willamette River, Ore.
Toledo—1896—Willamette River, Ore.
Winifred—1896—Lake Washington, Wash.
*Zinita—1896—No. of Grays Harbor, Wash.
Wm. F. Monroe—1896—Skagit River, Wash.
Benito—1896—Pt. Arena, Calif.
Columbia—1896—Near Pigeon Pt., Calif.
Caspar—Oct. 22, 1897—Saunders Reef, near Pt. Arena, Calif.
Daisy—Oct., 1897—Near Edmonds, Wash.
Truckee—Nov. 8, 1897—No. spit Umpqua River, Ore.
Lily—1897—Off Cape Flattery, Wash.
Matilda—1897—Near Tatoosh Is., Wash.
Quickstep—1897—Lake Washington, Wash.
Samaria—1897—Seattle for San Francisco.
Thistle—1897—Juan de Fuca Strait.
Lila&Mattie—1897—Tillamook Bay Bar, Ore.
Yaquina—1897—Hueneme, Calif.
Elnorah—1897—Off Pacific Coast.
New York—March 13, 1898—Halfmoon Bay, Calif.
Bobolink—March 22, 1898—Kent's Pt., Mendocino, Calif.
J. Eppinger—July 2, 1898—W. of Pt. Reyes, Calif.
Helen W. Almy—May 21, 1898—Off Golden Gate, Calif.
*Lydia Thompson—Dec. 12, 1898—Shagg Rk., Orcas Is., Wash.
Jewel—Dec. 12, 1898—No. of Caspar, Calif.

Shipwrecks of the Pacific Coast

W. H. Starbuck—Dec., 1898—Off Pacific Coast.
Venita—1898—Grays Harbor Bar, Wash.
Townsend—1898—Port Townsend, Wash.
Penelope—1898—Juan de Fuca Strait.
Forest Queen—1898—Tacoma for San Francisco.
Hat—1898—Off Cape Flattery, Wash.
Keystone—1898—15 mi. So. Columbia River, Ore.
J. F. West—1898—Near San Miguel Is., Calif.
Bismarck—1898—Willamette River, Ore.
*Gamecock—1898—On Columbia River Bar.
Andelana—Jan. 14, 1899—Tacoma Harbor, Wash.
W. S. Phelps—Feb., 1899—Eureka for San Pedro.
Chilcat—April 2, 1899—Humboldt Bay, Calif.
City of Kingston—April 23, 1899—Near Tacoma, Wash.
*Columbia River No. 50—Nov. 29, 1899—McKenzie Head, Wash.
Eureka—Nov. 30, 1899—North Coquille Bar, Ore.
Carita—1899—Everett, Wash.
*Wilna—1899—Tacoma, Wash.
Weott—1899—Humboldt Bay Bar, Calif.
*Clara Brown—1899—Alki Point, Wash.
Portia—1899—Stewart's Pt., Calif.
*Sequoia—1899—Near Duxbury Reef, Calif.
Henriette—1899—Near Duxbury Reef, Calif.
*Novo—1899—Duxbury Reef, Calif.
*Orizaba—1899—Near Punta Gorda, Calif.
Leelenaw—1899—Near Pt. Montara, Calif.

SHIPWRECKS—1900-1910

Protection—Jan. 1, 1900—Off Columbia River.
City of Florence—March, 1900—Near Pt. Pedro, Calif.
Laguna—July 17, 1900—Klamath River, Calif.
May Flint—Sept. 8, 1900—San Francisco Bay, Calif.
Sunol—Oct. 23, 1900—Little River, Calif.
Five Brothers—Oct. 24, 1900—Drakes Bay, Calif.
Daisey Rowe—Nov. 21, 1900—Pt. Bonita, Calif.
*Poltalloch—Nov. 26, 1900—Willapa Bay (North Spit), Wash.
Elfin—Dec. 2, 1900—Houghton, Wash.
Andrada—Dec. 11, 1900—Off Columbia River.
Pioneer—Dec. 17, 1900—Nestucca Beach, Ore.
Gypsy—1900—Willamette River, Ore.
*Jeanie—1900—Near Pt. Arena, Calif.
*Cleone—1900—Near Punta Gorda, Calif.
Viscata—1900's—Near Golden Gate, Calif.
Joseph and Mary—Jan. 3, 1901—Near Alsea Bay, Ore.
*Fearless—Jan. 13, 1901—Off Bolinas, Calif.
*Flottbek—Jan. 13, 1901—White Rock, Wash.
Cape Wrath—Jan. 16, 1901—Off Columbia River.
Falcon—Jan. 18, 1901—Off Pacific Coast.
Barbara Hernster—Jan. 24, 1901—Pt. Arena, Calif.
City of Rio de Janeiro—Feb. 22, 1901—Fort Point, San Francisco, Calif.
Monitor—March 24, 1901—20 mi. off Columbia River.
San Rafael—Nov. 30, 1901—San Francisco Bay (off Alcatraz), Calif.
*Skagit Chief—Dec. 1, 1901—Off Bainbridge Island, Wash.
Matteawan—Dec. 2, 1901—Off Cape Flattery, Wash.
Condor—Dec. 2, 1901—Off Cape Flattery, Wash.
Ernest Reyer—Dec. 7, 1901—Mouth Quinault River, Wash.
*Pinmore—Dec. 11, 1901—Near Pt. Grenville, Wash.
*Minnie A. Caine—Dec. 26, 1901—Smith Island, Wash.

Major Shipwrecks on Coastal, Offshore and Inland Waters

*Henriette—Dec. 27, 1901—Near Astoria, Oregon.
*Asie—Dec. 30, 1901—Portland, Ore.
*Shianano Maru—Dec. 30, 1901—Juan de Fuca Strait.
Vermont—1901—Near Port Orchard, Wash.
Wheeler—1901—Yaquina Bay, Oregon.
*Capital City—1901—Brown's Point, Wash.
Mary F. Perley—1901—Off Alki Point, Wash.
Ajax—1901—Off Oregon Coast.
Lily and Maud—1901—Fletchers Bay, Wash.
*Fearless—1901—Near Bolinas Bay, Calif.
*Pomona—1901—Near Bolinas Point, Calif.
*Iaqua—1901—Duxbury Reef, Calif.
Walla Walla—Jan. 2, 1902—Off Cape Mendocino, Calif.
E. D. Smith—Jan. 25, 1902—West Seattle, Wash.
Laura Pike—Feb. 7, 1902—Off Cape Mendocino, Calif.
Occidental—Feb. 9, 1902—Near Point Gorda, Calif.
Reporter—March 13, 1902—South of Grays Harbor, Wash.
Eureka—June 19, 1902—Point Lobos, Calif.
Charles H. Merchant—Aug. 11, 1902—Nehalem Bay Bar, Ore.
Rogue River—Nov. 16, 1902—Rogue River, Ore. (Boiler Riffle)
Nettie Sundberg—Dec. 28, 1902—Siuslaw Bar, Ore.
Florence—Dec., 1902—Off Cape Flattery, Wash.
Seaside—1902—Budd Inlet, Wash.
Enola—1902—Hadlock, Wash.
Glide—1902—Mukilteo, Wash.
Kate and Annie—1902—San Miguel Island, Calif.
Amethyst—1902—Between San Francisco and Coquille, Ore.
City of San Diego—1902—Ozette Beach, Wash. (only wreckage found)
Clan McDonald—1902—Chuckanut Bay, Wash.
Prince Arthur—Jan. 2, 1903—12 mi. South, Ozette River, Wash.
Crescent City—Jan. 30, 1903—Fish Rock, Calif.
*Alsternixie—Feb. 9, 1903—Peacock Spit, Wash.
Bay City—Feb. 12, 1903—Shilshole Bay, Wash.
Albion River—April 3, 1903—Bodega Bay, Calif.
North Pacific—Aug. 19, 1903—Off Marrowstone Point, Wash.
Gifford—Sept. 28, 1903—Mussel Rock, Calif.
South Portland—Oct., 1903—Off Cape Blanco, Ore.
*C. A. Thayer—Nov. 8, 1903—Grays Harbor Bar, Wash.
Ruth—Nov. 11, 1903—Beilers Point, Calif.
Cavour—Dec. 8, 1903—Peacock Spit, Wash.
Mary Buhne—Dec. 13, 1903—8 mi. off Humboldt Bar, Calif.
*C. A. Klose—1903—Coquille Light, Ore.
*Tanner—1903—West of Port Angeles, Wash.
Imnaha—1903—Snake River, Wash.
*Iaqua—1903—Near Punta Gorda, Calif.
*Alliance—1903—Near Punta Gorda, Calif.
*La Conner—1903—Deception Pass, Wash.
Lady of the Lake—1903—West Seattle, Wash.
George W. Prescott—1903—Off Columbia River.
Clallam—Jan. 9, 1904—Strait of Juan de Fuca.
Alcalde—Feb. 14, 1904—Grays Harbor Bar, Wash.
Gem—Feb. 15, 1904—Double-Headed Rock, Ore.
Frank W. Howe—Feb. 22, 1904—Near Seaview, Wash.
*Queen—Feb. 27, 1904—Off Oregon Coast.
Mabel Gray—March 11, 1904—Redondo Beach, Calif.
Fannie Adele—May 23, 1904—San Francisco, Calif.
*Zampa—July 17, 1904—Point Leadbetter, Wash.
City of Denver—July, 1904—Sullivan Slough, Wash.
*City of Topeka—Sept. 12, 1904—Pier A, Seattle, Wash.

Alice Kimball—Oct. 12, 1904—Siuslaw River Bar, Ore.
Challenger—Nov. 7, 1904—Willapa River, Wash.
Western Home—Nov. 13, 1904—Coquille River Bar, Ore.
Web Foot—Nov. 21, 1904—Off Tillamook Rock Light, Ore.
Quickstep—Nov. 24, 1904—Off Yaquina Bay, Ore.
Pearl—Dec., 1904—Off Golden Gate, Calif.
Camano—1904—Upper Columbia River.
Drumbarton—1904—Point San Pedro, Calif.
*Point Arena—1904—Near Point Arena, Calif.
*Northland—1904—Point Pinos, Calif.
Santa Cruz—1904—Near Port San Luis, Calif.
George W. Elder—Jan. 21, 1905—Near Reuben, Ore.
Onward—Feb. 25, 1905—Coquille River Bar, Ore.
C. A. Klose—Mar. 26, 1905—North Beach Pen., Wash.
Volunteer—June 5, 1905—Off Bodega Head, Calif.
Robert Sudden—June 11, 1905—Surf, Calif.
Tricolor—July 26, 1905—North of Cape Mendocino, Calif.
U.S.S. Bennington—July 21, 1905—San Diego, Calif.
Gypsy—July 27, 1905—China Point, Monterey, Calif.
J. M. Colman—Sept. 3, 1905—San Miguel Island, Calif.
W. H. Harrison—Sept. 22, 1905—Alsea Bay, Ore.
St. Paul—Oct. 5, 1905—Punta Gorda, Calif.
Sacramento—Oct. 15, 1905—Coos Bay Bar, Ore.
Katie Flickinger—Nov. 20, 1905—Redondo Beach, Calif.
Mainlander—Nov., 1905—Off West Point, Wash.
Elwood—1905—Port Susan, Wash.
*Cascade—1905—Point Dume, Calif.
*Les Adelphus—1905—Off Cape Flattery, Wash.
Gerome—1905—Upper Columbia River.
Alexander Griggs—1905—Entiat Rapids, Wash.
*Santa Barbara—1905—Del Mar Landing, Calif.
*Prentiss—About 1905—Albion, Calif.
*Oregon—About 1905—Off Humboldt Bay, Calif.
Junk (name unknown) —About 1905—Near Point Leadbetter, Wash.
*Portland—Jan. 16, 1906—Off Hueneme Point, Calif.
Regulator—Jan. 24, 1906—Willamette River, near Portland, Ore.
Nicholas Thayer—Jan., 1906—Off Cape Flattery, Wash.
Newsboy—March 31, 1906—Humboldt Bay, Calif.
Selkirk—May 15, 1906—Rock Island Rapids, Wash.
Volunteer—June 5, 1906—Near Bodega, Calif.
Corinthian—June 11, 1906—Near Humboldt Bar, Calif.
Argus—June 13, 1906—Near Destruction Island, Wash.
*Portland—June 19, 1906—North Island, San Diego, Calif.
W. H. Kruger—July 11, 1906—Off Point Arena, Calif.
*Shna Yak—July 14, 1906—Near San Francisco, Calif.
Chico—July 18, 1906—Shelter Cove, Calif.
Reaper—July 21, 1906—Port Ludlow, Wash.
Celia—Aug. 28, 1906—Point Joe, Calif.
Falcon—Aug., 1906—Lake Washington, Seattle, Wash.
Shasta—Oct. 5, 1906—Point Conception, Calif.
W. H. Pringle—Oct. 9, 1906—Off Harper, Wash.
Peter Iredale—Oct. 25, 1906—Clatsop Beach, Ore.
Galena—Nov. 13, 1906—Clatsop Beach, Ore.
Emma Claudina—Nov. 14, 1906—Off Grays Harbor, Wash.
Dix—Nov. 18, 1906—Off Alki Point, Wash.
Bella—Nov. 25, 1906—Ocean Beach, Ore.
Great Admiral—Dec. 6, 1906—175 mi. S. W. Cape Flattery, Wash.
Sea Witch—Dec. 7, 1906—Off Cape Flattery, Wash.
*Melanope—Dec., 1906—Off Columbia River.

Major Shipwrecks on Coastal, Offshore and Inland Waters

Drumcraig—1906—Off Columbia River.
*Bee—1906—Oakland, Calif.
Garden City—1906—Blake Island, Wash.
Ella G.—1906—Juan de Fuca Strait.
*Winslow—1906—Duncan Rock, Wash.
*Del Norte—1906—Near Punta Gorda, Calif.
*Thomas L. Wand—1906—Duxbury Reef, Calif.
*City of Topeka—1906—Point Reyes, Calif.
*City of Para—1906—Near Point Ano Nuevo, Calif.
Welcome—Jan. 11, 1907—Myrtle Point, Coquille River, Ore.
Alice Gertrude—Jan. 11, 1907—Slip Point Reef, Wash.
Sequoia—Jan. 14, 1907—Humboldt Bay Bar, Calif.
Success—Jan. 23, 1907—Madison Park, Lake Washington, Wash.
Maxim—Jan., 1907—Between San Francisco and Eureka.
Alpha—Feb. 3, 1907—9 mi. north, Umpqua River, Ore.
Solano—Feb. 5, 1907—North of Ocean Park, Wash.
Wm. F. Witzemann—Feb. 5, 1907—4 mi. north, Bolinas Bay, Calif.
Corona—March 1, 1907—Humboldt Bay Bar, Calif.
Chinook—April 12, 1907—South Spit Coos Bar, Ore.
Wizard—May 29, 1907—Punta Gorda, Calif.
Alcazar—June 10, 1907—Needle Rock, Calif.
Louis—June 19, 1907—South Farallon, Calif.
Columbia—July 21, 1907—Off Shelter Cove, Calif.
*San Pedro—July 21, 1907—Off Shelter Cove, Calif.
*Liberty—Aug. 21, 1907—Bandon, Ore.
La Conner—Aug. 24, 1907—La Conner, Wash.
Tellus—Sept. 21, 1907—No. entrance Grays Harbor, Wash.
Antelope—Sept. 30, 1907—Nehalem River Bar, Ore.
Queen Christina—Oct. 12, 1907—Near Point St. George, Calif.
J. N. Teal—Oct. 22, 1907—Portland, Ore.
Novelty—Oct. 23, 1907—14 miles north, Cape Arago, Ore.
*Washtucna—Nov. 10, 1907—So. jetty, Columbia Bar, Ore.
Berkeley—Nov. 14, 1907—E. of Pt. Conception, Calif.
*Wavertree—Nov. 29, 1907—Desdemona Sands, Columbia River, Ore.
Sotoyome—Dec. 7, 1907—14 mi. S. W., Cape Mendocino, Calif.
Puritan—1907—Jones Island, Wash.
Blue Star—1907—Mud Bay, Wash.
*National City—1907—Hermosa Beach, Calif.
*Annie Comings—1907—Willamette River, Ore.
*San Gabriel—1907—Near Pt. Reyes, Calif.
Hartfield—Jan., 1908—Off Cape Flattery, Wash.
Emily Reed—Feb. 14, 1908—South of Nehalem River, Ore.
Berwick—Mar. 13, 1908—Near Siuslaw River, Ore.
Mildred—Mar. 16, 1908—Grays Harbor Bar, Wash.
Pomona—Mar. 17, 1908—Fort Ross, Calif.
Lydia—Mar. 30, 1908—Admiralty Inlet, Wash.
*Minnie E. Kelton—May 2, 1908—Off Yaquina Head, Ore.
Ida Schnauer—June 17, 1908—Near Tillamook Bay Bar, Ore.
*Anubis—July 20, 1908—San Miguel Is., Calif.
*Colorado—Aug. 15, 1908—Liplip Pt., Wash.
Gotoma—Dec. 25, 1908—Willapa Harbor, Wash.
Brodick Castle—Dec., 1908—Off Columbia River.
*Roma—1908—Near Pt. Montara, Calif.
*Shna Yak—1908—Pt. Arena, Calif.
Acme—1908—Lake Wash., Wash.
Sibyl Marston—Jan. 12, 1909—Surf, Calif.
Alice—Jan. 15, 1909—1 mi. N. Ocean Park, Wash.
Ensign—Jan. 20, 1909—Near Naples, Calif.
R. D. Inman—Mar. 20, 1909—Duxbury Reef, Calif.

Marconi—Mar. 23, 1909—Coos Bay Bar, Ore.
Matterhorn—Mar. 27, 1909—70 mi. off Umatilla Reef, Wash.
Charles E. Falk—Mar. 31, 1909—Copalis Rks., Wash.
Roderick Dhu—Apr. 26, 1909—Pt. Pinos, Calif.
F. M. Smith—May 30, 1909—Alameda, Calif.
Sea Lion—June 9, 1909—Juan de Fuca Strait.
Yosemite—July 9, 1909—Orchard Narrows, Wash.
Grayling—July 25, 1909—Off Coos Bay, Ore.
Winnebago—July 31, 1909—Pt. Arena, Calif.
*Fair Oaks—Aug. 25, 1909—Grays Harbor Bar, Wash.
St. Croix—Nov. 20, 1909—Off Pt. Dume, Calif.
Argo—Nov. 26, 1909—Tillamook Bay Bar, Ore.
Majestic—Dec. 5, 1909—Off Pt. Sur, Calif.
Susie M. Plummer—Dec. 23, 1909—Off Cape Flattery, Wash.
*Standard Oil No. 91—1909—Near Astoria, Ore.
*Blanche—1909—Off Pier 14, Seattle, Wash.
Columbia—1909—Near Bellingham, Wash.
L. T. Haas—1909—Lake Wash., Wash.
Czarina—Jan. 12, 1910—Coos Bay Bar, Ore.
San Buenaventura—Jan. 13, 1910—Rogue River Bar, Ore.
Silver Wave—Mar. 23, 1910—Near Seattle, Wash.
*George Curtis—Apr. 4, 1910—San Francisco Bay, Calif.
Ajax—April 7, 1910—Pier 18, Seattle, Wash.
*Santa Clara—April 14, 1910—Off Table Bluff, Calif.
Edith—May 8, 1910—Waada Is., Wash.
Ply—May 13, 1910—Off West Pt., Wash.
J. Marhoffer—May 18, 1910—Off Yaquina Bay, Ore. (charred hull drifted into
    Boiler Bay)
*Charles R. Wilson—May 20, 1910—Pt. Reyes, Calif.
Dora Bluhm—May 26, 1910—Santa Rosa Is., Calif.
N. T. No. 2—June 11, 1910—U. O. Dock, Seattle, Wash.
Annie E. Smale—July 9, 1910—Pt Reyes, Calif.
Dode—July 20, 1910—Off Marrowstone Pt., Wash.
San Joaquin No. 3—July 25, 1910—Sacramento, Calif.
*Albion—Aug. 2, 1910—Off West Point, Wash.
James Rolph—Aug. 3, 1910—Point Pedro, Calif.
*Phoenix—Aug. 13, 1910—Off Pt. Arena, Calif.
*Daniel Kern—Aug. 18, 1910—Cooper Pt., Columbia River.
F. A. Kilburn—Aug. 22, 1910—Oakland, Calif.
*Watson—Sept. 1, 1910—Waada Is., Wash.
*Wildwood—Sept. 19, 1910—Lk. Washington, Wash.
*A. W. Sterrett—Sept. 26, 1910—Near Tacoma, Wash.
Selja—Nov. 9, 1910—Off Pt. Reyes, Calif.
Sea Prince—Nov. 19, 1910—San Francisco Bay off Angel Is., Calif.
*J. M. Weatherwax—Nov., 1910—Off Cape Flattery, Wash.
*Northwestern—Dec. 1, 1910—Near Roche Harbor, San Juan Is., Wash.
ABC VIII—1910—Near Seattle, Wash.
Thornton—1910—Santa Cruz Is., Calif.
*Alaskan—1910—San Diego, Calif.
*Alice McDonald—1910—Near Pt. Loma, Calif.
*Damara—1910—Fort Pt., S. F., Calif.
*Charles Nelson—1910—Near Pt. Arena, Calif.
*Tailac—1910—Near Pt. Reyes, Calif.

SHIPWRECKS—1911-1920

Elk—Jan. 1, 1911—Keyport, Wash.
Oshkosh—Feb. 13, 1911—So. Jetty, Columbia Bar, Ore.
*E. L. Dwyer—Feb. 25, 1911—Seattle, Wash.

Major Shipwrecks on Coastal, Offshore and Inland Waters

*Tampico—Apr., 1911—Dock, Seattle, Wash.
Capistrano—April, 1911—Mission Flats, Calif.
*Hazel Dollar—May 3, 1911—Possession Pt., Wash.
Whidby—May 9, 1911—Oak Harbor, Wash.
*Wasp—May 21, 1911—Off Cape Sebastian, Ore.
Washcalore—May 21, 1911—Cape Sebastian, Ore.
Valiant—May, 1911—Napa Creek, Calif.
Signal—June 27, 1911—Pt. Lobos, Calif.
M. F. Henderson—June, 1911—Columbia River.
Sonoma—July 1, 1911—Pt. Reyes, Calif.
Santa Rosa—July 7, 1911—Pt. Arguello, Calif.
Transport—Aug. 27, 1911—Off San Juan Is., Wash.
*Aurelia—Aug., 1911—Columbia River Bar.
Comet—Sept. 2, 1911—San Miguel Island, Calif.
*Wm. Nottingham—Oct. 9, 1911—Off Columbia River.
Perdita—Oct. 10, 1911—Near Point Ludlow, Wash.
*Hunter—Oct. 15, 1911—Bush Pt., Wash.
McKinley—Oct. 17, 1911—Wollochet Bay, Wash.
Multnomah—Oct. 27, 1911—Off Pier 57, Seattle, Wash.
Columbia—Oct., 1911—Near Northport, Wash.
*Fairhaven—Nov. 3, 1911—Pier 3, Seattle, Wash.
*Washington—Nov. 17, 1911—Peacock Spit, Wash.
Vashon—Nov. 28, 1911—Anacortes, Wash.
*Westerner—Nov., 1911—Pillar Rock, Columbia River.
Hoosier Boy—1911—Off Pt. Wilson, Wash.
Stockholm—1911—Near Cape Flattery, Wash.
A. R. Robinson—1911—Near Port Madison, Wash.
Trilby—1911—San Francisco Bay, Calif.
*Quinault—1911—Near Pt. Reyes, Calif.
*Bowdoin—1911—Near Pigeon Pt., Calif.
Mascot—1911—(Willamette or Columbia)
Winchester—1911—Off San Juan Is., Wash.
Admiralen—1911—Off Eureka, Calif.
Mary C.—Jan. 11, 1912—Near Port Blakely, Wash.
Admiral—Jan. 13, 1912—South jetty, Columbia Bar, Ore.
North Star—Jan. 20, 1912—Coos Bay Bar, Ore.
Rene—Jan., 1912—East of Dungeness, Wash.
*Independent—Feb. 22, 1912—PCC Dock, Seattle, Wash.
Ida McKay—Feb., 1912—Off California Coast.
*Rosecrans—Mar. 12, 1912—North of Santa Barbara, Calif.
*Telegraph—April 25, 1912—Elliott Bay (Seattle, Wash.)
Vida—April 27, 1912—Tillamook Bay Bar, Ore.
Neptune—April, 1912—Deception Pass, Wash.
*George R. Vosberg—May 3, 1912—So. spit, Nehalem Bar, Ore.
*C. T. Hill—July 30, 1912—So. spit, Nehalem River, Ore.
Lillebonne—Aug. 29, 1912—San Francisco Bay, Calif.
*Wm. G. Irwin—Aug., 1912—San Francisco Bay, Calif.
*Wilhelmina—Aug., 1912—Siuslaw River, Ore.
Nebraska—Aug., 1912—Neah Bay, Wash.
J. J. Loggie—Sept. 19, 1912—Pt. Arguello, Calif.
*Rosecrans—Sept., 1912—Gaviotta, Calif.
*Dauntless—Oct. 13, 1912—Off Fort Bragg, Calif.
Pilgrim—Oct., 1912—Yaquina Bay Bar, Ore.
*F-3—Oct., 1912—Off Port Angeles, Wash.
Osprey—Nov. 1, 1912—Coos Bay Bar, Ore.
Herald—Nov. 4, 1912—Oakland, Calif.
Condor—Nov. 17, 1912—Yaquina Bay Bar, Ore.
Golden Fleece—Dec. 23, 1912—Warm Springs, Calif.
Sea Gull—1912—Near San Francisco, Calif.

Shipwrecks of the Pacific Coast

*G. C. Lindauer—1912—Near Pt. Arena, Calif.
W. R. Todd—1912—Near Pasco, Wash.
*Sarah Dixon—1912—Columbia River.
Leona—1912—Willamette River, Ore.
Juanita—About 1912—Cedar River Bar, Wash.
Rosecrans—Jan. 7, 1913—Peacock Spit, Wash.
Pathfinder—Jan. 15, 1913—Pt. Diablo, San Francisco Bay, Calif.
Samoa—Jan. 28, 1913—Pt. Reyes, Calif.
*Vicksburg—Feb. 10, 1913—Bremerton, Wash.
Mimi—Feb. 14, 1913—So. entrance, Nehalem Bar, Ore.
Advent—Feb. 16, 1913—Coos Bay Bar, Ore.
*Pinta—Feb., 1913—San Francisco Bay, Calif.
Albion—Mar. 21, 1913—Stewarts Pt., Calif.
John D. Spreckles—Mar. 29, 1913—Off Pt. Reyes, Calif.
Maryland—June 5, 1913—San Rafael Creek, Calif.
Riverside—June 19, 1913—Blunts Reef, Calif.
Casco—June 27, 1913—Pt. Piedras Blancas, Calif.
J. H. Lunsmann—July 12, 1913—Black Pt., San Francisco Bay, Calif.
Point Arena—Aug. 9, 1913—Pigeon Pt., Calif.
Calcium—Aug. 7, 1913—Off Camano Is., Wash.
Glenesslin—Oct. 1, 1913—Neah-Kah-Nie Mt., Ore.
Merced—Oct. 15, 1913—Point Gorda, Calif.
Kake—Nov. 1, 1913—South jetty, Columbia Bar, Ore.
Col. Baker—Nov. 6, 1913—Drakes Inlet, Calif.
Aloha—Nov. 30, 1913—Off Destruction Is., Wash.
Balboa—Dec. 1, 1913—Grays Harbor Bar, Wash.
Torrisdale—Dec. 28, 1913—Grays Harbor Bar, Wash.
Pomo—Dec. 31, 1913—Off Pt. Reyes, Calif.
*John A. Hooper—1913—Pt. Lobos, Calif.
*Guard—1913—Near Richardson, Wash.
*Tamalpais—1913—Blunts Reef, Calif.
*Acme—1913—San Francisco Bay, Calif.
*Navajo—1913—San Pablo Bay, Calif.
*Washtenaw—1913—Near Pt. Gorda, Calif.
*Iaqua—1913—Pt. Arena, Calif.
Helen Hale—1913—Upper Columbia River.
Seminole—1913—Off Angel Is., San Francisco Bay, Calif.
*H. J. Corcoran—1913—Off Angel Is., San Francisco Bay, Calif.
*Sentinel—Jan. 14, 1914—E. Waterway, Seattle, Wash.
Pathfinder—Jan. 15, 1914—Point Diablo, San Francisco Bay, Calif.
Polaris—Jan. 16, 1914—Duxbury Reef, Calif.
Urania—Feb. 12, 1914—Lake Washington, Wash.
Petaluma—Mar. 22, 1914—Petaluma, Calif.
Argo—April 1, 1914—Off Pt. Wilson, Wash.
*Charles Nelson—April 23, 1914—Fields Landing, Calif.
Admiral Sampson—Aug. 26, 1914—Off Point No Point, Wash.
Scotia—Aug. 27, 1914—Purisima Pt., Calif.
America—Aug. 31, 1914—San Juan Is., Wash.
*Lorne—Aug. 31, 1914—San Juan Is., Wash.
Francis H. Leggett—Sept. 8, 1914—60 miles S.W. Columbia River.
Rochelle—Oct. 21, 1914—Clatsop Spit, Ore.
*Santa Catalina—Oct. 23, 1914—Portland, Ore.
Hanalai—Nov. 23, 1914—Near Bolinas, Calif.
*Oakland—Oct. 27, 1914—San Francisco Bay, Calif.
Dredger No. 1—Oct. 1914—Near La Conner, Wash.
Coos Bay—Dec. 18, 1914—Ventura, Calif.
*Wilhelmina—1914—Off Golden Gate, Calif.
*City of Topeka—1914—Pt. Reyes, Calif.
Albatross—1914—Near Quillayute River, Wash.

Major Shipwrecks on Coastal, Offshore and Inland Waters

Trifolicum—1914—Land's End, Calif.
*Sioux—1914—Dungeness Spit, Wash.
*Katy—1914—Elliott Bay, Seattle, Wash.
Brigit—1914—San Francisco Bay, Calif.
*Archer—1914—Off Duxbury Reef, Calif.
Magnolia—1914—Off Crescent City, Calif.
Eureka—Jan. 8, 1915—Pt. Bonita, Calif.
*Repeat—Jan., 1915—Off Tillamook Bay, Ore.
Monarch—April 13, 1915—San Pablo Bay, Calif.
Randolph—April 24, 1915—Coquille River Bar, Ore.
Claremont—May 22, 1915—Coos Bay Bar, Ore.
*West Coast—June 18, 1915—John's Pass, Wash.
Aggi—June, 1915—Santa Rosa Is., Calif.
Okanogan—July 8, 1915—Wenatchee, Wash.
North Star—July 8, 1915—Wenatchee, Wash.
Columbia—July 8, 1915—Wenatchee, Wash.
Chelan—July 8, 1915—Wenatchee, Wash.
*Decorah—July 15, 1915—Clatsop Spit, Ore.
*Admiral Watson—Aug. 29, 1915—Pier, Seattle, Wash.
Alliance No. 2—Oct. 17, 1915—Malpass Rk., Pt. Arena, Calif.
Graywood—Oct. 25, 1915—Off Umatilla Lightship, Wash.
Seeam—Oct. 31, 1915—No. of Whidbey Is., Wash.
Santa Clara—Nov. 2, 1915—Coos Bay Bar, Ore.
Sausalito—Dec., 1915—Waada Is., Wash.
St. Paul—1915—Wenatchee, Wash.
Walter Hackett—1915—San Francisco, Calif.
La Sota—1915—Near Los Angeles, Calif.
*Noyo—1915—La Jolla Pt. and San Diego, Calif.
Catania—1915—Near Pt. Sur, Calif.
*Georgiana—1915—Duxbury Reef, Calif.
*Albatross—1915—Dungeness Spit, Wash.
Swan—1915—Manette (Bremerton, Wash.)
Venus—1915—Puget Sound, Wash.
*President—1915—Camano, Wash.
*O. N. Clark—1915—Clatsop Spit, Ore.
Letitia—About 1915—Off So. San Francisco, Calif.
*Victor II—Jan. 15, 1916—Off Pt. Defiance, Wash.
Aberdeen—Jan. 23, 1916—San Francisco Bar, Calif.
Excelsior—Feb. 7, 1916—San Francisco Bay, Calif.
Fifield—Feb. 21, 1916—Coquille River Bar, Ore.
Ruby—Mar. 21, 1916—Off Golden Gate, Calif.
*Oakland—April, 1916—Nehalem Beach, Ore.
Roanoke—May 10, 1916—Off Port San Luis, Calif.
Washington—June 10, 1916—Off Grays Harbor, Wash.
Bear—June 14, 1916—Bear River, Cape Mendocino, Calif.
*Shna Yak—June, 1916—Near San Francisco, Calif.
*Bandon—Aug. 30, 1916—Near Port Orford, Ore.
*Congress—Sept. 14, 1916—Off Coos Bay, Ore.
Aliceil—Dec. 13, 1916—Pt. Loma, Calif.
*H-3—Dec. 14, 1916—Samoa Beach, Calif.
*Daisy Gadsby—1916—Pt. Reyes, Calif.
*Triton—1916—Off Mercer Is., Wash.
C. C. No. 38—1916—So. of Copalis Beach, Wash.
*Harriet G.—1916—Off Cape Flattery, Wash.
*Brooklyn—1916—Near Pt. Arena, Calif.
*Shna Yak—1916—Near Pt. Sur, Calif.
*Resolute—1916—Near Dungeness, Wash.
Grace Barton—1916—Near San Francisco, Calif.
*James Higgins—1916—Pt. Hueneme, Calif.

Jim Bludso—1916—Wood Is., Calif.
Milwaukee—Jan. 17, 1917—Samoa Beach, Calif.
Thistle—April 18, 1917—President Channel, Wash.
Coronado—April 27, 1917—Off Pt. Arena, Calif.
Alcatraz—May 2, 1917—10 miles North, Pt. Arena, Calif.
W.T. & B. No. 3—May 25, 1917—Puyallup River, Wash.
McCulloch—June 13, 1917—Off Pt. Hueneme, Calif.
*Sinaloa—June 15, 1917—Cape Blanco, Ore.
Del Norte—July 27, 1917—Pt. Arena, Calif.
*Irene—Aug., 1917—Duwamish River, Seattle, Wash.
Tolo—Oct. 5, 1917—Off Bainbridge Is., Wash.
Quinault—Oct. 9, 1917—Pt. Gorda, Calif.
Caroline—Nov. 18, 1917—Sausalito, Calif.
Kenkon Maru—Nov., 1917—Saturna Is., B. C., (near U. S. border)
*Hyak—Dec. 17, 1917—Poulsbo, Wash.
F-1—Dec. 17, 1917—Off Pt. Loma, Calif.
Capt. James Fornance—Dec. 21, 1917—Near Cape Disappointment, Wash.
Hero—1917—Elliott Bay, Seattle, Wash.
Hope—1917—Near San Francisco, Calif.
*Raymond—1917—Near Pt. Sur, Calif.
*Coquille River—1917—Near Caspar, Calif.
*Wergeland—1917—Off Cape Flattery, Wash.
*N. D. Tobey—1917—Agate Pass, Wash.
*Simla—About 1917—Pt. Gorda, Calif.
*Canada Maru—Jan. 31, 1918—Near Cape Flattery, Wash.
*Uwanto—Feb. 7, 1918—10 mi. south, Bellingham, Wash.
Chetco—Feb. 19, 1918—Summerland, Calif.
Noyo—Feb. 26, 1918—Pt. Arena, Calif.
Americana—Feb. 28, 1918—Off Columbia River.
Chesley No. 5—Mar. 1, 1918—Seattle, Wash.
*Phyllis—April, 1918—Point Vicente, Calif.
Fairhaven—June 6, 1918—La Conner, Wash.
Paloma—June 7, 1918—Willamette River, Ore.
Rosalie—June 22, 1918—Duwamish Waterway, Seattle, Wash.
Newburg—Oct. 8, 1918—North of Bodega, Calif.
Mandalay—Oct. 27, 1918—Crescent City, Calif.
A. J. Fuller—Oct. 30, 1918—Off Harbor Is., Seattle, Wash.
Wallacut—Nov. 2, 1918—Off Cape Arago, Ore.
Bertha Dolbeer—Nov. 3, 1918—Off Calif. Coast.
Della—Dec. 9, 1918—Near Port Orford, Ore.
Sehome—Dec. 14, 1918—San Pablo Bay, Calif.
George Loomis—Dec. 19, 1918—Off Blunts Reef, Calif.
Steven Quinn No. 1—1918—Near San Francisco, Calif.
*Caroline—1918—Near San Francisco, Calif.
Dunkerque—1918—Near Pt. Arena, Calif.
International—1918—Off Santa Cruz Is., Calif.
*Amazon—1918—Off Dash Pt., Wash.
Jupiter—1918—Off Willapa Bay, Wash.
Lief E.—1918—Off Cape Flattery, Wash.
Norfolk—1918—Pt. Gorda, Calif.
Janet Carruthers—Jan. 22, 1919—No. of Grays Harbor, Wash.
*Santa Clara—Jan. 25, 1919—Drydock, San Francisco, Calif.
*San Jose—March 23, 1919—Oakland, Calif.
Albert—April 2, 1919—No. of Pt. Reyes, Calif.
(unnamed Ferris type hull)—May 9, 1919—On ways, Aberdeen, Wash.
Hunter—May 13, 1919—Near Cape Johnson, Wash.
John G. North—May 14, 1919—Off Cape San Lucas, Calif.
*Owl—May 15, 1919—Near Bolinas Bay, Calif.

Major Shipwrecks on Coastal, Offshore and Inland Waters

Rustler—Aug. 24, 1919—So. of Rogue River, Ore.
North Fork—Sept. 21, 1919—10 mi. W., Shelter Cove, Calif.
Alert—Sept. 26, 1919—Rio Vista, Calif.
J. A. Chanslor—Dec. 19, 1919—Near Cape Blanco, Ore.
Girlie Mahoney—Dec. 23, 1919—Albion Harbor, Calif.
*Helen P. Drew—1919—Duxbury Reef, Calif.
*Unimak—1919—Duxbury Reef, Calif.
*G. C. Lindauer—1919—San Francisco Bay, Calif.
*San Jacinto—1919—Humboldt Bay, Calif.
Sentinel—1919—Near San Francisco, Calif.
*Nippon Maru—1919—Golden Gate, Calif.
Alert—1919—Coquille R., Ore.
*Daisy Putnam—1919—Point Arena, Calif.
*Mary E. Foster—1919—W. of Port Angeles, Wash.
*Bradford—1919—Near Pigeon Pt., Calif.
*Frank H. Buck—1919—Near Pigeon Pt., Calif.
*Celilo—1919—Near Pt. Arena, Calif.
Hammond—Jan. 25, 1920—10 mi. So. Columbia R., Ore.
French—Jan. 25, 1920—Off Oregon Coast.
Coquhon—Feb. 28, 1920—Off Grays Harbor, Wash.
Ituna—Mar. 13, 1920—Near San Francisco Lightship, Calif.
*Fred Baxter—May 22, 1920—Near Pt. Townsend, Wash.
Horace Templeton—June 22, 1920—Off Pt. Arena, Calif.
State of Washington—June 23, 1920—Off Tongue Pt., Oregon.
Lizzie Theresa—July 10, 1920—Suisun Bay, Calif.
Douglas—Aug. 7, 1920—Near Priest Rapids, Wash.
Melvina—Oct. 10, 1920—San Francisco Bay, Calif.
P.C.C. Co. No. II—Oct. 30, 1920—Madison Park, Wash.
North Star—Nov. 4, 1920—Catalina Is., Calif.
Joan of Arc—Nov. 16, 1920—Near Rogue River Bar, Oregon.
Gold—Nov. 20, 1920—Petaluma, Calif.
W. J. Pirrie—Nov. 26, 1920—Off Cape Johnson, Wash.
Alviso—Dec. 15, 1920—Brytes Bend, Sacramento, Calif.
Weitchpec—Dec. 15, 1920—Brytes Bend, Sacramento, Calif.
Annie—Dec. 27, 1920—Near San Rafael, Calif.
Bella—Dec. 1920—Near Port Orford, Oregon.
Fay No. 4—1920—Near San Francisco, Calif.
*Oregon—1920—Nehalem Bar, Oregon.
*Tillicum—1920—Ballard Channel, Wash.
*Santa Flavia—1920—San Francisco Bay, Calif.
*South Coast—1920—Near St. George Reef, Calif.
Arakan—1920—Near Pt. Reyes, Calif.
*Ernest H. Meyer—1920—Pt. Reyes, Calif.
*Yosemite—1920—Pt. Reyes, Calif.
Allenaire—1920—Near San Francisco, Calif.
*Umatilla—1920's—Off Neah Bay, Wash.
*Grace Dollar—about 1920—Coquille River Bar, Oregon.
*City of Sydney—1920's—Three miles north, Humboldt Bay, Calif.
Merillie—1920's—Mercer Slough, Wash.
*Martha—1920's—Klamath R., Calif.

SHIPWRECKS—1921-1930

Klamath—Feb. 5, 1921—Del Mar Landing, Calif.
Los Angeles T. C. Co. No. I—Feb. 18, 1921—Ocean Park, Calif.
Governor—April 1, 1921—Off Pt. Wilson, Wash.
*Arizonan—Summer 1921—Near Lime Kiln, Wash.
Canadian Exporter—Aug. 1, 1921—Willapa Bay Bar, Wash.

Shipwrecks of the Pacific Coast

Alaska—Aug. 6, 1921—Blunts Reef, Calif.
Cleopatra—Oct. 16, 1921—Port Discovery, Wash.
Neponset No. 2—Nov. 12, 1921—Georgiana Slough, Calif.
Sea Eagle—Nov. 20, 1921—Off Yaquina Head, Oregon.
Tokuyo Maru—Nov. 1921—60 miles off Columbia R.
Athlon—Dec. 17, 1921—Near Port Ludlow, Wash.
*Virginia IV—Dec. 28, 1921—Dock, Tacoma, Wash.
Oriole—1921—Near San Francisco, Calif.
Lotus—1921—Pt. Conception, Calif.
Thomas Crowley—1921—Pt. Conception, Calif.
*G. C. Lindauer—1921—Pt. Sur, Calif.
Conestoga—1921—San Francisco for Hawaii.
Whittier—May 1, 1922—Saunders Reef, Calif.
Hugh Hogan—May 18, 1922—Off Cape Blanco, Oregon
Welsh Prince—May 28, 1922—Altoona Head, Col. River, Wash.
Arctic—July 5, 1922—Pt. Arena, Calif.
Henry T. Scott—July 16, 1922—Ent. of Juan de Fuca Strait.
King Cyrus—July 17, 1922—Pt. Chehalis, Grays Harbor, Wash.
Calista—July 27, 1922—West Point, Wash.
*H. F. Alexander—Aug. 6, 1922—Cake Rock, Wash.
Washtucna—Aug. 17, 1922—Umpqua R. Bar, Oregon.
Zinfandel—Sept. 5, 1922—Sacramento R., Calif.
Lyman Stewart—Oct. 7, 1922—Off Pt. Lobos, Calif.
*City of Honolulu—Oct. 12, 1922—600 mi. off Pacific Coast.
Portland—Oct. 14, 1922—Willamette R. near Portland, Ore.
Golden Shore—Oct., 1922—Off Butchertown, San Francisco Bay, Calif.
Willie A. Higgins—Dec. 7, 1922—Blaine, Wash.
Orteric—Dec. 11, 1922—10 mi. No., Pt. Arena, Calif.
Stockton City—Dec. 28, 1922—Russian Gulch, Calif.
H. F. Harper—1922—Pt. Arena, Calif.
Golden West No. 2—1922—Humboldt Bay Bar, Calif.
*Claremont—1922—Near Los Angeles, Calif.
*Grays Harbor—1922—Near Pt. Montara, Calif.
*Thomas L. Wand—1922—Pt. Sur, Calif.
*Virginia Olson—1922—San Pedro, Calif.
*Pacific—1922—Pt. Loma, Calif.
*James Tuft—Jan. 5, 1923—Off Destruction Is., Wash.
Tyee—Feb. 3, 1923—Commencement Bay, Tacoma, Wash.
Nika—Feb. 14, 1923—Off Umatilla Lightship, Wash.
Alta—Feb. 20, 1923—San Pedro for Bellingham.
Watson A. West—Feb. 23, 1923—San Miguel Is., Calif.
*Georgie Burton—Feb. 1923—Portland, Oregon
Babina—March 3, 1923—Off Santa Cruz Is., Calif.
Fresno—April 4, 1923—Near Kennydale, Wash.
Evelyn N.—April 10, 1923—Off Three Tree Pt., Wash.
*Bahada—Apr. 23, 1923—San Pedro Harbor, Calif.
Brush—Apr. 26, 1923—Off Cape Arago, Ore.
Lake Gebhart—May 9, 1923—Toleak Pt., Wash.
Fidalgo—May 23, 1923—Strait of Juan de Fuca.
Lifeline—May, 1923—Off Manzanita Beach, Oregon.
Fox—May, 1923—Coos Bay Bar, Ore.
Rainier—July 28, 1923—Juan de Fuca Strait (beached Appletree Pt.)
*Otsego—July, 1923—Grays Harbor, Wash.
*Rubaiyat—Aug. 30, 1923—Near Tacoma, Wash.
Cuba—Sept. 8, 1923—San Miguel Is., Calif.
Woodbury—Sept. 9, 1923—Off Honda near Pt. Arguello, Calif.
S. P. Lee—Sept. 9, 1923—Off Honda near Pt. Arguello, Calif.
Nicholas—Sept. 9, 1923—Off Honda near Pt. Arguello, Calif.
Young—Sept. 9, 1923—Off Honda near Pt. Arguello, Calif.

Major Shipwrecks on Coastal, Offshore and Inland Waters

Chauncey—Sept. 9, 1923—Off Honda near Pt. Arguello, Calif.
Delphi—Sept. 9, 1923—Off Honda near Pt. Arguello, Calif.
Fuller—Sept. 9, 1923—Off Honda near Pt. Arguello, Calif.
*Equator—Oct. 23, 1923—Quillayute R. Bar, Wash.
Phoenix—Nov. 5, 1923—Tillamook Bay Bar, Oregon.
T. W. Lake—Dec. 5, 1923—Off Lopez Is., Wash.
Flavel—Dec. 14, 1923—Cypress Pt., Calif.
C. A. Smith—Dec. 16, 1923—Coos Bay Bar, Oregon.
Astorian—Dec. 20, 1923—Four Mile Rk., Seattle, Wash.
Dauntless—Dec. 30, 1923—Meadow Pt., Wash.
*Admiral Goodrich—1923—Humboldt Bay, Calif.
Rough & Ready—1923—Near San Francisco, Calif.
Crovate—1923—Pt. Sal, Calif.
*Sierra—1923—Farallon Islands, Calif.
Iolanda—1923—Near Piscadero Pt., Calif.
*Cascade—about 1923—Pt. Dume, Calif.
*Norwood—Jan. 29, 1924—City dock, Seattle, Wash.
*Agnes—Jan. 30, 1924—Grays Harbor, Wash.
Columbia—Feb. 17, 1924—No. jetty, Coos Bar, Oregon.
Burton—Feb. 22, 1924—Gig Harbor, Wash.
*Wakena—April, 1924—Lummi Is., Wash.
*Frank H. Buck—May 4, 1924—Pt. Pinos, Calif.
G. C. Lindauer—May 16, 1924—Umpqua R. Bar, Oregon.
*Admiral Nicholson—May 16, 1924—Umpqua R. Bar, Oregon.
Oakland—June 24, 1924—Off Cape Mendocino, Calif.
Mary Hanlon—June 24, 1924—Cape Mendocino, Calif.
Issac Reed—July, 1924—Off Bodega Bay, Calif.
Catherine M.—Aug. 21, 1924—Near Destruction Is., Wash.
Quadra—Summer, 1924—San Francisco, Calif.
Alpha—Sept. 19, 1924—Klipsan Beach, Wash.
Albion—Sept. 21, 1924—Foulweather Bluff, Wash.
La Feliz—Oct. 1, 1924—No. of Santa Cruz, Calif.
Chaco—Oct. 16, 1924—Near Pt. Defiance, Tacoma, Wash.
Elsie—Oct. 28, 1924—Partridge Pt., Wash.
Alden Anderson—Oct. 29, 1924—Avon, Calif.
Acme—Oct. 31, 1924—Coquille R. Bar, Oregon.
Bianca—Dec. 15, 1924—Near Clallam Bay, Wash.
Chinook—1924—Elliott Bay, Seattle, Wash.
Corona—1924—Near Bodega Head, Calif.
Ruth—1924—Oakland Estuary, Calif.
Caoba—Feb. 5, 1925—North Beach, Wash.
*Avalon—Apr. 29, 1925—Cape Shoalwater, Wash.
Ryba—April 30, 1925—Grays Harbor Bar, Wash.
Georgia—June 1, 1925—Port Orchard, Wash.
Eleanor W.—June 25, 1925—Lowell Pt., Wash.
Flavel—June 28, 1925—Off Newport, Oregon.
Muriel—July 3, 1925—Balboa, Calif.
Nemaha—July 12, 1925—Shelter Cove, Calif.
Transit—July 13, 1925—Titlow Beach, Wash.
Cornelia Cook—July 29, 1925—Port Angeles, Wash.
Mountaineer—Oct. 5, 1925—Hood Canal, Wash. (hull beached on Bainbridge Island, Wash.)
Halco—Nov. 30, 1925—Grays Harbor, Wash.
Sea Monarch—Dec. 9, 1925—Off Marrowstone Pt., Wash.
*Potlatch—1925—Huckleberry Is., Wash.
Stockton No. 2—1925—San Joaquin River, Calif.
Whale—1925—Port San Luis, Calif.
Yosemite—Feb. 7, 1926—Pt. Reyes, Calif.

Shipwrecks of the Pacific Coast

Wm. Bowden—Feb. 12, 1926—Redondo Beach, Calif.
*Alice Cooke—Feb., 1926—Off Washington Coast.
Sierra—March 3, 1926—San Pedro, Calif.
Horaisan Maru—March 8, 1926—Grays Harbor Bar, Wash.
David C. Meyer—March 9, 1926—Pt. Fermin, Calif.
*Wellesley—April 11, 1926—Near Astoria, Ore.
Norlina—Aug. 4, 1926—Horseshoe Pt., Calif.
City of Edmonds—Aug. 24, 1926—Port Gamble Bay, Wash.
Prosper—Aug. 27, 1926—Hoquiam River, Wash.
Everett—Oct. 29, 1926—Off Table Bluff, Calif.
Dart—Nov. 9, 1926—Houghton, Wash.
Bremerton—Nov. 9, 1926—Houghton, Wash.
Reliance—Nov. 9, 1926—Houghton, Wash.
*Solana—Nov., 1926—Pt. Purisima, Calif.
Bahada—Nov., 1926—Off Saddlebag Is., Wash.
*Ryo Yei Maru—Dec. 5, 1926—Off Cape Flattery, Wash.
Mohican—1926—San Diego, Calif.
Daisy—1926—Near San Francisco, Calif.
*Helene—1926—Off Crescent City, Calif.
Chas. B. Kennedy—1926—San Francisco Bay, Calif.
San Ubaldo—1926—Near Los Angeles Harbor, Calif.
Despatch No. 5—1926—Pt. Loma, Calif.
Rollo—1926—Everett, Wash.
Swallow—1926—Near Long Beach, Calif.
Rainier—1926—Apple Tree Point, Wash.
Esther Buhne—Feb. 13, 1927—Newport Beach, Calif.
Mary E. Moore—Feb. 23, 1927—Coquille River Bar Buoy, Ore.
Golden City—April 24, 1927—San Francisco Bay, Calif.
Port Saunders—May 6, 1927—San Francisco Bay, Calif.
Indiana Harbor—May 18, 1927—Pt. Gorda, Calif.
Warren—May 24, 1927—Off Protection Is., Wash.
City of Nome—June 3, 1927—Aberdeen, Wash.
Crescent City—July 7, 1927—Santa Cruz Light, Calif.
Dolphin—July 11, 1927—Stockton, Calif.
Northland—July 21, 1927—San Francisco Bay, Calif.
*Virginia—July, 1927—Shilshole Bay, Seattle, Wash.
Linnea—Sept. 27, 1927—Sacramento, Calif.
W. A. Fletcher—Oct. 7, 1927—Mokelumne River, Calif.
Ellen—Oct. 12, 1927—San Francisco Bay, Calif.
Coos Bay—Oct. 22, 1927—Golden Gate, Calif.
Henrietta—Nov. 6, 1927—Pt. Reyes, Calif.
Emily F. Bichard—Nov. 17, 1927—San Francisco Bay, Calif.
Tenpaisan Maru—Dec. 1, 1927—Copalis Beach, Wash.
Diamond—Dec., 1927—22 miles south of San Pedro, Calif.
Shark—1927—Near Crescent City, Calif.
Winifred O'Donnell—1927—Pt. Arguello, Calif.
Carrier Dove—1927—Near Coos Bay, Ore.
*North Bend—Jan. 5, 1928—Peacock Spit, Wash.
Red Wing—Feb. 21, 1928—San Nicholas Is., Calif.
John—Feb. 21, 1928—San Joaquin River, Calif.
Wespac No. 2—May 31, 1928—Magdalena Bay, Calif.
*Andrew Foss—July 24, 1928—Port Angeles, Wash.
*Petroleum II—Aug. 21, 1928—Pt. Wells Dock, Wash.
Floridian—Sept. 1, 1928—65 miles South of Tatoosh Is., Wash.
Washtenaw—Sept. 22, 1928—Wilmington Harbor, Calif.
Utility—Oct. 3, 1928—San Francisco, Calif.
*Forester—Nov. 20, 1928—Grays Harbor, Wash.
Bay Island—Nov. 30, 1928—Off Mukilteo, Wash.
J. D. Loop No. 1—1928—Oceanside, Calif.

Major Shipwrecks on Coastal, Offshore and Inland Waters

*Tourist—1928—Lake Washington, Wash.
Wahkeena—Jan. 24, 1929—Grays Harbor Bar, Wash.
*George M. Brown—Jan. 25, 1929—Siletz River, Ore.
Sujamico—Mar. 1, 1929—North of Coos Bay, Ore.
Explorer—Mar. 16, 1929—Los Angeles Breakwater, Calif.
City of Clinton—March 23, 1929—Mukilteo, Wash.
K. & W. No. 1—May 4, 1929—Pillar Pt., Wash.
Farwest—June 7, 1929—Orcas Is., Wash.
Rose No. 4—June 8, 1929—Puget Sound, Wash.
Gig Harbor—June 10, 1929—Gig Harbor, Wash.
Multnomah—June 16, 1929—Columbia River Bar (towed to Astoria, later
  scuttled).
Laurel—June 16, 1929—Peacock Spit, Wash.
Emrose—June 23, 1929—Lake Washington Ship Canal, Wash.
Hartwood—June 27, 1929—Pt. Reyes, Calif.
Jane L. Stanford—Aug., 1929—Off Santa Cruz Is., Calif.
San Juan—Sept. 29, 1929—Off Pigeon Pt., Calif.
Bretagne—Oct. 15, 1929—SW of Cape Flattery, Wash.
Irene—Nov. 1, 1929—Long Beach, Calif.
Daisy Putnam—Nov. 22, 1929—Pt. Gorda, Calif.
Skagway—Dec. 15, 1929—Off Tatoosh Is., Wash.
San Juan II—Dec. 25, 1929—Off Blakely Is., Wash.
*Suremico—1929—Off Cape Flattery, Wash.
Monarch—1929—Near San Francisco, Calif.
*Evanger—1929—Near Newport Beach, Calif.
Simla—Jan. 7, 1930—Oakland Estuary, Calif.
Farquhar—Jan. 22, 1930—Strait of Georgia, Wash.
Admiral Benson—Feb. 15, 1930—Peacock Spit, Wash.
*City of Lille—Feb. 19, 1930—Newport Beach, Calif.
*Agnes W.—Feb., 1930—Near Alki Pt., Wash.
Rhine Maru—Feb., 1930—Pt. Sur, Calif.
J. D. Peters—Apr. 11, 1930—Crescent Bay, Wash.
Richfield—May 8, 1930—Pt. Reyes, Calif.
*Dorothy L.—May, 1930—Off Richmond Beach, Wash.
South Coast—Sept. 16, 1930—16 miles SW Cape Blanco, Ore.
Gretchen—Oct., 1930—Near Neah Bay, Wash.
Brooklyn—Nov. 8, 1930—Off Humboldt Bay, Calif.
*Kekoskee—1930—Smith's Cove, Seattle, Wash.
Valiant—1930—Catalina Is., Calif.
*Charcas—1930—Near Los Angeles Harbor, Calif.
Prospector—1930—Oceanside, Calif.
Ida May—1930—Pt. Pinos, Calif.
Wilmington—1930—Off Humboldt Bay, Calif.
Oriental—1930—Pt. Dume, Calif.
Continental—1930—Near Los Angeles, Calif.
*Tamiahua—1930—Pescadero Pt., Calif.
Buckeye—1930—Stavis Bay, Hood Canal, Wash.
*A. G. Wells—1930's—Near San Francisco, Calif.

SHIPWRECKS—1931-1940

*Maliko—Jan., 1931—U. P. Dock, Seattle, Wash.
*Barbara Foss—Feb. 15, 1931—Off Lummi Is., Wash.
Sea Foam—Feb. 23, 1931—Pt. Arena, Calif.
Cleone—Apr. 9, 1931—Humboldt Bay, Calif.
Harvard—May 30, 1931—4 mi. No., Pt. Arguello, Calif.
Munleon—Nov. 7, 1931—Pt. Reyes, Calif.
M. F. Sterling—Nov. 12, 1931—Eagle Harbor, Winslow, Wash.

Shipwrecks of the Pacific Coast

Alameda—Nov. 28, 1931—Seattle, Wash.
*Emidio—1931—Pt. Arguello, Calif.
*Sinaloa—1931—San Pedro Breakwater, Calif.
G. Marconi—1931—Off Ventura, Calif.
*Admiral Sebree—1931—No. of Hoh Head, Wash.
Cowlitz—1931—Columbia River.
Windward—1931—Near San Clemente Is., Calif.
Agnes—1931—Near San Francisco, Calif.
Sea Products No. 3—1931—San Diego, Calif.
Tom—1931—Seattle, Wash.
*Nehalem—1931—Salmon Bay, Seattle, Wash.
Foss No. 2—1931—Off Tillamook Head, Ore.
Washington—Feb. 15, 1932—Humboldt Bay, Calif.
City of Mukilteo—Apr. 11, 1932—Columbia Beach, Wash.
Gratia—Apr. 20, 1932—Redondo Beach, Calif.
Thos. P. Emigh—Apr. 20, 1932—Redondo Beach, Calif.
*Truxillo—July 3, 1932—Tillamook Bay Bar, Ore.
Emperor—July 15, 1932—Off Santa Barbara Is., Calif.
Mt. Baker—Aug. 1, 1932—Birch Pt., Wash.
Horizon—Aug. 31, 1932—Pt. Dume, Calif.
Valiant—summer 1932—Catalina Is., Calif.
Fort Bragg—Sept. 7, 1932—Coos Bay Bar, Ore.
New Life—Sept. 7, 1932—Off Santa Barbara, Calif.
Advance—Sept. 8, 1932—Catalina Is., Calif.
Colusa—Sept. 15, 1932—Broderick, Calif.
Sacramento—Sept. 16, 1932—Broderick, Calif.
Fred Ball No. 4—Sept. 27, 1932—San Joaquin River, Calif.
*Eagle—Sept. 29, 1932—Brighton Beach, Calif.
Jacinto—Sept. 30, 1932—Broderick, Calif.
Flora—Sept. 30, 1932—Broderick, Calif.
San Joaquin No. 4—Sept. 30, 1932—Broderick, Calif.
San Joaquin No. 2—Sept. 30, 1932—Broderick, Calif.
San Jose—Sept. 30, 1932—Broderick, Calif.
Valletta—Sept. 30, 1932—Broderick, Calif.
Sea Wolf—Oct. 27, 1932—Off Davenport, Calif.
Tiger—Nov. 4, 1932—So. of Bellingham, Wash.
Mayflower—Nov. 17, 1932—Gig Harbor, Wash.
Sea Thrush—Dec. 4, 1932—Clatsop Spit, Ore.
Virginia—Dec. 14, 1932—Off Half Moon Bay, Calif.
Sealand—Dec. 14, 1932—Gig Harbor, Wash.
*Gedney—1932—Salmon Bay, Seattle, Wash.
Sunlight—1932—Off Santa Barbara, Calif.
Californian—1932—Half Moon Bay, Calif.
Garcia—1932—Off Pt. Vicente, Calif.
Fidelity—1932—Near San Francisco, Calif.
Charles Brown—1932—Laguna, Calif.
Yellowstone—Feb. 24, 1933—Humboldt Bay, Calif.
Pescawha—Feb. 27, 1933—No. jetty, Columbia River Bar, Wash.
Tiverton—Mar. 13, 1933—Humboldt Bay Bar, Calif.
*President Madison—Mar. 25, 1933—Todd Shipyard, Seattle, Wash.
Lindberg—Apr. 7, 1933—Off Sucia Is., Wash.
Wm. H. Smith—Apr. 14, 1933—Monterey, Calif.
Margaret C.—May 3, 1933—Catalina Is., Calif.
*Peralta—May 6, 1933—Oakland, Calif.
Belvedere—May 28, 1933—San Joaquin River, Calif.
Nippon Maru—May 28, 1933—Pt. Honda, Calif.
S. C. C. Co. No. I—June 27, 1933—Oceanside, Calif.
Valencia—June 29, 1933—San Clemente Is., Calif.
Helgeland—July 30, 1933—President Channel, Wash.

Major Shipwrecks on Coastal, Offshore and Inland Waters

Lahaina—Oct. 5, 1933—Pt. Vicente, Calif.
Swastika—1933—Near San Francisco, Calif.
Philippine—Jan. 1, 1934—Terminal Is., Calif.
Hercules—Jan. 5, 1934—Three Mile Rapids, Ore.
*Tai Yin—Mar. 14, 1934—5 mi. No. Pt. Reyes, Calif.
Diamond O.—Apr. 26, 1934—Portland, Ore.
*Childar—May 3, 1934—Peacock Spit, Wash.
Belle Isle—June 12, 1934—Out of San Diego, Calif.
J. B. Stetson—Sept. 3, 1934—Cypress Pt., Calif.
*Virginia V—Oct. 22, 1934—Olalla, Wash.
*M. T. 21—Oct., 1934—Partridge Pt., Wash.
*W. T. & B. No. 11—Oct., 1934—Smith Cove, Seattle, Wash.
*W. T. & B. No. 10—Oct., 1934—Smith Cove, Seattle, Wash.
*W. T. & B. No. 58—Oct., 1934—Smith Cove, Seattle, Wash.
*W. T. & B. No. 60—Oct., 1934—Smith Cove, Seattle, Wash.
Acalin—1934—Off Pt. Lobos, Calif.
Greenland—1934—Off Pt. Pinos, Calif.
Oregon—1934—Off Monterey Bay, Calif.
Parker No. I—1934—Near Astoria, Ore.
Adela Hobson—1934—Near Richmond, Calif.
Service—1934—Near San Francisco Bay, Calif.
Yours Truly—1934—Southern Calif. Coast.
NSK No. 2—1934—Huntington Beach, Calif.
LaCrescentia—Jan. 7, 1935—Off Port San Luis, Calif.
Aurora—Jan. 18, 1935—Monterey, Calif.
Hokuman Maru—Jan. 21, 1935—Off Wash. Coast.
Noyo—June 10, 1935—Pt. Arena, Calif.
Casino—Aug. 22, 1935—Off Long Beach, Calif.
San Domenico—Dec. 26, 1935—So. of Pt. Reyes, Calif.
Wilhelmina—1935—San Joaquin River, Calif.
Georgina—1935—Redondo Beach, Calif.
E. L. Smith—Jan. 1, 1936—Off Coquille River, Ore.
Verona—Jan. 10, 1936—Dock, Seattle, Wash.
Iowa—Jan. 12, 1936—Peacock Spit, Wash.
Silver Wave—Feb. 18, 1936—Off Newport Beach, Calif.
Phyllis—Mar. 9, 1936—Near Humbug Mt., Ore.
Nedra—Mar. 23, 1936—Off San Clemente, Calif.
*Santa Flavia—Apr. 7, 1936—Lake Union, Seattle, Wash.
New Crivello—Sept. 18, 1936—Off Pescadero Pt., Calif.
Standard—Sept. 24, 1936—Santa Barbara, Calif.
George U. Hind—Sept., 1936—Off Carlsbad, Calif.
Santiam—Oct. 14, 1936—Aberdeen, Wash.
Ohioan—Nov. 7, 1936—Near Pt. Lobos, Calif.
Golden West—Nov. 29, 1936—Coquille River Bar Jetty, Ore.
Necanicum—1936—San Pablo Bay, Calif.
T. G. Condare—1936—Near Albion, Calif.
Irene—Jan. 28, 1937—Off Redondo Beach, Calif.
Ione—Feb. 4, 1937—Near Copeys Rock, Ore.
Chris C.—Feb. 4, 1937—Pt. Hueneme, Calif.
Cottoneva—Feb. 10, 1937—Near Port Orford, Ore.
*Feltre—Feb. 17, 1937—Near Prescott, Ore. (Col. River).
Pronto—Mar. 1, 1937—Off Catalina Is., Calif.
Frank H. Buck—Mar. 6, 1937—Pt. Lobos, Calif.
Normandie—Mar. 10, 1937—Off Eureka, Calif.
Trinidad—May 7, 1937—North Spit, Willapa Bar, Wash.
Efin—May 11, 1937—Near Ilwaco, Wash.
W. T. & B. Co. No. 66—May 30, 1937—Puget Sound, Wash.
Capitol—June 15, 1937—Dana Pass, Olympia, Wash.
*West Mahwah—July 9, 1937—Pescadero Pt., Calif.

Eight Bros.—Sept. 25, 1937—Off Bodega Bay, Calif.
Garfield No. 6—Oct. 7, 1937—LaPush, Wash.
Hai Da—Oct., 1937—Off Cape Flattery, Wash.
*Florence Olson—Oct., 1937—Umpqua Jetty, Ore.
Shasta—Nov. 14, 1937—Alameda, Calif.
Pal—Nov. 27, 1937—6 mi. No. Pt. Hueneme, Calif.
Sunlight—Dec. 7, 1937—7 mi. S. E. San Francisco Lightship.
*Lebec—1937—Pt. Arena, Calif.
Koka—1937—San Clemente Is., Calif.
*Golden Bear—1937—Off Oregon Coast.
*City of Blaine—Jan. 3, 1938—Shipyard, W. Seattle, Wash.
Yukon—Jan. 6, 1938—Santa Cruz Is., Calif.
E. Antoni—Jan. 31, 1938—Drakes Bay, Calif.
*Nisqually—Mar. 26, 1938—Clatsop Spit, Ore.
Golden West—Mar. 26, 1938—San Joaquin River, Calif.
Melrose—Mar., 1938—Off San Pedro, Calif.
Coaster—Aug. 25, 1938—Off Pt. No Pt., Wash.
Harvester—Oct. 11, 1938—Smith Cove, Seattle, Wash.
*Vancouver—Nov. 3, 1938—San Francisco, Calif.
Dorothy Wintermote—Nov. 22, 1938—Fish Rock near Pt. Arena, Calif.
International No. 3—1938—Humboldt Bay, Calif.
*M. T. 6—1938—Hoquiam, Wash.
*Hagan—1938—West Seattle, Wash.
Danti Alighieri—1938—Santa Barbara Is., Calif.
Virgil Bogue—Jan. 28, 1939—Oakland Estuary, Calif.
Temple Bar—Apr. 8, 1939—Quillayute Needles, Wash.
Glen Mayne—July 13, 1939—Near Carlsbad, Calif.
No. XLV D.L. Co.—July 14, 1939—Near LaPush, Wash.
Bokuyo Maru—July 18, 1939—Off Calif. Coast.
Humanity—Sept. 12, 1939—Off Pt. Dume, Calif.
Redwood—Sept. 18, 1939—Humboldt Bay Breakwater, Calif.
Minnie A. Caine—Sept. 24, 1939—Santa Monica, Calif.
Paragon—Sept. 24, 1939—Ent. Newport Beach, Calif.
Canada—Nov. 9, 1939—Off Marrowstone Pt., Wash.
*Point Lobos—1939—Near Golden Gate, Calif.
Oakland—Jan. 27, 1940—Oakland, Calif.
Lone Eagle—Apr. 8, 1940—Off Pt. Arguello, Calif.
Horace—Apr. 14, 1940—Seattle, Wash.
Daisy Matthews—May 4, 1940—Pt. St. George, Calif.
Schatleben—May 11, 1940—Off Pt. Loma, Calif.
Agram—May 18, 1940—San Clemente Is., Calif.
*Claremont—June 14, 1940—Grays Harbor Bar, Wash.
Hellenic Skipper—July 13, 1940—125 mi. off Grays Harbor, Wash.
J. R. McDonald—Aug. 11, 1940—Sequim Bay, Wash.
Olympic II—Sept. 4, 1940—Off San Pedro, Calif.
El Dorado—Sept. 8, 1940—Bacon Is., Stockton, Calif.
Buster—Oct. 17, 1940—10 mi. above Astoria, Ore.
Star of the Sea—Oct. 22, 1940—2 mi. W. Pedro Pt., Calif.
North Bend—Oct. 23, 1940—Off Coos Bay, Ore.
Jugo Slavia—Nov. 10, 1940—2 mi. S. E. Pt. Montara, Calif.
Steelhead—Nov. 24, 1940—Off Meadowdale, Wash.
Gleaner—Dec. 6, 1940—Skagit River, Wash.
*Tyee—Dec. 6, 1940—Tillamook Bay Bar, Ore.
*Whitney Olson—Dec. 16, 1940—Clatsop Beach, Ore.
*Oregon Express—Dec. 29, 1940—Bush Pt., Wash.
*Wm. H. Harrison—Dec., 1940—Near Los Angeles, Calif.
West Maco—Dec., 1940—8 mi. off Pt. Fermin, Calif.
Harmony—1940—Off Bolinas Pt., Calif.
Manuel Espinosa—1940—Off Golden Gate, Calif.

Major Shipwrecks on Coastal, Offshore and Inland Waters

Lone Eagle—1940—Off Pt. Arguello, Calif.
*Anna Schafer—1940—Near Golden Gate, Calif.
Bloomfield—1940—Near San Francisco, Calif.

SHIPWRECKS—1941-1950

Lincoln—Jan. 1, 1941—Off Crane Is., Wash.
Katherine Donovan—Jan. 24, 1941—So. of Humboldt Bay, Calif.
*Bandon—Feb. 8, 1941—Off Trinidad Head, Calif.
*W. R. Chamberlain Jr.—Feb. 10, 1941—Near San Diego, Calif.
*Lumberman—Feb. 15, 1941—Lake Union, Seattle, Wash.
George Billings—Feb., 1941—Santa Monica, Calif.
Vazlav Vorovsky—Apr. 3, 1941—Peacock Spit, Wash.
*Iowan—June 12, 1941—Pt. Conception, Calif.
Brothers—Oct. 10, 1941—Catalina Is., Calif.
*Snohomish—Oct. 25, 1941—Skipjack Is., Wash.
Willapa—Dec. 4, 1941—Near Gold Beach, Ore.
Gen. Hugh L. Scott—Dec. 7, 1941—Off Calif. Coast.
Cynthia Olson—Dec. 7, 1941—700 mi. off San Francisco, Calif.
Mauna Ala—Dec. 10, 1941—Clatsop Beach, Ore.
Emidio—Dec. 22, 1941—Near Blunts Reef, Calif.
Montebello—Dec. 23, 1941—Off Piedras Blancas Pt., Calif.
*Absaroka—Dec. 24, 1941—Off Long Beach, Calif.
*Dorothy Phillips—Dec. 24, 1941—Off Calif. Coast.
*Nightingale (AM 18) —Dec. 26, 1941—Columbia R. Bar Buoy 11.
Sakuri—Dec., 1941—Off Palos Verdes, Calif.
*Port Saunders—1941—San Francisco Bay, Calif.
American Eagle—1941—Off Crescent City, Calif.
Umatilla—1941—Columbia River.
Columbia Contract—1941—Near Los Angeles, Calif.
Nordic Pride—1941—Pt. Arena, Calif.
Ruby—1941—Near Catalina Is., Calif.
Pacific Star—1941—Near Luguna, Calif.
Jitney—About 1941—Whidbey Is., Wash.
Coast Trader—Jan. 7, 1942—40 mi. off Cape Flattery, Wash.
Star of Scotland—Jan. 23, 1942—Off Santa Monica, Calif.
Chickaree—Jan., 1942—Near Bremerton, Wash.
Barbara Foss—Mar. 31, 1942—So. of Pt. Wilson, Wash.
Larry Doheny—Oct. 5, 1942—Off Cape Sebastian, Ore.
Camden—Oct. 10, 1942—Off Willapa Harbor, Wash.
Susan Olson—Nov., 1942—Southern Ore. Coast.
Empress—1942—San Nicholas Is., Calif.
Annie M. Rolph—1942—Off Long Beach, Calif.
Amazon—1942—Off So. Calif. Coast.
Mt. Vernon—1942—Skagit River, Wash.
Los Angeles—1942—Pt. Arguello, Calif.
Progress—1942—Monterey Bay, Calif.
Orion—1942—Near Santa Cruz, Calif.
Liberty Girl—1942—Off San Pedro, Calif.
Stimson No. 5—1942—Smith Slough, Quillayute River, Wash.
YFD No. 20—Jan., 1943—Off Bolinas, Calif.
San Wan—Feb. 11, 1943—Near Santa Barbara, Calif.
May—Feb. 14, 1943—Between Portland, Ore., and Vancouver, Wn.
YMS-133—Feb. 20, 1943—Coos Bay Bar, Ore.
Lamut—March 31, 1943—Quillayute Rocks, Wash.
La Paloma—July 13, 1943—Off Laguna, Calif.
*Toloa—July 18, 1943—Drydock, Seattle, Wash.
P. S. B. & D. Co. No. 14—Nov. 15, 1943—Off Columbia River.
C. W. W. 26—Dec. 5, 1943—San Nicholas Island, Calif.

Shipwrecks of the Pacific Coast

Stanford—Dec. 8, 1943—S.W. of Davenport, Calif.
Chicago—Dec. 15, 1943—South of Catalina Island, Calif.
Unimak—1943—San Francisco, Calif.
Prosperity—1943—Near San Francisco, Calif.
City of San Rafael—1943—San Francisco Bay, Calif.
Esmeraldo—1943—Near Antioch, Calif.
Cascades—1943—Columbia River, Ore.
Electra—Jan. 26, 1944—Clatsop Spit, Ore.
Motormates—March 4, 1944—San Joaquin River, Calif.
*Nabob—March, 1944—Near Point Roberts, Wash.
Henry Bergh—May 31, 1944—Farallon Island, Calif.
George L. Olson—June 23, 1944—Coos Bay Bar, Ore.
Illitch—June 24, 1944—Drydock, Portland, Ore.
Quinault Victory—July 17, 1944—Port Chicago, Calif.
E. A. Bryan—July 17, 1944—Port Chicago, Calif.
F. A. Douty—August 9, 1944—San Francisco Bay, Calif.
Blue Fin—Sept. 3, 1944—Off Santa Rosa Island, Calif.
Southland—Sept. 24, 1944—Off Pescadero Point, Calif.
Infallible—Oct. 26, 1944—2 mi. North of Santa Cruz, Calif.
Mobile Point—Dec. 23, 1944—Off Cascade Head, Ore.
* (Sub Chaser) —1944—Lopez Island, Wash.
Republic—Feb. 7, 1945—Off Columbia River Bar.
Alvarado—March 17, 1945—8 mi. North of Coos Bay, Ore.
Falcon—March 23, 1945—El Segundo, Calif.
New World—March 23, 1945—Near Coronado, Calif.
Sea Hawk—May 18, 1945—Off Point Loma, Calif.
*Cadaretta—May 28, 1945—James Island, Wash.
Robert B.—June 15, 1945—McDonald Island, San Joaquin River, Calif.
Marclay—July 30, 1945—Portland, Ore.
Dorothy Joan—Sept. 13, 1945—Off Yaquina Head, Ore.
Arrogant—Sept., 1945—Off Cape Flattery, Wash.
H. M. Adams—Oct. 30, 1945—Off Cambria Pines, Calif.
Foss 99—Nov. 23, 1945—Off Ballard, Wash.
*Rainier—Dec. 4, 1945—Coos Bay Bar, Ore.
Reliance—Dec. 17, 1945—Pier 23, San Francisco, Calif.
Matagorda—Feb. 18, 1946—35 mi. off Coos Bay, Ore.
Sea Pirate—Feb. 28, 1946—Off Point Gorda, Calif.
Martha Foss—May 20, 1946—Near Port Angeles, Wash.
Frank Lawrence—May 24, 1946—10 mi. off Point Sur, Calif.
K. & W. No. 1—Aug. 30, 1946—Port Angeles, Wash.
YP-636—Sept. 12, 1946—Half Moon Bay, Calif.
El Commodore—Oct. 28, 1946—Surf, Calif.
Hwa Tung—Dec. 14, 1946—300 mi. off San Pedro, Calif.
*Oneida Victory—1946—Point Conception, Calif.
*W. L. R. Emmet—1946—Point Conception, Calif.
Nancy Lee—1946—Near Santa Cruz Island, Calif.
*John H. Marion—1946—Near Long Beach, Calif.
Mindanao—1946—Off Point Loma, Calif.
P. T. & B. Co. No. 1684—Jan. 18, 1947—Peacock Spit, Wash.
P. T. & B. Co. No. 1685—Jan. 18, 1947—Peacock Spit, Wash.
Drexel Victory—Jan. 20, 1947—Off Columbia River Bar.
Markay—Jan. 22, 1947—Berth 168, Los Angeles Harbor, Calif.
Arrow—Feb. 13, 1947—North Beach Peninsula, Wash.
*Lawrence Victory—March 19, 1947—Foulweather Bluff, Wash.
Georgia—Apr. 9, 1947—Off Whidbey Island, Wash.
Smile—April 22, 1947—Tillamook Bay, Ore.
F. H. Marvin—April, 1947—Budd Inlet, Wash.
*Frej—May 7, 1947—Richmond, Calif.
W. H. McFadden—May 9, 1947—Off Dungeness Spit, Wash.

304

Major Shipwrecks on Coastal, Offshore and Inland Waters

Bialchi—June 4, 1947—San Francisco Bay, Calif.
*Skookum Chief—Aug. 12, 1947—Dofflemeyer Point, Wash.
Diamond Knot—Aug. 13, 1947—6 mi. West of Port Angeles, Wash.
Rossino II—Aug. 22, 1947—NW of Catalina Island, Calif.
White Crest—Aug. 29, 1947—Hoquiam, Wash.
Zarembo III—Sept. 13, 1947—W.S.W. Cape Blanco, Ore.
*W. E. Mahoney—Sept., 1947—Off Sauvies Island, Ore.
Juanita—Dec., 1947—Monterey, Calif.
*Tyee—1947—Dock, Bellingham, Wash.
Leader—1947—Near Point Vicente, Calif.
*Claire—Jan., 1948—Camas Slough, near Portland, Ore.
Garrison—Feb. 3, 1948—South of Crescent City, Calif.
*Colorado—Feb. 6, 1948—Otter Rock, Coos Bay, Ore.
Rose Ann—Feb., 1948—Off Columbia River.
*Mary Francis—Feb., 1948—Des Moines, Wash.
Joseph Aspdin—April 12, 1948—½ mi. off Yaquina Bay, Ore.
Ace No. 1—April 28, 1948—At Dana Point, Calif.
Pennsylvania—May, 1948—Near Carroll Island, Wash.
Robarts—June 15, 1948—Near Portland, Ore.
Stranger—July 17, 1948—West of San Onofre, Calif.
Sea Lion—July, 1948—Off Willapa Bay, Wash.
Leta B—Aug. 21, 1948—Off Coos Bay, Ore.
Diana—Aug., 1948—Near Point Loma, Calif.
Redondo—Aug., 1948—San Francisco, Calif.
West Coast—Summer, 1948—San Pedro, Calif.
Silver Gate—Sept. 4, 1948—Off Point Vicente, Calif.
*Olympic—Oct., 1948—San Diego, Calif.
American Clipper—Oct., 1948—Monterey Bay, Calif.
*Los Angeles—Nov. 13, 1948—Tacoma, Wash.
*Ruby VIII—Nov. 15, 1948—Off Point Wilson, Wash.
Neptune—Nov. 16, 1948—9 mi. off Columbia River.
Goodnews—Nov. 22, 1948—Off Oregon Coast.
*Irene—Dec. 17, 1948—Shelton, Wash.
*Bellingham—1948—Near Deer Harbor, Wash.
Western Fisher—1948—Off Point Dume, Calif.
*Peter—Feb., 1949—Oregon City, Willamette River, Ore.
Adele—March 19, 1949—Umpqua River, Ore.
LCM—April 21, 1949—Off Washington Coast.
Columbia—April, 1949—Off Golden Gate, Calif.
Waldero—May 14, 1949—North of Point Gorda, Calif.
Nuchek—May 19, 1949—Lake Washington Ship Canal, Seattle, Wash.
Sonoma—May 21, 1949—Off Ventura, Calif.
Ioannis G. Kuíukundis—July 11, 1949—Point Arguello, Calif.
Vashon—Aug., 1949—Off Catalina Island, Calif.
Pacific Enterprise—Sept. 9, 1949—Point Arena, Calif.
Liberty Girl—Sept. 16, 1949—Boundary Bay, Calif.
Forty Fathom No. 4—Sept. 26, 1949—Monterey Bay, Calif.
Mercer—Sept., 1949—Off West Point, Wash.
Salina Cruz—Oct. 17, 1949—Off Grays Harbor, Wash.
Yankee Mariner—Oct. 19, 1949—N.W. of Point Arguello, Calif.
Howkan—Oct. 26, 1949—Bellingham, Wash.
Ceres—Oct. 27, 1949—Off Port Orford, Ore.
San Francisco—Oct. 31, 1949—Off Anacapa Island, Calif.
Crowley No. 64—Nov. 1, 1949—Santa Monica Bay, Calif.
Andalusia—Nov. 5, 1949—4 mi. East of Neah Bay, Wash.
Tamara Sun—Nov., 1949—Off Sand Island, Ore.
*Hawaiian Rancher—Dec. 2, 1949—Alameda, Calif.
St. James—Dec. 11, 1949—S.W. of Pt. Fermin, Calif.
Aquila—Dec. 12, 1949—Off Point Fermin, Calif.

Shipwrecks of the Pacific Coast

Helori—Dec. 21, 1949—Off Umpqua River, Ore.
M. T. No. 6—Dec. 31, 1949—Off Harbor Island, Seattle, Wash.
*Invader—1949—John Day Rapids, Ore.
Equator—1949—Anacapa Island, Calif.
Balboa—1949—Anacapa Island, Calif.
Hopestill—1949—North of Santa Barbara, Calif.
Pride of the Sea—1940's—Off Santa Barbara, Calif.
Star of the West—1940's—Off Farallon Island, Calif.
*Dividend—Jan. 18, 1950—Bellingham, Wash.
Johnny Boy—Jan. 28, 1950—Off Laguna Beach, Calif.
*Umatilla—Jan. 30, 1950—North of McNary, Wash.
Onward—Feb. 22, 1950—S.W. of Catalina Harbor, Calif.
Wilmar—March 9, 1950—West of La Jolla, Calif.
Nooya—March 12, 1950—Seattle, Wash.
Kalama—March 14, 1950—Carrolls, Wash.
Bertha—March, 1950—Coos Bay Jetty, Ore.
Doris E.—April 17, 1950—South of Friday Harbor, Wash.
Oregon Cove—May 9, 1950—Off shore from Golden Gate, Calif.
*Deneb—May 15, 1950—North Beach Peninsula, Wash.
*Penguin—June 3, 1950—Lake Union, Seattle, Wash.
Seaport—June 22, 1950—Off Columbia River Bar.
Island Queen—July 7, 1950—Off Cypress Island, Wash.
Lucky—July 16, 1950—Off Columbia River Lightship.
Point Loma—July 18, 1950—Crescent City, Calif.
Milmar—Aug. 22, 1950—Off Santa Barbara Island, Calif.
Benevolence—Aug. 26, 1950—Off Golden Gate, Calif.
Islander—Aug. 30, 1950—Skagit Island, near Deception Pass, Wash.
Spray—Sept. 5, 1950—North of Umpqua River, Ore.
Alice H.—Sept. 23, 1950—Near Port Orford, Ore.
*Western Clipper—Sept., 1950—Point Fermin, Calif.
YBI—Oct. 1, 1950—100 mi. off Columbia River.
St. Peter—Nov. 4, 1950—Everett, Wash.
YTB-286—Nov. 19, 1950—Off Grays Harbor, Wash.
Louis B.—Nov. 30, 1950—Near Everett, Wash.
Del Monte No. 3—Nov. 30, 1950—Mouth of Noyo River, Calif.
San Guiseppe—Dec. 19, 1950—Off Anacapa Island, Calif.
*Bear—Dec., 1950—Portland, Ore.
Radio—1950—San Diego, Calif.
Pan Pacific—1950—Off Point Dume, Calif.
Yankee Boy—1950—Off Laguna, Calif.
Helen P. Drew—1950—Oakland Estuary, Calif.

SHIPWRECKS—1951-1960

*Oleum—Jan. 2, 1951—Columbia River Bar.
Rose—Feb. 2, 1951—Off Umatilla Lightship, Wash.
*T-6—Feb. 3, 1951—Off Golden Gate, Calif.
American Girl—Feb. 8, 1951—Portuguese Bend, Calif.
Helen E.—March 9, 1951—4 mi. North of Coos Bay, Ore.
L. A. McLeod—March 18, 1951—Northport, Wash.
*Kenkoku Maru—April 28, 1951—Stewart's Point, Calif.
Elsie I—April 29, 1951—Off Huntington, Calif.
Retriever—April 29, 1951—Near Redondo Beach, Calif.
Active—Aug. 27, 1951—Dock, Everett, Wash.
Morgan Shell—Sept. 25, 1951—San Francisco Bay, Calif.
Snoopy—Sept., 1951—Off Cascade Head, Ore.
Lourakis—Oct. 2, 1951—Anderson's Cove, Calif.
Linde—Oct. 5, 1951—Near Port Hueneme Breakwater, Calif.
Ommaney—Oct. 6, 1951—80 mi. off Cape Blanco, Ore.

Major Shipwrecks on Coastal, Offshore and Inland Waters

J. C. Freese Co. No. 7—Oct. 23, 1951—Richmond, Calif.
L. H. Coolidge—Oct. 29, 1951—Coquille River Jetty, Ore.
San Joaquin—Nov. 2, 1951—Mouth of Sacramento River, Calif.
Glory of the Sea—Nov. 2, 1951—Breakwater, Neah Bay, Wash.
George Walton—Nov. 6, 1951—Off Cape Flattery, Wash.
No. 4413—Dec. 5, 1951—San Nicolas Island, Calif.
*Erria—Dec. 20, 1951—Off Tongue Point, Ore.
El Padre—Dec. 22, 1951—Near Los Angeles, Calif.
Associated Oil Co. No. 8—Jan. 9, 1952—Rock off Point Richmond, Calif.
Susan—Jan. 21, 1952—Peacock Spit, Wash.
Esperia III—Jan. 25, 1952—Long Beach, Calif.
Golden Gate—Jan. 30, 1952—Santa Cruz Island, Calif.
*P. S. No. 91—Jan., 1952—South of Heceta Head, Ore.
*Baer—Feb. 13, 1952—Allan Island, Wash.
New Rex—April 29, 1952—3 mi. off Laguna, Calif.
Prelude—May 19, 1952—Near Orcas Island, Wash.
Resolute—May 30, 1952—S.W. of Gaviota, Calif.
Healy No. 1—June 8, 1952—Houghton, Wash.
*Cynthia Olson—June 9, 1952—Coquille River Bar, No. Jetty, Ore.
*Go Getter—June 12, 1952—South Jetty, Columbia Bar, Ore.
*Victor H. Kelly—July 12, 1952—Pier, San Francisco, Calif.
*Yorkmar—Sept. 9, 1952—North of Grays Harbor Bar, Wash.
Eagle—Oct. 3, 1952—Tulalip Bay, Wash.
*YTB-268—Oct. 8, 1952—San Francisco Bay, Calif.
Del Rio—Oct. 28, 1952—Off Anacapa Island, Calif.
Aurora—Nov. 7, 1952—Santa Cruz Island, Calif.
Blue Sky—Nov. 17, 1952—Catalina Island, Calif.
American Rose—Dec. 8, 1952—Near San Clemente Island, Calif.
Fernstream—Dec. 11, 1952—Off Alcatraz Island, Calif.
Phyllis—Dec. 15, 1952—Gaviota, Calif.
Periwinkle—Jan. 19, 1953—North Spit, Grays Harbor Bar, Wash.
Rosana—Feb. 27, 1953—Off San Mateo Coast, Calif.
*BARC—March 18, 1953—Off Pigeon Point, Calif.
Caroga—March 29, 1953—Portuguese Bay, Calif.
(A. C. Dutton) barge—March, 1953—Bodega Beach, Calif.
Lazy Days—May 9, 1953—Near San Diego, Calif.
Captain Ludwig—June 25, 1953—Off Newport, Ore.
Jacob Luckenbach—July 14, 1953—S.W. of San Francisco Lightship, Calif.
*Racquette—Sept. 24, 1953—Near Astoria, Ore.
*Ticonderoga—Sept. 28, 1953—Off Southern Calif. Coast.
Georgene M.—Oct. 4, 1953—Near Point Arena, Calif.
Ocean Cape—Oct. 10, 1953—Iceberg Pt., Lopez Is., Wash.
*Tajlum—Nov. 1, 1953—Whidbey Island, Wash.
*Otsega—Nov. 11, 1953—No. of Long Beach, Wash.
Oliver Olson—Nov. 3, 1953—South Jetty, Coquille River, Oregon.
Andrew D.—Nov. 13, 1953—South of Point Dume, Calif.
Western Pilot—Nov. 14, 1953—South of Dana Point, Calif.
*Barge No. 16—Nov. 22, 1953—Columbia River Bar.
No. 510 Port of Pasco—Dec. 12, 1953—North Jetty, Coos Bar, Ore.
Ida Mae—1953—Off Cape Disappointment, Wash.
*Galveston—Jan. 25, 1954—Near Neah Bay, Wash.
Sea Lion—Feb. 1, 1954—Off Point Conception, Calif.
Intrepid—Feb. 23, 1954—North Beach Peninsula, Wash.
Nichols I—Feb. 23, 1954—North Beach Peninsula, Wash.
Andrew Jackson—May 2, 1954—S.W. of Gold Beach, Ore.
St. George—May 2, 1954—West of La Jolla, Calif.
*Patria—June 21, 1954—Santa Rosa Island, Calif.
American Beauty—June 24, 1954—Off San Clemente Island, Calif.
*Western—July, 1954—Near Vancouver, Wash.

Shipwrecks of the Pacific Coast

*Mule Duzer—Aug. 21, 1954—Near Bonneville Dam, Ore.
North Head—Sept. 25, 1954—Off Catalina Island, Calif.
Holy Cross—Nov. 15, 1954—Off Whidbey Island, Wash.
My Pride—Dec. 13, 1954—Near Golden Gate Bridge, Calif.
Bob-Don—Dec. 15, 1954—Sequim Bay, Wash.
Mary Ann—Jan. 26, 1955—W.S.W. of Cape Elizabeth, Wash.
*Baby Doll—Feb. 28, 1955—Off Oregon Coast.
Santa Maria—March 10, 1955—Off Point Wells, Wash.
Benjie Boy—April 13, 1955—Off Catalina Island, Calif.
Suomi—April 21, 1955—North of Santa Barbara, Calif.
Northern Light—June 28, 1955—Near San Diego, Calif.
Dolly C.—Aug. 11, 1955—Near Smith Island, Wash.
*Tancred—Aug. 13, 1955—Off Golden Gate, Calif.
Gypsy Q—Aug. 24, 1955—Off Anacapa Island, Calif.
*Paula Jean—Aug., 1955—Columbia River, near Cathlamet, Wash.
*Normandie—Sept. 18, 1955—Near San Diego, Calif.
Selma S.—Sept. 26, 1955—Off Umpqua River, Ore.
Casco—Sept. 28, 1955—Off Vashon Island, Wash.
St. Anne of the Sunset—Oct. 17, 1955—Off Anacapa Island, Calif.
*Thetis—Nov. 5, 1955—Lake Union, Seattle, Wash.
Point Augusta—Nov. 7, 1955—Off Lummi Island, Wash.
Bear—Nov. 9, 1955—Bellingham Bay, Wash.
*Lightship No. 16 (Sandheads) —Nov. 10, 1955—Pt. Roberts, Wash.
Ocean Pride—Nov. 11, 1955—Off Cape Lookout, Ore.
New Saturnia—Nov. 14, 1955—West of Dana Pt., Calif.
Discovery—Dec. 20, 1955—Off Los Angeles, Calif.
*Del Norte Woodsman—Dec., 1955—Near Crescent City, Calif.
*Steel Chemist—1955—Off Southern California Coast.
Helen T.—Jan. 20, 1956—Roche Harbor, Wash.
Barge No. 14—Jan., 1956—Off Rogue R. Bar, Ore.
No. 506—Feb., 1956—Near Castle Rock, Ore.
Howard Olson—May 14, 1956—Off Pt. Sur, Calif.
Thorvald—May 15, 1956—N.W. of Blunts Reef, Calif.
(Associated Oil) barge—June 29, 1956—San Francisco, Calif.
Achille Paladini—Sept. 2, 1956—Off Pt. Laguna, Calif.
Seagate—Sept. 7, 1956—Sonora Reef and Taholah, Wash.
John W.—Sept. 13, 1956—Koitlah Pt., Wash.
Skagit Chief—Oct. 29, 1956—12 mi. W. Grays Harbor, Wash.
LSM-455—Nov. 20, 1956—San Clemente Is., Calif.
American Boy—Nov. 26, 1956—Off Malibu, Calif.
New Home II—Dec. 6, 1956—5 mi. S.S.E. Oceanside, Calif.
Gov. Markham—Jan. 9, 1957—Off La Jolla, Calif.
Pronto—Jan. 6, 1957—Grays Harbor, Wash.
Landing Craft (unnamed) —Jan. 9, 1957—Off La Jolla, Calif.
*Henry B.—Jan. 14, 1957—Willamette River, Ore.
*Jeanny—Jan. 30, 1957—Alameda, Calif. (drydock)
Kumalong—March 30, 1957—Off Yaquina Point, Ore.
Companion—July, 1957—San Francisco to Astoria.
William T. Rossell—Sept. 10, 1957—Coos Bay Bar, Ore.
Pacific Queen—Sept. 17, 1957—Old Town Dock, Tacoma, Wash.
Gosling—Jan. 18, 1958—San Pedro, Calif.
Klihyam—Sept. 27, 1958—Mouth Siuslaw River, Ore.
*Wainaku—Sept. 27, 1958—Mouth, Siuslaw River, Ore.
*Cape Douglas—Dec. 29, 1958—Between Vashon Island and Three Tree Pt., Wash.
*Midway—March 10, 1959—Off Partridge Point, Wash.
*Lois Ann—March 26, 1959—Swamped off Alki Point, Wash.
North American—July 11, 1959—Between Double Bluff and Bush Point, Wash.
*Lipari—Oct. 25, 1959—Off Grayland, Wash.

308

Major Shipwrecks on Coastal, Offshore and Inland Waters

Brant—May, 1960—20 miles off Santa Barbara, Calif.
Avalon—July 18, 1960—Off Long Beach, Calif.
Humboldt Woodsman—Aug. 18, 1960—Mouth of Siuslaw River, Ore.
*Kalamas—Sept. 6, 1960—Simpson Reef, Cape Arago, Ore.
Coos—Nov. 10, 1960—Off Cape Meares, Ore.
Elizabeth Olson—Nov. 30, 1960—Coquille River bar, Ore.
Texmar—Dec. 30, 1960—Grays Harbor, near Moon Island, Wash.
*Skagit Belle—1960—Skagit River, Wash.

SHIPWRECKS—1961—FEBRUARY, 1962

Three U. S. Coast Guard vessels (including the motor lifeboat *Triumph*) ; a 36-foot motor lifeboat; a 40-foot Coast Guard patrol craft; and a commercial fish boat, the *Mermaid*—All lost on the Columbia River Bar, Jan. 14, 1961.
Dominator—March 13, 1961—Palos Verdes Cliffs, Calif.
*Rebel—March 27, 1961—Coquille River Bar, Ore.
*Island Mail—May 29, 1961—Just west of Smith Island, Wash.
ex Western—June 15, 1961—South shore Tomahawk Island, Ore.
Alaska Reefer—Aug. 29, 1961—Whalem Point, Indian Island, Wash.
Star of the Sea—Oct. 5, 1961—Point Arena, Calif.
*Morning Star—Oct. 1961—South jetty, Yaquina Bay bar, Ore.
Bristol—Nov. 29, 1961—Southwest of Bellingham, Wash.
Chickasaw—Feb. 7, 1962—Santa Rosa Island, Calif.
Aloma—Feb. 11, 1962—15 mi. south, Destruction Island, Wash.
Olympic—Feb. 16, 1962—Off Camano Island, Puget Sound, Wash.

INDEX

A

Abby Palmer, ship, 248
Abercorn, bark, 46, 47
Abila, Jean, 222
Abrego, Capt. Jose, 257
Active, tug, 246
Agge, Capt. Niels, 180, 181
Agwiworld, tanker, 262
A. J. Fuller, ship, 93, 94
Alaska, str., 213, 214, 215, 216, 217
Alaskan, str., 159, 161, 162
Alice, bark, 64
Alliance No. II, power schr., 222
American Eagle, str., 240
Andalusia, str., 73, 74, 75
Andelana, bark, 95, 96
Anderson, Capt. Sam, 53
Anyox, str., 214, 215, 216, 217
Arapahoe, Navy tug, 190
Argo, str., 130, 131, 132, 133
Arneson, A., 225
Asturian Prince, str., 40
Aubert, Capt., 64
Austria, ship, 28, 30

B

Baldwin, H. H. ,146
Bear, str., 209, 210, 212, 213
Beaver, str., 210
Bendixsen, H. D., 198
Bennington, USS, 270
Beresford, Lord Charles, 39
Bergman, John, 144, 145
Blackburn, Capt. David, 34, 35
Blairmore, ship, 246, 247, 248
Blanco, brig, 140, 141
Blanco, trawler, 36, 38
Blunts Reef Lightship, 207, 210, 212
Bonaparte, Napoleon, 257, 258
Bonham, C. G. cutter, 157
Bose, Capt., 163, 164
Boyd, Capt., 200
Bragg, Frank, 195, 196
Bremen, ship, 232, 233
Bremmer, A., 115
British Knight, str., 115
Brooklyn, st. schr., 204, 205, 206
Brother Jonathan, str., 183, 184, 186, 187, 188
Brown, Capt., 10
Buhne, Capt. H. H., 192, 194, 195, 198
Bulagin, Capt. Nikolai, 5, 6, 7, 8, 9

C

Caavinen, John, 115
Cairny, Capt., 52
Camden, tanker, 263
Captain Lincoln, Govt. schr., 145, 146, 147
Carey, Capt., J. J., 235, 236, 237
Carlos III (King), 229
Carmarthan Castle, ship, 133
Cavendish, Thomas, 227
Caw, Capt. John, 246, 247
Cermenon, Capt. Sebastian, 228
Charles Levi Woodbury, power schr, 222
Chauncey, destroyer, 264
Cherry, E. M., 106
Cheyenne, monitor, 190
Christensen, Gustav, 200
Chrysopolis, str., 241
City of Dublin, ship, 101, 102
City of Everett, str., (whaleback), 149
City of Rio de Janeiro, str., 249, 250, 251, 255
Clallam, str., 85, 86, 87, 88
Clan McKenzie, str., 175, 176
Clarke, Samuel A., 106
Clevedon, MS., 180
Coast Trader, str. 263
Colefield, John, 115
Collins, Capt. G., 50
Collins, John, 92
Colman, J. M., 92, 93
Col. P. S. Mitchie, Govt. dredge, 151
Columbia, str., 37
Columbia, str., 70, 71, 218, 219, 220
Columbia, steamboat, 162
Combs, James, 165
Commodore, str., 184
Concomly, Chief, 102
Condor, HMS, 35, 36, 37, 38, 39, 40, 41
Congress, str., 150, 151, 152
Conick, Capt., 64
Connor, Capt., 82
Contra Costa, str., 241
Conway, Capt., 60
Coronado, str., 133
Corona, str., 199, 200, 201
Cook, James, 72
Cottoneva, st. schr., 165
Cousins, Capt. N. E., 150
Crosscup, Capt. H. B., 39, 40
Crowe, Capt., 125

311

Index

313

Index

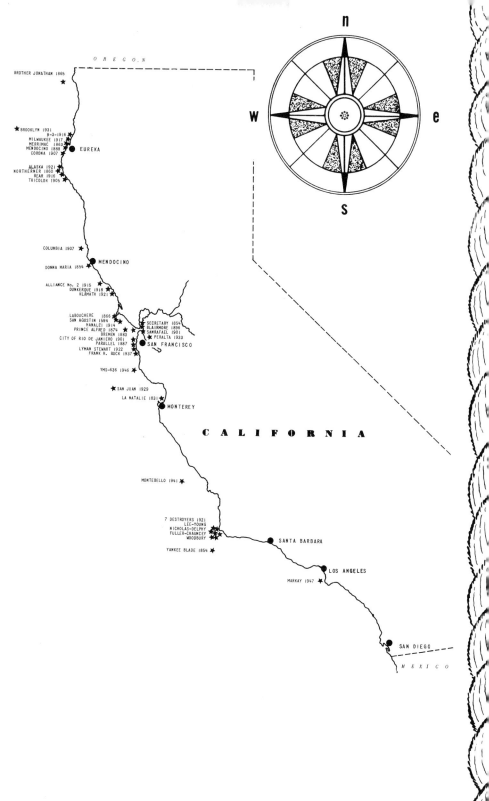